THE ORDEAL OF CONSCIOUSNESS IN HENRY JAMES

The case prescribed for its central figure a sick young woman, at the whole course of whose disintegration and the whole ordeal of whose consciousness one would have quite honestly to assist.

Henry James, *The Wings of the Dove*, p. vi

BY THE SAME AUTHOR

Three Traditions of Moral Thought (1959)

THE ORDEAL OF CONSCIOUSNESS IN HENRY JAMES

BY

DOROTHEA KROOK

Lecturer in English in the Hebrew University, Jerusalem

CAMBRIDGE

AT THE UNIVERSITY PRESS

1967

CAMBRIDGE UNIVERSITY PRESS
Cambridge, New York, Melbourne, Madrid, Cape Town, Singapore,
São Paulo, Delhi, Dubai, Tokyo, Mexico City

Cambridge University Press
The Edinburgh Building, Cambridge CB2 8RU, UK

Published in the United States of America by
Cambridge University Press, New York

www.cambridge.org
Information on this title: www.cambridge.org/9780521094498

First published 1962
First paperback edition 1967
Re-issued 2010

A catalogue record for this publication is available from the British Library

ISBN 978-0-521-05494-2 Hardback
ISBN 978-0-521-09449-8 Paperback

To

JUNE HOOPER

CONTENTS

PREFACE

THIS book was originally planned as a supplementary volume to my book *Three Traditions of Moral Thought*. Under the title *The Figure in the Carpet: A Study of Henry James* it was to have included an introductory chapter and two concluding chapters setting out an hypothesis about James's development, particularly in his last or 'late' period, towards a view of life which I proposed to call 'religious-humanist' in the sense defined in my earlier book; and I had hoped to be able to show, on the basis of certain external evidences as well as the internal evidences provided by some of the most important novels and stories of the late period, that Henry James might be counted as one of the greatest representatives of the modern Humanist tradition.

This part of the original plan, however, had to be abandoned, chiefly for reasons of space, and the material of the discarded chapters has been reserved for a shorter work, to be published separately. This leaves the present book as a collection of purely elucidatory studies of a selected number of James's works, connected by the theme of 'being and seeing'—the exploration and definition of consciousness in James's particular meaning of the term. I have also attempted from time to time to trace broad connexions between the individual works discussed, in an effort to show the continuity of James's principal preoccupations through the various periods of his creative life.

The choice of my texts has been determined by two main considerations: first, their representativeness; second, their comparative difficulty and consequent need of detailed elucidation. *The Portrait of a Lady* and *The Tragic Muse* were accordingly chosen as representative and sufficiently complex examples of James's early and middle periods; *The Turn of the Screw*, *The Awkward Age* and *The Sacred Fount* were chosen to represent the 'transition' between the middle and late periods, and *The Wings of the Dove* and *The Golden Bowl* the works of the late period. The omission of *The Ambassadors* from the last group, I should perhaps explain, was not invidious: I consider it to be quite as great as the other two, and have frequently referred to it in various connexions. Since, however, it appears to be the most widely read and the best understood of James's late works, and since it has also had full critical justice done to it (particularly by Mr Percy Lubbock in his masterly account in *The Craft of Fiction* and more recently by Mr F. C. Crews in the excellent, workmanlike study contained in his book *The Tragedy of Manners: Moral Drama in the Later Works of Henry James*), I felt I had no sufficient reason to give it a separate chapter.

Though the final judgement of the book must rest with the James specialist, who is familiar with the critical problems and has the fullest relevant experience to bring to the works, its method and style of presentation have been designed with a view particularly to the needs of the non-specialist. I have accordingly assumed no intimate knowledge of any of the works except perhaps *The Turn of the Screw*; nor have I hesitated, for instance, to re-tell the 'story' where this seemed to facilitate the task of elucidation. The fullness of the quotations has likewise been intended to help the Johnsonian common reader of Henry James: I wanted him to have the relevant passages immediately available as a direct 'check' on my comments and interpretations; and, even more, I wanted the voice of the author to be heard as often as possible, believing this to be the best way of ensuring the closest contact between author and reader (and minimising the critic's power of interference between them). I hope that the losses entailed by this method of exegesis will seem to be compensated for by the gains in relative clearness and completeness.

I wish to acknowledge very gratefully the encouragement and help I received from Mrs Joan Bennett in the writing of this book. Mrs Bennett read the whole manuscript, first in parts and then as a whole, and her numerous criticisms and suggestions not only saved me from many mistakes but were a constant stimulus to the rethinking or restatement of some of the main problems. My debt of gratitude to her is large indeed. My friend Enid Welsford contributed almost as much to this as to my first book by the enthusiasm and discernment she brought to our early discussions of Henry James, and by the generous interest with which she followed the work in progress. She also read with great care the chapters on *The Golden Bowl* and suggested many valuable improvements of the original drafts. Of the undergraduates who attended my lectures and seminars on Henry James at Cambridge and contributed so much by their questions, comments and general interest, I am especially grateful to Mr Edwin Stein, of New York, formerly at Pembroke College, Cambridge, who drew my attention to an important problem in *The Portrait of a Lady* which I should otherwise have missed, and to my sister Anita Greenberg, whose ardent interest in Henry James and intelligent, loving participation in my work made the writing of this book assume almost the character of a family undertaking. Mr Tony Becher, of the Cambridge University Press, who read the book in its final form and suggested many last improvements, was again of the greatest help to me. I am much indebted to Newnham College for electing me into a research fellowship for one year, to enable me to write this book; and for a supplementary grant from the Stuart Research Endowment Fund; and to the Committee of the Michael Behrens Research Fund for the generous award which enabled me to finish it.

I am grateful to Mr T. S. Eliot for his permission to reproduce the long extract from his article on Henry James (originally published in *Vanity Fair*, in the issue of February 1924) which appears at the opening of Chapter I. I also wish to thank the Editors of *The London Magazine* and *The Cambridge Journal* for allowing me to use the substance of articles which were first published in their periodicals: in Appendix C (ii), the material of an article on 'The Method of the Later Works of Henry James' (*The London Magazine*, July 1954), and in Chapters VII and VIII, that of two articles on 'The Wings of the Dove' and 'The Golden Bowl' (*The Cambridge Journal*, August and September, 1954). Permission has been granted for the use of the material from the standard New York edition of James's works by John Farquharson Ltd., on behalf of the Estate of the late Henry James.

D. K.

JERUSALEM
September, 1961

Quotations from the following works of Henry James are used by permission of Charles Scribner's Sons (New York).

From *The Sacred Fount* (1901).

From THE NOVELS AND TALES OF HENRY JAMES (New York Edition): *The Awkward Age* (Volume IX), *The Portrait of A Lady* and Preface (Volumes III and IV), *The Tragic Muse* (Volumes VII and VIII), *The Turn of the Screw* and Preface (Volume XII). Copyright 1908 Charles Scribner's Sons; renewal copyright 1936 Henry James.

The Golden Bowl (Volumes XXIII and XXIV), *The Wings of the Dove* (Volumes XIX and XX). Copyright 1909 Charles Scribner's Sons; renewal copyright 1937 Henry James.

NOTE ON THE TEXTS

EXCEPT where otherwise indicated, the quotations from the works of Henry James discussed in this book are taken from the 35-volume Library Edition of the Novels and Stories of Henry James published by Macmillan (London) in 1921–3. The page-references are to this edition, which uses the revised texts of the New York Edition of 1907–1909.

CHAPTER I

MATERIAL AND METHOD

In the issue dated February 1924 of a once popular American periodical called *Vanity Fair*, the curious student of Henry James will find a short article by T. S. Eliot bearing the title '*A Prediction in regard to Three English Authors: Henry James; J. G. Frazer; F. H. Bradley.*' The section on James is hardly more than a thousand words long; but it succeeds in compressing into this small space as brilliant and penetrating an account of James's greatness as any that may be hoped for; and since it has never been reprinted, it has seemed to me a service to reproduce it here in full. Mr Eliot writes:

Henry James is an author who is difficult for English readers, because he is an American; and who is difficult for Americans, because he is a European; and I do not know whether he is possible to other readers at all. On the other hand, the exceptionally sensitive reader, who is neither English nor American, may have a position of detachment which is an advantage. One thing is certain, that the books of Henry James form a complete whole. One must read all of them, for one must grasp, if anything, both the unity and the progression. The gradual development, and the fundamental identity of spirit, are both important, and their lesson is one lesson.

James has suffered the usual fate of those who, in England, have outspokenly insisted on the importance of technique. His technique has received the kind of praise usually accorded to some useless, ugly and ingenious piece of carving which has taken a very long time to make; and he is widely reproached for not succeeding in doing the things that he did not attempt to do. With 'character', in the sense in which the portrayal of character is usually expected in the English novel, he had no concern; but his critics do not understand that 'character' is only one of the ways in which it is possible to grasp at reality: had James been a better hand at character, he would have been a coarser hand altogether, and would have missed the sensibility to the peculiar class of data which were his province. And the fact that, an American, his view of England—a view which very gradually dissolves in his development—was a romantic view is a small matter. His romanticism implied no defective observation of the things that he wanted to observe; it was not the romanticism of those who dream because they are too lazy or too fearful to face the fact; it issues, rather, from the imperative insistence of an ideal which tormented him. He was possessed by the vision of an ideal society; he *saw* (not fancied) the relations between the members of such a society. And no one, in the end, has ever been more aware—or with more benignity, or less bitterness—of the disparity between possibility and fact. If his completed work failed to prove that, his last unfinished novels (*The Sense of the Past* and *The Ivory Tower*) could hardly fail to do so.

The example which Henry James offered us was not that of a style to imitate, but an integrity so great, a vision so exacting, that it was forced to the extreme of care and punctiliousness for exact expression. James did not provide us with 'ideas', but with another world of thought and feeling. For such a world some have gone to Dostoevsky, some to James; and I am inclined to think that the spirit of James, so much less violent, with so much more reasonableness and so much more resignation than that of the Russian, is no less profound, and is more useful, more applicable for our future.

In view of the date at which it was written, it is not surprising that there should be a faint period flavour about one or two of Mr Eliot's comments. Few critics of James nowadays would make an issue, for instance, of his 'portrayal of character' (though not everyone, even nowadays, understands that character in a novel is 'only one of the ways in which it is possible to grasp at reality'); and though James's late style is still a stumbling-block to many of the faithful, the sally about the useless, ugly and ingenious piece of carving is probably no longer fair to most of James's modern critics. It is also possible, I feel, to pick a small quarrel with Mr Eliot's use of the word 'resignation' in the comparison with Dostoevsky. He reiterates the idea in the concluding paragraph of the article when he speaks of his three authors as 'infinitely more *disillusioned*' than (for instance) Bernard Shaw, Anatole France and Thomas Hardy; and if 'resigned' means 'disillusioned', I think it is not applicable to Henry

James.[1] One has only to remember the 'insolence of health and joy' he proudly finds in *The Awkward Age* when he re-reads it for the New York edition at the age of over sixty, or the remark in the Notes to *The Ivory Tower*, written almost ten years later, about his hero Gray Fielder's 'enjoyment' of his knowledge born of suffering, or the wonderful letter to Henry Adams, written at the age of seventy, in which he proclaims himself to be still 'that queer monster, the artist, an obstinate finality, an inexhaustible sensibility', to feel that 'resignation' in the sense of 'disillusionment' is not the right word. 'Acceptance' would do better, and 'reconciliation' perhaps best of all—in the positive affirmative spirit of the famous lines in *King Lear*,

> Men must endure
> Their going hence, even as their coming hither;
> Ripeness is all;

and this would accord better too with Mr Eliot's other defining terms, all profoundly accurate—the lack of 'violence', the sweet 'reasonableness' and (best of all) the 'benignity' and absence of 'bitterness'.

Apart from this, however, the interest and value of Mr Eliot's main *obiter dicta* seem to me indisputable. The first chapter of this book, though written before I came upon Mr Eliot's piece, and indeed many things in the chapters that follow, seem to me now to be hardly more than a fuller statement of some of Mr Eliot's points; and this was a further reason for quoting it, as an extended epigraph, so to speak, for the book.

Henry James's social material is, or appears to be, severely limited. Like Jane Austen, who wrote always and only about the English provincial middle-classes she knew intimately and at first hand, James writes always and only about the social

[1] Not, at any rate, without careful qualification. The kind and quality of disillusion that is to be discerned in some of his late works is discussed in the last chapter of this book (ch. x below).

classes he happened to know with the same inside knowledge, namely, the moneyed classes of the expanding America of his day, the titled and propertied classes of Edwardian England, and the decaying aristocracies of France and Italy. The 'lower orders', as they were called in James's day, have virtually no place in his stories except as footmen and parlour-maids in the town-houses and country-houses of his moneyed, propertied and titled folk; and this to many, especially those who find an unqualified virtue in the greater variety and range of the social material of a Tolstoy, a Dostoevsky, a George Eliot and even a Dickens, has always seemed to set a fatal limitation on Henry James's greatness.[1]

The critical problems that the Jamesian social material

[1] Among James's major works, *The Princess Casamassima* is the only instance of a significant departure from this otherwise consistent homogeneity of the Jamesian social material. Here James does attempt to render from the inside the lives of people from the lower ranks of London society in the 1870's, in particular a group of English anarchists of the period. This part of the novel, however, seems to me not to be a conspicuous success; and I think that Mr Lionel Trilling, in his otherwise brilliant essay on *The Princess Casamassima* (reprinted in *The Liberal Imagination*, London 1951), has overrated the anarchist portion of the story. In my judgement, the best parts of *The Princess Casamassima* are the characteristically Jamesian parts—that is, the story of 'little' Hyacinth Robinson and his Princess; the uncharacteristic parts, those dealing with the anarchists and the rest, are—by Jamesian standards, at any rate—second-hand, at best imperfectly 'realised', at worst merely rhetorical in the opprobrious sense of the word. These points cannot be pursued here; but the validity of the last objection at least could be argued from a passage such as this:

'He felt hot and nervous; he got up suddenly and, through the dark tortuous greasy passage communicating with the outer world, went forth into the street. The air was foul and sleety but refreshed him, and he stood in front of the public-house and smoked another pipe. Bedraggled figures passed in and out and a damp tattered wretched man with a spongy purple face, who had been thrust suddenly across the threshold, stood and whimpered in the brutal blaze of the row of lamps. The puddles glittered roundabout and the silent vista of the street, bordered with low black houses, stretched away in the wintry drizzle to right and left, losing itself in the huge tragic city where unmeasured misery lurked beneath the dirty night, ominously, monstrously still, only howling, for its pain, in the heated human cockpit behind him. Ah what could he do? What opportunity would rise? The blundering divided counsels he had been listening to but made the helplessness of every one concerned more abject.' (*The Princess Casamassima*, I, 21, p. 316.)

Besides *The Princess Casamassima* there are also two stories, *Brooksmith* and *In the Cage*, in which the central figures are drawn from the proscribed social raises are to be considered presently. First, however, it may be useful to indicate briefly some of the more prominent features of its several constituent parts, the English, the European, and the American.

We may begin with the English. As every reader of James knows, the English national character remained for James to the end of his life an inexhaustible source of wonder, perplexity, amusement and delight; and it was also to the end one of his best beloved subjects. The English in James's stories are sometimes rich, like Lord Warburton in *The Portrait of a Lady*, but more often poor (by Edwardian upper-class standards, at any rate, which are not quite the same as those of the Welfare State); and when they are poor in this sense, they are generally exceedingly rapacious. But whether rich or poor, they are always beautifully cultivated, well-bred and charming; this breeding and charm, moreover, are of a kind that would seem in theory to be incompatible with their extreme rapacity, but in practice are not so at all; and this (we are meant to see) is one of the strange, wild graces of an old civilisation—that it should be able so competently, indeed so exquisitely, to reconcile the seemingly irreconcilable.

Another vital aspect of this perfect breeding and charm of the English is that it is un-intellectual. This, of course, does not mean it is unintelligent. Lord Warburton in *The Portrait of a Lady*, Lady Agnes and Julia Dallow in *The Tragic Muse*, Mrs Brookenham, Kate Croy, Lord Mark are all liberally endowed with the kind of practical, resourceful intelligence that built the British Empire, the House of Commons, the City and other monuments to the British genius for political life; and for this kind of intelligence the

class. But in both instances they are such 'refined' specimens of their type, are seen (like the Cockney model and the Italian manservant in *The Real Thing*) so much through upper-class eyes, and derive their interest in the story so entirely from their relation to the upper-class characters that they cannot, I think, count as genuine exceptions to the Jamesian practice of denying the 'lower orders' any significant place in the world of his novels.

English have the greatest admiration and respect. But they are *not* intellectual, often indeed positively anti-intellectual. In the story called *An International Episode* Lord Lambeth, the English nobleman on his first visit to America, is shown to be as bewildered as he is fascinated by the torrent of *generalisation*—about men, women, life, love, America and the Americans, England and the English—that seems to pour in an endless stream from his American hosts and hostesses, in particular the hostesses:

> Lord Lambeth listened to her [his American hostess] with, it must be confessed, a rather ineffectual attention. . . . He had no great faculty for apprehending generalisations. There were some three or four indeed which, in the play of his own intelligence, he had originated and which had sometimes appeared to meet the case—any case; yet he felt he had never known such a case as Mrs Westgate or as her presentation of *her* cases. But at the present time he could hardly have been said to follow this exponent as she darted fish-like through the sea of speculation.[1]

The American passion for 'speculation' is itself, of course, not exempt from James's irony. But if the Americans' cultivation of this noble passion errs by excess, that of the English certainly errs by defect—as we learn from another of James's early impressions of the English national character, contained in a letter to William James dated 8th March 1870, in which he sets down an imaginary scrap of dialogue with an Englishman of the type, presumably, of Lord Lambeth:

> 'Have you ever been to Florence?'
> 'Oh yes.'
> 'Isn't it a most peculiarly interesting city?'
> 'Oh yes, I think it's so very nice.'
> 'Have you read *Romola*?'
> 'Oh yes.'
> 'I suppose you admire it?'
> 'Oh yes, I think it so very clever.'

[1] *An International Episode*, p. 272. At another point in the story, when Lord Lambeth's friend Percy Beaumont expresses his Englishman's sense of Bessie Alden's complex American virtues by calling her 'sharp', we are reminded in parenthesis that 'Percy's critical categories remained few and simple. (*Ibid.* p. 285.)

Upon which James comments: 'The English have such a mortal distrust of anything like "criticism" or "keen analysis" (which they seem to regard as a kind of maudlin foreign flummery) that I rarely remember to have heard on English lips any other intellectual verdict (no matter under what provocation) than this broad synthesis—"so immensely clever". What exasperates you is not that they can't say more, but that they wouldn't if they could. Ah, but they are a great people for all that. . . .'[1]

So the English are not interested in 'ideas'; they are not 'critical' or 'analytical'; and being like that themselves, they are naturally disposed to view with suspicion, and certainly with distaste, that class of person whom they call, comprehensively, 'clever'. These are the people who do take seriously ideas, criticism and analysis, the chief offenders under this head being the poor American heroines in James's novels—Milly Theale in *The Wings of the Dove* is a notable instance—who always, and chiefly for this reason, come to a bad end in English society. Or, if they are not American but English, like Nick Dormer in *The Tragic Muse* or Nanda Brookenham in *The Awkward Age*, they come to a bad end (we are meant to understand) because they are still too young and too inexperienced to be properly English—to have learnt, that is, the value for the ends of self-preservation of curbing their disposition to pursue ideas further than their elders have thought necessary for happiness or virtue.

These are some of the features of the English national character that James is continually exhibiting in his stories; and we shall meet them in almost all the works I propose to discuss: in their simpler forms in the earlier works, *The Portrait of a Lady* and *The Tragic Muse*; in their more complex and subtle forms in the works of the later period, *The Awkward Age*, *The Wings of the Dove* and *The Golden Bowl*.

Turning from the English to the Europeans, we are to

[1] *Letters*, ed. Lubbock, I, p. 27.

meet a pure, native specimen of the type in the Prince in *The Golden Bowl*, a more artificial graft in Gilbert Osmond in *The Portrait of a Lady*. For the fullest, most direct portrayal of the Europeans, we would have to go to *The American* among James's early works and *The Ambassadors* among the late; for it is in these two works in particular that he exposes, openly and sharply in the first, more ambiguously in the second, the decadence of the old European aristocracies, with their ferocious pride of race, their fanatical adherence to traditional forms, and their ripe Old World sophistication issuing in the more insidious varieties of moral corruption. *The Portrait of a Lady*, however, gives us an indirect but sufficiently powerful insight into the simpler forms of this corruption, in the intimations we receive of what it was that shocked Isabel Archer in the life of the fashionable Roman society into which she is drawn by her marriage to Gilbert Osmond; and in *The Golden Bowl* we are shown the same corruption in its subtlest, most complex, most dangerously deceptive form—the form it takes when the aesthetic criterion (the 'touchstone of taste', as the Prince is to call it) is substituted for the moral in the conduct of life, and is proved to serve almost as well as the moral. Nevertheless, in his treatment of the Europeans, from *The American* to *The Golden Bowl*, James's principal (and characteristically Jamesian) object is always to show also the beauty and the grace that co-exist with this corruption in a really old society, and to indicate what a fatal fascination these can have for a susceptible young mind, especially if the mind happens to be American. This, conspicuously, is the case of Isabel Archer in *The Portrait of a Lady* and Maggie Verver in *The Golden Bowl* where, in both instances, the tragedy turns upon the impact of the 'corrupt' European mind upon the 'innocent' American.

The Americans themselves are almost always rich, often exceedingly rich. This means, in the first place, that they are free of the material wants that have already for generations been harassing the impoverished Europeans, and are now beginning to harass also the cultivated Edwardians. Their freedom from material cares, moreover, is matched in James's Americans by their freedom from conventional forms. Coming from a new and consciously democratic society, they are unimpeded by those rigid conventional forms that regulate the life of older societies. Consequently they have a freshness and a vitality in their approach to life, an absence of inhibitions, as we would say nowadays, and a lack of sophistication that together add up to the famous American innocence (as the Europeans call it); and this fine American innocence inspires the most mixed feelings in the sophisticated Europeans. In so far as it is crude and provincial (as it is, often enough), it makes them shudder with distaste: this is the feeling that Henrietta Stackpole, for instance, who is wholly and hopelessly American, inspires in Gilbert Osmond and his friends in *The Portrait of a Lady*. On the other hand, in so far as it is fresh, charming and 'original', they find it, at least at the start, fascinating, amusing and even delightful; and this on the whole is the feeling that Isabel Archer in *The Portrait of a Lady*, Milly Theale in *The Wings of the Dove*, and Maggie Verver in *The Golden Bowl* inspire in the Europeans. But almost always (alas) what the Europeans at the start find engaging and fascinating in the American national character they find in the end desperately irritating and intolerably boring; and it is out of this interaction of the American mind with the European that James's grand theme is born—the so-called international theme, of which *Daisy Miller* is the famous specimen in miniature. What is likely to happen (James, the curious, interested and 'amused' observer of human tangles, asks himself) when the European mind is confronted at close quarters with the American mind, and in particular when they are intimately entangled by love or marriage? What happens, or can happen, James takes pleasure in showing over and over again, with the nicest variations in the details—in the complications of the plot, the degree of seriousness, the scale and scope of the fable, the pitch and tempo of the treatment—in a dozen or more of his best stories and in some of his greatest novels. Among the last are *The Portrait of a Lady, The Wings of the Dove* and *The Golden Bowl*; and in James's handling of the international theme in these works in particular what we shall chiefly find cause to admire is the way in which he makes it serve the double purpose of every great dramatist: that of a radical criticism of society at the turn of the last century on the one hand, and, on the other, of a 'criticism of life' in Matthew Arnold's sense—a radical exposure, sometimes in its comic aspect, more often in its tragic aspect, of some of the fundamental and permanent predicaments of human life.

Leaving further discussion of the international theme to the chapters in which *The Portrait of a Lady, The Wings of the Dove* and *The Golden Bowl* are to be more fully treated,[1] I return to the critical problems raised by James's social material as such. Why (it has been asked, with varying degrees of distaste and disapproval) does James confine himself so exclusively to this highly selected fragment of society? Why does he deal, always and only, with the titled and the moneyed, or those aspiring after titles or money or both? And if the reason is that the titled and moneyed happened to be the only people James knew anything about, why in that case must they be so excessively titled and moneyed? Why, in short, choose such thoroughly unrepresentative types of common humanity as counts and princes, millionaires and heiresses for his heroes and heroines? Such personages (it is argued), leaving aside their other disqualifications, have never seriously known the pressure of material want; and since this, as everyone knows, is one of the principal determinants of human character and conduct in real life, it must necessarily be present, with all the proper modifications, in the rendering of life in the novel.

[1] Chs. II, VII, VIII and IX below.

This, according to these critics, is the basic 'unreality' of the Jamesian world. And from it follows the crowning unreality of keeping these millionaires and heiresses and titled folk confined to their town-houses and country-houses, or even only the drawing-rooms and terraces of the town-houses and country-houses, for the sole purpose, it would seem, of engaging in the analysis of their intricate personal relations and the processes of their own consciousnesses. By the time the novels of the late period have been reached, this really seems to be their exclusive preoccupation; and it is conducted in those late novels with a minuteness and subtlety so exhausting, and an adherence to the 'indirect' method of presentation so fantastically (or fanatically) rigid, that it has led some critics to dismiss the works of the late period as, in quite a definable sense, pathological. According to Dr F. R. Leavis, for instance, James by this period had succumbed to an occupational disease which he calls an 'hypertrophy of sensibility', of which the main symptom is an interest in technique for its own sake, resulting in an excess of 'doing' over what is actually 'done', and having its source in 'some failure about the roots and at the lower levels of life': poor James has by this time 'run excessively to consciousness'; and this is taken to account for the fatal deterioration that Dr Leavis has persuaded himself to see in all James's later works.[1]

In my chapters on the late works I will try to show that this account of the works of James's maturity is wide of the mark: so wide indeed that it misses completely both their intention and their achievement. At this point, I am concerned only with the more general problem raised by James's social material, namely, whether its effect upon his criticism of life in Arnold's sense was in fact as restrictive as some

[1] F. R. Leavis, 'Henry James', in *Scrutiny*, v, 4, pp. 405, 406, 409, 410, 414, 416–17. The last passage appears to have been excised from Dr Leavis's revised version of this essay printed in *The Great Tradition* (1948). The rest, however, is retained unaltered. (See *The Great Tradition*, pp. 158, 161, 163, 165, 166, 170, 171.)

have thought. Why (to return to our question) this exclusive preoccupation with the uppermost classes of his society? Why only, or almost only, counts and princes, millionaires and heiresses? Why—and this is the crux of the present problem—why all this emphasis upon *money*: the possession of money, the desire for money, the consequences of having or not having money? Does it show in James (as some critics have thought) merely an unhealthy fascination with this unhealthy phenomenon of the modern world? Or does it show something quite different?

I believe it does show something quite different; and what it shows can be considered in two distinct, though intimately related, aspects. The first is, or ought to be, fairly obvious. James, like every great novelist whose criticism of life is also and at the same time a criticism of society, is passionately interested in the ultimate source of power in the society which he seeks to depict. His interest is not of course that of the economist or political scientist, or even that of the social psychologist: James is not concerned with power as a function of the ownership of the means of production or of the distribution of parties and pressure-groups or of the status-seeking propensities of modern man. He is concerned with it solely in its moral aspect, in the broadest sense of the term 'moral'; and the questions he accordingly asks about it are: What, in our society, is the supreme instrument of power; who in our society are the people that possess it; and what difference does the possession of it make to the quality and the conduct of life?

Having asked these questions, James has no difficulty in finding the answers. The supreme instrument of power in the modern world is money, and the possessors of supreme power in the modern world are the moneyed classes. The novelist who wishes to discover the nature and operations of power, and the effects of the possession of power upon the quality of life in the modern world, must therefore go to the moneyed classes: not to the poor and virtuous working-classes, or the noble and impecunious intellectual classes, or the less noble and less impecunious trading classes, or the Civil Service or the House of Commons, but only to the moneyed classes. It is not a question here of what ought to be but of what is; and since the supreme instrument of power in the modern world is money, the class possessing this supreme instrument becomes the aristocracy of the modern world, and as such stands in the same relation to our dominantly commercial society as the old aristocracy stood to the dominantly feudal societies of earlier ages, for instance, Shakespeare's.

To understand this is, I believe, of immediate help in understanding the dramatic function of the millionaires and heiresses in James's novels. James's millionaires and heiresses have in his novels exactly the same dramatic function as the kings, queens and princes in Shakespeare's plays. They are 'representative' of all humanity in the modern world in exactly the same sense as Shakespeare's kings, queens and princes are representative: in the sense that they are the acknowledged symbols of supreme power and prestige in their society, and are therefore 'the glass of fashion and the mould of form, the observ'd of all observers'. They embody, in short, the dominant (though not necessarily the exclusive) ideal of human possibility in that society; consequently, what 'happens' to them—their vicissitudes, their 'rise and fall', their suffering and joy—is exemplary and instructive for the purposes of drama in exactly the way that Shakespeare conceived the fate of a Hamlet, a Macbeth, a Lear to be exemplary and instructive. This accordingly is one reason that James chooses millionaires and heiresses for his heroes and heroines.

The parallel between the Jamesian drama and the Shakespearian can be extended in at least one further point. In Shakespeare's historical plays in particular, the kings, queens and princes always have their Norfolks and Northumberlands and Westmorlands for their supporting cast—those noble dukes, earls, knights and their ladies who simultaneously pay homage to their kings and princes and pursue their own political and personal designs under cover of these acts of homage. In the world of the Jamesian novel, the impoverished and rapacious aristocracy of the Old World perform a similar dramatic function. The French vicomtes, Italian princes, English lords and *grandes dames* pay rapturous homage to the American millionaires and heiresses who have descended on Europe in their search for culture. They cover them with their praise and adoration—and in the intervals between the banquets and balls 'work' them as hard as they can, the ultimate form of working them being, of course, to arrange as many marriages as possible between the rich Americans and their own sons and daughters.

This, I suggest, is the dramatic framework of some of James's most brilliant and most mordant criticism of society in such novels as *The Portrait of a Lady, The Wings of the Dove, The Golden Bowl* and in dozens of the stories; and it is also the chief dramatic reason (and justification) for the money *motif* in these works. In this connexion it should perhaps be added, without pursuing the point at this stage, that those modern critics who believe that James is identifying himself with the inglorious money-values of this money-obsessed world—that he himself joins in the chorus of praise and adulation of the moneyed Americans, speaking of them as 'wonderful', 'beautiful' and 'prodigious' where the critics can only find them prodigiously nauseating—are totally misreading James's intention. The money-values are there always for exposure, never for praise. They happen, however, in James's works, to be exposed not as part of a social system or an ethical code or any other abstraction but as the destructive element in particular concrete human beings (Mrs Brookenham, Mrs Lowder, Adam Verver) who are in fact wonderful and prodigious in ways irresistibly stimulating to the imagination, sympathy, and general powers of appreciation of such an observer of life as Henry James. Consequently the Jamesian exposure of the money-values is conducted in a medium so generously and tenderly 'appreciative' as to invite misunderstanding from the literal-minded; and since this is only one instance among many of the fatal effects of literal-mindedness in the reading of James's works, its remedy (if there is a remedy) is to be sought in a more imaginative, more receptive, less blunt and less literal reading.

There are two further aspects of the 'representativeness' of the Jamesian heroes and heroines to be discerned. I have suggested one sense in which they may be seen as 'high personages', comparable for the purposes of drama with Shakespeare's kings, queens and princes. This turns upon their being the repositories of supreme power and prestige in their society. But, besides this (or as a consequence of this), they are also rich, often very rich; they are generally handsome; they are well-bred; they live in elegant surroundings; they wear fine clothes; they have cultivated tastes and every opportunity to indulge them. In this more limited sense, too, they are 'uncommon': not of the common people; raised far above the common level of the majority of men and women, whose lives are a perpetual struggle for even a small share of the goods of life which these Jamesian heroes and heroines enjoy in such abundance. And in this too they resemble the high personages of the Shakespearian drama.

There is, however, still another, more important, sense in which they are 'high personages'. They are, one and all, very superior people; and the respects in which they are so superior may be readily collected from any representative selection of James's works. They are all, these Jamesian heroes and heroines, endowed in an extraordinary degree with the gifts of intelligence, imagination, sensibility, and a rare delicacy of moral insight; and they are all extraordinarily articulate about all that they see and understand. The intelligence is not of course of the academic kind, the sensibility is not 'trained' (as we now say in the academies); and the moral insight appears to owe nothing to the offices of teachers or preachers. On the contrary, it appears to owe everything only to their inordinate capacity for *being* and *seeing* (the phrase applied to one of the remarkable heroines, Kate Croy): for life, that is, and for consciousness; for living and for understanding. And since their inordinate capacity for enjoyment and suffering is matched by their inordinate passion for knowledge, especially self-knowledge, their suffering is not the blind, brute suffering of common humanity, which is always pitiful, often indeed heartbreaking, but never tragic. Their suffering is the kind peculiar to the highly intelligent and highly imaginative—'full vessels of consciousness' (James calls them), 'those on whom nothing is lost', who are all the time 'exposed' (another favourite Jamesian term) to the impact of living experience, and fully cognisant, all the time, of the operation and effect of that experience.

Of course (one hastens to add, having received the hint from James himself) they must not be *too* fully cognisant: they must not be so intelligent, so conscious of all the implications of what is happening to them, so full of the light of understanding, that they cease to be capable of making any mistakes, or of suffering any of the uncertainties, confusions and bewilderments to which their fellow-creatures are so desperately prone. This danger for the novelist who chooses to make his heroes and heroines really full vessels of consciousness James touches upon in the Preface to *The Princess Casamassima*:

> They may carry too much [light] for our credence, for our compassion, for our derision. They may be shown as knowing too much and feeling too much—not certainly for their remaining remarkable, but for their remaining 'natural' and typical, for their having the needful communities with our own precious liability to fall into traps and be bewildered. . . .[1]

[1] *The Princess Casamassima*, p. xi.

So they *must* be full vessels of consciousness, but only so full as may be compatible with their retaining this 'needful community' with the rest of suffering humanity in point of their liability—in spite of all their intelligence and all their imagination—to fall into traps and be bewildered. But, given this requisite degree of nescience (without which, as James adds, there would be no story to tell), their suffering remains of the kind peculiar to the highly developed, the highly intelligent and imaginative. And since, as the great tragic dramatists have always known, it is the rise and fall of great spirits, of personages endowed with gifts and graces, weaknesses and vices, far above the common level, that is the only proper material for tragedy, it is because the suffering of the Jamesian heroes and heroines is of this kind—because it is suffering illuminated by understanding, or the passionate aspiration after understanding—that it is redemptive, even when in the end it destroys them; and because redemptive in this way, therefore also truly tragic—truly exemplary and instructive.

The picture, however, is not yet quite complete. We have seen so far that the Jamesian heroes and heroines, besides being in the highest degree intelligent, imaginative and sensitive, are also in the highest degree what would commonly be called 'morally earnest'. This is true equally of the 'bad' and 'good' Jamesian characters—of Mrs Brookenham, Kate Croy, the Prince and Charlotte equally with Nanda Brookenham, Milly Theale, Maggie Verver. The bad are as passionately preoccupied as the good with the strictly moral analysis of motives—what Vanderbank in *The Awkward Age* calls 'getting at the idea of things'. They all mind passionately about doing what is morally right even when what they in fact do is morally wrong: of this the Prince and Charlotte in *The Golden Bowl* are perhaps the most instructive instance; and they all suffer intense moral conflict in the making of important moral choices—witness Kate Croy's desperate efforts in the opening chapter of *The Wings of the Dove* to persuade her dreadful father to let her stay with him instead of forcing her to go to Aunt Maud. In short, they all exhibit a remarkable moral energy, whether the ends to which it happens to be directed are good or bad; and it is in this sense that they may all justly be described as morally earnest.

There is, however, a last fine stroke in the picture that sets the bloom of perfection upon the whole. Though morally earnest in this intense degree, they are never portentous, never boring, never violent or brutal, but always charming and civil and good-tempered. There is a phrase in *The Princess Casamassima* which makes this point with memorable force. The hero Hyacinth Robinson, at the precise point in the story at which his premonitory consciousness of the suffering to which he is doomed is most acute, is praised for 'his composure, his lucidity, his good humour'.[1] In the moral world that James has created, these three, perfect lucidity, perfect composure and perfect good humour, are (we come to see) the transcendent virtues of man as man, by which the greatness and the dignity of the human spirit are affirmed in the very midst of suffering in itself degrading and demoralising. The lucidity is the mark of the human intelligence at its furthest reach, which seeks to understand, to render fully intelligible to itself, its own deepest experience of life. The composure is the mark of the human spirit at its highest reach—'spirit' in the Platonic sense, meaning the courageous, the heroic, element in the soul of man: this composure that James commends to our praise is the supreme expression of this element of 'spirit', by which a man may retain inviolate his command of himself even while he is exposed to the deepest anguish and humiliation. And the good-humour (taking the word in the large sense in which James uses it) is the supreme mark of the civilised temper, which will not stoop to rail at life, whatever the provocation—will not revile or recriminate, but seeks instead to come to terms with life

[1] *The Princess Casamassima*, ch. 24.

by understanding it. This is the vision of human perfection that lights the way of the Jamesian vessels of consciousness with a radiance consistently splendid; and its special interest for the literary mind is that it owes its existence and its reality solely to the novelist's art.

If this is a substantially true account of what it is that makes the Jamesian heroes and heroines so 'superior', such uncommon personages in the largest sense of the word 'uncommon', it still remains to ask: How can the tragic condition of man be exhibited through such uniformly superior personages, who would seem now to be as unrepresentative of common suffering humanity by virtue of this very superiority as they were already by their freedom from material cares? How can 'the essential passions of the heart' (as Wordsworth called them) be exhibited in and through such personages? How can they be rendered even credibly, let alone in an 'exemplary' way, in and through creatures so prodigiously, so elaborately, over-civilised?

The key-word is 'over-civilised', and the mention of Wordsworth in this connexion was deliberate. For it is by contrasting the ideal world of James's novels with the ideal world of the *Lyrical Ballads* (or, rather, of the Preface to the *Lyrical Ballads*) that one can, I have thought, best understand the ultimate aesthetic principle that determines James's choice of his *dramatis personae*; and, by understanding the principle, also further explain and justify his practice in this respect.

The point of the comparison is to draw attention to two principles of what may be called poetic idealisation (or poetic intensification, or even stylisation), which are so distinct as to stand at opposite poles to each other. Both are valid, in the sense that both are capable of producing great art; yet they are mutually exclusive as modes of rendering the fundamental realities of the human condition.

To take first the Wordsworthian extreme: Wordsworth,

we remember, deliberately chose to exhibit 'the essential passions of the heart' in and through a class of people representing the simplest, most primitive, most *uncomplicated* human material available to him as a poet. 'Humble and rustic life was generally chosen', he writes, 'because, in that condition, the essential passions of the heart find a better soil in which they can attain their maturity . . .; [and] because in that condition of life our elementary feelings co-exist in a state of greater simplicity, and consequently may be more accurately contemplated and more forcibly communicated.' In this sentence from a famous passage in the Preface to the *Lyrical Ballads,* Wordsworth sets out the principle of poetic idealisation that has determined his choice of his human material. On this principle, the 'ideal' man for the purposes of poetry—the man through whom the fundamental passions can be most instructively and most beautifully exhibited—is the man who stands as close as possible to the 'beautiful and permanent forms of nature', whose life is innocent equally of the surface encrustations and the internal complexities of more involved forms of life. One may call this the stripping principle. Observe man (it says in effect) in the minimum conditions necessary for the maintenance of life in a human community. Observe him in these simplest, least complicated of conditions, those in which he approximates to the simplicity of earth and rocks and trees. Observe him, that is, stripped, in the first place, of the external appurtenances of civilisation: stripped of money, of course, and all personal property in the shape of fine houses, fine furniture, fine dress; stripped, further, of the enjoyment of the formal arts—painting, literature and music, theatre, ballet and opera; and of the formal modes of social intercourse—the luncheon parties and dinner parties at which civilised people meet to exchange ideas and gossip; and the more intimate forms of exchange, in private sitting-rooms and enclosed gardens and wide terraces, where these people conduct their complicated personal relations.

Having stripped man of these external forms of a developed social life, strip him also (says Wordsworth) of the internal appurtenances of civilisation, in particular the appurtenance of *thought*. Divest him of the burden of consciousness, or rather self-consciousness, which is the burden, uniquely, of the civilised man. Show him in a condition of minimal self-consciousness, exercising his intelligence and his passion in a wholly un-selfconscious, 'objective' way, directing them in this way upon nature, his fellow-men, himself, but never turning the intelligence upon itself—never, that is, performing the defining act of the reflective mind, that of the mind become conscious of its own activities. Strip man of all this; and then, and only then (Wordsworth concludes), you have him in the condition in which the fundamental passions may be most accurately contemplated and most forcibly communicated.

This is one valid form of poetic idealisation, one self-consistent mode of achieving that intensification which is the necessary condition of the poetic rendering of life. It is a mode of intensification or simplification that has been employed often enough in the history of English literature, to say nothing of other literatures. The pastoral convention is one of the well-known historic forms it has assumed; Wordsworth's own 'realistic pastoralism' (if one may so call it) is another; and Shakespeare used it frequently in his comedies, and at least once with intensely tragic effect—when King Lear, that night on the heath, is stripped of every particle of his kingliness, and reduced to a condition below the primitive—a condition of nakedness and madness—in order that he may learn the meaning of total deprivation and by this means purge his soul of the sin of pride.

The principle of idealisation that regulates the art of Henry James stands at the opposite pole to the Wordsworthian. James does not say, Strip and reduce; he says instead, Load. Load your human material (he says), first, with all the external appurtenances of civilisation. Let them live in the finest houses filled with the finest furniture; let them wear the finest clothes; give them the most cultivated tastes; let them spend all, or almost all, their time at luncheon parties, dinner parties and evening parties, observing rigidly all the conventions of these forms of social intercourse—engaging in the right kind of conversation in the right kind of idiom with the right persons for the prescribed length of time. Then, on top of these cultivated tastes and habits, give them also the most refined sensibilities, the most delicate perceptions, and a developed power of articulating all that they feel and see; and, passing in this way from the external appurtenances of civilisation to the internal, endow them with gifts of insight and powers of discrimination and analysis, in the field of moral relations in particular, far exceeding the reach of men in real life. Finally, endow them with the supreme gift of consciousness—specifically, self-consciousness. Steep them and saturate them in this self-consciousness, until they are all, like Kate Croy in *The Wings of the Dove*, 'made for being and seeing'[1]: made, that is, with the power to be actively and deeply involved in the objective world, which is to be made for 'being'; and at the same time made with the power to be intensely and minutely conscious of all that this involvement in the objective world implies, which is to be made for 'seeing'.

And, further: let this self-consciousness of theirs be not only intense and minute, but also active without intermission, ever awake, ever watchful; registering every bend and turn in the stream of consciousness as the eye of the soul moves perpetually back and forth, between the activity of apprehending the objective world and the activity of apprehending its own apprehensions. Make them, in short, full 'vessels of consciousness'—those on whom not a single implication of the meaning of their life's experience is lost; and at the same time keep them actively and keenly exposed to every fresh impact of experience, sparing them neither the pain, the

[1] *The Wings of the Dove*, I, 1, 2, p. 30.

anguish and the humiliation of life as lived, nor the greater pain, anguish and humiliation of understanding, to the last particle of meaning, the nature of that experienced pain, anguish and humiliation. And, in the midst of their suffering, let them remain always, like 'little' Hyacinth Robinson, perfectly lucid, perfectly composed and perfectly good-humoured: never breaking down under the burden of their consciousness; never betraying this most sacred trust of their humanity by a single failure in intelligence or self-command; and even if it destroys them (as it does several of them—Hyacinth Robinson himself, and Milly Theale in *The Wings of the Dove*) make them carry it forward, still lucid, composed and good-humoured, into the ranks of death.

Now (says James), given such human material, which is not, like Wordsworth's, stripped and denuded, but on the contrary complicated to the last degree—loaded and weighed down, encumbered and encrusted, to the furthest limit of the poetic imagination, with all the goods, internal and external, of the civilised life: given such human material, let us see whether (adapting Wordsworth's phraseology) it is not in this condition rather than the other that the essential passions of the heart find the best soil in which they can attain their maturity; whether it is not in this condition of life that our elementary feelings may be most accurately contemplated and most forcibly communicated.

This, I believe, is the claim that James is implicitly making: that (to recapitulate) it is in this infinitely encumbered and encrusted condition of life that the fundamental human passions can be exhibited in a way more instructive and more beautiful than they could in any other. For, James argues (or, rather, the novels and stories argue, very cogently and persuasively), it is in this condition that both the noble and the destructive passions show with an 'ideal' intensity, complexity and completeness such as could not be attained under the condition of primitive simplicity that the Wordsworthian ideal postulates. In this, the Jamesian condition, the noble passions, on the one side, can appear so much more noble than in the Wordsworthian because they have here to sustain their nobility against powers and principalities more subtle, insidious and deceptive than any that could be conceived of in the Wordsworthian world. And the powers and principalities, the bad destructive passions, on their side, are so much more dangerous and destructive because, in this supremely civilised world, they carry such a lustre and a bloom: like everything else in that world, they, too, are overlaid with its beauty and civility, saturated in its characteristic delicacies and refinements. This makes it very difficult to recognise them for what they are; and it is because they are so appallingly deceptive that they are so dangerous and destructive.

This is the sense in which it is true to say that in the Jamesian world the fundamental human passions co-exist in forms the most complex, most subtle, most elusive. And if (the argument concludes)—if in this ideal or perfect state of complexity the fundamental passions can in fact be exhibited with the maximum poetic intensity, if a radical poetic criticism of life can in fact be bodied forth from such human material under such conditions, then the Jamesian heroes and heroines are rendered fully intelligible, and the Jamesian principle of poetic idealisation is artistically vindicated.

The task of showing in more detail what James achieves on this aesthetic principle is to be reserved for later chapters. For the present, it remains to add that the sketch I have tried to give of the Jamesian world is more fully applicable to the later than the earlier novels, and most fully—along with *The Ambassadors*—to the late works I have chosen to discuss, namely, *The Awkward Age*, *The Sacred Fount*, *The Wings of the Dove* and *The Golden Bowl*. But the tendency to create the poetic world I have tried to describe is there from the beginning, and may be discerned not only in *The Portrait of a Lady*, *The Princess Casamassima* and *The Tragic Muse* but already in works as early as *The American* and *The Europeans.* For this reason it seemed legitimate to indicate the mode of operation of this aesthetic principle of James's art at, so to speak, its furthest point of development in the final products of his genius.

CHAPTER II

'THE PORTRAIT OF A LADY'

REVIEWING the genesis of *The Portrait of a Lady* in his Preface to the New York edition, James recalls that it was produced in those early years of his life in London when to his dazzled sense the 'international light' lay especially 'thick and rich upon the scene'. Written when James was at the height of his powers in his early, 'direct' mode, *The Portrait of a Lady* may indeed be taken as his grand definitive statement of the international theme in that mode, which he was to surpass only in the great works of his later period, *The Ambassadors, The Wings of the Dove* and *The Golden Bowl*; and since in *The Portrait* (James tells us) it is 'the light in which so much of the picture hung', it is virtually as important as the picture and will be treated accordingly.

In the picture itself, however, the richest element is the 'engaging young woman', Isabel Archer; and in the same Preface James firmly directs our attention to her as the centre of interest in his story. She was the 'seed' from which the story sprang, the seminal 'idea entertained' which carries its own 'lurking forces of expansion', its own 'necessities of upspringing' and 'beautiful determinations . . . to grow as tall as possible, to push into the light and air and thickly flower there'. For the novelist—for a James as for a Turgenev—she was one of those persons 'who hovered before him, soliciting him, . . . interesting him, and appealing to him just as they were and by what they were'; and once thus ensnared, the novelist was left but with one task, namely, 'to find for them the right relations, those that will most bring them out; to imagine, to invent and select and piece together the situations most useful and favourable to the sense of the creatures themselves, the complications they would be most likely to produce and to feel'.[1] Isabel Archer

[1] *The Portrait of a Lady*, p. viii.

accordingly is brought out in three principal relations: first, her relation with Lord Warburton, her very upper-class English suitor; next, with Caspar Goodwood, her very provincial American suitor; and, last, with Gilbert Osmond, the cosmopolitan American whom she finally marries. Of these the last is the most important for the main tragic theme of the story, and is the most profoundly explored and most fully exhibited. But all three are equally important for James's international theme; and each on its own scale is a masterpiece of the novelist's art.

The bare story of *The Portrait of a Lady* is enough to bring before us, very vividly and richly, the international light in which the picture is hung. Isabel Archer is a young, intelligent and charming American girl of modest means, who has been born and brought up in Albany, New York, the ancestral seat of the James family consecrated in *A Small Boy and Others* as one of the principal scenes of James's own childhood. She is rescued from this provincial backwater by her aunt Mrs Touchett, an energetic, outspoken, commonsensical expatriate American. Mrs Touchett is one of these cosmopolitan Americans of the last century who cannot bear to live anywhere but in Florence, and accordingly lives there most of the year, leaving her wealthy husband, a retired banker, and her son Ralph to enjoy the pleasures of English country life in their charming house Gardencourt, which stands on the Thames some forty miles from London. Mrs Touchett carries Isabel straight to Gardencourt; and there, with her arrival on a lovely summer's afternoon, Isabel's story begins.

Isabel finds everything and everybody at Gardencourt enchanting; and she herself in turn enchants them all, in particular her old uncle and her cousin Ralph. Ralph is an immensely clever, imaginative, passionate young man, who instantly falls in love with Isabel. But being consumptive, he cannot propose to her, chooses instead to conceal his passion behind a smoke-screen of witty disenchanted levity, and contents himself with making Isabel's career the object of his detached and amused contemplation. Ralph's attitude to Isabel plays an important part in the story.

Besides Ralph, however, Lord Warburton, a young nobleman living in the neighbourhood and a frequent visitor to Gardencourt, also falls in love with Isabel; and in refusing Warburton's proposal of marriage, James's engaging young woman receives the first important extension of her life's experience.

Warburton himself is offered to us as the perfect specimen of an Englishman of the uppermost crust of English society, and though his appearances are comparatively few and brief, James renders him with the finest comic-ironic verisimilitude. Mr Touchett's introductory account of him, though not free of some gentle American animus, is meant to be taken as accurate enough:

> Lord Warburton's a very amiable young man—a very fine young man. He has a hundred thousand a year. He owns fifty thousand acres of the soil of this little island and ever so many other things besides. He has half a dozen houses to live in. He has a seat in Parliament as I have one at my own dinner-table. He has elegant tastes—cares for literature, for art, for science, for charming young ladies. The most elegant is his taste for the new views. It affords him a great deal of pleasure—more perhaps than anything else, except the young ladies. . . . His views don't hurt anyone as far as I can see; they certainly don't hurt himself. And if there were to be a revolution he would come off very easily. They wouldn't touch him, they'd leave him as he is: he's too much liked.[1]

So Lord Warburton is exceedingly likeable; and easily the most likeable feature of his character (we are soon made to see) is his complete and perfect simplicity. In this well-bred, thoroughly honest and sincere, and most satisfyingly ardent Englishman, perfect breeding wears the richer aspect of a delicacy utterly natural, unforced, un-learnt; and this naturalness is somehow compatible with its being at the

[1] *The Portrait of a Lady*, I, 8, pp. 90–1.

same time the product of a highly artificial form of social life—that secure and tranquil life in solid, handsome country-houses set in the midst of a lovely countryside that had been lived for long generations by Englishmen of Lord Warburton's class. Lord Warburton is the product of a culture which, compared with the primitive simplicities and crudities of the American culture that has produced Isabel Archer herself and (even more) her American suitor Caspar Goodwood, is infinitely complex and full of subtle variety. Yet he remains astonishingly simple, modest and unselfconscious about it all; and this is his most representatively English—as well as his most engaging—characteristic.

It is to be expected, however, that a price should be paid for this. In the end Lord Warburton is seen to be not only touchingly simple-hearted, but also (alas) simple-minded. This comes out most clearly in the delightful scene in which he asks Isabel to marry him.[1] Warburton there shows himself to be totally incapable of understanding Isabel's reasons for refusing him; and this failure, we are meant to understand, is to be referred to another of the grand characteristics of the English national character—its conspicuous helplessness in respect to the deeper, more elusive, more inaccessible motives of human conduct, and its consequent ineptitude in the face of situations demanding an insight into such motives. It is the quality of this blankness, this remarkable incomprehension, of Lord Warburton's that James renders with the finest dramatic economy and the nicest sense of its comic incongruity in the scene of the proposal.

Isabel has tried to explain, rather confusedly and clumsily and even a trifle crudely, that she believes she will not do as a wife for him. 'It's not what I ask', she says, 'it's what I can give. I don't think I should suit you; I really don't think I should.' Warburton evidently cannot take this seriously. He answers lightly: 'You needn't worry about that. That's my affair. You needn't be a better royalist than the king.'

[1] *The Portrait of a Lady*, I, 12.

Isabel tries again, but with no greater success, and finally has to give up. 'I'm afraid I can't make you understand', she says. 'You ought at least to try', he replies. 'I've a fair intelligence.' And then: 'Are you afraid—afraid of the climate? We can easily live elsewhere, you know. You can pick out your climate, the whole world over.' [1]

The passage that follows expresses Isabel's sense of the charm of Warburton's ignorance and innocence and incorruptible good nature:

> These words were uttered with a breadth of candour that was like the embrace of strong arms—that was like the fragrance straight in her face, and by his clean, breathing lips, of she knew not what strange gardens, what charged airs. She would have given her little finger at that moment to feel strongly and simply the impulse to answer: 'Lord Warburton, it's impossible for me to do better in this wonderful world, I think, than commit myself, very gratefully, to your loyalty.' But though she was lost in admiration of her opportunity she managed to move back into the deepest shade of it, even as some wild, caught creature in a vast cage. The 'splendid' security so offered her was *not* the greatest she could conceive. What she finally bethought herself of saying was something very different—something that deferred the need of really facing her crisis. 'Don't think me unkind if I ask you to say no more about this to-day.' [2]

The scene ends soon after this on a similar note; but not before we have received a hint of the real reason for Isabel's refusal of Warburton. She has said she will write to him and he agrees to wait, though (he says) the waiting will seem long. She answers:

> 'I shall not keep you in suspense; I only want to collect my mind a little.'
>
> He gave a melancholy sigh and stood looking at her a moment, with his hands behind him, giving short nervous shakes to his hunting-crop. 'Do you know I'm very much afraid of it—of that remarkable mind of yours?' [3]

There is the rub. Lord Warburton finds Isabel Archer en-

[1] *The Portrait of a Lady*, I, 12, pp. 133–4.
[2] *Ibid.* pp. 134–5.
[3] *Ibid.* pp. 135–6.

chanting in every respect except that in which she is disposed to value herself—the quantity designated, with deliberate vagueness, her mind, her 'remarkable mind'. The thought of her mind fills Lord Warburton with nervous apprehension; yet what is it but her mind that sets Isabel Archer apart from all the other enchanting young women with whom Lord Warburton might have fallen in love? More exactly, it is her desire to *use* her mind, in ways as yet not fully specified or specifiable; to enlarge it, develop it, so that it may become the instrument for satisfying her passion for knowledge and experience, and her desire for the fullest self-realisation: it is this that makes Isabel Archer 'remarkable'—so much more remarkable, it seems, than Lord Warburton can find altogether comfortable. And it is because Isabel knows this about herself, though so dimly and confusedly, and knows also that to marry Lord Warburton would mean the end of her aspiration after this self-development, that she refuses his offer of marriage.

Of this awkward quantity of mind in Isabel Archer we are to hear a great deal more as the story progresses. In the meantime, James makes sure that we shall not miss the significance of the hint that has been thrown out here. 'Do you know, I'm very much afraid of it—of that remarkable mind of yours?' Warburton has said; and upon this follows:

> Our heroine's biographer can scarcely tell why, but the question made her start and brought a conscious blush to her cheek. She returned his look a moment, and then with a note in her voice that might almost have appealed to his compassion, 'So am I, my lord!', she oddly exclaimed.[1]

But Warburton's compassion is not stirred—not for lack of good nature or good will but for lack of imagination; and the scene ends on a note which strikes again the exact pitch and accent of his incomprehension:

'There's one thing more,' he went on. 'You know, if you don't

[1] *The Portrait of a Lady*, I, 12, p. 136.

like Lockleigh [his stately home]—if you think it's damp or anything of that sort—you need never go within fifty miles of it. It's not damp, by the way; I've had the house thoroughly examined; it's perfectly safe and right. But if you shouldn't fancy it you needn't dream of living in it. There's no difficulty about that; there are plenty of houses. I thought I'd just mention it; some people don't like a moat, you know, Good-bye.'

'I adore a moat,' said Isabel. 'Good-bye'.[1]

This is said, of course, in all earnestness and under the stress of deeply agitated feeling. It is exactly what Lord Warburton and every Englishman of his type would say in such a situation under the stress of such feeling—something just so exquisitely inept and just so touchingly, disarmingly sincere; and in this consists the perfect dramatic felicity of the passage.

Later in the story we are to see that there is a seamier side to Lord Warburton's innocence and ignorance—and a less unqualified grace perhaps in what old Mr Touchett had noted as his taste for charming young ladies.[2] When Warburton reappears in Isabel Archer's life some years after her marriage to Gilbert Osmond, to become almost immediately the suitor of Osmond's daughter Pansy,[3] it is of course never explicitly said, or at any rate not emphasised, that it is any serious discredit to Warburton, now aged forty-two, to wish to marry Pansy, aged nineteen, and still very much the little convent-flower. But the situation itself sufficiently intimates that it *is* rather pitiable, rather pathetic, even the least bit sordid; nor is it the less but the more so for being enacted in the tainted air of the Roman *beau monde*, and for being intensely desired by Osmond as a 'great' match for his daughter. We are in any case left in no doubt that this kind of immaturity ('arrested development', as the psychologists call it) is the heavier price one has to pay for those weaknesses in Lord Warburton that appeared so amiable, touching and amusing in the scene of the proposal. And when in the end Warburton leaves Rome without proposing to Pansy

[1] *The Portrait of a Lady*, I, 12, p. 136.

[2] P. 28 above. [3] *The Portrait of a Lady*, II, 40–1.

and soon afterwards marries instead a young lady of the English nobility (a 'Lady Flora, Lady Felicia—something of that sort', Mrs Touchett reports to Isabel)[1], we are meant to see in this last light thrust of irony at once a confirmation of the arrested development and a vindication of Isabel's intuition when she told Warburton that she didn't, she really didn't, think she would suit him as a wife.

In the meantime, our attention is invited to the next important situation designed to 'bring out' James's engaging young woman. This is her relationship with Caspar Goodwood, her American suitor, who comes to Gardencourt soon after Isabel's refusal of Warburton, to press his suit.

James's earliest full study of 'the American' had been Christopher Newman in *The American*, and Caspar Goodwood is a fresh rendering of the type, accomplished with an economy and intensity greatly surpassing that of the earlier study. For here, almost for the first time, an important character is presented exclusively through a single centre of consciousness (Isabel's), and—by all that it demonstrably gains in dramatic clarity and force—triumphantly vindicates what was to become a cardinal principle of James's method.[2]

In Caspar Goodwood, James desires to give us a type standing as nearly as possible at the opposite pole to Lord Warburton (and also, as we shall see, to Gilbert Osmond). A Bostonian, the son of a prosperous cotton industrialist, he has, though still young, been running the family business for some years; and he is offered to us as the late nineteenth-century variant of the modern American tycoon. He is a man in whom the practical intelligence and the practical imagination predominate to the exclusion of other sorts of intelligence and imagination: a man of resolute will; completely single-minded in his pursuit of particular practical ends; incapable of being deflected from his purpose. He has all the gifts and energies required for conceiving and executing

[1] *The Portrait of a Lady*, II, 54, p. 356.

[2] See Appendix B below, pp. 399-401.

large practical projects of the kind (as the newspapers would put it) that 'change the face of an industry overnight'; and he is liberally endowed also with the gift of what is called leadership—the power to master men, to kindle their interests and direct their wills to the accomplishment of large practical enterprises. He is distinctly a manly man, or (as Isabel puts it to herself) 'a stubborn fact'—a very stubborn fact.

The type is by no means unattractive to a young woman of sensibility and imagination; and Isabel finds herself sufficiently susceptible to Caspar Goodwood in his character (as she puts it) of 'a mover of men', which she is quite disposed to view in a heroic, even a romantic, light. Besides this, however, she feels also, less romantically and less comfortably, the influence upon her of a certain impersonal force in him, a sheer impersonal energy of assertion and domination. This is the distinctively 'male' quality that D. H. Lawrence was to make so much of in his heroes, whose potency Henry James recognises here as elsewhere, but always keeps in perspective, never exaggerating (as Lawrence often did) either its importance or its interest.

Isabel Archer reflects upon this quality in Caspar Goodwood on receiving from him a letter announcing his intention to come to Gardencourt:

> It was in no degree a matter of his 'advantages'—it was a matter of the spirit that sat in his clear-burning eyes like some tireless watcher at a window. She might like it or not, but he insisted, ever, with his whole weight and force: even in one's usual contact with him one had to reckon with that. . . . Sometimes Caspar Goodwood had seemed to range himself on the side of her destiny, to be the stubbornest fact she knew; she said to herself at such moments that she might evade him for a time, but that she must make terms with him at last—terms which would be certain to be favourable to himself.[1]

This deeper aspect of Isabel's relationship with Caspar

[1] *The Portrait of a Lady*, I, 13, p. 143.

Goodwood is, however, to remain more or less submerged until the very end of the story, when it asserts itself in one of the most vivid episodes in the whole book.[1] In the meantime, she takes refuge from these more disturbing thoughts by reflecting upon his disqualifications. These, she recognises, are indeed superficial; yet they are not so superficial (we are meant to see) as not to play an important part in determining the affections of a young woman with a marked taste for certain refinements of disposition, behaviour, and even appearance in the man she is to marry. The reflections that follow, it is to be understood, are made in the context of a considerable general respect and regard for Caspar Goodwood, and are to be taken as genuinely reflective, not as merely censorious: Isabel is trying, in James's favourite phrase, to 'make out' Caspar Goodwood, to understand the grounds of her resistance to him:

She wished him no ounce less of his manhood, but she sometimes thought he would be rather nicer if he looked, for instance, a little differently. His jaw was too square and set and his figure too straight and stiff: these things suggested a want of easy consonance with the deeper rhythms of life. Then she viewed with reserve a habit he had of dressing always in the same manner; it was not apparently that he wore the same clothes continually, for, on the contrary, his garments had a way of looking rather too new. But they all seemed of the same piece; the figure, the stuff, was so drearily usual. She had reminded herself more than once that this was a frivolous objection to a person of his importance; and then she had amended the rebuke by saying that it would be a frivolous objection only if she were in love with him. She was not in love with him and therefore might criticise his small defects as well as his great—which latter consisted in the collective reproach of his being too serious, or, rather, not of his being so, since one could never be, but certainly of his seeming so. He showed his appetites and designs too simply and artlessly; when one was alone with him he talked too much about the same subject, and when other people were present he talked too little about anything. And yet he was of a supremely strong, clean make—

[1] *The Portrait of a Lady*, II, 55. See Appendix A for further discussion of this episode.

which was so much: she saw the different fitted parts of him as she had seen, in museums and portraits, the different fitted parts of armoured warriors—in plates of steel handsomely inlaid with gold. It was very strange; where, ever, was any tangible link between her impression and her act? Caspar Goodwood had never corresponded to her idea of a delightful person, and she supposed that this was why he left her so harshly critical.[1]

From this it is clear enough what in Isabel's view is the matter with Caspar Goodwood. She can respect and admire him; but she cannot, she finds, *like* him. He is too stiff, too sober, too inflexible; too much lacking in the qualities of naturalness, easiness, grace—the last in particular. She can admire his integrity, his solidity, his seriousness; but she cannot help feeling just a little irritated by his manners. ('He showed his appetites and designs too simply and artlessly; when one was alone with him he talked too much about the same subject, and when other people were present he talked too little about anything.') His whole disposition, his bearing, his very clothes suggest 'a want of easy consonance with the deeper rhythms of life'. He is altogether too much of an artifact: too obtrusively put together—constructed, or, rather (what is worse), self-constructed. ('She saw the different fitted parts of him as she had seen, in museums and portraits, the different fitted parts of armoured warriors—in plates of steel handsomely inlaid with gold.')

What it all in the end amounts to is that Caspar Goodwood does not correspond to Isabel Archer's idea of 'a delightful person.' With all his virtues, he lacks the one virtue without which the others lose their savour—that sacred charm which belongs so naturally, it seems, to the well-bred Englishman of Lord Warburton's type, and also (as we shall see) to the cultivated European of Gilbert Osmond's. And this, we recognise, is indeed the perennial, irremediable defect of the American of Caspar Goodwood's type, in our own day as in James's. He may be full of all the shining virtues of character and disposition that no disinterested mind can

[1] *The Portrait of a Lady*, I, 13, pp. 145–6.

fail to recognise and admire; but he always falls short in respect of that ineffable quality that Englishmen of an earlier generation called breeding: he always remains just that shade 'common' (as the same Englishmen would have called it)—just that shade provincial, gauche, crude, in fact *non-U*, to give it its most contemporary name; and this no Englishman or European of sensibility can fail to take in, whatever he may choose to do about it. Isabel Archer, already in imagination able to take the English and European view of the American, takes all this in about Caspar Goodwood, and, having taken it in, decides that she cannot live at close quarters with it. And so she turns him down when he comes to Gardencourt to ask her to marry him, leaving the stage clear for the central relationship of the book, her meeting with and final marriage to Gilbert Osmond.

First, however, her uncle, old Mr Touchett, dies, leaving her a very handsome fortune. He had intended to leave her a more modest inheritance, but is persuaded by his son Ralph to add to this Ralph's own much larger share. So, instead of a mere £5,000 Isabel receives £60,000 and emerges from Gardencourt an heiress—without knowing, of course, that her cousin Ralph has been responsible for this important change in her situation.

The last dialogue between the dying Mr Touchett and his son Ralph[1] is worth pausing over, for it gives us our first significant warning of a possible weakness in Isabel Archer's moral constitution that we may have cause to remember as the story advances. Old Mr Touchett has agreed to do as Ralph asks, namely, to leave Isabel his share of the family fortune; but he has doubts about the wisdom of what Ralph has proposed. Ralph explains that his reason for wishing to make Isabel rich is that she shall be free—'free to meet the requirements of her imagination'. He wants (he says) 'to put wind in her sails', to see her 'going before the breeze'. His father chides him with doing it all merely for

[1] *The Portrait of a Lady*, I, 18.

his own amusement; and Ralph does not deny this: it is true that he is doing it largely (though not wholly) from a detached 'aesthetic' interest in Isabel and her imaginative possibilities. Then follows the crucial portion of the dialogue:

'Well, I don't know' [says Mr Touchett]. 'I don't think I enter into your spirit. It seems to me immoral.'

'Immoral, dear daddy?'

'Well, I don't know that it's right to make everything easy for a person.'

'It surely depends upon the person. When the person's good, your making things easy is all to the credit of virtue. To facilitate the execution of good impulses, what can be a nobler act?'

This was a little difficult to follow, and Mr Touchett considered it for a little while. At last he said: 'Isabel's a sweet young thing; but do you think she's so good as that?'

'She's as good as her best opportunities', Ralph returned.

'Well,' Mr Touchett declared, 'she ought to get a great many opportunities for sixty thousand pounds.'

'I've no doubt she will.'

'Of course I'll do what you want', said the old man. 'I only want to understand it a little.'[1]

The crucial question ('Isabel's a sweet young thing; but do you think she's so good as that?') is deliberately put in this vague way to make it clear that Mr Touchett has no specific moral weakness in mind, but only a general, unanalysed impression of Isabel's moral quality as a whole which leads him to feel that she may be just not 'so good as that'. That there is such a moral weakness and what exactly it is the story will in due course disclose; in the meantime, Mr Touchett's doubt is meant to be noted and borne in mind as a first suggestion that Isabel may have her share of moral responsibility for the disaster that overtakes her.

For the present, however, Isabel, now an heiress, is taken to Florence by her aunt; and there, by the discreet machinations of Madame Merle, her aunt's cosmopolitan friend, with whom she herself has become fast friends, Isabel meets Gilbert Osmond.

[1] *The Portrait of a Lady*, I, 18, pp. 232–3.

Osmond is also an American by birth, who having lived in Europe since childhood is completely Europeanised; like Charlotte Stant in *The Golden Bowl*, he is a classic case of the Jamesian expatriate, deracinate American. He lives now with his young daughter Pansy in a charming villa on a hill just outside Florence. The villa is exquisitely appointed, and filled with *objets d'art* of a quality which cannot fail to proclaim Gilbert Osmond to be a man of unusually cultivated taste even in a community in which taste is not as rare as elsewhere. For Isabel Archer, however, he is more than merely a man of cultivated taste. He is poor; he is solitary; he is handsome, in the finest, least obtrusive way. He is grave and somewhat sombre, yet with an effect not at all depressing but only intriguing. He has evidently suffered, and this has left scars, but the scars are not disfiguring. And, above everything, he has personal distinction of a kind and in a degree overwhelming to her.

This is evident in every detail of his bearing, his manners, his conversation, his conduct; and it is this, more than anything, that makes him for Isabel the first really *interesting* man she has known. It is not until she meets Gilbert Osmond that she perceives how fundamentally uninteresting were the other men she had known—Lord Warburton, Cousin Ralph, Caspar Goodwood. For Osmond is not merely clever, witty and good-natured like Cousin Ralph Touchett. He is not merely well-bred, decent and kind like Lord Warburton; and he is not, like Caspar Goodwood, 'too serious'—serious, that is, in a way incompatible with being also 'a delightful person'. He does not, like poor Caspar Goodwood, 'show his appetites and designs too simply and artlessly': on the contrary (Isabel notes, we may imagine, with inexpressible pleasure and relief), he shows them either not at all, or with the utmost restraint—with the finest delicacy of consideration (as Isabel sees it) for the feelings of other people. He is all too evidently a man who is easily bored; but he appears not to find Isabel Archer boring. On the contrary, he finds her 'interesting': not, in the first instance, we are meant to note, enchanting or adorable or irresistible, but interesting; and he expresses this interest from the start in a way that entirely meets her conception of the way in which a man of cultivated mind and developed sensibility should express his interest in a woman. So here, at last, in the person of Gilbert Osmond, is a man who—to adopt Ralph Touchett's formula—satisfies the requirements of Isabel Archer's imagination.

There are numerous passages in this part of the book, all too long to quote, in which James renders for us the exact quality of Osmond's enchantment for Isabel. The following short passage, however, shows it admirably enough, with the aesthetic aspect of Isabel's view of Osmond properly emphasised:

> Isabel thought him interesting—she came back to that; she liked so to think of him. She had carried away an image from her visit to his hill-top which her subsequent knowledge of him did nothing to efface and which put on for her a particular harmony with other supposed and divined things, histories within histories: the image of a quiet, clever, sensitive, distinguished man, strolling on a moss-grown terrace above the sweet Val d'Arno and holding by the hand a little girl whose bell-like clearness gave a new grace to childhood. The picture had no flourishes, but she liked its lowness of tone and the atmosphere of summer twilight that pervaded it.[1]

Their friendship develops and Osmond confides in her little by little the story of his life. He tells her of the death of his wife, of whom he says little—which Isabel takes as a mark of his habitual restraint about matters that have affected him deeply. He speaks of his devotion to Pansy, his young daughter; speaks little of his poverty, though it is evident to Isabel that he finds it oppressive; and speaks much of Italy and art and literature in a way that Isabel of course finds enchanting but also peculiarly touching: what touches her is his noble contentment, as she sees it, in the pursuit of his cultivated tastes—in spite of the poverty that forces him to pursue them on a scale so gallingly modest.

[1] *The Portrait of a Lady*, I, 26, p. 352.

And so Isabel Archer (like Desdemona) comes more and more to love him for the dangers he has passed, and he in his own way comes to love her that she does pity them. Their courtship proceeds; and against the wishes of her family and friends—chiefly, those of her Aunt Touchett, who expresses her dislike of Osmond with characteristic emphasis, but also against the advice of her cousin Ralph and her friend Henrietta, who both come to Rome for the express purpose of dissuading her from the marriage—Isabel becomes engaged to Gilbert Osmond, and in due course they marry.

At this point it may be useful to set out explicitly Isabel Archer's principal reasons for choosing to marry Gilbert Osmond. For in view of what happens to the marriage, it is important that these reasons should be 'good' or 'creditable' enough to save Isabel from being condemned as a mere simpleton who deserves what she gets for being such a fool as to marry a man like Osmond. Nor is it merely gratuitous to urge that these reasons *are* sufficiently good or creditable, since this very point has been disputed by some modern critics of *The Portrait of a Lady*: who have seen in Isabel Archer nothing but a half-educated American girl with a head stuffed full of sentimental nonsense about life and art and Europe and gracious living—the sort of 'sentimental idealism' which, as everyone knows, is the weaker side of the American national character, and therefore needs to be exposed rather than condoned as (according to these critics) James condones it in *The Portrait of a Lady*.

To take this view is, of course, to drain the whole central relationship of the book of its tragic meaning, and *a fortiori* to diminish almost out of existence Isabel Archer's stature as a tragic heroine. It is accordingly important for those who believe that this central relationship *is* tragic in the fullest sense of the word to establish the moral sufficiency of the reasons that led Isabel Archer to enter into her tragically disastrous marriage.

It has already been noted that what pre-eminently draws Isabel to Osmond is his sovereign personal distinction—the single quality that for her subsumes all his other qualities. But to this power of his to satisfy the requirements of her imagination must be added two vital elements of her own nature. The first is her ardent desire to develop her mind and her sensibilities: her need, that is, to give direction and form to her vague aspiration after knowledge and virtue—'experience' in the largest, noblest sense of the word. This, James desires us to understand, is one of the most engaging characteristics of his engaging young woman Isabel Archer; and for the reason chiefly that it argues the presence of that intellectual energy and moral spontaneity, so lamentably lacking in the English and Europeans, which James had already remarked as one of the most inspiring features of the American national character.[1]

To take this view of Isabel Archer's American 'idealism' helps us to understand, among other things, what James is referring to in a frequently misunderstood passage in the Preface in which he speaks of Isabel's *presumption*.[2] The word is used, I believe, with an irony at once comic and tragic, and in both aspects with a mitigating tenderness. The comic emphasis lies nearest the surface. It is to be detected in the many references to the vanity, self-centredness, even arrogance of his engaging young woman, which James exposes with so much pleasant wit in the earlier portions of the book. Even here, however, the irony is not directed so much against the vanity, self-centredness, arrogance as such, but is intended rather to direct our amused attention to the perpetual struggle in Isabel between these frailties of her all too feminine nature and the high moral principles to which she is, both by temperament and training, wholeheartedly committed. The struggle is genuine and equal because both sides are equally real and powerful: in Henry James's view of man's nature we will not find a trace of the

[1] Cp. pp. 6-7 above. [2] *The Portrait of a Lady*, p. xiv.

shallow realism which proceeds on the axiom that the baser elements in a human soul are always more real because more base; and its interest and amusement for us is precisely in the fact that it is exhibited as so thoroughly equal.

In its more serious aspect, Isabel Archer's 'presumption' may be seen as the natural concomitant of her passionate desire to grow in knowledge and virtue in a society which holds both in small esteem. It appears presumptuous to those around her (that is what *they* would call it, James is saying) because they are themselves so little moved by any passion of this kind, and can therefore barely recognise it for what it is; and the tenderness of James's irony is accordingly for all that is beautiful and noble in his heroine's spirit, and the irony itself for what she will have to suffer for being what she is in the society in which she finds herself.

But besides this, the irony has still another, deeper meaning. It suggests, first, that this kind of 'presumption' belongs inescapably to every genuinely adventurous, enquiring, questing mind—is in fact almost only another name for these admirable qualities; and, second, that it is the more dangerous for being a part of something essentially good and noble. Knowledge puffeth up, warned St Paul, meaning that knowledge need not but, alas, too often does make a man proud, vainglorious, 'presumptuous'; and for a young person especially (James, particularising Paul's wisdom, tells us) it is difficult not to feel the kind of pride or 'vainglory' in her growing knowledge which is, or may be, inimical to the soul's health. So Isabel Archer's love of appearances struggles with her love of truth and reality, and her disinterested passion for knowledge with her sense of personal power in the acquisition of it; and all this too is exhibited in those opening portions of the book with an irony equally penetrating and tender.

This is a theme that James is to return to, sometimes again with the comic emphasis, more often after *The Portrait of a Lady* with the tragic—this profound spiritual dilemma, shared by some of his most highly developed vessels of consciousness, arising from the co-presence in them of the creative passion for knowledge, which makes them the beloved of the gods, and the destructive pride this same passion generates, which is likely to put them if they are not very careful straight into the hands of the devil. *The Aspern Papers, The Sacred Fount* and *The Turn of the Screw* are among the works in which this theme is most prominent; indeed, in the last two it is the very heart of the moral fable. But it is present also, though not so prominently, in the story of Hyacinth Robinson in *The Princess Casamassima,* of Fleda Vetch in *The Spoils of Poynton,* Nanda Brookenham in *The Awkward Age,* Milly Theale in *The Wings of the Dove.* And in all these stories, as in *The Portrait of a Lady,* the destructive element is always and insistently shown as the obverse side of a nature essentially good—essentially generous, passionate and disinterested. 'I don't believe that such a generous mistake as yours can hurt you for more than a little', says Ralph Touchett almost with his last breath to his weeping cousin Isabel as she kneels by his bedside at Gardencourt a few hours before his death [1]. This may be taken as an epigraph for most of James's stories about the 'presumption' of his finest vessels of consciousness, from Isabel Archer and the governess in *The Turn of the Screw* to Milly Theale and Maggie Verver. It is the generosity of the mistake that in each instance redeems it, always gloriously, even when its visible consequences are deprivation or death.

Returning to Isabel's reasons for marrying Gilbert Osmond: the first, as we saw, is her ardent desire to enlarge and enrich her experience of life, to grow in wisdom and virtue under the guidance of this most superior of men. The second is her desire, equally ardent, to serve. More specifically, it is the desire to do something with her money that will be at once useful and imaginative; most specifically, to use her money in the service of someone she loves. These

[1] *The Portrait of a Lady,* II, 54, p. 364.

are the two fundamental needs of her nature; and in Gilbert Osmond she believes she has found someone who will satisfy both. Osmond, she believes, is a man to whom her fortune will be of real service, whose enjoyment of it she can intimately share. At the same time (she also believes) he is a man who in his turn will share her desire for self-development, and by virtue of his superior gifts and accomplishments will contribute everything in the world to the enlargement of her mind, the refinement of her sensibilities, indeed to the extension—the most splendid extension imaginable—of her life's experience. Thus by adding to the attraction of Osmond's great personal distinction these two conditions of her own nature, her desire for self-development and her desire to serve, and to these again her certainty that Osmond, supremely, will meet these needs of her nature, we arrive at a reasonably complete view of Isabel Archer's motives for marrying Gilbert Osmond. And if these can be seen as 'creditable', that is, as motives that could prevail only with an essentially noble nature, the tragic impact of the catastrophe that follows is ensured.

We do not meet Isabel and Osmond again until three years later; and this second part of the story opens with a memorable scene in the Osmonds' grand house in Rome, at one of Mrs Osmond's Thursday evening receptions. A young American named Rosier, who is in love with Pansy Osmond, now aged nineteen, and wishes to marry her, has learnt from Madame Merle that her father will not hear of the suit. Determined to seek Mrs Osmond's assistance, young Rosier goes to the Osmonds' house, and on entering the first *salon*, which is already full of people, sees Pansy's father standing by the fire and goes up to him to pay his respects.

This is our first view of Osmond since the time, three years back, when he and Isabel were wandering the streets of Rome full to the brim with their happiness in each other: when Gilbert Osmond saw Isabel as the most charming and graceful woman he had ever known, and Isabel felt that 'she had never known a person of so fine a grain' as Gilbert Osmond. It is this same Osmond whom young Rosier now approaches; and in the brief colloquy that follows, we have vividly suggested to us the appalling difference between the man Isabel had fallen in love with and the man she is now married to.

Osmond stood before the chimney, leaning back with his hands behind him; he had one foot up and was warming the sole. Half a dozen persons, scattered near him, were talking together; but he was not in the conversation; his eyes had an expression frequent with him, that seemed to represent him as engaged with objects more worth their while than the appearances actually thrust upon them. . . .

Rosier goes up to him:

Osmond put out his left hand without changing his attitude. 'How d'ye do? My wife's somewhere about.'

'Never fear; I shall find her', said Rosier cheerfully.

Osmond, however, took him in; he had never in his life felt himself so efficiently looked at. 'Madame Merle has told him, and he doesn't like it', he privately reasoned. . . . He had never especially delighted in Gilbert Osmond, having a fancy he gave himself airs. But Rosier was not quickly resentful, and where politeness was concerned had ever a strong need of being quite in the right. He looked round him and smiled, all without help, and then in a moment, 'I saw a jolly good piece of Capo di Monte to-day', he said.

Osmond answered nothing at first; but presently while he warmed his boot-sole, 'I don't care a fig for Capo di Monte', he returned.

'I hope you're not losing your interest?'

'In old pots and plates? Yes, I'm losing my interest.'

Rosier for an instant forgot the delicacy of his position.

'You're not thinking of parting with a—a piece or two?'

'No, I'm not thinking of parting with anything at all, Mr Rosier', said Osmond, with his eyes still on the eyes of his visitor.

'Ah, you want to keep but not to add', Rosier remarked brightly.

'Exactly. I've nothing I wish to match.'

Poor Rosier was aware he had blushed; he was distressed at his want of assurance. 'Ah, well, *I* have', was all he could murmur; and he knew his murmur was partly lost as he turned away.[1]

This is how James gives us Gilbert Osmond in his new character; and it is not often that a novelist succeeds in suggesting so much by means so simple and economical. All the strokes in this short scene are characteristically light and unemphatic; but they are brilliantly sufficient to administer a shock of apprehension and foreboding. There is something in the posture of the man, standing before the chimney with one foot up warming the sole of his boot, in the gesture with which he extends his left hand to the young man, in the 'dry impertinence' (as the young man is afterwards to name it to himself) of his remarks and rejoinders—something which shows us Gilbert Osmond in a light disconcertingly different from that in which we last saw him. What we receive from this new glimpse of Osmond is a clear intimation of some portentous, calamitous alteration in the relationship upon which our attention is focused. Osmond, astonishingly, now gives the impression of being coarse; and brutal, or at least brutalised; and cold and ruthless: in every way, in short, not 'a delightful person'. And if he is all this, he is appallingly unlike the man Isabel Archer had thought she was marrying; and if he is not what Isabel thought he was, what is he; and what has happened—to him, to her, to the marriage?

This is the effect upon the reader of that brief, brilliant opening scene between Osmond and young Rosier. From this point, we are launched into the second half of the story, which discloses to us exactly what has happened and how it happened, and culminates (though it does not end there) in Isabel's great midnight meditation when she sits before the dying fire of her sitting-room and reviews her whole relationship with her husband. In this meditative vigil[2] which is in effect a long and intense interior monologue, Isabel discloses the reasons for the failure of her marriage,

[1] *The Portrait of a Lady*, II, 37, pp. 90–1.

[2] *Ibid.* II, 42.

and this accordingly calls for the closest attention if we are to understand fully the principal tragic relationship of the book.[1]

What first emerges from Isabel's analysis of the failure of her marriage is the real character of Gilbert Osmond. He has indeed turned out to be a man very different from Isabel's first conception of him. He has indeed turned out to be a brute: morally coarse, to the last fibre; cold-hearted; appallingly egotistical; and capable of acts of calculated violence—'mental cruelty', as it is now technically called—that have a power to terrify far exceeding that of mere physical acts of violence. This is the man in whom Isabel Archer had believed herself to see the perfection of delicate feeling and moral refinement; and what makes the disclosure of his real character so terrible is, of course, the betrayal it implies of Isabel's trust and love: of her trust in his goodness upon which her love had been founded; and of all her dearest hopes of self-fulfilment through love and service of the man who had thus betrayed her.

The knowledge of how completely and cruelly she has been deceived induces in her a condition of utter wretchedness—a dry-eyed misery of despair (we are told)—which is most poignantly conveyed in certain passages of the midnight meditation. Before their marriage, she recalls,

> He had told her he loved the conventional; but there was a sense in which this seemed a noble declaration. In that sense, that of the love of harmony and order and decency and of all the stately offices of life, she went with him freely, and his warning had contained nothing ominous. But when, as the months had elapsed, she had followed him further and he had led her into the mansion of his own habitation, then, *then* she had seen where she really was.
>
> She could live it over again, the incredulous terror with which she had taken the measure of her dwelling. Between those four walls she had lived ever since; they were to surround her for the rest of her life. It was the house of darkness, the house of dumbness,

[1] It is worth noting that James himself thought this interior monologue 'obviously the best thing in the book'. (*The Portrait of a Lady*, p. xxiv.)

the house of suffocation. Osmond's beautiful mind gave it neither light nor air; Osmond's beautiful mind indeed seemed to peep down from a small high window and mock at her. Of course it had not been physical suffering; for physical suffering there might have been a remedy. She could come and go; she had her liberty; her husband was perfectly polite. He took himself so seriously; it was something appalling. Under all his culture, his cleverness, his amenity, under his good-nature, his facility, his knowledge of life, his egotism lay hidden like a serpent in a bank of flowers.[1]

Again:

She knew of no wrong he had done; he was not violent, he was not cruel: she simply believed he hated her. That was all she accused him of, and the miserable part of it was precisely that it was not a crime, for against a crime she might have found redress. He had discovered that she was so different, that she was not what he had believed she would prove to be.[2]

Then, recalling that he had told her she had 'too many ideas' she begins to see what it was in her that he found so repellent:

It had not been this, however, his objecting to her opinions; this had been nothing. She had no opinions—none that she would not have been eager to sacrifice in the satisfaction of feeling herself loved for it. What he had meant had been the whole thing—her character, the way she felt, the way she judged. . . . She had a certain way of looking at life which he took as a personal offence.[3]

Finally, she sees also the nature of her offence:

The real offence, as she ultimately perceived, was her having a mind of her own at all. Her mind was to be his—attached to his own like a small garden-plot to a deer-park. He would rake the soil gently and water the flowers; he would weed the beds and gather an occasional nosegay. It would be a pretty piece of property for a proprietor already far-reaching. He didn't wish her to be stupid. On the contrary, it was because she was clever that she had pleased him. But he expected her intelligence to operate altogether in his favour, and so far from desiring her mind to be a blank he had flattered himself that it would be richly receptive.[4]

[1] *The Portrait of a Lady*, II, 42, pp. 171–2.
[2] *Ibid.* p. 167.
[3] *Ibid.* p. 171.
[4] *Ibid.* p. 175.

James, speaking throughout this interior monologue through Isabel's consciousness, accommodates the analysis to her capacities, allowing her with his customary dramatic propriety all the pain, bewilderment and confusion that is bound to limit her insight into the ultimate grounds of Osmond's hatred of her. But within those dramatic limits, the analysis of Osmond's vicious aestheticism is made with precision, and the judgement upon it pronounced with clarity and firmness. Gilbert Osmond's fine aestheticism is a sham and a delusion, its real name being vulgar vanity and egotism. In his relations with his wife it expresses itself as a common desire to dominate her; and in his relation to the world, to 'society', it expresses itself in a curiously ambiguous attitude to the values and standards of that society. A sophisticated conventionality, one might call it, which is not the less but the more shabby and shoddy for being sophisticated, which affects to despise the world but in fact submits itself and conforms itself wholly to the standards of the world: this, we are meant to see, is the last refinement of Osmond's vulgar vanity and egotism. It implied, Isabel discovers,

> a sovereign contempt for every one but some three or four exalted people whom he envied, and for everything in the world but half a dozen ideas of his own. That was very well; she would have gone with him even there a long distance; for he pointed out to her so much of the baseness and shabbiness of life, opened her eyes so wide to the stupidity, the depravity, the ignorance of mankind, that she had been properly impressed with the infinite vulgarity of things, and of the virtue of keeping one's self unspotted by it. But this base, ignoble world, it appeared, was after all what one was to live for; one was to keep it for ever in one's eye, in order not to enlighten or convert or redeem it, but to extract from it some recognition of one's own superiority. On the one hand it was despicable, but on the other it afforded a standard.[1]

So it is the discovery of Osmond's base worldliness and the corrupt values springing from it that first undermines and finally destroys the loving trust in his essential goodness

[1] *The Portrait of a Lady*, II, 42, pp. 172–3.

with which Isabel entered into the marriage; and it is this, along with Osmond's egotism, coldness and brutality, that constitutes the betrayal which is the heart of the tragedy. Nevertheless, if this were in fact the whole tragedy of *The Portrait of a Lady* there would be, paradoxically, no tragedy in the proper sense of the word. The heroine, Isabel Archer, would be the totally innocent and helpless victim of a cruel combination of circumstances which she had been powerless to avert; and she would then bear no responsibility for the disaster following from them. The story of *The Portrait of a Lady* would in that case be a story pitiful and heart-breaking indeed, as a story of human suffering always is; but it would not be a tragedy, for a mere victim cannot be a tragic hero or heroine: the tragic effect in drama depends upon our recognising that the hero shall be in some sense and in some degree responsible for the fate that overtakes him.

Now Isabel Archer, we discover, is not in fact a mere victim. On the contrary, she carries a proper share of the moral responsibility for the disaster that overtakes her. Nor is Osmond, on his side, merely a vicious brute. He too (we discover) has been deceived, in a subtly interesting way; he too has been misled into a fatal error of judgement which has helped to precipitate the catastrophe; and it is in James's dramatic exposé of this joint responsibility for the tragic catastrophe that his gift of moral analysis is perhaps at its most brilliant.

What we discover first is that Osmond's original motives for wishing to marry Isabel had not been as base as might be supposed. He had certainly not been a mere adventurer who was marrying her for her money—like another Morris Townsend in *Washington Square* who was only less crude in his tactics. If Isabel, we are made to understand, had been in the least (for instance) like her impossible friend Henrietta Stackpole, he would not have married her were she ten times the heiress she was. Nor had he been merely the aesthetic dilettante (as some critics have thought him), who merely desired to possess Isabel Archer as the finest piece in his collection of 'fine things'. The money-motive had indeed not been absent, and the aesthetic motive had certainly been present; but his main reason for wanting to marry her was, simply, that he liked her: that he found her really charming and graceful (as he tells Madame Merle); that he was in fact, to his capacity, in love with Isabel—genuinely, even ardently, in love.

This genuineness of his feeling for Isabel comes out most clearly in his several 'speeches' during the period of the courtship; and since they are generally overlooked by those readers who see Osmond as nothing but an aesthetic dilettante or vulgar adventurer or both (and consequently miss the finer points of James's conception and execution of Gilbert Osmond), it is perhaps worth quoting two of them. In the first passage Osmond is commenting on her relations' disapproval of their engagement:

> Of course [he says] when a poor man marries a rich girl he must be prepared for imputations. I don't mind them; I only care for one thing—for your not having the shadow of a doubt. I don't care what people of whom I ask nothing think—I'm not even capable perhaps of wanting to know. I've never so concerned myself, God forgive me, and why should I begin today, when I have taken to myself a compensation for everything? I won't pretend I'm sorry you're rich: I'm delighted. I delight in everything that's yours—whether it be money or virtue. Money's a horrid thing to follow, but a charming thing to meet. It seems to me, however, that I've sufficiently proved the limits of my itch for it: I never in my life tried to earn a penny, and I ought to be less subject to suspicion than most of the people one sees grubbing and grabbing. I suppose it's their business to suspect—that of your family; it's proper on the whole they should. They'll like me better some day; so will you, for that matter. Meanwhile my business is not to make myself bad blood, but simply to be thankful for life and love.[1]

Then, on another occasion:

[1] *The Portrait of a Lady*, II, 35, p. 70.

It has made me better, loving you; it has made me wiser and easier and—I won't pretend to deny—brighter and nicer and even stronger. I used to want a great many things before and to be angry I didn't have them. Theoretically I was satisfied, as I once told you. I flattered myself I had limited my wants. But I was subject to irritation; I used to have morbid, sterile, hateful fits of hunger, of desire. Now I'm really satisfied, because I can't think of anything better. It's just as when one has been trying to spell out a book in the twilight and suddenly the lamp comes in. I had been putting out my eyes over the book of life and finding nothing to reward me for my pains; but now that I can read it properly I see it's a delightful story. My dear girl, I can't tell you how life seems to stretch there before us—what a long summer afternoon awaits us. It's the latter half of an Italian day—with a golden haze, and the shadows just lengthening, and that divine delicacy in the light, the air, the landscape, which I have loved all my life and which you love to-day. Upon my honour, I don't see why we shouldn't get on. We've got what we like—to say nothing of having each other. We've the faculty of admiration and several capital convictions. We're not stupid, we're not mean, we're not under bonds to any kind of ignorance or dreariness. You're remarkably fresh, and I'm remarkably well-seasoned. We've my poor child to amuse us; we'll try and make up some little life for her. It's all soft and mellow—it has the Italian colouring.[1]

It is typical of James's high conscience as an artist that he should have insisted at this point on presenting Osmond so directly. The technical difficulty of getting the speeches just 'right' must have been enormous—to show Osmond's feeling as genuine and attractive enough to make psychological and dramatic sense of his irresistible charm for Isabel at this critical stage of their relationship, yet at the same time to make it only the kind and degree of genuineness and attractiveness that would be consistent with the character he is to disclose after the marriage. James, one could argue, need not have made things so difficult for himself; he might have evaded altogether this difficult and delicate task and given us Osmond entirely by description—and probably no one would have noticed the difference. But he has done it the

[1] *The Portrait of a Lady*, II, 35, pp. 70–1.

difficult way; he has done it with brilliant success; and it does make—or ought to make—a great difference for our understanding of Osmond's side of the affair. For though in such passages as those quoted above the sincerity, exhilaration and ardour are of course tainted with sophistication, and though the aesthetic emphasis is of course dangerously present ('It's all soft and mellow—it has the Italian colouring'), yet the feeling is genuine and strong. Osmond really does 'like' Isabel; he really does look forward to finding in his marriage with her the perfection of personal happiness; he really does have the highest expectations of their life together—expectations, in their way, quite as high as Isabel's own. Consequently (James means us to see) *his* disappointment of *his* expectations, though not morally justifiable and never justified, is yet as genuine as Isabel's, his sense of betrayal as strong; and this—which, as we shall see, Isabel herself comes to recognise—is an important aspect of the tragedy which may be ignored only on pain of losing half its truth, power and subtlety.

So (to return) the interest that Isabel Archer has for Osmond is genuine, and his 'liking' for her is genuine. There is, however, one thing that Gilbert Osmond does not like in Isabel Archer; and upon this, we already know, hangs the greater part of the tragedy.

It happens to be the very same thing that had filled Lord Warburton with nervous apprehension. Lord Warburton had called it her mind, her 'remarkable mind'; Osmond calls it her ideas. It is her ideas that Osmond does not like, and in particular (we soon come to realise) the moral emphasis of her ideas. These he sees as the regrettable product of her provincial upbringing in her native town of Albany; and to a man of developed aesthetic sensibility there is nothing more distasteful than moral ideas in a charming woman, especially when she happens to take them really seriously. He is confident, however, that he can cope with this flaw—serious indeed but not (he believes) irremediable—in an otherwise delightful nature; and to cope with it means of course, for Gilbert Osmond, not to accept it or accommodate himself to it but to master it: to suppress it if necessary; or, if it proves stubborn, to eradicate it—destroy it root and branch. He intimates this intention to Madame Merle early on in the story, in a brief exchange with her:

> 'She's really very charming. I've scarcely known anyone more graceful.'
> 'It does me good to hear you say that' [she replies]. 'The better you like her the better for me.'
> 'I like her very much. She's all you described her, and into the bargain capable, I feel, of great devotion. She has only one fault.'
> 'What's that?'
> 'Too many ideas.'
> 'I warned you she was clever.'
> 'Fortunately they're very bad ones', said Osmond.
> 'Why is that fortunate?'
> '*Dame*, if they must be sacrificed!'[1]

From this it is clear just how intensely Gilbert Osmond dislikes Isabel Archer's 'ideas', how ruthlessly determined he is to get rid of them, and how assured of his competence to accomplish this desirable end without undue inconvenience to himself.

But in this last supposition he is fatally mistaken. Isabel's ideas, it turns out, are not so easily suppressed. Though she desires above everything to be a loyal and loving wife to Gilbert Osmond ('She had no opinions—none that she would not have been eager to sacrifice in the satisfaction of feeling herself loved for it'[2]), it is impossible for her, being what she is, not to voice her ideas—her moral ideas—about many things in the life of her husband and the life of the society into which she has been drawn by her marriage. In particular (we learn) it is impossible for her not to express her opinions about the degenerate morals of the fashionable Roman society in

[1] *The Portrait of a Lady*, I, 26, pp. 363–4. [2] *Ibid.* II, 42, p. 171.

which her husband chooses to live; and since he identifies himself with the values of that society, it is unavoidable that her criticisms should by implication be directed also against him personally.

And this is what Gilbert Osmond cannot bear: that her criticisms should be directed against *him*—against his standards, his attitudes, his 'assumptions'. This is an assault upon his vanity and egotism for which nothing can compensate; and it is perhaps not surprising that it should lead him in the end to hate his wife with a cold, implacable hatred. This is how Isabel herself comes to see it:

> It was her scorn of his assumptions, it was this that made him draw himself up. He had plenty of contempt, and it was proper his wife should be as well furnished; but that she should turn the hot light of her disdain upon his own conception of things—this was a danger he had not allowed for. He believed he should have regulated her emotions before she came to it; and Isabel could easily imagine how his ears had scorched on his discovering he had been too confident. When one had a wife who gave one that sensation there was nothing left but to hate her.[1]

This expresses the final tragic horror of Isabel Archer's situation: that she should be hated not for what is worst but for what is best in her—for her free enquiring mind, for her moral purity, for her desire to uphold, to her capacity, what she believes to be right and good. And this, we are meant to see, is indeed one of the profoundest of the tragic ironies of life: to be rejected and despised—hated, as Osmond comes to hate Isabel—for what is best in one, and by those in whom one had placed one's most loving trust.

Yet Isabel herself, it has already been suggested, bears her share of responsibility for the tragedy. The nature of that responsibility, or part of it at least, emerges very clearly in certain passages of her interior monologue, in which she recognises that she herself had encouraged Osmond before their marriage to suppose that her free enquiring mind and

[1] *The Portrait of a Lady*, II, 42, p. 176.

her moral ideas were not a serious matter, and had to this extent positively deceived him, or at any rate helped him in his self-deception. 'Scanning the future with dry, fixed eyes,' Isabel in her midnight meditation feels, strangely, that 'there were times when she almost pitied him':

For if she had not deceived him in intention she understood how completely she must have done so in fact. She had effaced herself when he first knew her; she had made herself small, pretending there was less of her than there really was. It was because she had been under the extraordinary charm that he, on his side, had taken pains to put forth.[1]

And again:

She lost herself in infinite dismay when she thought of the magnitude of *his* deception. It was a wonder perhaps, in view of this, that he didn't hate her more. . . . She had known she had too many ideas; she had more even than he had supposed, many more than she had expressed to him when he had asked her to marry him. Yes, she *had* been hypocritical; she had liked him so much.[2]

'She had been under the extraordinary charm that he . . . had taken pains to put forth'; 'she had liked him so much'. Of course there is every excuse, one is tempted to say. If she deceived him, if she was 'hypocritical', it was out of love and for the sake of love; and who, remembering Osmond's sovereign personal power over her, could hold her morally culpable for thus deceiving him?

All this is true; and the punishment, as always in tragedy, is or seems to be far in excess of the crime. Yet (James answers us—or, rather, his fable answers us) a deception is a deception; a lapse from truth carries its own punishment; the wages of sin, as religious people say, is death—in this instance, spiritual death. Isabel has to suffer because she had not the courage to *be herself*, completely and uncompromisingly, against all temptations. Because for the sake of love she lapsed from truth, the love for which she lapsed failed her; and this is one truth about the human condition

[1] *The Portrait of a Lady*, II, 42, p. 167. [2] *Ibid.* pp. 170–1.

that the central story of *The Portrait of a Lady* presses upon our attention.

But there is a further and deeper aspect of Isabel's culpability to take account of. This is to be discovered in the fatal aestheticism that she herself is tainted with; and it is this, we are meant to see, that was from the beginning the real common ground, and to the end remains the deepest bond, between herself and Osmond. In her it is never, of course, as vicious as it is in Osmond; compared with his indeed it is innocent. And yet not so innocent as not to be culpable, and therefore doomed to earn its own retribution.

The evidences for Isabel's aestheticism are scattered throughout the book, and cannot all be cited in detail. We have already noted [1] James's early ironic references, with all the necessary mitigations, to her vanity, her self-centredness, her tendency to self-dramatisation—all functions, as we saw, of her desire to appear good as well as be good, and therefore also the first signs of her growing commitment to the aesthetic view of things. The next important sign is her tremendous enthusiasm for Madame Merle as a personage 'rare, superior, pre-eminent', possessed of a 'greatness' that Isabel finds peculiarly (and dangerously) fascinating. ('To be so cultivated and civilised, so wise and so easy, and still make so light of it—that was really to be a great lady, especially when one so carried and presented one's self. It was as if somehow she had all society under contribution, and all the arts and graces it practised.') [2] It reaches a peak in her receptiveness to Osmond's charm, expressed in her many private reflections upon his 'fineness'.[3] It is to be discerned in the very midnight vigil in which she is seeking to understand the reasons for the disastrous failure of her marriage: we remember that 'when he pointed out to her so much of the baseness and shabbiness of life, opened her eyes so wide to the stupidity, the depravity, the ignorance of

[1] Pp. 42-3 above. [2] *The Portrait of a Lady*, I, 19, p. 239.
[3] *Ibid.* I, 23, p. 313; I, 24, pp. 332–3; I, 26, pp. 352–3.

mankind . . . she had been properly impressed with the infinite vulgarity of things, and of the virtue of keeping one's self unspotted by it;'[1] and it is significant that when she decides to support her husband in encouraging Warburton's suit with Pansy, the *amusement* she will derive from it has a place in her calculations. ('It would occupy her, and she desired occupation. It would even amuse her, and if she could really amuse herself she perhaps might be saved'.[2]) Isabel herself never becomes fully conscious of this taint in herself; she does not to the end see it face to face, she knows it only by its effects. But the reader is expected to see it, and to give it the weight that is due to it. The sense of beauty is one thing, aestheticism, the 'touchstone of taste' (as James is to call it in a later work), is quite another thing. For aestheticism seeks always to substitute the appearance for the reality, the surface for the substance, the touchstone of taste for the touchstone of truth: that truth which in the life of man (Henry James comes more and more to insist) is in the first instance moral and only secondarily and derivatively aesthetic. Isabel Archer is too susceptible—just that shade too susceptible—to fine appearances, to a brilliant surface, to the appeal, in short, of the merely aesthetic, to be morally altogether sound. And this perhaps is what old Mr Touchett dimly recognised when he asked Ralph whether he really thought his cousin Isabel was 'so good as that'[3]; and for this Isabel has to suffer, and through her suffering learn that the aesthetic is not coextensive with the moral, and that the touchstone of taste is not the touchstone by which a good life can be lived.

This conflict of the aesthetic and the moral in a highly civilised society is to emerge in James's later novels as one of his great themes, perhaps his very greatest. In *The Portrait of a Lady* it receives only its first and more or less tentative statement. We may judge the tentativeness, even

[1] Cp. p. 50 above. [2] *The Portrait of a Lady*, II, 41, p. 153.
[3] P. 38 above.

the inconclusiveness, from the course of the fable itself. Nothing 'happens' as a result of this discovery; neither Isabel herself nor Osmond is significantly affected by it: neither is altered by it as (for instance) the Prince in *The Golden Bowl* is profoundly and irrevocably altered when he discovers that 'his touchstone of taste is all at sea'.[1] The theme is further developed in several of the works that follow *The Portrait of a Lady*—in *The Princess Casamassima, The Awkward Age* and, most particularly, in *The Ambassadors*. But for its definitive rendering we have to wait until *The Golden Bowl*, where we will find the whole fable directed to the single end of exhibiting the triumphant supersession of the aesthetic by the moral.

In the foregoing account of *The Portrait of a Lady* I have concentrated on that part of the story to which the title directs our attention in the belief that this, the story of Isabel Archer, is most in need of critical elucidation, and that first things must in any case come first. The exclusion of all, or almost all, subsidiary matters has thus been unavoidable; and since these happen in *The Portrait of a Lady* to be of absorbing interest this has been a real sacrifice. Ralph Touchett and the Gardencourt *milieu* are perhaps the most important part of the sacrifice; Henrietta Stackpole (whom James himself dismissed, unjustly, as a mere *ficelle*) is another; the 'case' of Madame Merle is still another; and that of Countess Gemini yet another. These gaps have to remain; but there are two critical problems directly precipitated by the main story that cannot be left untouched. The first is the problem raised—for contemporary critics in particular—by the *dénouement*, which may be reduced to the bald question, Why does Isabel go back to Osmond? To this the text seems to me to yield a wholly satisfactory answer. The second, which is more complex, turns upon the treatment of the sexual theme in *The Portrait of a Lady*;

[1] P. 272 below.

and here, it seems to me, we encounter some real difficulties which are worth elucidating even if they cannot be finally resolved. These two problems are discussed in Appendix A,[1] where I suggest an analysis of each broadly consistent with the account of the main story set out in this chapter.

[1] Pp. 357–69 below.

CHAPTER III

'THE TRAGIC MUSE'

The Tragic Muse, published some ten years after *The Portrait of a Lady*, is perhaps the most distinguished novel in the group of novels and stories of James's 'middle' period which includes *The Bostonians, The Princess Casamassima, The Reverberator*, and the group of stories recently republished under the title *The Lesson of the Master*. There has been a tendency to neglect it among James's works of this period [1]—a neglect wholly undeserved in view of the rich and varied interest it offers, and especially regrettable since it is not at all 'difficult' like the later works, and is therefore likely to be read by most people with the same kind of immediate enjoyment as *The Portrait of a Lady*. The present chapter has been included partly in an effort to remedy the situation, but chiefly with the object of examining James's gifts as a novelist in a work sufficiently different both from his earlier and his later works to be rewarding for this purpose.

Among its more immediate claims to notice *The Tragic Muse* is the first of James's major works to deal almost exclusively with Englishmen, Englishwomen and English life. The American or 'international' interest is completely absent; and what is not English in it is French, or, more exactly, Parisian. But even Paris is only a light presence in the book, not the dominating affair it is in *The American*, for instance, and *The Ambassadors*; and the main emphasis throughout falls upon the English theme. The fuller treatment of the English national character that his theme invites is among James's happiest achievements in this book: it is chiefly remarkable, we will find, for what one may call his

[1] The only recent discussion of *The Tragic Muse* I have come upon is Mr W. W. Robson's, published in *Mandrake* (II, 10, 1954–5). This contains many sound, illuminating observations, but has left enough of importance unsaid to justify a fresh and more extended account.

loving discrimination in respect to the English, the discrimination being always as exact and severe as the love is sincere and tender.

The central theme of *The Tragic Muse* turns upon the conflicting claims of the world of art on the one side, the world of affairs on the other, the two persons in whose lives the conflict is chiefly exhibited being a young man, Nick Dormer, and a young woman, Miriam Rooth. Nick Dormer, scion of an English political house, son of Sir Nicholas Dormer, deceased elder statesman, and Lady Agnes, Sir Nicholas' passionately political widow, sacrifices a brilliantly promising career in the House of Commons for the hazardous career of a portrait-painter; and Miriam Rooth, the Tragic Muse, turns down the offer of a splendid marriage with a clever and cultivated young diplomat, Peter Sherringham, choosing, after a prolonged conflict of wills with her lover, to remain an actress rather than become the wife of a future ambassador.

There are accordingly two distinct stories and two distinct sets of personal relationships to take account of in *The Tragic Muse*: on the one side, the story of Nick Dormer, the young politician turned artist, and his relations in particular with his mother Lady Agnes and his betrothed Julia Dallow; and on the other side, the story of the rise to fame of Miriam Rooth, and her relation with her lover Peter Sherringham. The two stories are linked, in the first instance, by neatly contrived family ties: it is because Peter Sherringham happens to be Julia Dallow's brother and Nick Dormer's cousin that the Bohemian Miriam Rooth first comes to be introduced to the Dormers; and this first contact is presently extended by Nick Dormer's undertaking to paint Miriam's portrait, which brings Miriam still more closely and intimately into the Dormer circle, with important consequences for the affairs of that circle. There are other, more subtle links—those, for instance, turning upon the bond between Nick and Miriam as artists and that between

Lady Agnes, Julia Dallow and Peter Sherringham as the representatives of the English ideal of public service—which are to be discussed in their place.

It is easy to see the kind of challenge that this double story presents to the novelist. What it chiefly demands is that he shall render the two distinct kinds of life represented by the two stories with equal, or almost equal, power and persuasiveness: on the one side, the life political, the world of public affairs, which Nick Dormer and Miriam Rooth both reject; on the other, the life of the artist and the world of art which they both in the end choose. James does not fail to meet the challenge. In view of his own unconcealed partisanship—for there is never a doubt, of course, that he himself stands firmly on the side of the angels, that of the artist and his world—he does achieve a remarkable degree of impartiality in his treatment of both sides. His sympathetic insight into both is almost equally profound, his critical detachment almost equally ruthless; and the main distinction of *The Tragic Muse* is in the mastery with which he handles this varied material under the binding conditions imposed by the art of the novel.[1]

The political or 'public' theme representing the dominant ideal of English national life is bodied forth principally in the persons of the two Englishwomen, Nick's mother Lady Agnes and Nick's betrothed Julia Dallow. Each represents a distinct artistic triumph, and as such deserves the closest attention.

To begin with Julia Dallow: Mrs Dallow, we are made to understand, is by nature and training formed to perfection for the role of a great political hostess. She is beautiful; she

[1] It is characteristic of James's novels of this period that the material should be so varied, and that the world of these novels should consequently be more variously and richly peopled than that of the later novels. *The Tragic Muse*, like *The Bostonians* and *The Princess Casamassima*, is much more directly in the mainstream of the contemporary English tradition— the fictive art as practised by Thackeray, Dickens, George Eliot—than are the works of James's late period, for reasons to be touched upon in later chapters.

is wealthy; she possesses in a marked degree the kind of intelligence peculiar to this type of Englishwoman—the strictly administrative, executive, organising kind of intelligence, which nowadays receives all the public recognition due to it in the persons of those women J.P.s and Q.C.s, Permanent Secretaries and Principals of women's colleges who have made their mark in public life. In Julia Dallow's day, however, such opportunities for the exercise of this kind of intelligence did not exist; and a woman like Julia had therefore to be content to restrict her sphere to that of the political hostess. But in this ambition (we learn) Julia had already been disappointed. She had been married at an early age to George Dallow, an amiable but ineffectual man, who had failed to do anything remarkable in public life; and Julia's disappointment in him, though silent, had been bitter. And so, since the death of her husband, some years before the opening of the story, her hopes had been gradually transferred to her cousin Nick Dormer, whom she had known since childhood, was genuinely in love with, and believed in implicitly as capable of doing something 'great' in public life.

This is why Julia wishes to marry Nick. We are left in no doubt that she is genuinely in love with him—that her attachment to Nick is passionate and not merely calculating. But (we also understand) she is so genuinely and passionately in love with him at least partly, or even principally, because she sees in him the opportunity of fulfilling her own dearest ambition, that of using her money, her intelligence and her beauty in the service of the English political ideal; and this strange mixture of motives in Julia Dallow (James further intimates) is entirely typical of the Englishwoman of what used to be called the ruling class. It is accordingly of the utmost importance that the reader of *The Tragic Muse* should take the mixture exactly as James gives it to us. He must not minimise what is noble and fine in it, and must at the same time recognise and give full weight to its less admirable side; for to appreciate this delicate balance of the noble and the base in Julia Dallow is the only way of understanding with James's own inward understanding her otherwise unsympathetic personality and conduct in the story.

In her ambition for Nick, Julia is of course passionately supported by Nick's mother Lady Agnes. Lady Agnes is devoted to the memory of her husband, Sir Nicholas Dormer, with a curious cold passion of devotion which James (it seems) had observed to be another peculiarity of the Englishwomen of this class; and it is with the same kind of passion that she desires that her son Nick shall achieve all that the father had failed to achieve for the lack of a single commodity—namely, money. This precious commodity Julia is happily in the position to bestow as liberally as may be wished upon Nick; and it is therefore little wonder that Lady Agnes should desire Nick's marriage with her above everything in the world. But, alas (and this is the central episode in this part of the story): Nick, having already secured a seat in the House of Commons as Member for Harsh, Julia's own constituency, presently resigns it in order to devote himself wholly to his portrait-painting; Julia, through whose brilliant management the seat had been secured, breaks off their engagement; and Lady Agnes is left heart-broken.

The significance of this episode in the 'political' story of *The Tragic Muse* is multifold indeed. Nick Dormer, we have noted, cruelly disappoints his passionately political mother and cousin by his decision to give up public life for the life of art. But Nick's choice is more than merely disappointing to them. It is an outrage; and the reason that it should be so is meant to throw a light upon certain important features of the class to which Nick belongs. It is an outrage precisely because it is for *art*, of all things, that Nick is making his wanton sacrifice. Now neither Lady Agnes nor Julia Dallow knows anything or cares anything about art; this has already been abundantly demonstrated in earlier parts of the story. Indeed (as we shall see) Lady Agnes and Julia habitually regard art and the life of the artist with the deepest suspicion; and when, as in this instance, art presumes to set up claims for itself against the claims of a life of public service, neither Lady Agnes nor Julia Dallow has any difficulty in heartily detesting and despising it. And since this is their attitude (to which Matthew Arnold had already and for all time given the name *philistine*), it is perhaps not surprising that they should find Nick's choice not only bitterly disappointing but positively outrageous because, simply, incomprehensible.

Some of the best things in *The Tragic Muse* are those portions of it that give us the measure of this characteristically English incomprehension of Nick Dormer's choice. We receive our first glimpse of Lady Agnes's incomprehension in the enchanting opening scene of the whole novel, set at an exhibition of modern art in Paris, to which Nick has taken his mother and sisters. It is not until we have advanced a good way into the story that we are able to see, retrospectively, the perfect artistic propriety of this opening scene: how much it does to precipitate us straight into the very centre of Lady Agnes's world, and how deftly and economically this is accomplished—at exactly the right pace, with exactly the right emphasis, and with every surface detail made to yield the maximum intensity of evoked life. Even before this, however, it is not difficult to take a keen pleasure in James's opening picture of this typically English upper-class family behaving as such families apparently always do when they are abroad:

> They had about them the indefinable professional look of the British traveller abroad; that air of preparation for exposure, material and moral, which is so oddly combined with the serene revelation of security and of persistence, and which excites, according to individual susceptibility, the ire or the admiration of foreign communities.[1]

They are sitting in the central court of the Palais de l'Industrie, resting after their course among the pictures on

[1] *The Tragic Muse*, I, 1, pp. 3–4.

the upper floor, united (we are told) by their 'fine taciturnity', and thoroughly confirming the French view of the English—that they are 'as a general thing, an inexpressive and speechless race, perpendicular and unsociable, . . . unaddicted to enriching any bareness of contact with verbal or other embroidery'.[1] Presently there is some desultory conversation, turning upon where and when they are to meet for lunch, and whether their guests (Julia Dallow and cousin Peter Sherringham) will or won't be punctual. Nick suggests to his sister Biddy that they might in the meantime look at one of the sculptures nearby—a group composed of 'a man with the skin of a beast round his loins, tussling with a naked woman in some primitive effort of courtship or capture'. As Nick points in the direction of this conspicuously modern work of art,

> Lady Agnes followed the direction of her son's eyes, and then observed:
>
> 'Everything seems very dreadful. I should think Biddy had better sit still. Hasn't she seen enough horrors up above?'[2]

Nick, however, does persuade Biddy to take a turn with him round the court, and while he walks about discoursing to her with animation about the marbles and bronzes, Lady Agnes remains seated with her other daughter Grace, speechlessly registering her profound dislike of all the surrounding futility.

This first direct glimpse of Lady Agnes's attitude to art is to be confirmed, again and again, in the course of the story, and in particular of course by her violent reaction to Nick's decision to become a portrait-painter. This, for instance, is how Nick later in the story finds occasion to describe his mother's ideas about art:

> She has the darkest ideas about it—the wildest theories. I can't imagine where she gets them; partly, I think, from a general conviction that the 'esthetic'—a horrible insidious foreign disease—is eating the healthy core out of English life (dear old English

[1] *The Tragic Muse*, I, 1, p. 3. [2] *Ibid.* p. 7.

life!), and partly from the charming drawings in *Punch* and the clever satirical articles, pointing at mysterious depths of contamination, in the other weekly papers. She believes there's a dreadful coterie of uncannily artful and desperately refined people who wear a kind of loose faded uniform and worship only beauty—which is a fearful thing; that Gabriel has introduced me to it, that I now spend all my time in it, and that for its sweet sake I've broken the most sacred vows.[1]

And Julia Dallow's attitude, we learn, is essentially the same. We receive the first hint of this in the same opening scene at the exhibition in Paris. Lady Agnes has suggested that Nick might like to wait for Julia and take her instead of Biddy to look at the 'horrors' around them. Nick answers good-naturedly: 'Mother, dear, she doesn't care a rap about art. It's a fearful bore looking at fine things with Julia.' To which Lady Agnes replies, rather irrelevantly: '*Don't* say nasty things about her!'[2] And later in the story, when Julia is asked her opinion of the portrait of Miriam Rooth that Nick is painting, her reply is almost identical with that of the imaginary Englishman in James's letter to his brother William some fifteen years back: 'Is the portrait good?' 'I haven't the least idea—I didn't look at it. I daresay it's clever.'[3]

So it is through the mutual relations of these three, Nick Dormer, his mother Lady Agnes and his cousin Julia Dallow, that James exhibits the ultimate motives and passions, the gains and losses, belonging to the English political ideal and the life of the English political families of his day. These are projected with the characteristic Jamesian intensity; and in this connexion the critical point that needs to be stressed is that this intensity, this vividness, owes everything to James's art as a novelist and nothing to those extrinsic

[1] *The Tragic Muse*, II, 37, p. 187. [2] *Ibid.* I, 1, p. 7.

[3] *Ibid.* II, 28, p. 74. Cp. pp. 6-7 above. The last sentence occurs in this form in the original edition of *The Tragic Muse* published in 1890. In the revised 'New York' text it is altered to 'I daresay it's like'.

aids to verisimilitude with which less gifted novelists are so often obliged to eke out the deficiencies of their art. In *The Tragic Muse* the most striking proof of this is that James's rendering of English political life is conspicuously free of all 'documentary' matter. There are no quasi-dramatic scenes in the House of Commons; no novelised tit-bits of lobby-gossip; no political table talk even; and the great election itself, from which Nick emerges as Member for Harsh, is never described directly but only by its effects, principally upon Nick's relations with his mother and with Julia Dallow.

It is worth pausing over this last episode to see just how James does it. Nick at the time of the election is already deeply divided by the conflicting claims of his private inclinations and his public and family commitments—that is, by his undeveloped desire to paint on the one hand, and on the other his desire, equally strong, not to disappoint his mother's hopes in him. In this divided state of mind, Nick perceives three unexpected effects upon him of his successful election campaign: first, that he had enjoyed it all a great deal more than he would have supposed possible; second, that his mother's appeal to him not to throw away chances of political success by his 'perversity' (as she sees it) had moved him more than he would have supposed possible—especially as it had been made in the moment of his triumphant return from the election, in the handsome drawing-room of Julia's handsome country-house on the outskirts of the village of Harsh; and, third, that Julia's own part in the business of securing his election had deepened and strengthened his feeling for her in an unexpected way. This is how he recalls the fun and excitement of the election itself:

He had risen to the fray as he had risen to matches at school, for his boyishness could still take a pleasure in an inconsiderate show of agility. He could meet electors and conciliate bores and compliment women and answer questions and roll off speeches and chaff adversaries—he could do these things because it was amusing and slightly dangerous, like playing football or ascending an Alp, pastimes for which nature had conferred on him an aptitude not so very different in kind from a due volubility on platforms.[1]

This admirably evokes, by its rhythm equally with the nice collocation of details, the spirit in which a young man of Nick Dormer's class could, in an age less competitive than the present, take in his stride an election-campaign in which he himself was the principal figure. It also suggests that Henry James knew all that a novelist needs to know about some of the more important effects of the great public schools upon the English national character—how, it seems, not only the battle of Waterloo, but also a Parliamentary election might be won on the playing-fields of Eton or Harrow or Winchester.

Then (still to show how James gives us the election solely by its effects) we have the scene of Nick's reception by his mother after the election:

Lady Agnes was alone in the large bright drawing room. When Nick went in with Julia he saw her at the further end; she had evidently been walking up and down the whole length of it, and her tall, upright, black figure seemed in possession of the fair vastness after the manner of an exclamation-point at the bottom of a blank page. The room, rich and simple, was a place of perfection as well as of splendour in delicate tints, with precious specimens of French furniture of the last century ranged against walls of pale brocade, and here and there a small, almost priceless picture. . . . All around were flowers in rare vases, but it looked a place of which the beauty would have smelt sweet even without them.

Lady Agnes had taken a white rose from one of the clusters and was holding it to her face, which was turned to the door as Nick crossed the threshold. The expression of her figure instantly told him—he saw the creased card that he had sent her lying on one of the beautiful bare tables—how she had been sailing up and down in a majesty of satisfaction. The inflation of her long plain dress and the brightened dimness of her proud face were still in the air. In a moment he had kissed her and was being kissed, not in quick repetition, but in tender prolongation, with which the perfume of the white rose was mixed. But there was something else too—

[1] *The Tragic Muse*, I, 14, pp. 231–2.

her sweet smothered words in his ear: 'Oh my boy, my boy—oh your father, your father!' Neither the sense of pleasure nor that of pain, with Lady Agnes—as indeed with most of the persons with whom this history is concerned—was a liberation of chatter; so that for a minute all she said again was: 'I think of Sir Nicholas and wish he were here'; addressing the words to Julia, who had wandered forward without looking at the mother and son.

'Poor Sir Nicholas!' said Mrs Dallow vaguely.

'Did you make another speech?' Lady Agnes asked.

'I don't know. Did I?' Nick appealed.

'I don't know!'—and Julia spoke with her back turned, doing something to her hat before the glass.[1]

The last bit of dialogue is intended, of course, as another perfect English conversation-piece—to show again how the English behave under extreme emotional stress.

Finally, we have Nick's vivid recollection of Julia Dallow during the election campaign: of a Julia who had appeared at her most brilliant and beautiful and gracious, and had as a consequence become for her cousin Nick 'a still larger fact in his consciousness than active politics':

She had been there at each of the moments, passing, repassing, returning, before him, beside him, behind him. She had made the business infinitely prettier than it would have been without her, added music and flowers and ices, a finer charm, converting it into a kind of heroic 'function', the form of sport most dangerous. It had been a garden-party, say, with one's life at stake from pressure of the crowd. The concluded affair had bequeathed him thus not only a seat in the House of Commons, but a perception of what may come of women in high embodiments and an abyss of intimacy with one woman in particular.

She had wrapped him up in something, he didn't know what—a sense of facility, an overpowering fragrance—and they had moved together in an immense fraternity. There had been no love-making, no contact that was only personal, no vulgarity of flirtation: the hurry of the days and the sharpness with which they both tended to an outside object had made all that irrelevant. It was as if she had been too near for him to see her separate from himself; but none the less, when he now drew breath and looked back, what had happened met his eyes as a composed picture—a picture of

[1] *The Tragic Muse*, I, 13, pp. 211–13.

which the subject was inveterately Julia and her ponies: Julia wonderfully fair and fine, waving her whip, cleaving the crowd, holding her head as if it had been a banner, smiling up into second-storey windows, carrying him beside her, carrying him to his doom. He had not reckoned at the time, in the few days, how much he had driven about with her; but the image of it was there, in his consulted conscience, as well as in a personal glow not yet chilled: it looked large as it rose before him. The things his mother had said to him made a rich enough frame for it all and the whole impression had that night kept him much awake.[1]

It is this vivid recollection of Julia Dallow during the election campaign that leads him, the next day, to propose to her.

So this is how James gives us the election: none of it directly, all of it by its effects; and only those effects that are strictly relevant to the principal relationships of his story. It is one instance of James's disciplined artistry in *The Tragic Muse*; some of the others, equally exemplary, are to be mentioned presently.

Though Lady Agnes and Julia Dallow are the principal 'political' figures in the book, they are supported in this function by one of James's highly successful *ficelles* (his own designation for his minor characters). This is old Mr Carteret, Nick's prospective benefactor, who is offered to us as the perfect type of the retired parliamentarian. Mr Carteret once sat in the House of Commons with Sir Nicholas Dormer, and his whole life since his retirement has revolved about the recollected splendours of those days. He has the exactest memory for all the election figures of all years in all places; his letters of advice and exhortation to Nick are thick with parallels drawn from British constitutional history; and his wise parliamentary saws are delivered in the meticulous idiom of an earlier generation that James appears to have had the gift of catching and reproducing to perfection. Nick's several interviews with Mr Carteret are among the most tenderly funny things in the book.

Lady Agnes and Julia Dallow remain, however, the

[1] *The Tragic Muse*, I, 14, pp. 233–4.

principal representatives of the political life that Nick in the end rejects; and it is through them that James recreates for us, with the most persuasive vividness, the traditional splendours of the life to which they are dedicated, which is best pictured in the setting of the fine spacious country-houses—such as Julia's in the story—of the political families of England in the last age. Lady Agnes and Julia, for all their indifference to art and their cold hostility to the class of person that practises it, are not for that reason meant to be seen as merely contemptible. On the contrary, James in various delicate ways engages our sympathy for each of them and thus for the life that they together represent; and one of the important artistic consequences of presenting Lady Agnes and Julia in this sympathetic light is, of course, to make Nick's dilemma as real as possible. The choice between the life of art and the life of public service, we are made to see very clearly, is a real and a difficult one, certainly for an Englishman of Nick's class and upbringing; and not only at that time and in that place, but whenever and wherever the ideal of public service is a living ideal, and can as such justly command the devotion of intelligent men and women.

With the artistic integrity already noted, James, however, consistently keeps his political *motif* subordinated to his story—its visible operations, that is, strictly confined within the limits of the main personal relationships. We accordingly receive the full measure of Julia's stature in the scene between her and Nick when she breaks off their engagement,[1] and of Lady Agnes's in the scene (in both senses of the word) in which she lets her son Nicholas know exactly what she thinks of him when she hears that he has resigned his seat in the Commons, so ruining his political career and blasting all their hopes.[2] These two scenes are among the best in this part of the story, and deserve to be fully examined.

The scene with Julia is precipitated by her coming into Nick's studio one day and finding him in an apparently

[1] *The Tragic Muse*, II, 27. [2] *Ibid.* II, 34.

compromising attitude with Miriam Rooth, bending over her chair as she sits there looking at Nick's portrait of herself. Julia does indeed leap to the conclusion, entirely false, that Nick is infatuated with Miriam Rooth, and forthwith breaks off their engagement. But Julia's motive is not wholly, or even chiefly, mere jealousy of Nick's supposed infatuation with Miriam. It is, rather, bitter grief and disappointment at the implications of Nick's choosing to consort on such terms with such a person. It is a bitter blow, not in the first instance to Julia's personal pride, but to her pride in Nick. This man, she now knows for certain, will never do anything remarkable in the world of public affairs; and with such a man—a man (as his mother is to say afterwards) 'who is determined to remain a nobody'—she cannot, simply cannot, link herself in marriage. That is why she breaks off the engagement; and it is the fact that she really still loves Nick, that he still has a real hold upon her curiously passionate nature, that gives her resolution something of the character of the heroic. None of this is lost upon Nick himself, through whose consciousness this strange heroism of Julia's single-mindedness is brought home to us. The whole impassioned exchange between them is too long to reproduce; but the following passage records Nick's reflections on what has just passed between them:

As Nick stood there before her, struggling sincerely with the force that he now felt to be strong in her, the intense resolution to break with him, a force matured in a few hours, he read a riddle that hitherto had baffled him, saw a great mystery become simple. A personal passion for him had all but thrown her into his arms (the sort of thing that even a vain man—and Nick was not especially vain—might hesitate to recognize the strength of); held in check at moments, with a strain of the cord that he could still feel vibrate, by her deep, her rare ambition, and arrested at the last only just in time to save her calculations. His present glimpse of the immense extent of these calculations didn't make him think her cold or poor; there was in fact a positive strange heat in them and they struck him rather as grand and high. The fact that she could drop him

> even while she longed for him—drop him because it was now fixed in her mind that he wouldn't after all serve her resolve to be associated, so far as a woman could, with great affairs; that she could postpone, and postpone to an uncertainty, the satisfaction of an aching tenderness and plan for the long run—this exhibition of will and courage, of the larger scheme that possessed her, commanded his admiration on the spot. . . . He ached, on his side for the moment, to convince her that he would achieve what he wouldn't, for the vision of his future she had tried to entertain shone before him as a bribe and a challenge. It struck him there was nothing he couldn't work for enough with her to be so worked with by her.[1]

From this passage, and from the dialogue that precedes and follows it, one recognises that Julia Dallow has an honourable place in the line of James's strong-minded heroines, of whom the least sympathetic is Olive Chancellor in *The Bostonians* and the greatest, the most magnificently conceived and executed, is Kate Croy in *The Wings of the Dove*.

Something of the same quality is disclosed in Lady Agnes on the occasion of her great show-down with Nick, on the day she learns that his engagement to Julia has been broken off, that he has resigned his seat in the Commons, and that he has told his benefactor Mr Carteret what he has done, thus forfeiting the fortune that Mr Carteret was going to leave him when he married Julia. The news at first quite prostrates Lady Agnes: she weeps bitterly, a thing her children have rarely seen her do. But she recovers sufficiently to speak her mind to Nick as never before; and it is a sure proof of James's success in enlisting our sympathies for her side of the affair (though we know that hers is the 'wrong' side) that we feel positively pleased and relieved to hear Lady Agnes speak her mind with such freedom and force; and positively glad, too, to see her give her son Nick the most unpleasant hour of his existence as the price of his liberty to pursue his artist's life.[2]

[1] *The Tragic Muse*, II, 27, pp. 65–6.

[2] Another brilliant instance of James's power to produce this unexpected kind of pleasure and relief in his reader occurs in *The Spoils of Poynton* when

This scene, for once, is not projected in the form of direct dialogue but entirely as recollected by Nick; but it loses nothing on this account in dramatic force and verisimilitude. The passage owes its exquisite comic effect chiefly to what it exhibits of the sheer impurity of Lady Agnes's motives for execrating Nick's action. She execrates it because he has betrayed her, because he has betrayed Julia, because he has lost Julia's money, because he has lost Mr Carteret's money, because he has deprived his poor sisters of their last chance of being successfully married, because (even) he has deprived her, his mother, of the country-house that Julia was in the habit of lending her. It is all a wonderful illogical muddle, this which we have disclosed to us of the contents of Lady Agnes's enraged mind. But neither the impurity of her motives nor the defective logic of her argument has the power to alienate our sympathies. Her case may be bad, but she distinctly has a case, we still feel at the end of her fine tirade; and we are glad again and again, as we listen, that she has a chance to put it—with every note, accent and emphasis and every lapse in logic of her incensed-mother's argument brilliantly reproduced.

The scene begins with Nick's telling his mother about the immediate cause of the rupture with Julia—the episode in the studio with Miriam Rooth, which had up to then been concealed from her. He reminds his mother that she had met Miss Rooth in Paris; but Lady Agnes stops him in her most imperious way:

Lady Agnes's mind and memory were a blank on the subject of Miss Miriam Rooth and she wanted to hear nothing whatever about her: it was enough that she was the cause of their ruin and a part of his pitiless folly. She needed to know nothing of her to allude to her as if it were superfluous to give a definite name to the class to which she belonged.

Mrs Gereth, 'with the very best of her coarseness', tells her protégée Fleda Vetch exactly what she thinks of her for having turned away her son Owen when he was on the point of proposing to her. (*The Spoils of Poynton*, 18, pp. 193–4.)

But she gave a name to the group in which Nick had now taken his place, and it made him feel after the lapse of years like a small, scolded, sorry boy again; for it was so far away he could scarcely remember it—besides there having been but a moment or two of that sort in his happy childhood—the time when his mother had slapped him and called him a little fool. He was a big fool now—hugely immeasurable; she repeated the term over and over with high-pitched passion. The most painful thing in this painful hour was perhaps his glimpse of the strange feminine cynicism that lurked in her fine sense of injury. Where there was such a complexity of revolt it would have been difficult to pick out particular wrongs; but Nick could see that, to his mother's imagination, he was most a fool for not having kept his relations with the actress, whatever they were, better from Julia's knowledge. . . . The form in which the consequences of his apostasy appeared most to come home to Lady Agnes was the loss for the Dormer family of the advantages attached to the possession of Mrs Dallow. The larger mortification would round itself later; for the hour the damning thing was that Nick had made that lady a gift of an unforgivable grievance. He had clinched their separation by his letter to his electors—and that above all was the wickedness of the letter. Julia would have got over the other woman, but she would never get over his becoming a nobody.

Lady Agnes challenged him upon this low prospect exactly as if he had embraced it with the malignant purpose of making the return of his late intended impossible. She contradicted her premises and lost her way in her wrath. What had made him suddenly turn round if he had been in good faith before? He had never been in good faith—never, never; he had had from his earliest childhood the nastiest hankerings after a vulgar little daubing, trash-talking life; they were not in him, the grander, nobler aspirations—they never had been—and he had been anything but honest to lead her on, to lead them all on, to think he would do something: the fall and the shame would have been less for them if they had come earlier. Moreover, what need under heaven had he to tell Charles Carteret of his cruel folly on his very death-bed?—as if he mightn't have let it all alone and accepted the benefit the old man was so delighted to confer. No wonder Mr Carteret would keep his money for his heirs if that was the way Nick proposed to repay him; but where was the common sense, where was the common charity, where was the common decency of tormenting him with such vile news in his last hours? Was he trying what he could invent that would break her heart, that would send her in sorrow down to her grave? Weren't they all miserable enough, and hadn't he a ray of pity for his wretched sisters?

The relation of effect and cause, in regard to his sisters' wretchedness, was but dimly discernible to Nick, who, however, perceived his mother genuinely to consider that his action had disconnected them all, still more that she held they were already disconnected, from the good things of life. Julia was money, Mr Carteret was money—everything else was the absence of it. . . . For days, for weeks and months to come, the little room on the right of the hall was to vibrate for our young man, as if the very walls and window-panes still suffered, with the odious trial of his true temper.[1]

The sustained energy and finely controlled pace of this piece of recollected dialogue is remarkable; and one may have to look far to find this kind of thing done so well anywhere else. Indeed, one may have to look as far back as the famous 'mad' mothers of the Elizabethan and Jacobean drama; or (best of all perhaps) to a certain famous father in Shakespeare—the incensed old Capulet giving his daughter Juliet a piece of his mind in accents not essentially dissimilar to Lady Agnes's:

> God's bread, it makes me mad,
> Day, night, hour, tide, time, work, play,
> Alone, in company, still my care hath been
> To have her match'd. And having now provided
> A gentleman of noble parentage,
> Of fair demesnes, youthful, and nobly train'd,
> Stuff'd, as they say, with honourable parts,
> Proportion'd as one's thought would wish a man:
> And then to have a wretched puling fool,
> A whining mammet, in her fortune's tender,
> To answer, I'll not wed, I cannot love:
> I am too young; I pray you pardon me.
> But, an you will not wed, I'll pardon you.[2]

Allowing for the differences between the Shakespearian blank verse and the Jamesian prose, there is surely a point of comparison in the quality of dramatic verisimilitude achieved here by these two masters of the English drama.

[1] *The Tragic Muse*, II, 34, pp. 160–3. [2] *Romeo and Juliet*, III, v, 177 ff.

Passing now to the other side of James's theme in *The Tragic Muse*, that concerned with the world of art and the life of the artist in which Miriam Rooth and Nick Dormer are the central figures, we will find it rewarding to glance at James's Preface for a detailed and very illuminating discussion of the special artistic problems involved in this part of his story. The chief of these, James tells us, was the difficulty of portraying in a novel the character and life of the artist *qua* artist—in other words, the difficulty of making a hero of a practising artist. Re-reading *The Tragic Muse* after an interval of some eighteen years, James is struck by the fact that his artist hero Nick Dormer 'is not quite so interesting as he was fondly intended to be'. This appears to be the case, James adds, 'in spite of the multiplication, within the picture, of his pains and penalties'; and goes on to explain the 'singularly charming and touching' reason for this failure:

> Any presentation of the artist *in triumph* must be flat in proportion as it really sticks to its subject—it can only smuggle in relief and variety. For, to put the matter in an image, all we then—in his triumph—see of the charm-compeller is the back he turns to us as he bends over his work. 'His' triumph, decently, is but the triumph of what he produces, and that is another affair. His romance is the romance he himself projects; he eats the cake of the very rarest privilege, the most luscious baked in the oven of the gods—therefore he mayn't 'have' it, in the form of the privilege of the hero at the same time.[1]

This is the crux of the difficulty, which James goes on to develop, with insight and eloquence, in the rest of this part of the Preface. The artist as artist cannot be shown as a hero. If we want the artist as hero, it is only as man and not as artist that we can have him so. He can be a hero only (in James's phrase) 'as the interesting and appealing and comparatively floundering *person*' [2]—only (in Mr Eliot's phrase) as the man that suffers, not as the mind that creates. And this difficulty, of course, the novelist, will encounter equally

[1] *The Tragic Muse*, p. xxiv. [2] *Ibid.*

with the creative philosopher, scholar, scientist (the last in spite of what the glamour-advertisements would like us to believe): he will encounter it, in short, whenever he attempts to make a 'hero' of those whose heroic achievements are accomplished in silence and solitude, with only, as James says, their backs visible as they bend over their work.

One can see how real the difficulty is. Nevertheless there are ways in which the gifted novelist can, without cheating, make his artist *qua* artist 'interesting'; and James in *The Tragic Muse* exploits several of these very effectively—much more effectively than he gives himself credit for in his own final appraisal of his artist-hero. He can use, for instance, the episode of Nick's visit to the National Gallery [1] as a means of exhibiting to us the alternating cycles of elation and depression which form such a familiar part of the inner life of the artist. Nick has by this time given up politics for his portrait-painting, and is engaged upon his portrait of Miriam Rooth. He happens just then to be rather pleased with the way it is progressing, and accordingly goes off to the National Gallery in a mood of modest elation. We see him entering the National Gallery in this mood—and then, an hour later, coming away thoroughly miserable and depressed, and no longer the least bit pleased with his work. The reason for this change of mood is meant to throw a further light on the interior workings of the artist's life:

If the experience was depressing this was not because he had been discouraged beyond measure by the sight of the grand things that had been done—things so much grander than any that would ever bear his signature. That variation he was duly acquainted with and should taste in abundance again. What had happened to him, as he passed on this occasion from Titian to Rubens and from Gainsborough to Rembrandt, was that he found himself calling the whole exhibited art into question. What was it after all at the best and why had people given it so high a place? Its weakness, its limits broke upon him; tacitly blaspheming he looked with a

[1] *The Tragic Muse*, II, 42.

lustreless eye at the palpable, polished, 'toned' objects designed for suspension on hooks. That is, he blasphemed if it were blasphemy to feel that as bearing on the energies of man they were a poor and secondary show. The human force producing them was so far from one of the greatest; their place was a small place and their connection with the heroic life casual and slight.[1]

This is how the cycles of elation and depression can produce corresponding vacillations in the young artist's attitude to the very art that he is practising. When he is in the elated mood, he will feel (as Nick feels most of the time) that the art of the portrait-painter is one of the sublimest expressions of the creative spirit and that no claim for its sublimity can be too extravagant—not even that of his friend Gabriel Nash, that 'there are more ideas, more of those that men live by, in a single room of the National Gallery than in all the statutes of Parliament'. And then, when the other mood seizes him, he will find himself (like Nick here) 'calling the whole exhibited art into question', and 'tacitly blaspheming' as he looks at the world-famous performances in the National Gallery with a lustreless eye.

So this is one way of exhibiting 'the pains and penalties' of the life of the artist—these vacillations between the brightest faith and the blackest pessimism in respect to the sacred art itself; and James gives us other delightful instances of their occurrence in Nick Dormer. There is, however, an even better way open to the novelist by which to expose the inner life of his artist-hero. This is the way of conversation—the kind of conversation about art in which *The Tragic Muse* abounds, which has the power to render, indirectly, it is true, yet very vividly and precisely, the distinctive quality of the life of any creative artist. It gives scope, in the first place and most obviously, for generalisations about art and the artist—the kind of generalisation, philosophical, historical, and technical, that Nick's friend Gabriel Nash has such a wonderful facility for; and this by itself is illuminating. But it gives

[1] *The Tragic Muse*, II, 42, p. 233.

scope also for other, more subtle, things. It can communicate, for instance, the excitement and the sense of adventure that the artist enjoys in his 'good' periods; or the more sober satisfaction he receives from his sense of growing mastery of his art—his growing understanding of its complexities and his growing facility in the management of its technicalities. And, chiefly perhaps, it can communicate the pleasure that the artist—especially the Jamesian artist—will find in the criticism and analysis of his own work: how he will enjoy seeing his 'idea' really working itself out in the paint on the canvas, or (more commonly) seeing it work out here but not there, and trying to understand why here and not there. These are some of the things that can be conveyed by good—that is, properly dramatised—'art-talk' in a novel; and in *The Tragic Muse* they are in fact superbly conveyed by the numerous conversation-pieces between Nick Dormer and his super-aesthetic friend Gabriel Nash.

Nash is quite the best subsidiary character in *The Tragic Muse*, a work by no means deficient in excellent subsidiary characters. He is James's quintessential aesthete of the period, and being a Jamesian aesthete, he is a very much more impressive affair than anything to be found in Oscar Wilde—an Hyperion to those satyrs.[1] His gospel is substantially that

[1] Since writing this I came across an article by Mr Oscar Cargill entitled 'Mr James's Aesthetic Mr Nash' (in *Nineteenth-Century Fiction*, XII, 3, Dec. 1957, pp. 177–87) in which the author argues very persuasively that Nash is in fact drawn from Oscar Wilde. I had dismissed this possibility because (as I have indicated above) I thought Nash so much more interesting than Wilde; I did not know the piquant confirmatory detail Mr Cargill mentions (*op. cit.* p. 181), that James on meeting Wilde at the time of his visit to America had described him as 'a fatuous fool, a tenth-rate cad'. My own guess as to a possible living model for Nash (besides Herbert Pratt, who is of course the most obvious candidate) had been John La Farge, the American painter who is described at vivid length in *Notes of a Son and Brother* (*Autobiography of Henry James*, ed. W. F. Dupee, ch. 4, pp. 287 ff.): the resemblance in personality and outlook seemed to me very close, and the effect he appears to have had on Henry and his brother William remarkably similar to that of Nash on Nick Dormer. Most probably Nash, like most of James's recognisably contemporary characters, was a composite study based on more than one living model, and in view of the evidences Mr Cargill has produced it now seems to me very likely that Wilde was at least one of these. In that case, however, I

of Walter Pater, which he preaches with as much passion as the master and a great deal more wit. He repudiates absolutely every form of mere activity: the great thing, in his view, is to 'be', not to 'do'; and because to do, or to want to do, is the ultimate outrage, he undertakes to disengage (he says, to save) his friend Nick Dormer from all his public commitments—with the not surprising result that he arouses the coldest hostility in Nick's mother Lady Agnes and Nick's cousin Julia Dallow. Nash defiantly believes in art and beauty ('I make it my business', he tells Nick, 'to take for granted an interest in the beautiful'). He believes in the free play of intelligence and the ironic view of things; he believes in living one's life with a certain personal style. 'Life', he tells Nick, as they walk along the banks of the Seine towards Notre Dame,

> consists of the personal experiments of each of us, and the point of an experiment is that it shall succeed. What we contribute is our treatment of the material, our rendering of the text, our style. . .'
>
> 'Don't you think your style's a trifle affected?' Nick asked for further amusement.

would want to argue that Gabriel Nash was a deliberately Jamesian 'idealisation' of the actual—what the great aesthete of the age *would* have been if Henry James had had the making of him, and what he *should* have been if he had had the wit and the imagination that the living pretender to the title did not have. As such Nash would represent a conscious criticism of the historic Oscar more radical and subtle than Mr Cargill appears to give James credit for; and would also explain what puzzles Mr Cargill, namely, that James should, have treated Wilde with such seeming 'mildness' (*op. cit.* p. 186). The mildness would then turn out to be of the deadly kind that James knew admirably how to use for the exposure of fatuous fools and tenth-rate cads; and at the same time the portrait of Nash would not be merely a destructive critique of the current aestheticism but, as I have suggested, an imaginative rendering of the ideal possibility (with all its limitations) of the phenomenon. In this connexion, I may perhaps add that I was as surprised as Mr Cargill to find that Mr Quentin Anderson in his book *The American Henry James* (Rutgers University Press 1957) believes James's father, the elder Henry James, to have been the model for Nash (*The American Henry James*, pp. 101 ff.). It is just possible that the physical features Mr Anderson mentions (*op. cit.* p. 122 n.) may have been taken from the elder James; but the 'gift for talk' would have been common, one imagines, to a large number of James's friends and acquaintances; and the kind of talk—its exclusively secular character, its defiant amoralism, and particularly its European sophistication—strikes me as very different from the kind one would expect to have heard from the elder Henry James.

'That's always the charge against a personal manner: if you've any at all people think you've too much.'[1]

And on the same occasion he repudiates, with genuine indignation, the suggestion that he is 'self-conceited' or 'impudent'. (This had been very much Julia Dallow's impression of him when Nick had presented him to her.) 'Heaven help us all,' Nash pleads, 'What do people mean by impudence?'

Upon my word I have literally seen mere quickness of intelligence or of perception, the jump of a step or two, a little whirr of the wings of talk, mistaken for it. Yes, I've encountered men and women who thought you impudent if you weren't simply so stupid as they. The only impudence is unprovoked, or even mere dull, aggression, and I indignantly protest that I'm never guilty of *that* clumsiness.[2]

Above all, however, Nash believes in what he calls 'the faculty of appreciation', and the importance of cultivating this 'special sense' to its furthest limit. He urges this upon Nick at their first meeting at the art exhibition in Paris:

'We must train our special sense. It's capable of extraordinary extension. Life's none too long for that.'

'But what's the good of the extraordinary extension if there is no affirmation of it, if it all goes to the negative, as you say? Where are the fine consequences?' Dormer asked.

'In one's own spirit. One is one's self a fine consequence. That's the most important one we have to do with. *I* am a fine consequence', said Gabriel Nash.[3]

One can imagine the effect of a remark like the last on someone like Lady Agnes Dormer or Julia Dallow. Nick himself, of course, finds it irresistibly engaging and diverting; but the more normal British reaction is not left unrecorded, and is expressed by Nick's younger sister Biddy, who happens to be standing by, trying not to stare at her brother's strange friend to whom she has just been introduced. Biddy finds this remark so extraordinary that (we are told) she 'bent

[1] *The Tragic Muse*, I, 9, p. 154.

[2] *Ibid.* pp. 152–3.

[3] *Ibid.* I, 2, p. 29.

her eyes on the speaker with a heightened colour, an air of desperation, and the question, after a moment: "Are you an aesthete?"'[1]

So Gabriel Nash believes in everything that stands implacably opposed to the prevailing Philistine tradition 'of dreariness, of stodginess, of dull, dense, literal prose'. And his principal weapon of attack upon the enemy, we soon learn, is simply his talk, this being the thing that they, distinctly, don't 'go in' for. Gabriel Nash talks and talks—endlessly dissects and discriminates and comments and generalises; positively deluges Nick Dormer with the kind of criticism and keen analysis of which Nick (like James) had always felt the dearth in his immediate circle; and in this respect he is of real service to Nick, and Nick is properly grateful to him.

In the end, it is true, Nick grows very tired of all this talk of his friend Gabriel Nash. He becomes conscious of this one evening in his studio, shortly before Nash is to disappear out of his life for ever:

> Nash indeed was as true as ever to his genius while he lolled on a divan and emitted a series of reflexions that were even more ingenious than opportune . . . He had grown used to Gabriel and must now have been possessed of all he had to say. That was one's penalty with persons whose main gift was for talk, however irrigating; talk engendered a sense of sameness much sooner than action. The things a man did were necessarily more different from each other than the things he said, even if he went in for surprising you. Nick felt Nash could never surprise him any more save by mere plain perpetration.[2]

It is evident from this (if it was not sufficiently so before) that we are expected to take Gabriel Nash with the strictest reservations. It remains true nevertheless that his talk *is* 'irrigating':[3] first, in the obvious sense that Nick finds it

[1] *The Tragic Muse*, I, 2, p. 29. [2] *Ibid.* II, 35, p. 168.

[3] The word 'irrigating' in the 1890 text is changed to 'inspiring' in the revised New York Edition text. I have kept the original word because I think it better than the other.

immensely stimulating; but also in another sense—that it communicates, with remarkable vividness and intensity, the adventurous, romantic, *heroic* aspect of the whole artistic enterprise, and therefore also—by reflection, as it were—the romantic and heroic aspects of the artist-hero himself. This, technically speaking, is Gabriel Nash's principal (though not exclusive) function in the book: to celebrate, in his own flamboyant personal style and his own extravagant idiom, the world of art and the life of the artist; and to celebrate it in such a way as to evoke from the artist-hero the dramatically right responses, those that will exhibit him most fully in the character of the artist. And it is by performing this function that Gabriel Nash, 'whose main gift was for talk', assists James in solving the artistic problem he discussed in the Preface to *The Tragic Muse*, that of making his artist-hero as 'interesting' as the conditions of the case permit.[1]

The story of Miriam Rooth, the Tragic Muse, does not, it seems, offer the special difficulty that Nick Dormer's presents. For the art of acting is happily not one of those arts in which 'all we see of the charm-compeller is the back he turns to us as he bends over his work'. In this art the personality of the artist—the man (or the woman) that suffers—is more intimately a part of the mind that creates than in the art of portrait-painting, and it is commensurately easier to make a real honest-to-goodness heroine of Miriam Rooth even though she does happen to be an artist of genius.

The story of Miriam Rooth is the success-story of a very handsome, very crude and gauche young girl, who is possessed by the single purpose of becoming a great actress, and in fact achieves this purpose well before the end of the story. She achieves it by the only means (as the story is at

[1] Nash's other important function is to demonstrate an excess in devotion to the life of art exactly comparable to Lady Agnes's excess in her opposition to it; and in this he helps James to express his own impartiality in respect of the two worlds.

pains to teach us) by which success in this exacting profession can be achieved—by grindingly hard work, inflexible resolution, inexhaustible energy, and an illimitable power of learning from experience. It is such a success story as Henry James knew how to tell. As a drama, its breathless excitement is recreated by the large sweeping rhythms of the narrative; as a picture, with all the contours sharp and clear and all the colours heightened to maximum intensity, it is as dazzling in its total effect as it is minutely accurate in the details.

The story of Miriam's rise to fame is what James would have called 'foreshortened': that is to say, it is done rather too rapidly to be completely convincing; and one does feel this as a flaw, especially on a second reading of the novel. The flaw, however, is not fatal; and it is interesting in any case to see how James engineers this foreshortened impression of Miriam's career. It is done entirely 'scenically' (to use one of James's favourite dramaturgical terms), by showing Miriam in two acutely contrasting episodes, the first near the beginning of the book, the second about two hundred pages on. We have already had our first glimpse of Miriam in the memorable opening scene of the novel at the art exhibition in Paris. She and her rather dreadful mother have been brought there by Gabriel Nash, and while Nick Dormer and Nash talk together, Nick's younger sister Biddy gazes in astonishment and some apprehension at the two ladies Nash has been escorting. The younger, that is, Miriam,

> had a pale face, a low forehead, and thick dark hair. What she chiefly had, however, Biddy rapidly discovered, was a pair of largely-gazing eyes. . . . Her arms hung at her sides, her head was bent, her face lowered, so that she had an odd appearance of raising her eyes from under her brows; and in this attitude she was striking, though her air was so unconciliatory as almost to seem dangerous. . . . She only looked at Biddy from beneath her eyebrows, which were wonderfully arched, but there was ever so much of a manner in the way she did it. Biddy had a momentary sense of being a figure in a ballet, a dramatic ballet—a subordinate motionless figure, to be dashed at to music or strangely capered up

to. It would be a very dramatic ballet indeed if this young person were the heroine.[1]

We are meant, of course, to see in Miriam's striking appearance and the disturbing effect she produces upon Biddy Dormer the potential Tragic Muse who is before long to take London by storm. In the meantime, however, she is far from being even a good actress, let alone a great actress—as we learn from the first of the two scenes mentioned just now. This shows us Miriam receiving what would today be called an audition in the drawing-room of a famous old French actress, Madame Carré. Miriam (we are told) recites first a passage from a French tragedy, then a poem by de Musset,, then 'The Lotus Eaters' by Lord Tennyson, 'from which she passed directly, almost breathlessly, to "Edward Gray". . . . She uttered these dissimilar compositions in exactly the same tone—a solemn, droning, dragging measure suggestive of an exhortation from the pulpit and adopted evidently with the "affecting" intention and from a crude idea of "style". It was all funereal, yet was artlessly rough'.[2] Her performance, in short, is an excruciating failure, which sends a shudder of embarrassment through the assembled guests, agitates even the seasoned nerves of Madame Carré, and obliges her sponsor Peter Sherringham to admit to himself that 'the manner in which Miss Rooth had acquitted herself offered no element of interest'.[3] After this we hear little about Miriam's progress as an actress—until, nearly two hundred pages afterwards, not more than a year or so later in time, we see her doing Constance in Shakespeare's *King John* in the same drawing-room of Madame Carré. This time her performance keeps the hard professional gaze of the old actress ('hard, bright eyes, polished by experience like fine old brasses') fixed on her in a mute ecstasy of appreciation; and leaves Peter Sherringham,

[1] *The Tragic Muse*, I, 2, pp. 21, 23.
[2] *Ibid.* I, 7, pp. 115–16.
[3] *Ibid.* p. 117.

who is again present, dazzled and prostrated with admiration:

> Peter listened intently, arrested by the spirit with which she attacked her formidable verses. He had needed to hear her set afloat but a dozen of them to measure the long stride she had taken in his absence; they assured him she had leaped into possession of her means. . . . The ample and powerful manner in which Miriam handled her scene produced its full impression, the art with which she surmounted its difficulties, the liberality with which she met its great demand upon the voice, and the variety of expression that she threw into a torrent of objurgation. It was a real composition, studded with passages that called a suppressed tribute to the lips and seeming to show that a talent capable of such an exhibition was capable of anything. . . . She was now the finished statue lifted from the ground to its pedestal. It was as if the sun of her talent had risen above the hills and she knew that she was moving and would always move in its guiding light. This conviction was the one artless thing that glimmered like a young joy through the tragic mask of Constance, and Sherringham's heart beat faster as he caught it in her face.[1]

These two scenes, both directly described, mark the distance that Miriam Rooth has travelled on the way to becoming London's leading tragic actress; and what makes the second scene in particular remarkable as a testimony to James's integrity as a novelist is that, though directly rendered, it does not in the least suggest a scene from a play, and though profusely commented upon, the commentary never for a moment sounds like a piece of dramatic criticism. This point perhaps needs to be stressed, for it has sometimes been made an objection to *The Tragic Muse* that James 'does not know enough' about acting or about painting, the proof of this being (it is argued) that he does not talk about either like a professional. But that, it may be counter-argued, is precisely the novelist's merit of his handling of this ticklish material—that he never does talk like an art-critic or drama-critic in the weekly reviews, but always and only as a novelist. As he gave us the election of Harsh solely by its effects upon the

[1] *The Tragic Muse*, I, 19, pp. 297–300.

central personages and the central theme,[1] so here he gives us the piece of acting or the work of art: its quality is exhibited always and solely by its impact upon a particular consciousness; and this, we have already learnt, is for James the novelist's first and final act of submission to the supreme law of his art.[2]

Besides the 'acting' scenes which show Miriam Rooth's development as an actress, there is a splendid passage in connexion with the other art, the art of painting, which illustrates the same point. Peter Sherringham has dropped in at his cousin Nick Dormer's studio while Nick is out, and finds himself looking at the unfinished portrait of Miriam Rooth:

> Unfinished, simplified and in some portions merely suggested, it was strong, vivid and assured, and had already the look of life and the promise of power. Peter felt all this and was startled, he was strangely affected—he had no idea Nick moved with that stride. Miriam, seated, was represented in three-quarters, almost to her feet. She leaned forward with one of her legs crossed over the other, her arms extended and foreshortened, her hands locked together round her knee. Her beautiful head was bent a little, broodingly, and her splendid face seemed to look down at life. She had a grand appearance of being raised aloft, with a wide regard, a survey from a height of intelligence, for the great field of the artist, all the figures and passions he may represent. Peter asked himself where his kinsman had learned to paint like that. He almost gasped at the composition of the thing and at the drawing of the difficult arms. Biddy Dormer abstained from looking round the corner of the canvas as she held it; she only watched in Peter's eyes for this gentleman's impression of it.[3]

[1] See pp. 70-3 above.

[2] It may be added that if James does not give us drama criticism in his novels, it is not because he couldn't but because he wouldn't. He could do the professional stuff as well as the best of drama-critics, as a recent collection of his drama criticism, published under the title *The Scenic Art*, sufficiently shows. If he eschewed this kind of thing in his novels, it must be supposed it was for the doctrinal reason mentioned, that he believed it to be against the rules of the fictive art to indulge it by even a fraction beyond the needs of the theme and the story.

[3] *The Tragic Muse*, II, 29, pp. 99–100.

That is all; and that, it may be urged, is all that is needed—all indeed that it is legitimate—for a novelist as distinct from an art-critic to say about a picture in a novel. Add even a sentence or two, about the draughtsmanship or the composition or the colour values—and the novelistic effect is ruined. James stops just where he ought—not a moment sooner than he ought, but also not a moment too late; and that is one of the countless small ways in which he shows that he knows to perfection what he is about.

To return to the story of Miriam Rooth: this turns upon her remarkable personality and its impact upon the people around her, in particular (as we will see) upon one person, Peter Sherringham, the clever and cultivated young diplomat who first 'discovers' Miriam, acts as sponsor, guide and friend to her in the early ugly-duckling period of her career, and then, when she emerges as the Tragic Muse, finds himself, much against his will, in love with her. Peter Sherringham's unwillingness in this connexion is central to the story, and will be taken up presently. First, however, there is Miriam herself to take account of.

James has several times in his novels given us the type of the eternal Cleopatra, and of this type the finest Jamesian exemplar is probably Kate Croy in *The Wings of the Dove*. Miriam Rooth, however, does sufficient justice to the brilliance, if not the greatness, of the same conception. Her personal power, like the original Cleopatra's, springs from her infinite variety. This (which alternately delights and torments her lover Peter Sherringham) is the source of her personal magnetism, as they called it in those days; and it has of course a great deal to do with her rapid rise to fame. Her artistic genius and her personal genius are inseparably one: she shows the same resolution, the same single-mindedness, the same ruthlessness in the exercise of both. Her striking beauty is matched by her boundless vitality; she is vulgar, in the most careless, most unself-conscious way; she is utterly unscrupulous in exploiting her power; and she is perpetually and astonishingly *good-humoured*. This perpetual high good humour of Miriam Rooth's is much emphasised; and rightly so since it is the other great source of her personal power. It is the humour of the artist in secure possession of her creative powers who is therefore at bottom happily and cheerfully contemptuous of everything else—of everything, that is, but her art, herself as artist, and whatever can serve her as artist. Her perfect self-confidence as an artist is behind her contempt; her contempt is behind her cheerfulness, her wonderful good humour; and her wonderful good humour is behind her 'personal magnetism'. This is the interesting psychological sequence that James exhibits; and it is meant to illuminate for us one of the most persistent (and most fascinating) features of the mind and temper of a great actress.

What is even more illuminating, however, is James's analysis of the nature of Miriam's own insight into the art of acting. The crucial point here is that Miriam's understanding of the art she practises so consummately is wholly un-intellectual—'intuitive', she herself calls it. She always *knows* what to do, and she can never properly explain how or why she has done it. We are shown Miriam in Parisian cafés and London sitting-rooms listening avidly to the criticisms and suggestions of that experienced theatre-critic Peter Sherringham. It is plain that her understanding of what he is saying is, intellectually speaking, very imperfect. But she always, somehow, does 'see' the point; and can always—miraculously, it seems—execute to perfection what she has only imperfectly understood.

James makes a great deal of this peculiarity of the acting genius, which is, of course, generally recognised but not therefore the less astonishing and mysterious. 'How does she do it?' most of us have at one time or another asked ourselves as we have watched an actress whose mental powers are known to be at best commonplace rendering superbly a Medea or a Portia or a Cleopatra. The way she does it, James helps us to see, is the way Miriam Rooth does it in this story: by 'the perfect presence of mind, unconfused, unhurried by emotion, that any artistic performance requires and that all, whatever the instrument, require in exactly the same degree: the application, in other words, clear and calculated, crystal-firm as it were, of the idea conceived in the glow of experience, of suffering, of joy.'[1] This is how Peter Sherringham comes to see it, very vividly, during Miriam's performance of Constance in Madame Carré's drawing-room. He later puts it to Miriam herself; but she, we are told, 'was never able to present him with a neat theory of the subject. She had no knowledge that it was publicly discussed; she only ranged herself in practice on the side of those who hold that at the moment of production the artist can't too much have his wits about him.'[2] From this it appears that Miriam understands all she needs to understand. A perfect performance demands before everything perfect self-possession; and not for its own sake, so to speak, but because self-command is the necessary condition of the command of the ideas and emotions to be enacted. For the actor's emotion is always (to adapt Wordsworth's famous phrase) emotion re-enacted in tranquillity: in the first instance felt as intensely as possible, grasped and understood as intimately as possible; but enacted, or re-enacted, always in tranquillity. This is what James means by speaking of a perfect dramatic performance as 'an application, clear and calculated, crystal-firm, as it were, of the idea conceived in the glow of experience, of suffering, of joy'; and all this Miriam understands, by a process of understanding that never attains to the intellectual yet surpasses the intellectual—the mere grasp of the 'idea'—in the power it gives to translate the idea into act.

This is the nature of Miriam Rooth's genius; and it is impossible in a bare analysis to reproduce the brilliance of the

[1] *The Tragic Muse*, I, 19. p. 301. [2] *Ibid.* p. 301

style—the high colour, the rapid, almost breathless tempo, and the exquisite design—with which James renders it in *The Tragic Muse*. There is, however, another side to Miriam Rooth's genius, the human side, which is most prominent, as may be expected, in her personal relations, in particular in her relation with her lover Peter Sherringham. Inevitably, a price has to be paid for Miriam's genius: specifically, for the constant effort of self-discipline, the perpetual high tension that the exercise of that genius entails. This is how Gabriel Nash puts it in his characteristic style:

> You can't eat your cake and have it, and you can't make omelettes without breaking eggs. You can't at once sit by the fire and parade about the world, and you can't take all the chances without having some adventures. You can't be a great actress without nerves. Without a plentiful supply—or without the right ones—you'll only be second fiddle. If you've all the tense strings you may take life for your fiddlestick. Your nerves and your adventures, your eggs and your cake, are part of the cost of the most expensive of professions. You play with human passions, with exaltations and ecstasies and terrors, and if you trade on the fury of the elements you must know how to ride the storm.[1]

And this is how Peter Sherringham puts it to Miriam herself, commenting on her good humour and unscrupulousness:

> We can't have everything, and surely we ought to understand that we must pay for things. A splendid organization for a special end, like yours, is so rare and rich and fine that we oughtn't to grudge it its conditions'. 'What do you call its conditions?' Miriam asked . . . 'Oh, the need to take its ease, to take up space, to make itself at home in the world, to square its elbows and knock others about. That's large and free; it's the good-nature you speak of. You must forage and ravage and leave a track behind you; you must live upon the country you traverse. And you give such delight that, after all, you're welcome—you're infinitely welcome.'[2]

Sherringham says she is 'welcome, infinitely welcome', but his voice betrays the bitterness he in fact feels about it; and it is upon this reservation that the whole story of his relationship with Miriam virtually turns.

[1] *The Tragic Muse*, II, 36, pp. 176–7.
[2] *Ibid.* I, 21, p. 319.

Peter Sherringham, who is Julia Dallow's brother and Nick Dormer's cousin, looks (we are told) foreign and romantic, 'like one of those wonderful ubiquitous diplomatic agents of the sixteenth century'; but he is in fact distinctly modern and distinctly of his class and country. He is clever and charming, and has a passion for the theatre which he has been able to cultivate assiduously in Paris, where he has been for some years a member of the British Embassy. It is in Paris, we have already learnt, that he 'discovers' Miriam Rooth and her mother, and there, for his amusement as much as anything, adopts Miriam as his protégée, and puts up as best he can with her mother. (Mrs Rooth herself is one of those wonderful Dickensian characters which are not uncommon in James's novels of the middle period. She is typical of the dispossessed *émigré* of the last century, perpetually reading novels bought at the second-hand bookstalls of all the capitals of Europe, incurably snobbish and slatternly and untruthful; and she is so passionately devoted to her daughter's beauty and gifts and so obsessively governed by her ambition of fame for Miriam that she is genuinely incapable of recognising any means as too illegitimate or too improper to advance this end. She is another of James's several excellent *ficelles du théâtre* in *The Tragic Muse.*)[1]

Peter Sherringham does not seriously fall in love with Miriam until she is well on the way to fame; and from then on his life becomes a torment to him. We see him first, over a long stretch of the novel, resisting her growing fascination. His passion wrestles with the pride of class and the prejudice of fastidious habits. *Can* he marry her, he asks himself, having just come away from the Rooth's Bohemian lodgings in Balaklava Place:

> He disliked besmoked drawing-rooms and irregular meals and untidy arrangements; he could suffer from the vulgarity of Mrs

[1] Of these, Mr Carteret, Nick Dormer's benefactor, has already been mentioned. The others are Biddy, Nick's devoted younger sister, the perfection of the English *jeune fille*—a pure Gainsborough; Grace, Nick's foolish unmarriageable sister; and, of course, Gabriel Nash.

> Rooth's apartments, the importunate photographs which gave on his nerves, the barbarous absence of signs of an orderly domestic life, the odd volumes from the circulating library. . . . tumbled about with cups and under smeary glasses.[1]

It is easy to see how all this might well give on the nerves of a nephew of Lady Agnes Dormer with a taste for the more gracious forms of living which a young ambassador in foreign parts might enjoy; and this dislike of Peter Sherringham's for the Bohemianism of the 'histrionic life' is certainly one important reason for his inability to make up his mind. But the reason goes deeper than that, we presently learn. In the end passion conquers, and he does ask Miriam to marry him—but on condition that she gives up the stage. This proviso Miriam, of course, cannot accept; and it is in their last important scene together[2] that the deeper motive behind his agonies of vacillation discovers itself, and his poor divided passion is exposed in all its final shabbiness against Miriam's splendid integrity.

The full significance of the show-down between Miriam and her lover is, however, likely to be lost if one does not see Peter Sherringham in the exalted light in which Miriam herself sees him: that is, as an extremely gifted man, whose passion for the theatre is not merely a young man's infatuation with the superficial glamour of the stage, but is genuinely informed and discerning, and (most important for what follows) profoundly appreciative of the moral and spiritual significance of the whole theatrical art. The point is summed up by Miriam when she speaks of him as 'the best judge, the best critic, the best observer, the best *believer* that I've ever come across';[3] and it is precisely as 'believer' in all that is 'noble' and 'beneficent' in the art of the theatre that he has done so much for Miriam herself—has done everything in fact to create, develop and sustain in her that splendid faith in her art by which she has been carried to the top.

[1] *The Tragic Muse*, II, 37, p. 182.
[2] *Ibid.* II, 46.
[3] *Ibid.* II, 46, p. 551.

And so in this last great scene she taxes him specifically with his *treachery*—his betrayal of this splendid faith that he himself had first kindled in her. 'You're committed to it', she tells him; 'you're committed to it by everything you've said to me for a twelvemonth, by the whole turn of your mind, by the way you've followed us up, all of us, from far back.' [1] Yet here he is, turning traitor to their common cause, asking her to give up the noble and beneficent art in order to become his wife, the mere wife of a diplomat. Then, presently, she challenges him on his side to give up the world of affairs and share with her the life into which he first initiated her, to which, as she has said, he is so inescapably committed. Miriam speaks in this scene with the special lucidity characteristic of all the Jamesian heroes and heroines at the moments of their deepest insight, but also with a magnificent eloquence that belongs to her distinctively in her character as the Tragic Muse. Peter has reached the point of pleading with her to see the ugly squalid side of her profession, and reminds her that she herself had once seen it in just this way:

'You expressed to me then a deep detestation of the sort of self-exposure to which the profession you were taking up would commit you. If you compared yourself to a contortionist at a country-fair I'm only taking my cue from you.'

Miriam takes him up:

'Of course I'm a contortionist and of course there's a hateful side, but don't you see how that very fact puts a price on every compensation, on the help of those who are ready to insist on the *other* side, the grand one, and especially on the sympathy of the person who's ready to insist most and to keep before us the great thing, the element that makes up for everything?'

'The element—?' Peter questioned. . . . 'Do you mean your success?'

'I mean what you've so often been eloquent about, . . . the way we simply stir people's souls. Ah, there's where life can help us,' she broke out with a change of tone, 'there's where human

[1] *The Tragic Muse*, II, 46, p. 551.

relations and affections can help us; love and faith and joy and suffering and experience—I don't know what to call 'em! They suggest things, they light up and sanctify them, as you may say; they make them appear worth doing.'

She became radiant for a moment, as if with a splendid vision; then melting into still another accent, which seemed all nature and harmony and charity, she proceeded: 'I must tell you that in the matter of what we can do for each other I have a tremendously high ideal. I go in for closeness of union, for identity of interest. A true marriage, as they call it, must do one a lot of good!'[1]

She stops there; and Peter Sherringham asks himself (and we also by this time ask ourselves) how much of this is acting, how much *ex animo*? With Miriam it is impossible to say: Peter has already observed that 'she sometimes said things with such perfection that they seemed dishonest'; and this no doubt would be one of the several discomfiting features of being married to a great actress.

The main point, however, is that Peter Sherringham cannot respond to her appeal. And what in the end incapacitates him is, we discover, nothing other than that same British distrust and dislike of art that we have already met in his aunt Lady Agnes and his sister Julia Dallow. He had always sincerely believed himself to stand at the opposite pole to them in respect of their Philistinism about art; yet it is this same Philistinism that, to his own painful surprise and humiliation, he finds lurking beneath the surface of his acquired tastes and discriminations and devotions. '*Art be damned*',[2] cries his soul in reply to Miriam:

What commission after all had he ever given it to better him or bother him? If the pointless groan in which Peter exhaled a part of his humiliation had been translated into words, these words would have been as heavily charged with a genuine British mistrust of the uncanny principle as if the poor fellow speaking them had never quitted his island. Several acquired perceptions had struck a deep root in him, but an immemorial, compact formation lay

[1] *The Tragic Muse*, II, 46, pp. 308–9.

[2] This is the phrase used in the original 1890 text. In the revised edition it is changed to 'Art might yield to damnation'.

deeper still. He tried at the present hour to rest on it spiritually, but found it inelastic.[1]

So Peter Sherringham gives up Miriam Rooth and the great, noble and beneficent art of the theatre, and in the end marries his devoted cousin Biddy. And Miriam marries an equally devoted but not very remarkable fellow-actor named Basil Dashwood, whom the cynical Gabriel Nash had already declared exactly fitted for the role of a husband who will employ himself in 'writing her advertisements, living on her money, adding up her profits, having rows and recriminations with her agent, carrying her shawl, spending his days in her rouge-pot'.[2] In point of fact, however, Nash turns out to have underrated at least the business abilities of Miriam's husband; for before the end of the story Basil Dashwood has managed to buy a theatre of his own, and we last see Miriam playing Juliet, her first Shakespearian part, with surpassing brilliance and to a splendidly full house.

It is not difficult to see how Peter Sherringham's betrayal serves to weld together the two parts of James's story in *The Tragic Muse*, and how much ironic comment is contained in the final disclosure of the grounds of his defection. He cannot bear art any better than his aunt Lady Agnes and his sister Julia Dallow can bear it; and he would never have known this humiliating truth but for the crisis precipitated by his passionate entanglement with Miriam. And this ironic link between the two stories, and the two worlds, in *The Tragic Muse* is further reinforced by the promise of a reunion between Nick Dormer and Julia Dallow. The basis of this reunion is sketched by Gabriel Nash—as his last service, so to speak, to his friend Nick before he suddenly and mysteriously disappears. (We are never told where he has gone, and all that Nick is able to tell his sister Biddy when she asks him is that he is probably in India reclining upon a bank of flowers in the vale of Cashmere.) Nash

[1] *The Tragic Muse*, II, 46, p. 310. [2] *Ibid.* II, 36, p. 179.

makes a point of underlining all the dark discreditable aspects of the reunion:

'Mrs Dallow will send for you—*vous allez voir ça.*'

'She'll send for me?'

'To paint her portrait; she'll recapture you on that basis. She'll get you down to one of the country-houses, and it will all go off as charmingly—with sketching in the morning, on days you can't hunt, and anything you like in the afternoon, and fifteen courses in the evening; there'll be bishops and ambassadors staying—as if you were a 'well-known', awfully clever amateur. Take care, take care. . . . Your differences with the beautiful lady will be patched up and you'll each come round a little and meet the other half-way. The beautiful lady will swallow your profession if you'll swallow hers. She'll put up with the palette if you'll put up with the country-house. It will be a very unusual one in which you won't find a good north room where you can paint. You'll go about with her and do all her friends, all the bishops and ambassadors, and you'll eat your cake and have it, and every one, beginning with your wife, will forget there's anything queer about you, and everything will be for the best in the best of worlds; so that, together—you and she—you'll become a great social institution and every one will think she has a delightful husband; to say nothing of course of your having a delightful wife. Ah, my dear fellow, you turn pale, and with reason!' [1]

So Nick Dormer, we are warned, will compromise—will make his peace with Julia's world, will have his cake and eat it; and in so doing, he will of course, in Nash's view, turn traitor to the world of art: he will utterly betray it by this abject *rapprochement* with the enemy. And since Julia Dallow, soon after this, does intimate that she would like Nick to paint her portrait, it looks as if Nash's prophecy is likely to be fulfilled.

Nash, however, is mistaken, or at any rate leaves out of account the subtler, more interesting (and more creditable) reasons for the promised reunion between Nick and Julia. In this connexion, it is relevant to mention that James appears to have had in mind, at least as a theoretical possibility, an alternative ending for Nick's (and Miriam's)

[1] *The Tragic Muse*, II, 49, pp. 354–5.

story. He intimates this in the Preface to *The Tragic Muse*, where he calls attention again to the peculiarly exacting demands that 'the trade of the stage-player' makes upon the emotional and nervous energy of the actor or actress, particularly the actress, and suggests again (as he had already suggested in the story) that this trade 'must have so many detestable sides for the person exercising it that we scarce imagine a full surrender to it without a full surrender, not less, to every immediate compensation, to every freedom and the largest ease within reach.'[1] And the 'immediate compensation' he appears to have had in mind was that Miriam Rooth, instead of marrying the commonplace Basil Dashwood, should instead take Nick Dormer for her lover, whom she was not only several fathoms deep in love with but also genuinely respected as she never really could respect his cousin Peter Sherringham.

This alternative ending would obviously have made good dramatic sense: that the two dedicated artists in the story should enjoy together the only kind of relationship that would leave them both free to pursue their respective 'trades'. James mentions as one reason for abandoning it, if he ever seriously entertained it, the restrictive moral code to which a novel appearing 'serially' in *The Atlantic Monthly* had to conform. But he appears also to have had doubts about its intrinsic plausibility or 'workability'. '[This] presentment of the possible case for Miriam', he says in the Preface, 'would yet have been condemned—and on grounds both various and interesting to trace—to remain very imperfect'; [2] and in view of what is actually presented in the novel, it is difficult not to agree with him. Since James does not himself specify the grounds both various and interesting that he had in mind, the reader may perhaps be allowed to supply his own. One of them is surely that Nick Dormer does not seem to be made of quite the stuff of which one would expect a lover of Miriam Rooth to be made. He strikes one as rather

[1] *The Tragic Muse*, p. xxiii. [2] *Ibid.* p. xxiii.

too light-weight, emotionally too low-pitched, therefore liable (one feels) in an intimate relationship to become a bit of a bore to a woman of Miriam's calibre. This at any rate is the impression he gives in the novel as it stands; but it would, of course, have been open to James to alter him—intensify him, touch him up, so to speak—in ways that would have brought him into line with this alternative ending without making him lose his essential character.

There is, however, another more important reason, which happens also to bear intimately on Nick's promised reconciliation with Julia. Taking Nick Dormer as we find him, his affinities with Julia are shown to be much more real and much more binding than any that he might conceivably have with Miriam. The absence of such affinities with Miriam is mentioned explicitly in the Preface:

If the man [Peter Sherringham] . . . who holds her personally dear yet holds her extremely personal message to the world cheap, so the man [Nick Dormer] capable of a consistency and, as she regards the matter, of an honesty so much higher than Sherringham's, virtually cares, 'really' cares, no straw for his fellow struggler.[1]

And, in the story itself:

What was above all remarkable for our young man was that Miriam Rooth fetched a fellow, vulgarly speaking, very much less than Julia at the times when, being on the spot, Julia did fetch. He could paint Miriam day after day without any agitating blur of vision. . . . There are reciprocities and special sympathies in such a relation; mysterious affinities they used to be called, divinations of private congruity.[2]

The way in which James convinces us of the reality of these 'reciprocities and special sympathies', these 'mysterious affinities' and 'divinations of private congruity' between Nick and Julia is another of the major artistic triumphs of the book. It is accomplished by the cumulative effect of a score of unobtrusive strokes, none by itself decisive or even noticeable,

[1] *The Tragic Muse*, p. xxiii. [2] *Ibid.* II, 47, pp. 328–9.

and all qualified by a recognition of incompatibilities between them which are equally real and serious. At the opening of the story, for instance, Nick, while admiring afresh Julia's beauty and distinction, can feel nevertheless 'that her mind was less pleasing than her person';[1] and towards the end of the story, when he is particularly longing for Julia's presence, he can reflect on her charm with admirable detachment:

> This charm operated apparently in a very direct, primitive way: her presence diffused it and fully established it, but her absence left comparatively little of it behind. It dwelt in the very facts of her person—it was something that she happened physically to be; yet—considering that the question was of something very like loveliness—its envelope of associations, of memories and recurrences, had no great density. She packed it up and took it away with her quite as if she had been a woman who had come to sell a set of laces. The laces were as wonderful as ever when taken out of the box, but to admire again their rarity you had to send for the woman.[2]

Yet one has only to remember Nick's vivid recollection of Julia during the election,[3] or the idyllic beauty, laced with delicate irony, of their day together on the lake which ends in his proposing to her,[4] or the profoundly genuine sense of loss they both feel (though neither can properly articulate it) when the engagement is broken off,[5] to understand, very precisely and vividly, what James means when he speaks of 'reciprocities', 'special sympathies', 'mysterious affinities' and so on. It is these that Gabriel Nash, whose perception is limited by his cynicism, fails to discern and take account of; and so, while not missing the irony of Nick's reunion with Julia, he does miss the characteristic Jamesian tenderness which is also implicit in it. That Nick Dormer who had sacrificed a public career for art's sake should in the end marry Julia who cares nothing about art—as his cousin Peter Sherringham, who had been 'the best judge, the best critic, the best observer, the best *believer*', should in the end

[1] *The Tragic Muse*, I, 6, p. 80.
[2] *Ibid.* II, 47, p. 328.
[3] See pp. 72-3 above.
[4] *The Tragic Muse*, I, 15.
[5] *Ibid.* II, 27.

marry not Miriam Rooth but Nick's sister Biddy—is certainly meant to rub in the ironic truth that, among the English at any rate, the affinities springing from the common ground of family, class, education, social and domestic habits are immeasurably stronger than are those springing from the common pursuit of an artistic or quasi-artistic vocation. This is the truth that Gabriel Nash does not miss. But what James also intimates is that these affinities, though seemingly so artificially determined, are yet among the English profoundly natural; and being in this paradoxical manner not only natural but also infinitely touching and engaging, they are matter for interest, enjoyment, 'amusement' (in James's large sense of the word) rather than derision. And this is the sweeter, tenderer aspect of Nick's reunion with Julia that Gabriel Nash fails to see.

CHAPTER IV

'THE TURN OF THE SCREW'

The Turn of the Screw has in recent years received an amount of attention that Henry James would have found surprising, flattering and delightful. It has been staged, filmed and made into an opera; the opera was recently seen on television in a highly successful production; and it will soon no doubt become a favourite source of quotation and reference in the smarter type of advertisement. In short, it is well on the way to becoming a popular classic; and since it thoroughly deserves the distinction, one can only rejoice.

The popularity *The Turn of the Screw* has come to enjoy does not, however, solve the problems that this in some ways most baffling of James's stories raises. The interpretations that have from time to time been advanced are extremely diverse. One of the best known, that of Mr Edmund Wilson in his essay *The Ambiguity of Henry James*, is discussed in a later section, where it is shown to be interesting equally for its genuine perceptions and its exemplary errors.[1] In the meantime, it is encouraging to receive independent confirmation of the interpretation of *The Turn of the Screw* to be set out in this chapter—of its general direction at any rate, if not of its details—from another critic of Mr Wilson's essay. Mr R. B. Heilman, commenting on the intellectual climate that produced Mr Wilson's interpretation, remarks with justifiable animus: 'In that climate there is so strong a suspicion of the elements that are central in *The Turn of the Screw*—salvation, the supernatural, evil as an absolute—that the critic ripened in the climate runs into a mental block: he is compelled to find a "scientific" way round these irrationalities; and in doing so he is likely to lose sight of the

[1] See Appendix B, pp. 370–81 below.

proper imaginative values.'[1] Though Mr Heilman does not here attempt a complete account of *The Turn of the Screw*, what he says about its 'central elements' seems to me profoundly true. Indeed, on the view proposed in this chapter the story yields its full meaning when and only when it is read as a moral fable which powerfully dramatises certain fundamental facts of our spiritual experience—chiefly, the reality of evil ('evil as an absolute', in Mr Heilman's phrase), the reality of good, and the possibility of redemption ('salvation') for the victims of the evil by the power of human love.[2]

The principal claim for this approach to *The Turn of the Screw* is that it is genuinely inclusive. It is consistent, to begin with, with James's explicit statement of his intention in his Preface and in his note on *The Turn of the Screw* in the *Notebooks*. It makes the most coherent sense of all the principal episodes and relationships in the story; it suggests an account of the governess's 'guilt'—one of the most perplexing and elusive elements in the story—which is fully consistent with all the data; and it also attempts to explain, in the light of an hypothesis that aims to do justice to the level of James's treatment of it, that most perplexing and elusive element of all —the famous 'ambiguity,' which the attentive reader has rarely failed to respond to and yet has almost always found it difficult satisfactorily to account for.

Taking James's statement of his intention as our starting-point, we note first that (contrary to Mr Wilson's view) the children and the children's relations with the dead servants are to be taken as the centre of interest in the story. In his Preface he mentions that the anecdote which gave him the germ of his story centred upon 'a couple of small children

[1] R. B. Heilman, 'The Freudian Reading of *The Turn of the Screw*' in *Modern Language Notes*, Vol. LXII (Nov. 1947), p. 444.

[2] In a subsequent essay '*The Turn of the Screw*' *as Poem* (1948), Mr Heilman does set out a full interpretation of the story, which in many important points corroborates mine. I have discussed it in Appendix B, pp. 381-4 below.

in an out-of-the-way-place, to whom the spirits of certain "bad" servants, dead in the employ of the house, were believed to have appeared with the design of "getting hold" of them'.[1] The servants are described as 'hovering prowling blighted presences',[2] and again as 'abnormal agents' on whom 'there would be laid . . . the dire duty of causing the situation to reek with the air of Evil'.[3] In presenting them in this character, James adds, 'the essence of the matter was the villainy of motive in the evoked predatory creatures';[4] and, still more explicitly, in respect to the danger of anticlimax involved in his plan 'to bring the bad dead back to life for a second round of badness',[5]

What, in the last analysis, had I to give the sense of? Of their being, the haunting pair, capable, as the phrase is, of everything—that is of exerting, in respect to the children, the very worst action small victims so conditioned might be conceived as subject to.[6]

The entry about *The Turn of the Screw* in the *Notebooks* confirms these statements of intention in the Preface:

Saturday, January, 12th, 1895. Note here the ghost-story told me at Addington . . . by the Archbishop of Canterbury: . . . the story of the young children (indefinite number and age) left to the care of servants in an old country-house, through the death, presumably, of parents. The servants, wicked and depraved, corrupt and deprave the children; the children are bad, full of evil, to a sinister degree. The servants *die* (the story vague about the way of it) and their apparitions, figures, return to haunt the house *and* children, to whom they seem to beckon, whom they invite and solicit, from across dangerous places, the deep ditch of a sunk fence, etc.—so that the children may destroy themselves, lose themselves, by responding, by getting into their power. So long as the children are kept from them, they are not lost; but they try and try, these evil presences, to get hold of them. It is a question of the children 'coming over to where they are'. It is all obscure and imperfect, the picture, the story, but there is a suggestion of strangely

[1] *The Turn of the Screw*, p. xvii.
[2] *Ibid.* p. xxii.
[3] *Ibid.* p. xxii.
[4] *Ibid.* p. xxiii.
[5] *Ibid.* p. xxiii.
[6] *Ibid.* p. xxiv; cp. p. 115 below.

gruesome effect in it. The story to be told—tolerably obviously—by an outside spectator, observer.[1]

Our first task accordingly is to examine the strange and gruesome relationship between the children and the servants; and this in turn requires some understanding of James's intention in respect to the children themselves. What (we first have to ask) is he seeking to portray in those remarkable children Flora and Miles? What precisely is the nature of the evil to which they have fallen victim, and what is its moral interest and significance?

I believe that what James is seeking to portray in and through them is a prime fact about the moral constitution of young children, which many have recognised but few have grasped with James's fullness and intensity of understanding. This, stated baldly, is the co-existence of innocence with corruption in the young child. The corruption takes the form, especially in children of more than average intelligence and imagination, of a knowledge, or 'knowingness', that too evidently—and very strangely—exceeds any they could possibly have derived from their own experience of the world; and because this happens as often as not to be a knowledge of 'forbidden' things, disturbingly (so it seems) intimate and first-hand, it argues the presence of a corrupt element.

This, it appears, is the principal psychological insight (which is also a moral insight) that James is concerned to dramatise through the children in *The Turn of the Screw*. The children's innocence is really innocent and their corruption really corrupt—of this James convinces us by his masterly rendering of both; and it is this real, indisputable co-presence of elements so grossly incompatible that accounts for the peculiar mystery and horror of the phenomenon. James himself clearly felt it as such; and for that reason perhaps, among others, chose the traditional literary form of the 'thriller', reinforced by the supernatural —the 'supernatural thriller', one might call it—as the best form in which

[1] *The Notebooks of Henry James*, ed. Matthiessen and Murdock, pp. 178–9.

to project imaginatively the experience of that particular mystery and horror. The supernatural is there, in other words, in the interests of the children's side of the affair, not (as Mr Wilson's theory asks us to believe)[1] in the interests of the governess's: it is there to evoke, as powerfully as possible, the sense of the sheer mysteriousness and inexplicability, with the accompanying sense of horror, that the element of moral corruption in young children induces in a sensitive adult observer.

In this connexion, it is worth noting that if the presence of a corrupt element in the young child is a true inference from the observed phenomena, the theological doctrine of Original Sin would seem to have a sound basis in human experience.[2] Indeed, in so far as the doctrine of Original Sin emphasises, not the actual depravity of human nature from birth, but its inborn or inherited ('original') *disposition* to be depraved, it would seem to be a remarkably cogent explanation on theistic premises of this fact among other facts of our moral constitution. Whatever the theological truth of the matter may be, it is at any rate certain that on Henry James's strictly non-theistic account of the matter the child is not born with the corrupt element already present. As we see in *The Turn of the Screw*, it is precisely not born with it, but acquires it by adult influence and example. But it acquires it early—this seems to be a vital point; and it is therefore probably no accident that the children in *The Turn of the Screw* should be the age they are. Flora, we are told, is eight, Miles ten: they are old enough, that is, to be actively receptive to the corrupting influence of the servants and to show with distinctness the effects of their corruption; but they are not old enough to be morally culpable; and because not morally culpable, therefore innocent. Were they (it can be argued) even a few years younger, say, four and six, or

[1] See Appendix B below.

[2] Mr Heilman in '*The Turn of the Screw*' *as Poem* makes a similar point. See Appendix B, p. 384 below.

five and seven, they would be too young to show the effects of their corruption by the servants in a way interesting enough or instructive enough for the purposes of James's fable; were they, on the other hand, a few years older—Flora twelve, for instance, and Miles fourteen—they would indeed be old enough to be corrupted, but too old to be properly innocent. James in his genius has, it would seem, 'caught' his children at the right age—at the exact age when this co-existence of the innocence with the corruption may be most distinctly perceived and therefore most instructively exhibited.

The process by which the corruption of the children is effected in *The Turn of the Screw*, though left deliberately inexplicit, is not difficult to reconstruct. James had already, in another famous story of about the same period, *What Maisie Knew*, treated the theme of the attempted corruption of a young child of unusual intelligence and sensibility. Little Maisie Farange is the child of divorced parents who have both remarried, and the story turns upon the effects on the child of being exposed to the ugly violence of the two sets of parents, all—or at least three of them—bitterly hostile to one another, who use the child as a means of paying off their sordid scores. In this story the child Maisie survives, chiefly because she is not left completely unprotected, having her old nurse, the Dickensian Mrs Wix, to stand between her and the unscrupulous parents.

In *The Turn of the Screw*, James employs a favourite quasi-mathematical device, that of 'dropping' from a later story what was a decisive element in an earlier one, and so constructing a new 'equation' composed of all the essential elements of the old save this one element. He deliberately drops what was the saving element in *What Maisie Knew*, and asks us now to imagine the same type of child exposed to an evil adult influence in its immediate environment with no protection at all. 'But ah the exposure indeed, the helpless plasticity of childhood that isn't dear or sacred to *some*body

That *was* my little tragedy . . .', James writes to a perceptive correspondent,[1] making it plain where the emphasis ought to fall: it is the unprotected condition of the children, we are to understand, that leaves them so desperately exposed to the insinuating advances of the man-servant Peter Quint and the governess Miss Jessel.

'Wicked' and 'depraved' are the terms applied to the servants in the entry in the *Notebooks*;[2] and in the story itself all the hints and guesses about Quint and Miss Jessel are designed to give as morally sinister a meaning to these terms as they have ever received. The man, it is intimated, is openly and coarsely degenerate, the woman in a more genteel way ('She was a lady', we are told); and the man, besides, has a certain flamboyancy which an impressionable little boy might find especially attractive. That there was an illicit sexual relation between the man and woman seems certain; and equally certain that they made the details fully accessible to the children, communicating them in the confidential, insinuating, nudging-and-whispering way in which such people habitually talk about sexual matters, especially to the young. This no doubt was part of what Miles was 'told' by Quint and Flora by Miss Jessel; and the effect of these confidences (as anyone who as a child has had any experience of them will know) would be twofold: the children would find them, on the one hand, confusing and frightening, and on the other dangerously, unhealthily exciting and alluring.

Besides this, however, the existence of an erotic relation between the servants and the children themselves is strongly hinted at: indeed, of erotic exchanges of some kind, between Quint and Miles in particular, which if not actively homosexual at any rate expressed itself in 'talk'—intimate and sustained talk—about these matters. In that case, these principally were the 'things' that Quint told Miles, and Miles

[1] Letter to Dr Louis Waldstein, 21 October 1898 (*Letters*, ed. Lubbock, I, p. 305).

[2] See p. 108 above.

in turn told the boys at school—those he 'liked', as he tells the governess at the end, meaning those he regarded as his special friends, with whom therefore he would particularly want to share his valuable knowledge. And if these were the things that Miles said or did at school, his doing so would be consistent with the known practices at English preparatory schools, especially at the time at which James was writing; and would also make the best psychological and dramatic sense of the governess's reaction to it—both of the nameless horror which her intuitive sense of it inspires in her and of her ignorance to the end of what the 'things' actually were. ('Did you take letters?—or other things?' she can still ask Miles in the last scene when, in view of all that had already passed, probably only a young woman brought up in a remote country parsonage could remain quite so wide of the mark.)[1]

The final and most disastrous effect of the children's exposure to Quint and Miss Jessel would in that case also be clear. It would be to induce in them, and in Miles in particular, a craving for more and more 'knowledge' of this kind—for the fascination, the excitement, the stimulation, to the

[1] The view that the corruption of the children was sexual in character has been widely accepted from the beginning by the critics of *The Turn of the Screw*; and the specifically homosexual element has been held (very plausibly) to explain the significant comment of an early critic, William Lyon Phelps—that 'had he [James] spoken plainly the book might have been barred the mails'. (Quoted by Oscar Cargill in 'Henry James as Freudian Pioneer', *Chicago Review*, x, Summer 1956.) One recent critic who accepts this view chooses, however, to express a remarkably emancipated attitude to it. 'The hint of boyish homosexuality can scarcely be ignored', writes Joseph J. Firebaugh in 'Inadequacy in Eden: Knowledge and *The Turn of the Screw*' (*Modern Fiction Studies*, III, Spring, 1957). 'But', Mr. Firebaugh goes on, 'we need not be put off by this, unless we are as naive as the governess. If that is the nameless crime, it is still knowledge—a highly useful knowledge in the world as it is unfortunately constituted—and it is moreover the knowledge the child has been able to get from his limited sources.' Much rich and effectual comment (as Henry James might have said) could be made on this statement; but—remembering that the children are described in the *Notebooks* as 'bad, full of evil, to a sinister degree' and their corruption as 'the very worst action small victims so conditioned might be conceived as subject to'—it is perhaps enough to say that the view it expresses is as remote from and alien to James's own view of the matter as any could well be.

imagination and the senses, of a debased eroticism. And it is this craving for the illicit, the forbidden, in sexual knowledge (and potentially, of course, also in sexual practice) with which Quint and Miss Jessel had infected the children that would give them their hold over them. By this means they would have succeeded in possessing themselves of the hearts and minds of the children, attaching them inseparably to their own depraved persons; and it is this finally that would make it worth their while, so to speak, to come back 'for a second round of badness'—to 'beckon' to them, 'invite and solicit' them (as James says in the *Notebooks*) 'so that the children may destroy themselves, lose themselves, by responding, by getting into their power'.[1]

This, then, or something like this, is what James asks us to imagine as the process of the children's corruption by the servants.[2] The emphasis, it will be remembered, is all upon the word 'imagine'. For James nowhere explicitly tells us what it was that Peter Quint and Miss Jessel 'told' the children, or what it was they made them 'do', or what it was for which

[1] Cp. p. 108 above.

[2] In view of the fact that some modern critics have found James's pre-occupation with the corruption of the young in some of his later works 'unhealthy', 'morbid' and so on, it is perhaps worth suggesting a different view of the matter. I believe that James was moved to a compassion (and a horror) beyond the imagination of his critics by the sufferings of the helpless young in the society which he came to know so intimately. The injuries, psychological and moral, that irresponsible, self-centred, pleasure-seeking parents of the leisured class could inflict upon their children by simple neglect (as in *The Turn of the Screw*: 'Ah, the exposure indeed, the helpless plasticity of childhood that isn't dear or sacred to *some*body. That *was* my little tragedy'), or by positive exploitation (as in *What Maisie Knew*), or by still subtler forms of violation (as in *The Awkward Age*) was—and still is—a matter of daily observation in the life of this society; and James's concern with these phenomena, so far from being unhealthy and morbid, shows rather the healthiest moral revulsion from these unlovely aspects of the upper-class society of his day. Their exposure is never, of course, the only object of these works; I will try to indicate the remarkable variety of objects achieved, for instance, in *The Turn of the Screw* and *The Awkward Age*. But it is an important part of James's object; and the observable iniquities of 'bad' adults in respect to their children or dependants are, I believe, the basic empirical material of these stories. Besides *The Turn of the Screw*, *What Maisie Knew* and *The Awkward Age*, there are several shorter novels and stories—for instance, *A London Life*—to testify to James's passionate feeling about the matter.

Miles was expelled from his school; and this absence of explicit detail, we learn by glancing back at a memorable passage in the Preface, is entirely deliberate:

What, in the last analysis, had I to give the sense of? Of their being, the haunting pair [the servants], capable, as the phrase is, of everything—that is of exerting, in respect to the children, the very worst action small victims so conditioned might be conceived as subject to. . . . Only make the reader's general vision of evil intense enough . . . and his own experience, his own imagination, his own sympathy (with the children) and horror (of their false friends) will supply him quite sufficiently with all the particulars. Make him *think* the evil, make him think it for himself, and you are released from weak specifications.[1]

There is hardly a page of *The Turn of the Screw* that does not testify to James's magnificent success in this task of evoking a sense of evil intense enough to render superfluous any 'weak specifications'. One has only to recall two representative passages. The first is the description of the nightmare situation created for the governess in her daily relations with the children by her knowledge that they are holding communication with the dead servants under her very eyes;[2] and here the moral horror is all in the sense of the children's dreadful duplicity—in the diabolical skill with which they are able to maintain the appearance of perfect innocence while they are in fact responding to the evil presences in the schoolroom. The second passage is the dialogue between the governess and little Miles on their Sunday-morning walk to church,[3] when the boy asks to be sent back to school in order that (so he intimates) he may be free to communicate as often and as fully as he desires with his evil genius Peter Quint. Here again the horror is in the implied depths of cynical depravity in the boy—that he should be able to put this loathsome plan to the governess with a candour and a self-possession so charming and so seemingly guileless. The 'ambiguity', of course, contributes materially to the effect of the nameless

[1] *The Turn of the Screw*, p. xxiv. [2] *Ibid.* 13, pp. 216–18.
[3] *Ibid.* 14, pp. 220–4.

terror inspired by these passages,[1] but it is in any case indisputable that here as elsewhere in *The Turn of the Screw* James succeeds in conveying to us a powerful sense of the children's corruption without recourse to a single specific detail.

This, accordingly—the children's mysterious but palpable and ponderable corruption by the servants—is James's *donnée* in *The Turn of the Screw*; and upon this he constructs the first of his great fables of salvation, of which the greatest (though not the last) is to be *The Golden Bowl*. Viewed as a fable of salvation, *The Turn of the Screw* may be seen as James's rehandling, in a characteristically Jamesian setting and in the characteristically Jamesian idiom, of the 'Faustus' theme in so far as this turns upon the battle of the powers of good with the powers of evil for a soul that has sold itself to the devil but is still capable of being saved.[2] The souls that have been sold to the devil are the children's; the dead servants are the powers of evil; the governess is the power of good, seeking to save the children by the strength of her love; and the residual innocence of the children is their one remaining hope of redemption. Their innocence is, as it were, their last link with the good, the power of light; and it is to this that the governess repeatedly appeals—as the good angels in Marlowe's drama appeal repeatedly to Faustus's last lingering sense of the greatness and goodness of God.

The first scene in which the theme of salvation is struck with clarity and firmness is the scene in Miles's bedroom on the night the governess catches him outside on the lawn communicating with the apparition of Peter Quint.[3] She has taken him back to his room; and presently, kneeling at his bedside, she implores him in the name of his innocence and her love to confess what it was he had done to be expelled from his school, in order that, having confessed he may repent,

[1] For further discussion of the ambiguity, see pp. 130-4 below.

[2] Cp. R. B. Heilman on the 'Faustus' theme, Appendix B, p. 384 below.

[3] *The Turn of the Screw*, 17.

and having repented he may be forgiven and restored to the good:

In the tenderness of my pity I embraced him. 'Dear little Miles, dear little Miles—!'

My face was close to his, and he let me kiss him, simply taking it with indulgent good humour, 'Well, old lady?'

'Is there nothing—nothing at all that you want to tell me?'

He turned off a little, facing round toward the wall and holding up his hand to look at as one had seen sick children look. 'I've told you—I told you this morning.'

. . . 'That you just want me not to worry you?'

He looked round at me now as if in recognition of my understanding him; then ever so gently, 'To let me alone', he replied.

She almost gives up at this point. But the next moment she resumes her questioning; and her reason for going on is significant. 'I felt', she says, 'that merely, at this, *to turn my back on him was to abandon or, to put it more truly, lose him.*[1] So she repeats her question:

'What happened before?'

He gazed up at me again. 'Before what?'

'Before you came back. And before you went away.'

For some time he was silent, but he continued to meet my eyes. 'What happened?'

It made me, the sound of the words, in which it seemed to me I caught for the very first time a small faint quaver of consenting consciousness—it made me drop on my knees beside the bed and seize once more the chance of possessing him. 'Dear little Miles, dear little Miles, if you *knew* how I want to help you! It's only

[1] The ambiguity of the last phrase (and of the similar phrase—'seize once more the chance of possessing him' in the passage quoted below) is as significant as any that Mr Wilson saw and pounced upon. Is she afraid of 'losing' him (we are meant to ask) to the powers of good ('God') or—to herself? Is her love, in other words, as passionately disinterested and pure as she believes it to be—or is it as possessive, as neurotically (and erotically) possessive as Mr Wilson would wish us to believe? And even if not wholly possessive, is it not at least tainted with self-love, and therefore at least not completely and perfectly disinterested? That James intended the phrase to carry just such a weight of moral ambiguity seems certain in view of what emerges about the nature of the governess's love in the last scene of the story. It should be borne in mind as one of the many details in the earlier parts of the story which support the account of the governess's 'guilt' given below (pp. 125-9, 131).

that, it's nothing but that, and I'd rather die than give you a pain or do you a wrong—I'd rather die than hurt a hair of you. Dear little Miles'—oh, I brought it out now even if I *should* go too far—'I just want you to help me to save you!'[1]

But she *has* gone too far. As she pronounces the words, 'to save you', there is (we are told) 'an extraordinary blast and chill, a gust of frozen air and a shake of the room as great as if, in the wild wind, the casement had crashed in'.[2] As in the Faustus drama, Lucifer has appeared in the shape of Peter Quint to remind his young victim to whom his soul belongs, and to warn him that there is to be no backsliding.

So the powers of evil have won this round. But the governess will not give in: she will not desert them; she will persist in her efforts to save them. The situation is brought to a head by the scene beside the lake,[3] which ends in Flora's being sent away; and then the stage is set for the last great battle between the governess and Peter Quint, the good angel and the bad, for the soul of little Miles.

This scene, which stretches over the last two chapters of the story, seems to me to support in the most decisive way (both in its total structure and its often elusive details) the 'Faustus' interpretation I am proposing. James has chosen, it seems, to postpone the fullest and most nearly explicit statement of his theme of salvation to this last scene; and this ought accordingly to be taken as the key to the whole story, in the light of which all that has gone before is to be understood.

The governess, feeling that she has reached the end of her resources for dealing with the whole terrifying situation, has at last written to the children's guardian asking for an interview. But her letter, she discovers, has been removed from the hall table before it could be posted, and she rightly suspects Miles of having stolen it. So, at the opening of this last scene, she resolves to make one final effort to wrest

[1] *The Turn of the Screw*, 17, pp. 236–8. [2] *Ibid.* 17, p. 238.
[3] *Ibid.* 19.

from the child a confession of his wrongdoings, starting again with what it was he had 'done' at school to be expelled, and then passing on to the stolen letter itself. And, as the moment for the show-down approaches, we are given a further significant light on her character as a specifically Jamesian angel of light. Would it not be 'preposterous', she asks herself, 'with a child so endowed, to forgo the help one might wrest from absolute intelligence? *What had his intelligence been given him for but to save him*? Mightn't one, to reach his mind, risk the stretch of a stiff arm across his character?' [1] By taxing him with having stolen the letter, she means, she will be stretching a stiff arm over his character —appealing, that is, to his moral sense; then, having effected the moral exposure, she will hope to bring him to see with the eyes of his beautiful intelligence the foulness of the evil with which he is possessed, and so carry him at last to confession and repentance.

The last scene therefore begins with a prolonged verbal sparring-contest between the governess and little Miles, in the course of which it becomes apparent to her (she takes it in, she says, 'with a throb of hope') that the child is *uneasy* in a way she has never before known him to be. He is still on the surface composed and charming, and still speaks with his usual exquisite precision and civility. But in spite of this, it is clear that his resistance is beginning to break down and that he is in great anguish of spirit. And this change in Miles (we are perhaps meant to understand) is due to the check that the devil in the shape of Peter Quint has received by the removal of little Flora. This was a clear victory for the power of good represented by the governess; and Peter Quint's power over the boy has been correspondingly weakened. Indeed, as the scene advances it becomes clear that Miles at last *wants* to confess. But he is still mortally afraid of severing his connexion with his evil angel Peter Quint; and so he continues to resist—making a last-ditch stand,

[1] *The Turn of the Screw*, 22, p. 264. My emphasis.

as it were, against the solicitations of his good angel, the governess.[1]

The sparring-contest continues, growing more and more tense beneath the calm casual surface that is scrupulously maintained by both contestants; until the point is reached when Miles explicitly says that he will 'tell her everything' —only not just yet (he pleads): he first wants to go outside for a bit, and when he comes back he will tell her—he really *will* tell her—everything. What this signifies, we are meant to see, is that he wants first to confront Peter Quint and finally sever his connexion with the power of evil before he submits himself to the powėr of good. The governess consents to his going; but, just as he is about to leave the room, she darts at him the question that precipitates the last climactic scene and the final catastrophe. 'Tell me'—she asks, ever so casually —'Tell me if yesterday afternoon from the table in the hall, you took, you know, my letter.'[2]

The question has hardly been spoken when the apparition of Peter Quint appears at the window. Again, as in the scene in Miles's bedroom, 'the hideous author of their woe' had appeared 'to blight his confession and stay his answer'. The governess instantly leaps upon the child—'*it was like fighting with a demon for a human soul*', she explicitly says: she leaps at the child and seizes him in her arms to prevent him from seeing 'the white face of damnation' at the window. And she succeeds. Miles does not in fact see his evil angel, and, as he clings to her, he speaks the words that are to be the beginning of salvation for him. 'Yes, I took it', he says—meaning the letter; and as he speaks the words, the apparition of Peter Quint withdraws from the window, and moves away with a slow wheel like 'the prowl of a baffled beast'.[3]

So the power of good has for the moment triumphed, and the governess is exultant. And then, determined to complete her work of salvation, she presses Miles to tell her also what

[1] *The Turn of the Screw*, 23, pp. 266–9. [2] *Ibid.* 23, p. 270.
[3] *Ibid.* 24, pp. 271–2.

it was that he had done at school to be expelled. The child prevaricates; he is obviously unwilling to say more. She insists, however, and manages to wrest from him a few disjointed bits of information which, however, do not add up to a full confession.[1] She continues to press him, and in the end asks sternly, *What were those things?* (that he said or did at school); and as she pronounces the question, the apparition of Peter Quint reappears at the window. Again she leaps at Miles to shield him from the devil; again she is successful; and this time, it seems, her triumph is to be complete and final. For Miles, struggling in her arms, explicitly cries out (or appears to cry out) his repudiation of his evil angel: 'Peter Quint, *you devil*'.[2] Upon which the governess, in her triumph, wheels him round to the window to show him that it is clear of the evil presence. And then, suddenly and swiftly, follows the catastrophe:

> But he had already jerked straight round, stared, glared again, and seen but the quiet day. With the stroke of the loss I was so proud of he uttered the cry of a creature hurled over an abyss, and the grasp with which I recovered him might have been that of catching him in his fall. I caught him, yes, I held him—it may be imagined with what a passion; but at the end of a minute I began to feel what it truly was that I held. We were alone with the quiet day, and his little heart, dispossessed, had stopped.[3]

If this account, necessarily abridged, of the last scene of the story is substantially correct, the validity of the interpretation of *The Turn of the Screw* I have proposed is, I think, established and its principal moral theme explained. *The*

[1] *The Turn of the Screw*, 24, pp. 272–5.

[2] This is the crowning instance of the ambiguity that Mr Wilson made so much of. In the immediate context, 'you devil' could be addressed either to Peter Quint or to the governess. On the governess's reading of the situation it is of course addressed to Peter Quint; on Mr Wilson's, it is addressed to the governess herself. The ambiguity here is, I believe, as deliberate as everywhere else in *The Turn of the Screw*, and can only be understood in the light of James's larger purpose, to be examined presently, in employing this extraordinary device to such extraordinary effect.

[3] *The Turn of the Screw*, 24, p. 277.

Turn of the Screw is then chiefly (though not exclusively) a fable about the redemptive power of human love: the power of love—here the governess's love for the children—to redeem the corrupt element in a human soul, and so to ensure the final triumph of good over evil; though (as so often in tragedy) at the cost of the mortal life of the redeemed soul.

To recognise this as the basic theme is not yet, however, to exhaust the meaning of the story. There is still a further and final aspect to consider—one last turn of the screw, as it were, that the traditional Faustus *motif* receives; and to understand this is to understand the full scope of James's achievement in this story and the range, depth and subtlety of the insight into the nature of man and the conditions of man's salvation it exhibits.

This last aspect has to do with the prevailing ambiguity and with the matter of the governess's guilt; and it is best approached by considering the problem of little Miles's death at the very end. For it *is* a problem: Why (one finds oneself impelled to ask) does Miles die? Why does he *have* to die? Why, if he has renounced the devil, as religious people would say; if he has embraced, or is about to embrace, God again; if he has thrown himself upon God's mercy through the agency of the good angel in the shape of the governess—why then must he die? Where is the moral necessity; where therefore the artistic inevitability?

The answer, I believe, is to be found by looking more closely at the second 'movement', as one may call it, of the last scene. The first movement consists in the governess's effort to bring Miles to confess and repent that he may be saved. It reaches a climax with the appearance of Peter Quint in the moment that Miles is about to confess that he stole the letter; and comes to a triumphant resolution when it is evident that the child can no longer see his bad angel and Quint retires 'baffled'. This marks the triumph of the power of good over the power of evil; and here one might have expected the story to end.

But it does not end: there follows what is in effect a tragic reversal of the triumph we have witnessed in the first movement; and it is this tragic reversal that has to be accounted for. Why—that is now the question—does Peter Quint return? By what strength is the devil so suddenly revived and restored to power when it seemed that he had been totally vanquished? Or (to put the question in such a way as to bring us nearer to our answer): by what weakness, by what taint of evil or corruption, in the power of good itself was the devil revived and restored to power?

It is the governess who directs us to the answer in the important transition passages between the two 'movements' of the scene. Peter Quint has vanished; little Miles has fallen back exhausted; and the governess exults in her victory:

> What was prodigious was that at last, *by my success*, his sense was sealed and his communication stopped. . . . The air was clear again and—*by my personal triumph*—the influence [was] quenched . . . . *I felt that the cause was mine* and that I should surely get *all*.[1]

And so, determined to get all, she presses him. 'And you found nothing?' (in the letter he stole, she means):

> He gave the most mournful, thoughtful little headshake. 'Nothing.'
>
> 'Nothing, nothing!' I almost shouted in my joy.
>
> 'Nothing, nothing!' he sadly repeated.
>
> I kissed his forehead; it was drenched. 'So what have you done with it?' [with the letter].
>
> 'I've burnt it.'
>
> 'Burnt it?' It was now or never. 'Is that what you did at school?'
>
> Oh, what this brought up! 'At school?'
>
> 'Did you take letters?—or other things?'
>
> 'Other things?' He appeared now to be thinking of something far off and that reached him only through the pressure of his anxiety. Yet it did reach him. 'Did I *steal*?'[2]

[1] *The Turn of the Screw*, 24, pp. 272–3. My emphasis.

[2] *Ibid.* 24, p. 273.

It is evident that the child is in great anguish of spirit. He grows more and more vague as she continues to press him:

He looked [she observes] *in vague pain* all round the top of the room and drew his breath, two or three times over, as if with difficulty. He might have been standing at the bottom of the sea and raising his eyes to some faint green twilight.[1]

And yet she persists in her effort to wrest from him what it was that he had done at school. He tells her that he didn't 'steal', but had only 'said things'. To whom (she asks) had he said whatever it was he had said. He tries to remember, but can't. 'I don't know', he says. And then:

He almost smiled at me in the desolation of his surrender, *which was indeed practically, by this time, so complete that I ought to have left it there. But I was infatuated—I was blind with victory*, though even then the very effect that was to have brought him so much nearer was already that of added separation.[2]

She cannot stop, fatally cannot stop, though she can see that the child is receding from her. She can even feel that he is, in some way, turning back to the evil power that he has repudiated—perhaps appealing to it for help: 'Once more, as he had done before, he looked up at the dim day as if, of what had hitherto sustained him, nothing was left but an unspeakable anxiety'.[3] But still she cannot stop: she must now *get all*. And she almost does:

He turned to me again his little beautiful fevered face. 'Yes, it was too bad.'

'Too bad?'

'What I suppose I sometimes said. [Too bad] to write home.'[4]

If only she could have stopped there, even there. But she cannot:

I can't name the exquisite pathos of the contradiction given to such a speech by such a speaker; I only know that the next instant I heard myself throw off with homely force: 'Stuff and nonsense!'

[1] *The Turn of the Screw*, 24, pp. 273–4. My emphasis.
[2] *Ibid.* 24, p. 274. My emphasis.
[3] *Ibid.* 24, p. 275. [4] *Ibid.*

But the next after that I must have sounded stern enough. 'What *were* these things?' [1]

'My sternness', she adds, 'was all for his judge, his executioner.' But—'What were these things?', she demands, though she can see that the child is collapsing under the pressure. 'What were these things?' And as she brings this out, Peter Quint reappears: 'There again, against the glass, as if to blight his confession and stay his answer, was the hideous author of our woe—the white face of damnation'. And from this point the scene proceeds to the tragic catastrophe.

What are we to understand by all this? It is plain, I think, that we are to understand that the governess herself is directly responsible for the return of Peter Quint; that she is therefore indirectly responsible for Miles's death; that she is, in short, guilty of some awful moral lapse which precipitates the final catastrophe. And this lapse (we come now to see) is only the last and most disastrous expression of something in the governess of which we have been uneasily conscious all the time: some flaw, some fatal weakness, in her moral constitution that has, in some elusive way, been present throughout in all her relations with the two children.

The nature of this 'fatal flaw' is now not difficult to see. Its generic name is what Christians call spiritual pride; and the specific form it takes here is, first, the desire to know all—to 'get all' (in the governess's own phrase) in the sense of putting herself in complete possession of the child's soul by a complete knowledge of all that he has done. This is the aspiration after complete and perfect knowledge which by Christian definition belongs only to God and not to man; and this, which in the traditional Faustus story is shown as the glorious and damnable sin of Faustus himself, the soul that had sold itself to the devil, is here transferred to God's own emissary, the 'good angel' of the Faustus story.

[1] *The Turn of the Screw*, 24, p. 275.

This is how James radically modifies the structure of the great traditional fable while retaining all its essential elements, and in doing so extends and deepens in a remarkable way its moral scope.

The governess's determination to 'get all', however, also expresses another form of the Faustian pride. This may be called spiritual greed or possessiveness—the kind of greed which is an intrinsic constituent of spiritual pride if not actually co-extensive with it, and as such suggests a significant connexion between two of the seven deadly sins in the Christian scheme, vanity ('pride') and greed. It is her determination to 'get all' in this sense that makes her so desperately, so insanely, so pitilessly, insistent; and it is her insistence that kills little Miles—just this common, familiar, domestic form of the ruthlessness that can spring from spiritual greed. It is this that dispossesses the heart of the child—her compulsion to pursue him, to press him to a full confession of all his 'crimes' at a point when the child has been harrowed already to the furthest limit of his small moral resources, when he has gone as far as he can in the way of confession and repentance.

She does it (this is the vital point) still for the sake of the good. 'My sternness was all for his judge, his executioner', she says. She wants to purge his soul completely, to make him, as the Christian would say, a perfect vessel for God's grace; and in so far as this remains her principal motive to the end, she retains to the end her character of the good angel, the emissary of God.

But (as she herself comes to see afterwards but, fatally, does not see at the time)—this is not the sole spring of her action. She does it also out of that love of self which is inseparable from the Faustian pride, from the desire that *her* triumph, hers personally, may be complete. 'By my personal triumph . . . the influence [was] quenched . . .', she says; 'I felt that the cause was mine and I should surely get all'; 'I was infatuated—I was blind with victory'; and so on.

What we are shown in the last scene of *The Turn of the Screw* is the disastrous, the heart-rending, consequence of this lapse from grace. For the moment the love that inspired the governess in her effort to save Miles ceases to be wholly disinterested, ceases to be directed solely to its object for the sake of the object, it turns to positive cruelty—the cruelty (as we have seen) of harrowing a poor little soul beyond its powers of endurance, of pressing it to a degree of self-exposure that cannot but destroy it. It is as if the eye which only a moment before was full of the light of love were suddenly stricken with a blind insensibility, so that it could no longer see or feel the suffering it was causing the beloved: this is the fearful transformation that love undergoes the moment it becomes tainted by the love of self that springs from spiritual pride.

Spiritual pride, the religious writers tell us, is the last infirmity of the angels of light themselves. Speaking in the manner of men, what this means is that it is the last infirmity of the most intelligent, sensitive and imaginative—the most morally developed, in short—of the race of men. This, we know, happened to be the part of the race of men that Henry James particularly loved and always chose as his 'vessels of consciousness', his vessels equally of salvation and damnation; and it is because the governess in *The Turn of the Screw* is one of these Jamesian angels of light—not, as Mr Wilson asks us to believe, a neurotic Anglo-Saxon spinster seeking hallucinatory compensations for sex-starvation in apparitions on Freudian towers and lakes—that she is chosen to exhibit this infirmity in one of its most subtle and insidious forms.[1]

[1] The importance of the governess's romantic passion for the children's guardian must not, of course, be minimised. It is sufficiently emphasised in the opening sections and indeed throughout the story as the main additional motive for her desire to save the children; the pastoral love (as Mr Heilman aptly calls it), which is the primary spring of her redemptive effort, is reinforced by the sexual in a form dramatically appropriate to her age, 'station', and social opportunities. But this, in Henry James's view of the human soul, argues nothing pathological in the character of the governess. Her passion may be romantic but it is not therefore neurotic; and since in his later works

That the destructive power of this Faustian form of spiritual pride is the deeper aspect of James's moral theme in *The Turn of the Screw* is, on this analysis, sufficiently established by the internal evidences. But for those who see *The Turn of the Screw* as one of the inaugural works of James's late period, in point of its moral preoccupations if not yet in its style, and are concerned to follow the development of James's vision in this last and greatest period of his creative life, there is a special interest in seeing the connexion between *The Turn of the Screw* and his last complete novel *The Golden Bowl*. This, I believe, is a matter of seeing how the moral theme of *The Golden Bowl* completes and perfects that of *The Turn of the Screw*. For in *The Golden Bowl* the heroine Maggie Verver succeeds precisely where the governess in *The Turn of the Screw* had failed. Maggie triumphs, turns evil into good, restores what has been lost, by renouncing that last and subtlest form of spiritual pride which consists, in the common phrase, in 'being cruel in order to be kind'. 'My sternness', said the governess, 'was all for his judge, his executioner'—and the catastrophe of little Miles's death followed almost immediately upon those words. Maggie Verver deliberately renounces this 'sternness', this cruelty, which consists in pressing and pursuing and harassing those we love best for the sake of the good. Maggie saves her husband the Prince, whom she adores, precisely by *not* insisting. Instead, having first, in St Paul's phrase, 'given an impulse to sin'—made him conscious, that is, of his condition of moral turpitude, she then does what the governess in *The Turn of the Screw* was unable to do. She lets his knowledge of good and evil grow of itself:

James came to see passion, whether 'unrequited' or not, as the sacred fount of the most noble, most heroic, most interesting moral endeavour, it is consistent with this view that the governess in *The Turn of the Screw*—like May Server in *The Sacred Fount* and Maggie Verver in *The Golden Bowl*—should have undertaken her heroic enterprise at Bly 'for love, for love, for love'—not only of the children but also of their charming uncle. (For further discussion of this theme in the later works, see ch. VI, pp. 169, 188-9, 190-1, 192-4 and ch. VIII, pp. 258-9, 262-3, 264-6, 273-6, 282-4 below.)

watching, silently and in anguish, as he struggles in the pain of his new birth; loving him, keeping an unbroken vigil over his suffering, but doing nothing, literally nothing, to hasten the process of his conversion to the love of the good. The effort of self-discipline that this requires nearly destroys her: indeed it would have destroyed her if her love had not sustained her. But her love does sustain her; she succeeds where the governess failed; and *The Golden Bowl* accordingly stands as Henry James's final, most complete and perfect affirmation of the redeeming power of human love.

If the interpretation of the governess's guilt set out above is correct—if she is guilty of Miles's death, and for the reasons I have suggested, it becomes possible to suggest an explanation, first, of the supernatural element in *The Turn of the Screw* and, second, of the famous ambiguity which Mr Edmund Wilson first drew attention to but, in my view, misunderstood and misanalysed.

What the supernatural is chiefly intended to express, I suggest, is Henry James's sense of the mystery and final inexplicability of absolute evil as figured in Quint and Miss Jessel. This, the sheer inexplicability of the nature and origin of evil in the human soul, appears to have challenged and perplexed the minds of reflective men ever since reflection upon the phenomenon began. Shakespeare was among those to whom the mystery of evil was an intensely vivid reality. He declares his sense of it in certain memorable lines in *Othello*:

> Will you, I pray, demand that demi-devil
> Why he hath thus ensnared my soul and body?

This is the question that Othello puts to Iago when he is confronted with the fact of Iago's iniquity. Quietly, because he is so dazed with the shock of the discovery, he implores Iago to tell him why he did what he did. But Iago only answers curtly:

> Demand me nothing: what you know, you know—

an answer thoroughly unilluminating; nor are we meant to suppose that Iago knows more than he says.

In *The Turn of the Screw* Henry James appears to go even further than Shakespeare in leaving the nature and origin of evil unexplained and uncommented on. The exemplary figures, Quint and Miss Jessel, are rendered totally inarticulate by being rendered apparitional: they speak never a word, say literally nothing—not even as little as Iago—to 'explain' themselves and their actions; and this is the principal reason for their being apparitional—that is, the kind of apparition or 'demon-spirit' that James speaks of in the Preface. They are demon-spirits in the first instance, of course, in order to figure the terror of absolute evil; but they are the kind of demon-spirit they are in order that the mystery of evil may retain unimpaired its inexplicable, inexpressible mysteriousness.[1]

The ambiguity of *The Turn of the Screw* is closely connected with the supernatural, the connexion being that of mutual reinforcement. What this expresses, I suggest, is James's sense of a phenomenon as profoundly mysterious and finally inexplicable as absolute evil itself—namely, the co-existence or co-presence of good and evil in the human soul. This is figured here equally in the governess and the children. *The Turn of the Screw,* I have tried to show, is pre-eminently a Faustian fable of salvation in which the governess plays the part of the good angel; and to that extent the governess is

[1] In his valuable article 'Psychical Research and *The Turn of the Screw*' (in *American Literature*, xx, 1949, pp. 401–12), in which he sets out to show that James's known interest in the Reports of the newly founded Society for Psychical Research materially influenced the conception of his apparitions in *The Turn of the Screw*, Mr Francis X. Roellinger points out that 'for readers today who approach the story with preconceptions still largely derived from the familiar phantoms of Gothic fiction, it is important to realize that the ghosts of *The Turn of the Screw* are conceived to a surprising extent in terms of the cases reported to the Society [for Psychical Research]'. In the account that follows of the main differences between the 'old' and the 'new' ghosts, Mr Roellinger mentions that, in contrast to the wailing, shrieking, chain-clanking apparitions of the magazine ghost stories, the 'veridical' apparitions of the reports of the Society (and of James's Preface) are almost always soundless in their movements and totally silent during their appearances. If Mr Roellinger's general hypothesis is correct, it would be typical of James to utilise a small detail of this sort for a large artistic purpose.

'good' and 'innocent' and the children 'evil' and 'guilty' (of the corruption from which she is seeking to save them). But the governess is also guilty in the sense indicated (though not in Mr Wilson's sense); and to this extent the children are the victims of the evil in her and are themselves innocent. And this, precisely, is what the ambiguity is there to express—the mystery and inexplicability of this very phenomenon, this co-presence of good and evil, innocence and guilt, in the children and in the governess; and the final baffling, tormenting impossibility of determining the degree of innocence in the guilt and of guilt in the innocence.[1]

The old writers called it the 'mystery of iniquity' and the 'mystery of godliness' when they wished to give theological names to this experience of the final inexplicability, both in its nature and origin, of absolute evil and good in the human soul. Henry James eschewed the theological terms, but (on the view proposed) passionately embraced the experience. The mystery of the corruption that can poison the most innocent and tender (the children); the mystery of the evil that can lurk in the heart of the most intelligent, most sensitive, most morally developed (the governess): this appears to have been the phenomenon that persistently occupied his mind in his late period; and in *The Turn of the Screw*, as in other works of this period, it is shown to be at the heart of the tragic predicament—in this instance, the predicament equally of two beautiful children who have succumbed to an evil power which they are yet able to recognise as evil, and that of a high-minded and brave young woman who only seeks to do good and to be good, but fails in the end because her love of the good is tainted with a love of self springing from spiritual greed.

This may be called the moral aspect of the ambiguity of *The Turn of the Screw*. It has, however, another aspect, which goes even deeper; and this may properly be called metaphysical. To pursue the implications of the 'given case' as far

[1] Cp. *The Golden Bowl*, I, iii, 9; and ch. VIII, p. 234 below.

and as deep as do the principal vessels of consciousness in James's late works is to court the haunting fear that all intensely reflective minds are heir to. This is the fear of ceasing at some point—a point by its nature wholly unpredictable—to 'read out' of the situation what is really there and proceeding instead to 'read into' it some part of the contents of one's own mind. James refers to this in several passages in *Notes of a Son and Brother*, where he discusses it, with elaborate ironic modesty, as his own most interesting aberration. Recalling, for instance, his impressions of a visit to Mr Frank Sanborn's progressive school at Concord, he writes:

> I have to reckon . . . with the trick of what I used irrepressibly to read into things in front of which I found myself, for gaping purposes, planted by some unquestioned outer force: it seemed so prescribed to me, so imposed on me, to read more, as through some ever-felt claim for roundness of aspect and intensity of effect in presented matters, whatever they might be, than the conscience of the particular affair itself was perhaps developed enough to ask of it.[1]

And when in another passage he speaks of his 'wasteful habit or trick of a greater feeling for people's potential propriety or felicity or full expression than they seemed able to have themselves',[2] we are reminded of a similar passage in *The Sacred Fount*, in which the Jamesian narrator resolves—vainly, as it turns out—'not to yield further to my idle habit of reading into mere human things an interest so much deeper than mere human things were in general prepared to supply'.[3]

This is the problem inherent in the nature and operations of the fully conscious mind—the kind of mind that belongs to all the late-Jamesian vessels of consciousness, but particularly for this purpose to the governess in *The Turn of the Screw* and the narrator in *The Sacred Fount*. It is a mind

[1] *Notes of a Son and Brother*, 7, p. 367.
[2] *Ibid.* 2, p. 261.
[3] *The Sacred Fount*, 9, p. 123; cp. ch. VI, p. 185 below.

whose receptiveness to experience and powers of discrimination and analysis exceed by so much the capacities of the minds that surround it as to make it seem almost of a different species; and given such a mind, it is not surprising (James intimates) that a portentous question-mark should hang over all its operations and persistently threaten its peace. How much am I reading out of the situation, and how much am I reading into it? How much of what I am seeing is really ('objectively') there to be seen, and how much am I just 'seeing'? And since by definition there is no one else capable of seeing what I see, even if what I see is there to be seen, how can I ever in any particular situation know for certain which it is?

The answer is that he, the victim of this developed consciousness, can in fact never know. His is an absolute dilemma, admitting of no solution; and it is insoluble, alas, not only in logic, epistemology and metaphysics, which might be endured, but also and more important, in life itself. The narrator in *The Sacred Fount* can really *never* know whether the strange and sinister relations of the four guests at the week-end house-party were really there to be seen—or whether it was all a colossal delusion. Nor can the governess in *The Turn of the Screw* ever know for certain whether what she thought she saw of the children's relations with the dead servants was or was not there to be seen. And this, the ultimate dilemma of the highly developed mind, is I believe the other grand experience that James is figuring in the ambiguity of *The Turn of the Screw*. The ambiguity is intended to render, with all the immediacy and concreteness of a fully articulated poetic device, the mystery and the terror of this particular dilemma. It is so mysterious because, like the nature and origin of evil in the moral life, its origin too is inexplicable, and its nature wildly paradoxical (for is it not a cruel paradox that the most highly developed mind should, in the end, be incapable of knowing what it knows?); and it is so terrifying because the consequences for the conduct of life of not knowing what one knows may be disastrous.

'If he *were* innocent, what then on earth was I?', the governess in *The Turn of the Screw* cries to herself, expressing in that cry her terror of the moral implications of her possible self-deception. The problem for her is, very properly, entirely moral: she has no business with epistemology and metaphysics but only with conduct. But we, having been exposed to the impact of the Jamesian ambiguity, and having grasped its meaning, are expected to see the matter in a larger light. We are expected to see that our liability to this fundamental kind of self-deception is not, in the first instance, a moral phenomenon but a metaphysical and epistemological phenomenon. For it consists, at bottom, in a false or distorted view of reality, which is a metaphysical disaster, and in not knowing what we know, which is an epistemological disaster; and it is because it is, in the first instance, metaphysical and epistemological that it is, derivatively, moral: the moral infirmity (with all its consequences) is grounded in the metaphysical and epistemological incapacity. This no doubt is the reason, or one of the reasons, why the religious thinkers have always insisted that metaphysics is antecedent to morality, that truth is the necessary condition of goodness, that knowledge is virtue, that no man can be good—really, successfully good—whose vision of reality is false or distorted, and who therefore does not know whether what he knows is fact or delusion. And perhaps this, among other truths of the same order, is what Henry James in his un-theological way was re-discovering in the works of his later period, beginning with *The Turn of the Screw*.

CHAPTER V

'THE AWKWARD AGE'

The Awkward Age, published in 1899, may be regarded as the inaugural work of Henry James's late period. In bulk it is small compared, for instance, with *The Wings of the Dove* or *The Golden Bowl*; and its theme is correspondingly less ambitious. But in every important respect it stands close to the major works of James's last period and, most conspicuously, in respect of its moral preoccupations and its dramatic method.

The term 'dramatic' indeed, as applied to the novel, receives from *The Awkward Age* an extension of meaning that marks something of an epoch in the history of the English novel; and this aspect of James's achievement is to be touched on presently. My main object in this chapter, however, is to elucidate as fully as possible the theme of *The Awkward Age*, which is not generally well understood. It goes very much deeper, I believe, than even the best critics of *The Awkward Age*—Dr Leavis, for instance—have allowed; and since, apart from its intrinsic interest and value, it also looks forward in the most direct way to the themes of the major works of James's maturity, *The Ambassadors*, *The Wings of the Dove* and *The Golden Bowl*, it is important for the better understanding of all the works of James's late period to miss no part of its complex meaning.

The Awkward Age has in fact two themes, organically linked in the story, of course, but still clearly distinguishable. The one that lies nearer the surface (which does not mean that it is superficial, or merely an ostensible one) is what I shall name for convenience the 'social' theme. This is concerned to exhibit some of the consequences of an interesting flaw in the social arrangements of English upper class society in James's day, namely, the absence of any established method or 'machinery' (as it would be called nowadays) for dealing with the phenomenon of *the awkward age*—that is, of the 'coming out' of young girls into society. The awkwardness is created by the fact that they are at once old enough to be admitted into the drawing-room to take their place in their parents' adult circle and yet not old enough to be exposed to its unexpurgated conversation—its 'good talk', as it was called in those days. This means either that the good talk has to be expurgated, which ruins the parents' fun; or it is left unexpurgated, which may ruin the girl—ruin, that is, or at least gravely jeopardise, her chances of making the right kind of marriage. As a third alternative, the girl can, of course, where that is practicable, be sent to other people's drawing-rooms, so that if she *is* ruined the parents will not have her ruin so directly on their own consciences.

The dilemma (James explains in his Preface to *The Awkward Age*, where he discusses this aspect of his theme with great vivacity and wit) is entirely peculiar to English society, having no counterpart either on the Continent or in America. Among the French, for instance, 'their social scheme absolutely provides against awkwardness. That is, it would be, by this scheme, so infinitely awkward, so awkward beyond any patching-up, for the hovering female young to be conceived as present at "good" talk, that their presence is, theoretically, at least, not permitted till their youth has been promptly corrected by marriage—in which case they have ceased to be merely young'.[1] In other words—as we have already learnt from the case of little Pansy Osmond in *The Portrait of a Lady*, and are to learn again from the case of little Aggie in *The Awkward Age* and that of Madame de Vionnet's daughter in *The Ambassadors*—the female young in France are firmly and securely kept in a convent until they have reached the awkward age; and since this happens also to be the marriageable age, they are then

[1] *The Awkward Age*, p. xi.

'by arrangement' married off with the utmost expedition, thus leaving no awkward gap between their emergence from the convent as little convent flowers and their translation by marriage into the adult world with all the rights and privileges belonging to that status.

This is the French solution. The American is equally simple and effective. It is, James says, 'that talk should never become "better" than the female young, either actually or constructively present, are minded to allow it';[1] or, as Dickens might have put it, that the talk should never be such as to bring a blush to the Young Person's cheek. In other words, there is no 'good talk' in the drawing-rooms of Boston and New York, therefore no problem of the awkward age.

It is only in England, in poor dear England, with its passion of having its cake and eating it, that the problem arises. The English, it seems, want their young girls to have both the freedom (up to a point) of the greater world and the protection (up to a point) of the French convent; and this (says James) is just another instance of 'the inveterate English trick of the so morally well-meant and so intellectually helpless compromise'.[2] Because it is so intellectually helpless, it does not, of course, work; and because it is so morally well-meant, it produces as nice a complication of motives as any keen and loving observer of English manners could wish to disentangle.

Henry James, being the keenest and most loving observer of English manners, accordingly seizes upon this little social situation to tell the tale of the awkwardness created for the lovely and brilliant Mrs Brookenham by the emergence from the schoolroom of her daughter Nanda, aged eighteen; of her efforts to marry Nanda off to the rich and ugly Mitchy, who loves her; of the failure of Mrs Brookenham's scheme, because Nanda does not love the rich and ugly Mitchy but loves instead, quite hopelessly, the poor and handsome Vanderbank; who, in his turn, does not, can not and will not love

[1] *The Awkward Age*, p. xii.

[2] *Ibid.* p. xi.

Nanda because (among other things) he loves, or at any rate stands in some ambiguous relation to, Mrs Brookenham herself. So Mrs Brookenham's scheme fails; and the whole awkward situation is resolved by a patchwork of compromises. Mitchy marries little Aggie, the convent flower, not because he wants to but because Nanda persuades him to it; and, having married her, he discovers she is an outrageous flirt, who does not hesitate the moment she is married to go off with Lord Petherton, Mitchy's closest friend. Nanda leaves her parents' emancipated circle in Buckingham Crescent to go and live in the country with the old-fashioned and upright Mr Longdon, who had once loved Nanda's grandmother and now offers Nanda his beautiful loyalty; and Mrs Brookenham herself remains at Buckingham Crescent, with the handsome Vanderbank to take care of her but her temple of analysis ruined beyond repair by the awkward events of the story.

This is the surface theme of *The Awkward Age*, which James had promised himself to treat with 'light irony': 'it would be light and ironical or it would be nothing', he says in the Preface.[1] And certainly the irony in *The Awkward Age* is as light, subtle and exquisitely poised as it is mordant. The phrase 'light irony', however, is misleading if it leads one to suppose that *The Awkward Age* is no more than a brilliant comedy of manners. For it is essentially not a comedy at all, but a tragedy—the tragedy of Nanda Brookenham, the girl who is exposed to the full impact of the London *beau monde* figured in Buckingham Crescent. And the Jamesian irony, so far from being used merely 'lightly', is used here to expose to its roots the basic corruption, sordidness, destructiveness, and ultimate self-destructiveness of this world through its effects upon the mind and heart of Nanda Brookenham.

This is the deeper theme of *The Awkward Age*; and its moral implications, we will see, are profound indeed. The

[1] *The Awkward Age*, pp. xiii–xiv.

profundity and the morality are, however, intimately dependent upon James's method of projecting the world of Buckingham Crescent; and since this is to remain substantially the method of all his later works, it is worth examining in the first of these works.

In a letter to an old friend, the American novelist W. D. Howells, James makes a significant remark that has often been quoted and almost as often misunderstood. 'I find our art, all the while, more difficult of practice, and want, with that, to do it in a more and more difficult way; *it being really, at bottom, only difficulty that interests me*', writes James;[1] and this has generally been taken to mean that James, especially in his later works, loved mastering technical difficulties for their own arid sake. But this is not at all what he means. The 'difficulty' he is speaking of is rather that inherent in the exercise of what may be seen as the artist's ultimate fidelity to his material. This in Henry James's practice consists principally in doing the fullest, richest justice to the world or worlds he chooses to project in a given work: in exploring each world to its furthest limit, exhibiting each at the maximum reach of its beauty and glory, and in these most difficult of conditions, exposing also its characteristic limitations—its weaknesses and follies, its vices and corruptions.

We have already seen how this is accomplished in *The Tragic Muse*: how of the two juxtaposed worlds exhibited there, that of the artist on the one hand and that of English public life on the other, neither is minimised, neither merely satirised or caricatured. On the contrary, as we saw, each is presented in the most tenderly sympathetic light—and, within this large, generous tribute to its virtue, also ruthlessly exposed.

That, I believe, is what James meant when he spoke of loving and rejoicing in 'difficulty'; and it is to love difficulty as only the greatest of artists perhaps can afford to love it—

[1] *Letters*, ed. Lubbock, II, p. 123. My emphasis.

'with all the assurance of his fancy and his irony, and yet with that fine taste for the truth and the pity and the meaning of the matter which keeps the temper of observation both sharp and sweet'.[1] To what a pitch the sharpness and sweetness were to be carried in the latest of James's late works is to be examined in the next four chapters. But it is already sufficiently impressive in *The Awkward Age*; and it is in any case in this sense that James here chooses to make things as 'difficult' as possible for himself when he undertakes to expose the corruption of Buckingham Crescent by deliberately making the main representative personages of that world as devastatingly attractive as possible.

'Beautiful', 'wonderful', 'prodigious' are the favourite epithets applied to them. (They are to continue to be the epithets applied to the main characters in all the later novels.) And indeed, we soon come to see, they *are* wonderful and prodigious as perfect specimens of their 'type' (another favourite Jamesian word): the type of sophisticated worldliness engaged in the pursuit of worldly values; directing all its remarkable resources of intelligence, courage and wit to the encompassing of what are in the last analysis material ends. Yet this most unpromising type is presented in a light in which it shows as supremely 'interesting' (in James's extended sense of the word)—as supremely brilliant and vital. It is brilliant and vital in its whole style of life, which is brave, bold and free—distinctly an aristocratic, not a bourgeois, style; and it is equally brilliant and vital in its intellectual life. The free play of mind was never freer than it is here, 'good talk' was never better, perceptions and discriminations never finer or more subtle or more amusing; and it is this combination of intellectual with personal style that makes the brilliance and vitality of Buckingham Crescent so irresistible. To the young and inexperienced, as we shall see, it may be fatally irresistible—as it is to Nanda Brookenham, who falls under its spell, and presently comes to know

[1] *Letters*, ed. Lubbock, II, p. 233.

intimately the heavy price that has to be paid for the style of Buckingham Crescent.

The most wonderful and prodigious of all these wonderful and prodigious personages in *The Awkward Age* is Mrs Brookenham herself—'Mrs Brook', as they call her: the acknowledged leader of the Buckingham Crescent circle, the high priestess of her 'temple of analysis', the 'fixed star' to which they all pay homage as the source of their light and life. This is how Vanderbank expresses it to Nanda in one of the last scenes in the book:

> The great thing is that . . . one doesn't, one simply *can't* if one would, give your mother up. It's absurd to talk about it. Nobody ever did such a thing in his life. There she is, like the moon or the Marble Arch. I don't say, mind you . . . that everyone *likes* her equally: that's another affair. But no one who ever *has* liked her can afford ever again, for any long period, to do without her.

For (he explains),

> There are too many stupid people—there's too much dull company. That, in London, is to be had by the ton; your mother's intelligence, on the other hand will always have its price . . . She's fine, fine, fine . . . She's a fixed star.[1]

But this tribute comes late in the story, and only sums up all that has already been directly exhibited of the remarkable Mrs Brook. Though she is in her forty-first year, she is young and lovely: 'She had about her the pure light of youth—would always have it; her head, her figure, her flexibility, her flickering colour, her lovely, silly eyes, her natural, quavering tone, all played together towards this effect by some trick that had never yet been exposed.'[2] The 'lovely silly eyes' is the touch of genius here. Of course, one sees at once, the eyes *have* to be 'silly': as silly as they are lovely and as lovely as they are silly. For if they were not both, Mrs Brook would be merely devastatingly intelligent; and that would mean the end of her unique power in Buckingham Crescent.

[1] *The Awkward Age*, x, 2, pp. 460–1. [2] *Ibid.* II, 1, p. 38.

The loveliness and the silliness, however, are reserved almost exclusively for the drawing-room. In private, with her family—with her dreadful son Harold and her difficult daughter Nanda in particular—she always (we are told) strictly eschews gaiety. With them she cultivates instead a beautiful distractedness, a luxurious kind of woe: 'This (with them) was her special sign—an innocence dimly tragic. It gave immense effect to her other resources.'[1]

We do in fact first meet Mrs Brookenham in this domestic milieu, in an early scene with her son Harold, aged about twenty. (Harold, we are told, 'was small and had a slight stoop which somehow gave him character—character of the insidious sort carried out in the acuteness, difficult to trace to a source, of his smooth, fair face, where the lines were all curves and the expression all needles. He had the voice of a man of forty and was dressed . . . with an air of experience that seemed to match it.'[2]) We soon see that there is the nicest artistic point in first showing us Mrs Brookenham in this setting. It takes us 'off-stage' right at the start for a brief glimpse of some of the cruder realities that lie behind the brilliant surface of Buckingham Crescent, showing us, by a few fine rapid strokes, how seamy is its seamier side.

The situation is as follows. Mrs Brookenham, it seems, has ordered Harold to procure himself an invitation for Easter to one of the several country-houses on their visiting-list, and has also ordered him to go at once and stay away as long as possible—so as to be (we are meant to understand) as little in her way as possible. Harold, however, has not gone as expected because he needs money. (Harold, we learn as the story advances, is always needing money; and we are presently to encounter him again in a rather sordid little episode about a five-pound note that reinforces this particular moral of the present scene.) There has been, it seems, no other way of furnishing himself with the money he needs

[1] *The Awkward Age*, II, 1, p. 38. [2] *Ibid.* II, 1, p. 37.

than by taking it out of his mother's desk; and having taken it, he remains behind to tell her what he has done and receive her blessing before he finally goes. The dialogue that follows takes place when Mrs Brookenham enters the room and finds to her astonishment and fury that Harold has not gone after all; and as one listens to this exchange between the brilliant, charming, well-bred Mrs Brookenham and her brilliant, charming, well-bred son, one feels that James has succeeded here in rendering the very essence, the distinctive moral flavour and savour, of a situation which is an intimate part of the domestic life of sophisticated societies.

She opened the secretary with the key she had quickly found, then with the aid of another rattled out a small drawer; after which she pushed the drawer back, closing the whole thing. 'You terrify me—you terrify me', she again said.

'How can you say that when you showed me just now how well you know me? Wasn't it just on account of what you thought I might do that you took out the keys as soon as you came in?' Harold's manner had a way of clearing up whenever he could talk of himself.

'You're too utterly disgusting—I shall speak to your father': with which, going to the chair he had given up, his mother sank down again with her heavy book. There was no anger, however, in her voice, and not even a harsh plaint; only a detached, accepted disenchantment. Mrs Brookenham's supreme rebellion against fate was just to show with the last frankness how much she was bored.

'No, darling mummy, you won't speak to my father—you'll do anything in the world rather than that', Harold replied, quite as if he were kindly explaining her to herself. 'I thank you immensely for the charming way you take what I have done; it was because I had a conviction of that that I waited for you to know it. It was all very well to tell you I would start on my visit—but how the deuce was I to start without a penny in the world? Don't you see that if you want me to go about you must really enter into my needs?'

'I wish to heaven you'd leave me—I wish to heaven you would get out of the house', Mrs Brookenham went on without looking up.

Harold, however, like some mild, good-tempered Hamlet, continues to speak daggers to her:

'You know', he answered with his manner of letting her see her own attitude, 'you know you try to make me do things you wouldn't at all do yourself. At least I hope you wouldn't. And don't you see that if I so far oblige you I must at least be paid for it?'

His mother leaned back in her chair, gazed for a moment at the ceiling and then closed her eyes. 'You *are* frightful', she said. 'You're appalling'.

'You're always wanting me to get out of the house', he continued; 'I think you want to get us *all* out, for you manage to keep Nanda from showing even more than you do me. Don't you think your children are good *enough*, mummy dear? At any rate it's as plain as possible that if you don't keep us at home you must keep us in other places. One can't live anywhere for nothing—it's all bosh that a fellow saves by staying with people. I don't know how it is for a lady, but a man's practically let in—'.

'Do you know you kill me, Harold?' Mrs Brookenham woefully interposed.

Then presently:

She rose. . . turning her eyes about the room as if from the extremity of martyrdom or the wistfulness of some deep thought. Yet when she spoke it was with a different expression, an expression that would have served for an observer as a marked illustration of that disconnectedness of her parts which frequently was laughable even to the degree of contributing to her social success. 'You've spent, then, more than four pounds in five days. It was on Friday I gave them to you. What in the world do you suppose is going to become of me?'

Harold continued to look at her as if the question demanded some answer really helpful. 'Do we live beyond our means?'

She now moved her gaze to the floor. 'Will you *please* get away?'

'Anything to assist you. Only, if I *should* find I'm not wanted [at the country-house, he means, to which he is being banished for Easter]—?'

She met his look after an instant, and the wan loveliness and vagueness of her own had never been greater. '*Be* wanted, and you won't find it. You're odious, but you're not a fool.'

He put his arms about her now, for farewell, and she submitted as if it were absolutely indifferent to her to whose bosom she was pressed. 'You do, dearest', he laughed, 'say such sweet things!'

And with that he reached the door, on opening which he pulled up at a sound from below. 'The Duchess! She's coming up.'[1]

Then, as Harold departs and the Duchess enters, the back-drop falls into place, so to speak, shutting out what lies behind; and the next scene is played off in Mrs Brook's most brilliant public style. This style she maintains without a lapse through the rest of the book, excepting only once, in another domestic scene, this time with Nanda,[2] where again the talk is of money, money and money—about dress-maker's bills and the cost of coal and the difficulty of knowing *where* to send the younger children in the holidays, all conducted in that tone of intense brooding fretfulness which (James intimates) is characteristic of the Mrs Brookenhams of the world when they let themselves go on the one subject that really dominates their lives and exercises their minds in every waking moment.

None of this, however, shows in her drawing-room, where, we have already learnt, 'her resources are immense'. She is not only beautiful and gay, perceptive, imaginative and intelligent, witty and amusing—which means, of course, also diabolically malicious, since this is what it is to be amusing in such circles; Mrs Brook, besides all this, appears also to have a genuine passion for 'analysis'. This indeed is what makes her a late-Jamesian character—this passion, for self-analysis in the first instance, for 'getting to the bottom' of her own motives; but also for the analysis of other people's motives—for disentangling, understanding, seeing steady and whole, the intricate web of personal relations which makes up the life of the society of which she is the 'fixed star'. Her drawing-room accordingly is not misnamed the temple of analysis: once we have seen her at it, we can be in no doubt about this. And when she does go at it, it is not only with the lucid intelligence of all the late-Jamesian heroines, but with a boldness, an audacity, a high free spirit, which is the sign of intelligence reinforced by character.

[1] *The Awkward Age*, II, 1, pp. 38–41.

[2] *Ibid.* VI, 3.

While she remains as to details the perfect Edwardian hostess, not moving a step beyond the social forms prescribed by the social code of her day, she is yet a universal type; and in this universal character she has affinities with the great 'wicked' heroines of the Jacobean drama—Vittoria Corombona, for instance, and Middleton's Beatrice-Joanna and even in certain respects Shakespeare's Cleopatra. Mrs Brookenham's proper place, it may be argued, is in this tradition of dramatic heroines; at any rate, to see her in this larger context is of help in arriving at a just estimate of her stature.

One of Mrs Brook's principal appearances, which has a special significance for the main tragic theme of the book, is in her great analytical session with her two fondest admirers, Vanderbank and Mitchy.[1] (These three, we are told, form the 'inner circle' at Buckingham Crescent.) The main subject of their joint analysis is Nanda's situation: Nanda who, they all know, is hopelessly in love with Vanderbank, is herself hopelessly loved by Mitchy, and is likely, to all appearances, to end up quite hopelessly unmarried. Mrs Brookenham (we are meant to understand) is, to her capacity, genuinely worried about her trying daughter, and is presumably seeking the advice and help of her dear friends and admirers Vanderbank and Mitchy when she invites them to this session in her drawing-room.

What is so remarkable and revealing is the way in which they conduct their analysis of Nanda's situation. They dissect it with a candour so ruthless and a fullness so unsparing as to be quite terrifying in its effect—an effect that is not in the least mitigated but only intensified by the wit, the gaiety and the good humour with which the whole operation is performed. This, it seems, becomes apparent even to themselves, and Vanderbank at one point in the scene feels constrained to remark upon it. He does it ever so casually, of course:

'What stupefies me a little [he says] is the extraordinary

[1] *The Awkward Age*, VI, 2.

critical freedom—or we may call it if we like the high intellectual detachment—with which we discuss a question touching you, dear Mrs Brook, so nearly and engaging so your most private and most sacred sentiments. What are we playing with, after all, but the idea of Nanda's happiness?'

'Oh I'm not playing!' Mrs Brook declared with a little rattle of emotion.

'She's not playing'—Mr Mitchett gravely confirmed it. 'Don't you feel in the very air the vibration of the passion that she's simply too charming to shake at the window as the housemaid shakes the table-cloth or the jingo the flag?'.[1]

And there this little matter is, for the moment, allowed to rest.

The scene, however, is remarkable also for what it reveals of their depths of self-knowledge. There is positively nothing they do not 'know' about themselves and each other. There is nothing too delicate, too intimate or too painful to be legitimate matter for analysis and appraisal by these three of the inner circle at Buckingham Crescent. Mitchy, for instance, who is hopelessly in love with Nanda, is perfectly clear about the fact that his main disqualification as a suitor is his goodness—his 'moral beauty', as they call it. When Mrs Brookenham speaks of his 'genius' as of a kind 'to which middle life will be particularly favourable', he replies: 'Why, my moral beauty, my dear woman—if that's what you mean by my genius—is precisely my curse. What on earth is left for a man just rotten with goodness? It renders necessary the kind of liking that renders *un*necessary anything else.'[2] What he means is that his unfortunate 'moral

[1] *The Awkward Age*, VI, 2, p. 271.

[2] *Ibid.* VI, 2, p. 272. The last sentence, being the kind of 'cheap paradox' that is apparently proscribed at Buckingham Crescent, renders Mitchy liable to a fine of five pounds; and since it happens to be exactly the kind of paradox or 'epigram' in which Oscar Wilde's plays abound, it is difficult not to see this as a mild side-kick at the successful rival whose *An Ideal Husband* was being acclaimed at the Haymarket the very night of the *Guy Domville* disaster at the St. James's Theatre (see Leon Edel, *The Complete Plays of Henry James*, pp. 468–9). The money, which Mitchy puts on a table by Mrs Brookenham's side, is later appropriated by Harold, causing Mrs Brook fresh spasms of luxurious woe over her odious son (*The Awkward Age*, IX, 3; cp. p. 142 above).

beauty' induces the kind of 'liking' that, somehow, excludes passion; and since it is passion that above everything he would wish to inspire in Nanda, he feels, not surprisingly perhaps, a certain dispassionate revulsion from his own moral beauty. And the other two quite see the point. Of course, they assent (in the coolest, most candid, most charming way) Nanda will never have him because he is so 'rotten with goodness'; and he will have to marry Aggie instead, not because he wants to but because it is Nanda's dearest wish that he should—and he is incapable of refusing Nanda anything because he is so hopelessly in love with her.

So this is Mitchy's case in relation to Nanda. As for Vanderbank: in the same cool, candid, charming, and utterly ruthless manner they all agree that Vanderbank has just that which poor Mitchy lacks. He has what they call 'the sacred terror', meaning that personal charm, that sovereign personal power, which renders superfluous mere goodness, mere 'moral beauty', even in the eyes of a girl like Nanda Brookenham.[1] He is (as Mitchy is later to put it to Mr Longdon) a great case of privilege: 'There are people like that—great cases of privilege. . . . They go through life somehow guaranteed. They can't help pleasing. . . . They hold, they keep every one. It's the sacred terror.'[2] And this (they all agree) makes the wonderful and prodigious 'interest' of the whole situation: that Vanderbank, who does not love Nanda, will continue to be hopelessly loved by her because he 'can't help pleasing', while Mitchy, who hopelessly loves Nanda, will never be more than 'liked' by her because he is so 'rotten with goodness'. And to *see* the interest of the situation in this way—in a way so prodigiously clear-sighted and dispassionate—is what they themselves regard as their unique virtue. This is their passion for 'getting at the idea of things', upon which Vanderbank comments in the course of the scene: 'What *is* splendid, as we call it, is this extraordinary freedom and good-humour of our intercourse and the fact that we

[1] *The Awkward Age*, VI, 2, p. 273. [2] *Ibid.* IX, 4, p. 429.

do care—so independently of our personal interests, with so little selfishness or other vulgarity—to get at the idea of things'.[1] Or again, commenting to Mitchy on Mrs. Brookenham's dispassionate analysis of the reasons why he, Vanderbank, will not propose to Nanda (and so will leave her free to marry Mitchy, which is Mrs Brookenham's 'favourite plan'), he remarks:

'What's really "superior" in her is that, though I suddenly show her an interference with a favourite plan, her personal resentment's nothing—all she wants is to see what may really happen, to take in the truth of the case and make the best of that. She offers me the truth, as she sees it, about myself, and with no nasty elation if it does chance to be the truth that suits her best. It was a charming, charming stroke.'[2]

Upon this follows a kind of antiphonal on the theme of their sincerity, simplicity and naturalness which conveys, very vividly, the sense of community they genuinely enjoy in and through their admiration of each other and, in particular, their delight in each other's 'dim depths'. (The episode referred to occurs earlier in the scene when Mrs Brookenham, having been told by Vanderbank, presumably in the strictest confidence, that Mr Longdon has offered to settle a fortune on Nanda if he marries her, immediately communicates this news to Mitchy. Van at this is as angry as a member of the inner circle at Buckingham Crescent can ever be; but he sees presently how 'wonderful' Mrs Brook has been to do as she did.) Mrs Brook's is the first 'voice':

'If the principal beauty of our effort to live together is . . . in our sincerity, I simply obeyed the impulse to do the sincere thing. If we're not sincere, we're nothing.'

'Nothing!'—it was Mitchy who first responded. 'But we *are* sincere.'

'Yes, we *are* sincere', Vanderbank presently said. 'It's a great chance for us not to fall below ourselves: no doubt, therefore, we shall continue to soar and sing. We pay for it, people who don't like us say, in our self-consciousness—'

[1] *Ibid.* VI, 2, p. 267.
[2] *Ibid.*

'But people who don't like us', Mitchy broke in, 'don't matter. Besides, how can we be properly conscious of each other—?'

'That's it!'—Vanderbank completed his idea: 'without my finding myself, for instance, in you and Mrs Brook? We see ourselves reflected—we're conscious of the charming whole. I thank you', he pursued after an instant to Mrs Brook—' thank you for your sincerity'.

. . . She exchanged with Vanderbank a somewhat remarkable look, then, with an art of her own, broke short off without appearing to drop him. 'The thing is, don't you think?'—she appealed to Mitchy—'for us not to be so awfully clever as to make it believed that we can never be simple. We mustn't see *too* tremendous things —even in each other.' She quite lost patience with the danger she glanced at. 'We *can* be simple!'

'We *can*, by God!' Mitchy laughed.

'Well, we are now—and it's a great comfort to have it settled', said Vanderbank.

'Then you see', Mrs Brook returned, 'what a mistake you'd make to see abysses of subtlety in my having been merely natural.'

'We *can* be natural', Mitchy declared.

'We can, by God!' Vanderbank laughed.[1]

If this scene, like all the best scenes in *The Awkward Age*, triumphs essentially as drama, it does so principally because of James's rendering of the conversational idiom of Buckingham Crescent. The achievement is in the marvellous way in which speed and tautness are fused with the easiness, informality and essential *simplicity* characteristic of the actual speech of this class. Dr Johnson's dictum in praise of Shakespeare's comic dialogue comes to mind—'a speech above grossness and below refinement', which (Johnson suggests) is the staple of educated English speech in every age. Its essential simplicity, at any rate in its post-Shakespearian form, is to be discovered as much in what it is not as in what it is—specifically, in the absence of all that is recognisable as jargon in less cultivated English speech: the speech of Buckingham Crescent, we find, is never disfigured by bookish words or banal phrases or stiff clumsy cadences, but is always easy and flexible, and wonderfully fresh and vivid.

[1] *The Awkward Age*, VI, 2, pp. 267–8.

Nor, it seems, is this special kind of simplicity in the least incompatible with the late-Jamesian characteristics of the style of *The Awkward Age*: that it should also be oblique, allusive, elliptical; that every half-sentence, exclamation, long pause should bristle with crucial implications, of which not one must be lost on pain of losing the thread of a whole scene, if not indeed of the whole story. The main dramatic reason (and justification) for its being so intensely oblique, allusive and elliptical is not difficult to discern. It is the speech of a homogeneous, closely-knit social group, sharing common standards, attitudes, forms of behaviour; and precisely because so much is shared, no part of what is shared need ever be explicitly referred to. All that is shared is implicitly present, and recognised to be present, in every judgement, every detail of conduct—indeed in every movement, gesture, and look—of the members of this homogeneous group; and it is for this reason that they are able to practise (in James's own phrase) 'that economy of expression which is the result of a common experience'.

But this intensely dramatic rendering of the idiom of Mrs Brookenham and her set is, of course, only the means to James's ultimate object in *The Awkward Age*, which is to render the distinctive moral quality of their world. It is in order to give us the directest access to this world, to make it fully transparent by letting it expose itself to our view, that James in his late style reproduces, or rather re-enacts, the characteristic idiom of that world.

To bring us back to the central theme of *The Awkward Age* we may take a last glance at the scene in Mrs Brookenham's drawing-room between the three of the inner circle. There is something radically wrong, we are expected to see, with these fine goings-on in Mrs Brook's temple of analysis; and in case the brilliance of the performance should lead us to miss or to minimise this, James drops the hint that ought instantly to restore our moral perspective. It is done in two brief phrases very near the end of the scene. The men are about to leave, and Mrs Brookenham, 'thoughtful, wistful, candid', throws out a last observation:

> 'And yet to think that after all it has been mere *talk*!'
>
> Something in her tone again made her hearers laugh out; so it was still with the air of good-humor that Vanderbank rejoined: 'Mere, mere, mere. But perhaps it's exactly the "mere" that has made us range so wide.'
>
> Mrs Brook's intelligence abounded. 'You mean that we haven't had the excuse of passion?'
>
> Her companions once more gave way to mirth, but 'There you are!' Vanderbank said, after an instant, less sociably. With it too he held out his hand.[1]

So it *has*, after all, been 'mere talk'; and they have not had 'the excuse of passion'. The men laugh because Mrs Brook says it so lightly, so amusingly and charmingly. But the reader is expected to reflect rather more soberly upon the implications of this suggestion. If they have not had the excuse of passion, their marvellous free play of mind has been exercised at the expense of passion—at the expense, that is, of a real, deep, painful involvement in the issues. There has after all, it seems, been an ultimate refusal to take ultimate risks, an ultimate insincerity (in spite of their protestations to the contrary) in the whole dazzling performance. And it is this ultimate falsity and sterility of the 'good talk' in Mrs Brookenham's drawing-room that, more than anything, has corrupted and demoralised poor Nanda. For where the appearance is so profoundly at variance with the reality—where all that the naked eye can see is energy in abundance, an ardour of interest in the life of the mind, intelligence, vivacity, wit, and the radiant charm that lies over it all—it is difficult indeed for an inexperienced mind not to be confused and deceived by it almost beyond the hope of salvation. And when the inexperienced mind, growing less inexperienced as the months pass, does in the end see through it, does penetrate—though of course

[1] *The Awkward Age*, VI, 2, p. 277.

dimly and confusedly—to the sterile reality that lies beneath and behind ('We haven't had the excuse of passion', says Mrs Brookenham), the shock of recognition is almost more than it can bear. Nanda does not wholly break down; but she also does not wholly survive; and this is what now remains to be briefly examined—the manner of her destruction and survival.

Nanda, we are repeatedly told, comes to know 'everything'. This fine large vague word is constantly used by her mother and her mother's friends to signify the alarming, the terrifying, indeed the sinister depths of Nanda's 'knowledge'. Now it is generally supposed in the Buckingham Crescent circle that this knowledge is merely the kind of knowledge that the Duchess, guardian of little Aggie, the convent flower, would sooner die (as she tells Mrs Brookenham) than let *her* precious darling have any taint of. Nanda, we learn, has read certain French novels which (says the Duchess) her mother had no business to leave lying about in the drawing-room. She has also been allowed to make a close companion of one Tishy Grendon, an unhappily married young woman, who has talked to Nanda, as unhappily married young women will, about her woes; and this also has not helped to preserve Nanda's innocence. In general, Nanda has enjoyed a degree of freedom of thought, speech and movement, that (according to the Duchess) might well make a mother tremble for her chances of remaining acceptable as a wife to some good and true man.

And, on top of all this, 'it is a question' (remarks one of the men in the story to another of the men) 'whether she is pretty'. She is striking and interesting, of course; and elegant, as Mrs Brookenham's daughter might be expected to be; and wonderful and prodigious, like everyone else in that charmed circle; but pretty—there *is* a question as to that. Her mother confirms the dreadful doubt: 'The girl's as bleak as a chimney-pot when the fire's out', she says in private to her husband; and from this we are to understand that Nanda lacks some essential ingredient of what in that circle is comprehensively called 'charm.' She is not a charming girl; and her mother has cause to fear the worst.

The worst, it has already been indicated, does in fact happen. Nanda does not marry—neither Mitchy who loves her, nor Vanderbank whom she loves; and instead of love, she has to make do with the 'beautiful loyalty' of her beautiful old-fashioned friend Mr Longdon. And it is generally understood in the circle of her mother and her mother's friends that what has rendered her unmarriageable has been her unfortunate, her tragic, knowledge: by which they mean always her premature loss of the kind and degree of innocence that is still, it transpires, required of a young girl in a circle as free and as enlightened as Mrs Brookenham's. (The ultimate tragic consequence for Nanda of this ironic truth is exposed in a splendid scene between Nanda and Mitchy towards the end of the book.[1])

But this, of course, is only the surface explanation of Nanda's tragedy, which the Buckingham Crescent circle finds it convenient to take, or pretend to take, as the whole explanation. The 'knowledge' Nanda has acquired from Tishy Grendon and the French novels is as nothing compared to that which she has acquired by her direct exposure to her mother's world in the three months that have passed since she emerged from the schoolroom. It is what she has been able to 'make out' of the values that lie behind the good talk in her mother's drawing-room that has ruined her innocence, made her bleak as a chimney-pot, and left her only her precious Jamesian lucidity—her insight, her understanding of all that this world stands for—as her sole recommendation to the good and true man who might want to marry her.

But Vanderbank, the charming, graceful, adorable Van with whom Nanda is in love ('Nanda's fairly sick—as sick as a little cat—with her passion', the Duchess tells Mr Longdon),[2] cannot in the end find this a sufficient recommendation.

[1] See pp. 159-62 below. [2] *The Awkward Age*, v, 4, p. 222.

This emerges indeed only in the end; and more than half of the story turns precisely upon whether he will or will not ask Nanda to marry him. He is given every cause, means and will to do it .The will is there from the start: for Van is a thoroughly charming, obliging man, who hates, as such men do, not to do what is desired of him. And this goodwill presently receives the strongest additional incentive to action by an offer from Mr Longdon to settle a fortune on Nanda if he should marry her. The offer is made with the utmost delicacy and circuitousness, but it is definitely made; and it is made because Mr Longdon, besides himself liking Van enormously, is torn with compassion for Nanda and wishes to do what he can for her happiness.

But with all his goodwill and all his desire to oblige, and now with Mr Longdon's money to ease his way, Van still finds that he cannot love Nanda. He can admire her, oh ever so ardently, ever so passionately even; but he cannot love her. For (as Nanda herself later explains it to Mr. Longdon) he is after all too old-fashioned to love a girl who 'knows' what Nanda knows: this free, enlightened spirit, this ornament of Mrs Brookenham's temple of analysis, is too old-fashioned to take a wife who is not conventionally ignorant and innocent of the ways of the worldly world.

This in any event is the surface explanation of Van's rejection of Nanda—the top layer, so to speak, of the multi-layered motive that determines his final act of choice. The reasons for Van's withdrawal, however, go deeper than that. Van does not know it—or, if he knows, would never admit it even to himself; but the truth is that he not only cannot love Nanda, he finds her positively repellent. To begin with, her passion—her terrible sincerity and candour, which she can by no effort conceal—frightens him and makes him thoroughly uncomfortable. But what is worse even than her passion is her lucidity, the product of her ever-active, enquiring, probing, discovering mind. This more than anything Van finds he cannot take. For (Van can see) it is a mind that already, at the age of eighteen, has seen through the corruptions and falsities of 'the world'—his world, to which he is committed with all his heart and soul. Van can admire, find 'beautiful', 'wonderful' and 'charming', the unworldly world of Mr Longdon which, in that time and place, stands at the opposite pole to Buckingham Crescent; and in this we have an instance of what James in a later work was to call the 'fathomless depths of English equivocation', expressed here in the special kind of moral duplicity which enables the English with perfect sincerity, often indeed with ardour, to admire in others a way of life that they would not dream of adopting for themselves. But Van's own world is the world of Buckingham Crescent: he can no more detach himself from it than Nanda can be part of it; and it is Nanda's repudiation of the values of that world—crude, childish and helpless as her repudiation is—that beyond anything frightens and repels Van. This, he knows, he could not live with; and this is in the end why, with all the good-nature, grace and charm in the world, he rejects Nanda.

And Nanda knows this—knows what it is that Van finds repellent in her. She knows it obscurely at first, presently more clearly, and in the end with a dispassionate anguish of clarity that issues in the poignant heroism of her last scene with Van, when she bids him good-bye and entreats him to take care of her mother before withdrawing for ever to Mr Longdon's house in the country.

It is not difficult to see how this aspect of the tragic situation in *The Awkward Age* is a development and refinement of the central situation in *The Portrait of a Lady*. There, we remember, the tragic failure of Isabel Archer's marriage was likewise due to her misfortune in possessing a 'mind'—the kind of mind that (like Nanda Brookenham's) could not but be critical of the values of the world, and therefore could not but be as profoundly repellent to her husband Gilbert Osmond as Nanda's is to Vanderbank. The difference is only that while Osmond was essentially vain, egotistical and cruel, Van is good-natured, charming and kind—a difference that creates for James one of those 'difficulties' he came to love in his late period, that of showing a man like Van as capable of an act of rejection which, in its consequences if not in its motive, is as cruel and arbitrary as any that Gilbert Osmond might commit. In *The Golden Bowl,* we will find, the central relationship of the story, that between Maggie Verver and her husband the Prince, is still another rendering of the same essential situation. There it is pursued to the farthest limit of James's insight, and with the 'difficulty' correspondingly intensified; for the Prince is made even more adorable (and adored) than Van, yet is shown to be capable of an act of betrayal many times more reprehensible.

Nanda's last scene with Van[1] establishes this connexion with *The Golden Bowl* in a particularly decisive way. She 'lets him down easily', we are told: in other words, she loves him too much to despise him, though there is everything in Van's conduct in that last scene to expose him to her contempt. The charm, the good nature, the perfect breeding that everyone finds so adorable can in this last scene barely sustain his uneasiness, his discomfort and his embarrassment. And his fatal evasiveness, his constitutional incapacity to face up to a moral issue, which James by a hundred delicate hints throughout the story has shown us to be Van's fundamental moral deficiency, threatens at last in this scene to break the surface and expose itself, to Van himself, and to Nanda, for the mean, base, shabby thing that it is.

But (and this is the vital point, which is to be taken up again and given still greater prominence in *The Golden Bowl*): if it *should* break the surface and expose itself, it would destroy Van. The blow would be mortal because it would undermine, irreparably, the very foundation of his charm, his good nature, his beautiful breeding—everything, in short, that

[1] *The Awkward Age,* x, 1–2.

makes him so uniquely adorable, indeed defines his very individuality. It is this precious individuality expressing itself in his special charm, for which Nanda herself first loved him and still loves him, that above all she desires to leave unimpaired. She sees him as he is, steady and whole, but desires only to spare him—to let him down as easily as possible: 'To force upon him an awkwardness was like forcing a disfigurement or a hurt, so that at the end of a minute, during which the expression of her face became a kind of uplifted view of her opportunity, she arrived at the appearance of having changed places with him and of their being together precisely in order that he—not she—should be let down easily'.[1]

The thread of connexion, as strong as it is fine, which (I have suggested) is to be discerned between *The Portrait of a Lady*, *The Awkward Age* and *The Golden Bowl* may provisionally be stated as follows. While the central relationship in *The Portrait of a Lady* issues in the heroism of mere endurance (for that is all that is left to Isabel Archer when she returns to her husband), and while the corresponding relationship in *The Awkward Age* issues in the heroism of mere renunciation (for Nanda gives up Buckingham Crescent and goes to live with Mr Longdon), the essentially similar relationship in *The Golden Bowl* issues in a transformation, triumphant and glorious, of moral ignorance and turpitude into moral knowledge and goodness by the power of love. Maggie Verver, like Nanda Brookenham, seeks to restore what has been lost by sparing and sparing again, at the price of anguish, terror and humiliation to herself, the three persons most dear to her, and in particular her husband the Prince. But while Nanda's selfless love can in the end only be exercised in renouncing her world, Maggie's is directed towards a triumphant fulfilment; and it is this extension in *The Golden Bowl*, this final exploration to its very limits, of one of the central tragic themes of his greatest novels

[1] *The Awkward Age*, x, 1, pp. 443–4. Cp. ch. VIII, pp. 273-5 below.

that marks perhaps the furthest reach of James's vision of human possibility.

There is still another and final aspect of the tragedy of Nanda Brookenham to consider. It is disclosed to us in Nanda's remarkable dialogue with Mitchy in the scene in which she lets him know that she cannot marry him and urges him to marry little Aggie.[1] (She does not, of course, have to tell him that it is because she loves Van that she cannot marry him, since he knows this perfectly well.) The crucial portion of the exchange occurs when she is pressing Mitchy to see the beauty of Aggie's innocence:

> 'Now the beauty of Aggie [she says to him] is that she knows nothing—but absolutely, utterly: not the least little tittle of anything.'
>
> It was barely visible that Mitchy hesitated, and he spoke quite gravely. 'Have you tried her?'
>
> 'Oh yes. And Tishy has.' His gravity had been less than Nanda's. 'Nothing, nothing'. The memory of some scene or some passage might have come back to her with a charm.
>
> 'Ah, say what you will—it *is* the way we ought to be!'
>
> Mitchy, after a minute of much intensity, had stopped watching her; changing his posture and with his elbows on his knees, he dropped for a while his face into his hands. Then he jerked himself to his feet. 'There's something I wish awfully I could say to you. But I can't.'
>
> Nanda, after a slow head-shake, covered him with one of the dimmest of her smiles. 'You needn't say it, I know perfectly which it is.' She held him an instant, after which she went on: 'It's simply that you wish me fully to understand that *you're* one who, in perfect sincerity, doesn't mind one straw how awful—'
>
> 'Yes, how awful?' He had kindled, as she paused, with his new eagerness.
>
> 'Well, one's knowledge may be. It doesn't shock in you a single hereditary prejudice.'
>
> 'Oh, "hereditary!"—' Mitchy ecstatically murmured.
>
> 'You even rather like me the better for it; so that one of the reasons why you couldn't have told me—though not, of course, I know, the only one—is that you would have been literally almost ashamed. Because, you know,' she went on, 'it *is* strange'.

[1] *The Awkward Age*, VII, 2.

'My lack of hereditary—?'

'Yes, discomfort in the presence of the fact I speak of. There's a kind of sense you don't possess.'

His appreciation again fairly goggled at her. 'Oh, you do know everything!'

'You're so good that nothing shocks you', she lucidly persisted. 'There's a kind of delicacy you haven't got.'

He was more and more struck. 'I've only that—as it were—of the skin and the fingers?' he appealed.

'Oh, and that of the mind. And that of the soul. And some other kinds, certainly. But not *the* kind.'

'Yes'—he wondered—'I suppose that's the only way one can name it.' It appeared to rise there before him. '*The* kind!'

'The kind that would make me painful to you. Or rather not me perhaps', she added as if to create between them the fullest possible light; 'but my situation, my exposure—all the results of them that I show. Doesn't one become a sort of a little drain-pipe with everything flowing through?'

'Why don't you call it more gracefully', Mitchy asked, freshly struck, 'a little aeolian-harp set in the drawing-room window and vibrating in the breeze of conversation?'

'Oh, because the harp gives out a sound, and *we*—at least we try to—give out none.'

'What you take, you mean, you keep?'

'Well, it sticks to us. And that's what you don't mind!'

Their eyes met long on it. 'Yes—I see. I *don't* mind. I've the most extraordinary lacunae.'

'Oh I don't know about others', Nanda replied; 'I haven't noticed them. But you've that one, and it's enough'.

He continued to face her with his queer mixture of assent and speculation. 'Enough, my dear, for what? To have made me impossible for you because the only man you could, as they say, have "respected" would be a man who *would* have minded?' Then as under the cool, soft pressure of the question she looked at last away from him: 'The man with "*the* kind", as you call it, happens to be just the type you *can* love? But what's the use', he persisted as she answered nothing, 'in loving a person with the prejudice—hereditary or other—to which you're precisely obnoxious? Do you positively *like* to love in vain?'

It was a question, the way she turned back to him seemed to say, that deserved a responsible answer. 'Yes.'[1]

[1] *The Awkward Age*, VII, 2, pp. 315–18.

In that last sentence we receive at last, I suggest, the full measure of what Buckingham Crescent has done to Nanda. 'Do you positively like to love in vain?' asks Mitchy. 'Yes', replies Nanda. Coming where it does in the story, when we are already saturated with our sense of Nanda's suffering, this statement is, of course, inexpressibly heart-rending. But it is also deeply and dreadfully shocking. The perversity of it strikes one, for the moment, as monstrous: it is, or seems, as wanton, arbitrary and cruel as a self-inflicted wound. And for that moment Nanda Brookenham's stature as the central tragic figure in the story hangs in the balance. For if she *is* merely perverse, and if this perversity is merely wanton, arbitrary, inexplicable, her tragic stature is fatally undermined and her story loses commensurately in tragic significance.

But it is not inexplicable. This last piece of perversity, as it seems (along with all that goes before it in the exchange with Mitchy), is to be accounted for by the world of Buckingham Crescent. It is accounted for by the power of Buckingham Crescent ultimately to infect with its false values even a nature as constitutionally inaccessible to its influence as Nanda's; and it is the final proof of its diabolical badness that it should possess the power to confuse and demoralise in this way a nature so fine. For Nanda's ultimate tragedy, as this dialogue with Mitchy discloses (and as in a different, lighter key we have already had intimated to us in the analytical session in Mrs Brook's drawing-room [1]), is that she cannot love Mitchy precisely because he does not 'mind' in her the loss of her ignorance and innocence for which Buckingham Crescent has been directly responsible. Though he is so full of goodness, though he possesses every delicacy of the mind and the soul that Nanda, uniquely in that circle, knows how to value, she yet cannot love him. For he lacks the one delicacy, the 'hereditary prejudice', as she calls it, that Van does possess; and though Van is neither good nor

[1] See pp. 147-8 above.

delicate in mind or soul nor anything else that Mitchy is, it is for this that she loves him—for the very thing that disables him from loving her. This (we now see) is the deepest bond between them: that Nanda positively shares Van's 'hereditary prejudice'—and shares it because Buckingham Crescent has infected her with it, this being the last infirmity, the last moral taint, which she has not been able to resist, and from which not all her moral passion nor all her lucidity has been able to save her.

So Nanda Brookenham's tragic stature is after all established on the firmest ground. She is infected with this final destructive prejudice, and is to that extent 'responsible' for, indeed even the author of, her own misery. But besides being responsible, she is also fully conscious of her own responsibility, her own part in her unhappiness; and this was the meaning of her reply to Mitchy's question. Did she positively like to love in vain? Yes, she replies, meaning that she *knows* she likes it because she shares the prejudice which is the cause of it, and that she knows this is the cause of her suffering. Yet, knowing it, she is helpless by her intelligence, her 'knowledge', to exorcise this last corruption in her blood, and helpless therefore to save herself.

That, it appears, is the deepest aspect of Nanda Brookenham's tragedy. It is also, of course, one of the deepest aspects of the universal human tragedy—the ultimate helplessness of the human intelligence, even when it is an intelligence as wonderful and prodigious as that of the late-Jamesian vessels of consciousness, to secure men from destruction or suffering. And this aspect, too, of the tragic condition of man is taken up again and developed in the works that follow *The Awkward Age*, particularly in *The Wings of the Dove* and in the unfinished novel *The Ivory Tower*.

The tragic and the universal, however, though doubtless paramount, is not the only aspect of *The Awkward Age* that in the end commands our interest. The local and the temporal has its claim, too, in the shape of the 'social' theme to which James draws such pointed attention in the Preface; and it would be a loss indeed to miss the last brilliant refinement in James's handling of this theme, which happens also to disclose a last, unexpectedly tender, view of Mrs Brookenham.

If the *dénouement* of Nanda's story is her encounter with Van in Book X, the *dénouement* of Mrs Brookenham's is the great show-down at Tishy Grendon's dinner-party in Book VIII. In this remarkable 'crowd' scene, with all the cast, so to speak, present on the stage, Mrs Brookenham—like Kate Croy in a comparable scene in *The Wings of the Dove*—shows herself capable of an audacity and a courage (as well as a wit, malice and deviousness) which surpasses everything of this kind she has previously exhibited. As Kate in her midnight session with Milly Theale 'gives away, hand over hand' Lancaster Gate and all it contains, thereby risking the annihilation of her own grand design against Milly,[1] so Mrs Brookenham at Tishy Grendon's, in a series of deliberately provocative acts—starting with her publicly demanding of Mr Longdon that he give Nanda back to them and culminating in her exposure of Nanda in the episode with the French novel—'gives away' Buckingham Crescent: to Mr Longdon in the first instance, of course, but also to all the assembled guests, and in particular Vanderbank. In order to ensure beyond the possibility of a reversal that Nanda shall not marry Vanderbank and shall be taken away by Mr Longdon, Mrs Brookenham goes to the furthest lengths at once to show Mr Longdon just how 'bad' Buckingham Crescent is and to show Vanderbank how 'bad' Nanda is; and to achieve this extraordinary double end, she is willing to risk sacrificing herself in the process. She is willing, it seems, not only to be 'hated' by Mr Longdon—that is, to make herself an even greater object of horror to him than she has been up to now—but, even more, to alienate, irreconcilably if necessary, her own dear

[1] Cp. ch. VII, pp. 207-8 below.

Vanderbank, as well as Mitchy and Nanda, and indeed everyone present.

The problem of Mrs Brookenham's 'motives' is left unresolved to the end. In the series of scenes that follow in Book IX, each designed to illuminate the momentous evening at Tishy Grendon's three months after the event, it is never unambiguously disclosed why she did what she did: whether she did it (as the Duchess repeatedly intimates) because she wanted 'to keep Van for herself', and wanted Nanda out of the way so that she might enjoy the full benefit of having kept him; or whether she did it because, in her own strange way, she had come to see how bad Buckingham Crescent was, and really wanted to do the best she could for her daughter Nanda, morally as well as materially; or, finally, whether she did it from both these motives, having perceived (and not for the first time) that by doing what she knew to be best for Nanda she might by the same stroke be doing what was best for herself.[1] What is certain, at any rate, is that—again like Kate Croy—the risk she takes is genuine, and commensurate with the stakes she is playing for. For (as we learn in Book IX) Mr Longdon takes Mrs Brookenham at her word and sends Nanda back to Buckingham Crescent, where we find her three months later installed in her own private sitting-room, seemingly for good. Van, we discover, has stayed away from Buckingham Crescent all these three months, and has to all appearances no intention of resuming his former beautiful relation with Mrs Brookenham; Mitchy, who went abroad immediately after the events at Tishy Grendon's, has not written in all these months; and Edward, her husband, has spoken never a word about it, concealing his mystification behind his 'dead face' and perfect taciturnity.

So at the end of Book IX the success of Mrs Brookenham's design is by no means assured, and what exactly her motives

[1] Cp. p. 149 above. Van's comment on her 'charming, charming stroke' in the scene in Bk. VI, ch. 2: 'She offers me the truth, as she sees it, about myself, and with no nasty elation if it does chance to be the truth that suits her best.'

were remains obscure. The design, we know, does finally succeed, chiefly through Nanda's intercession with Van, while the motives remain obscure to the end. Yet that a concern for Nanda's moral welfare *was* a part of Mrs Brook's motive— however a confused a part, and however mixed with the imputed selfish motive of 'keeping Van for herself'—is irresistibly suggested by a multitude of details too elusive to analyse in a short space; and it is this aspect of her conduct at Tishy Grendon's that is meant to throw a last sympathetic light both on Mrs Brookenham herself and on the English solution to the problem of the awkward age.

For among the complex ends achieved by the scene at Tishy Grendon's is the direct, dramatic exhibition of the clash between the English and the French solutions discussed in the Preface.[1] As we follow the consummate logic of the Duchess' defence of her little Aggie's carryings-on with Lord Petherton ('my dear child was only perfectly bred and deliciously clever', she explains[2]) and presently observe the quondam convent flower displaying her perfect breeding and delicious cleverness before her husband and his friends, what we are invited to see is the relative moral virtue of the English solution, and consequently the relative moral virtue of Mrs Brookenham, its principal agent. We recall James's statement in the Preface about 'the so morally well-meant and so intellectually helpless compromise' of the English solution, and perceive that there are worse things than intellectual confusion and better things than scientific precision. The English solution may be intellectually abject, but it leaves a margin, however narrow, for a saving humanity and even a vestigial morality; the French solution, being ruthlessly scientific, may succeed where the English fails, but at the price of all morality and humanity. Indeed what finally insinuates itself into (or out of) the drama is a distinct preference on the part of Henry James for the English solution. He may marvel

[1] See pp. 135-7 above. [2] *The Awkward Age*, VIII, 4.

ceaselessly at the English capacity for muddles and half-measures (and always, of course, at the fathomless depths of English equivocation[1]), yet he cannot but love them—or at least find them touching and engaging—for their residual humanity; while he can admire the French for the perfection of their 'science' but can only find repellent the immorality and inhumanity which it entails.

In *The Awkward Age*, the final proof of the relative morality and humanity is the demonstrable difference between Nanda and Aggie. Nanda, the victim of the English solution, loses her happiness but retains unimpaired her moral integrity; Aggie, the flower of the French scheme, has her happiness but emerges (in the Edwardian idiom) as a coarse little baggage. And since Mrs Brook is the agent of the English solution as the Duchess is of the French, she, too, emerges from her ordeal trailing clouds of a relative moral glory: a glory frail and tenuous indeed, yet distinctly there compared with its total absence in the Duchess' flawless immorality. This, we now recognise, accounts for our persistent sense throughout the story, and in particular at its close, of a fugitive likeableness and even loveableness in Mrs Brookenham, which all her displayed vanity and greed, malice and destructiveness, have no power to diminish. It is as if, contrary to all conscious intention or desire, she were doomed to remain relatively 'good'—by the accident, merely of being English and having to find an English solution to her difficulties.

[1] Cp. p. 233 below.

CHAPTER VI

'THE SACRED FOUNT'

THAT there is a connexion between *The Sacred Fount*, published in 1901, and *The Turn of the Screw* published some three years earlier has not escaped the notice of the critics, among them Mr Edmund Wilson and Mr Leon Edel.[1] The connexion is indeed worth pursuing for the valuable light it throws on the intention and scope of the later work. For *The Sacred Fount* is, I believe, chiefly though not exclusively, a writing large of one of the subsidiary themes of *The Turn of the Screw* —what I called the 'epistemological' theme, which turns upon the final incapacity of the enquiring mind to know with certainty whether what it 'sees' is fact or delusion.[2] In *The Turn of the Screw* this was secondary, and subordinate to the principal moral theme of salvation; in *The Sacred Fount* this relation seems to be almost exactly reversed: what was subsidiary in *The Turn of the Screw* is here dominant; and the moral theme, or rather themes, indicated by the title, though themselves profoundly interesting and important, are treated strictly within the encompassing framework of the epistemological, with all its own moral implications. Nor is it an accident that the all-important narrator in *The Sacred Fount* should be an 'author'. For James the problem hinted at in *The Turn of the Screw* (and now expanded, elaborated and refined on a scale requiring for its treatment the full technical resources of his mature artistry) came to figure as the central 'philosophical' problem, or mystery, of the life of the creative artist; and it is accordingly as the irreducible,

[1] Mr Wilson has written about it in his essay *The Ambiguity of Henry James*, and Mr Edel in his introduction to the Grove Press edition of *The Sacred Fount*. Mr Wilson's discussion shows, in my view, the same weaknesses as his account of *The Turn of the Screw* (see ch. IV above, and Appendix A below); Mr Edel's, on the other hand, has seemed to me to be perceptive and illuminating.

[2] Cp. ch. IV, pp. 131-4 above.

insoluble mystery in the heart of the creative process itself that it is dramatised in the curious fable of *The Sacred Fount*.

As in *The Turn of the Screw*, all the extraordinary events of the story are projected entirely through the consciousness of the first-person narrator, the nameless author. His two confidantes, Ford Obert, an artist, and Mrs Brissenden, one of the four participants in the drama, only (like Mrs Grose in *The Turn of the Screw*) appear to confirm what *he* 'sees'; and when at the end the confidantes explicitly repudiate all they appear in the course of the story to have confirmed, we are left in no doubt that we have all along had his word and his alone—not only for what was supposed to be happening but also for what the others are supposed to have confirmed of what was happening.

On the train to Newmarch, the country-house in which the little week-end drama is to be enacted, the narrator finds himself in the same compartment as two of the *dramatis personae*, Gilbert Long and Grace Brissenden. He observes, or thinks he observes, that Mrs Brissenden, whom he had always thought of as incurably plain and quite as old as her forty or so years, has become remarkably young and pretty. This impression is apparently supported by Gilbert Long, who also gives him the hint for the explanation he is presently to arrive at—her marriage some four years back to a man very much younger than herself. But (as we have reason to recall later) Long in fact receives his 'cue' from the narrator. 'I had given him his cue by alluding to my original failure to place her', the narrator says explicitly: 'What in the world, in the year or two, had happened to her? She had changed so extraordinarily for the better. How could a woman who had been plain so long become pretty so late? It was just what he [Long] had been wondering . . .'[1]

In the meantime, the narrator has noticed, or thinks he has noticed, a change in Gilbert Long himself. He had

[1] *The Sacred Fount*, 1, p. 6.

previously seemed to him a 'heavy Adonis', handsome but stupid and rather boorish; he finds him now less obtrusively handsome but unexpectedly intelligent and amiable. This impression is confirmed—quite independently, it seems—by Mrs Brissenden:

> She put it to me frankly that she had never seen a man so improved: a confidence that I met with alacrity, as it showed me that, under the same impression, I had not gone astray. She had only, it seemed, on seeing him made him out with a great effort.[1]

She in turn suggests to the narrator the reason for the change in Long—that he has for some time past been on terms of intimacy with 'a very clever woman', Lady John, and that it is she who 'has given him a mind and a tongue'. When the narrator demurs, not having the same confidence in Lady John's cleverness, she insists: 'You yourself acknowledge the effect. If she hasn't made him clever, what has she made him? She has given him, steadily, more and more intellect'.[2] She also tells him that Lady John is to be at Newmarch that week-end.

On his arrival at the house, the narrator fails to recognise Mrs Brissenden's husband Guy because he has grown so extraordinarily *old* ('He looked almost anything—he looked quite sixty' [3]); and this introduces the third term in the equation. His impression of the change in Brissenden is, or appears to be, confirmed by Ford Obert, the artist friend; and this leads him, with Obert's amused co-operation, to frame his hypothesis about the Brissendens' relationship: that Mrs Briss has acquired her youth and beauty by 'draining' her husband of his; that the miracle has been made possible because he loves her 'passionately, sublimely'; that she is necessarily unconscious of the whole process, but he, 'the author of the sacrifice', is fully conscious; and (the narrator adds, as a 'final induction') that in all such cases 'the agents of

[1] *The Sacred Fount*, 1, p. 8.
[2] *Ibid.* 1, p. 10.
[3] *Ibid.* 2, p. 18.

the sacrifice are uncomfortable . . . when they suspect or fear that you can see'.[1]

Applying his hypothesis *mutatis mutandis* to the case of Gilbert Long, the narrator feels certain that Lady John is not the source of his remarkable growth in intelligence. For she, besides being only superficially clever, shows no signs of having been intellectually depleted as Guy Brissenden has been physically depleted; and the sacred fount from which Long is drawing his strength must accordingly be sought elsewhere. He succeeds in persuading Mrs Brissenden of the truth of this further induction, and enlists her enthusiastic co-operation in the hunt for the 'right' woman. (They both know *ex hypothesi* that she must be there at Newmarch that week-end.) But he soon has reason to regret her aptness as a pupil. For her choice finally alights on May Server, a lady whom the narrator knows to be as charming and graceful as she is intelligent; and he finds, from the moment she is named, that he desperately wants to protect her from the predatory acuteness of his confederate. (The fact that Mrs Brissenden is merely bettering her instruction only increases his alarm and vexation; nor are these mitigated by his perception of the irony of this situation.) He insists, at any rate, that he can see no change in Mrs Server; but Mrs Brissenden equally insists that there *is* 'something wrong' with her and that everyone has noticed it. 'She used to be so calm—as if she were always sitting for her portrait', she reminds him; but now she is 'all over the place'—rushing from one man to another, 'making up to them in the most extraordinary way and leaving them still more crazily'; and this (Mrs Briss declares with conviction) shows she is as nervous as a cat and flirting so wildly to conceal her real intimacy with Long. This impression of Mrs Server is, or appears to be, confirmed by Ford Obert, who had painted her a few years back, and also finds her strangely changed; and is finally confirmed by the narrator's own observation

[1] *The Sacred Fount*, 2, pp. 24–5.

when, in a conversation with her, he finds her not only as 'unhappy' as Obert has found her and as 'terrified' as Mrs Brissenden has said but also completely robbed of her intelligence.

The plot by this time has been further complicated by the narrator's perception, as he believes, of a special bond between Mrs Server and Guy Brissenden. On his hypothesis she is, of course, using all the men at the party as a 'screen' for her connexion with Gilbert Long; but she is using Brissenden conspicuously more than the others; and from this he infers that they are drawn together by their common plight as the 'sacrificed', she being fully conscious of this, he only dimly so. The narrator's compassion for Mrs Server grows steadily, and with it his desire to protect her. Though he is by this time quite sure that she is the woman who has wrought the miracle in Gilbert Long, he persists in denying it to Mrs Briss; and in the meantime, he is privately torn between elation at the wonderful 'palace of thought' he has erected and compunction at the dreadful exposure of human weakness and misery its erection has cost.

The *dénouement* on the last evening of the house-party is precipitated when the narrator, seeing Gilbert Long and Mrs Brissenden talking together, 'divines' that they, too, have become conscious of their bond (as the 'sacrificers'), and are warning each other—or, more exactly, Long is warning Mrs Briss—of their common danger of detection by the super-subtle narrator. There follows a glimpse of Mrs Briss and her husband together which appears to confirm this; and a subsequent glimpse of Long alone on the terrace appears to confirm it still further. The collapse of his palace of thought begins when he joins Ford Obert in the smoking-room, and hears from him that Mrs Server has 'changed back' —she is now, according to Obert, as 'clever' as before and no longer 'beastly unhappy'. It is finally demolished in his last grand encounter with Grace Brissenden, who comes down after midnight when all the guests have already gone to bed on purpose to tell him that she repudiates every part of his monstrous hypothesis. Gilbert Long, she tells him, is as stupid as he always was: she had found this out in a talk with him earlier that evening (the same talk, it transpires, in which the narrator had supposed him to be warning her of their common danger of exposure). Long, moreover, *was* Lady John's lover, as she had said from the beginning: she had had this authoritatively from her husband; and it was from 'poor old Briss' that she had also learnt that May Server had been making love to him, and was therefore not at all stupid but merely 'horrid'. If (Mrs Briss concludes) she had ever thought anything different—that Gilbert Long had become remarkably clever, that May Server had ceased to be remarkably clever, that Lady John was not the woman in the case and May Server was—it was entirely by his diabolical powers of suggestion that she had been led to think these things; and she now wished him to know that she completely renounced him and his suggestions, and pronounced him, poor dear, 'crazy'. As she sweeps off, leaving him to contemplate the ruins of his palace of thought, we are left with the impression of a man with head bloody indeed but essentially unbowed: 'I *should* certainly never again, on the spot, quite hang together again, even though it wasn't really that I hadn't three times her method. What I too fatally lacked was her tone'.[1]

Compared with *The Turn of the Screw*, *The Sacred Fount* offers a vastly enlarged field for the operation both of the late-Jamesian irony and of the famous ambiguity, in the interest chiefly of the epistemological theme common to both stories. The opportunities in fact are multiplied in exact proportion to the complications, subtleties and ingenuities of the plot; and these in turn are there to ensure the multiplication of opportunities. Since this is to be his final, definitive statement of the predicament of the creative mind, James is resolved here, it seems, to be as *exhaustive* as possible—to establish

[1] *The Sacred Fount*, 14, p. 249.

the reality of the phenomenon by exploring it in aspects as numerous and varied as possible and, in each instance, pursuing it to its furthest implications; and it is for this end that he allows himself the most generous scope for his treatment of the epistemological theme.

To begin with, accordingly, there is a significant increase in the number of independent witnesses. In *The Turn of the Screw* we had only Mrs Grose; in *The Sacred Fount* we have Ford Obert, Mrs Brissenden, Gilbert Long and (once at least) Lady John; and since all but Obert are themselves participants in the drama and therefore necessarily 'biassed', the opportunities they provide for exploring the variety of human motives for 'seeing' and not 'seeing' what is or may be there to be seen are correspondingly increased.[1] Again, the 'suggestibility' of the witnesses, which is only hinted at in *The Turn of the Screw*, is here explicitly and repeatedly emphasised. Ford Obert, who is an artist and may therefore be supposed to possess naturally a vision akin to the narrator's, is in fact the most independent of the witnesses. Yet even Obert at the end, when he finds that May Server has not after all 'changed', does not hesitate to charge the narrator with first having put the idea into his head. 'I assure you I decline all responsibility', he says at their last encounter in the smoking-room, 'I see the responsibility as quite beautifully yours'.[2] For (he explains)[3] it was by the 'torch of your analogy'—the narrator's hypothesis about the Brissendens, he means—that he had first been led to see a change in Mrs Server and then to seek the man who might be held to account for it. When the narrator congratulates him on all he has come to see, he repeats: 'I do see. But only . . . through your having seen first. You gave me the pieces.

[1] Guy Brissenden and Mrs Server, the victims in *The Sacred Fount*, correspond most closely to the children in *The Turn of the Screw*. Yet only Mrs Server is wholly exempted from the office of witness; Brissenden himself is twice brought in to give evidence against his fellow-victim—first to the narrator, finally to his wife.

[2] *The Sacred Fount*, 11, p. 166. [3] *Ibid.* 11, pp. 170–1.

I've but put them together'.[1] Grace Brissenden in their final show-down is even more explicit than Obert (and much less friendly) in blaming the narrator's powers of suggestion for what she had supposed herself to 'see'. 'You talk too much', she tells him, 'I mean you're carried away—you're abused by a fine fancy: so that with your art of putting things, one doesn't know where one is . . .'[2] Again, 'You talked me over', she says when he accuses her of having no compunction about sacrificing May Server.[3] When he pleads that he had persuaded her of nothing but that Long's metamorphosis was not the work of Lady John, she replies, 'You persuaded me that it was the work of somebody . . . It came to the same thing'[4]; and finally, when he is pressing her to tell him at what stage her 'sympathy' for their joint enterprise had been alienated, she is goaded into a passionate denial of the imputed sympathy: 'As soon as I was not with you—I mean with you personally—you *never* had my sympathy. . . . As soon as I was away from you I hated you . . . —hated your theory.'[5]

The fuller treatment of the epistemological theme in *The Sacred Fount* depends chiefly, however, on the rich complication of motives for 'seeing' and not 'seeing' that the principal witnesses provide. In *The Turn of the Screw* we had in effect only the governess's and Mrs Grose's motives to take account of: the governess's love of the children, with its taint of possessiveness, and her high-minded sense of duty reinforced by her infatuation with the children's guardian, explained what she 'saw' or believed herself to see; and Mrs Grose's 'simplicity' explained both what she herself did not see and what she believed the governess to have seen.[6] In *The Sacred Fount* what each principal—including, of course, the narrator—sees and does not see is determined partly indeed by his or her character but chiefly by the relation in

[1] *The Sacred Fount*, 11, p. 173. [2] *Ibid.* 12, pp. 203–4.
[3] *Ibid.* 13, p. 208. [4] *Ibid.* 13, p. 210. [5] *Ibid.* 13, p. 224.
[6] See Appendix B, pp. 377-8 below for further discussion of this point.

which he or she stands, or appears to stand, to the other principals; and since these relations, whether real or delusory, are very much more intricate than those in *The Turn of the Screw*, the motives of the principals are correspondingly more intricate, the incentives to deception and self-deception correspondingly stronger, and the ambiguities springing from these deeper and subtler.

At an early point in the story, Gilbert Long, we remember, fails to see the change in Guy Brissenden which the narrator presses upon his attention, and in his growing irritation at the narrator's insistence almost lapses back into his old boorishness.[1] Granted the change in Brissenden, does Long (we are meant to ask) fail to see it because (like Mrs Grose) he is in fact 'simple'—because (as Mrs Briss insists at the end) he has not changed but has remained as stupid as he always was? Or is his blindness, as the narrator's hypothesis invites us to suppose, a self-protective device which forbids him to see the resemblance between Grace Brissenden's 'eating up' of her husband and his own of May Server? Again, when Guy Brissenden appears to see but not to understand what is 'wrong' with May Server, is he, too, merely being as simple as Mrs Grose when she saw that there was something wrong with little Miles (why after all was he expelled from his school?) but did not understand what it could be? Or is he in his turn protecting himself from his recognition, or half-recognition, of the bond between himself and Mrs Server as the 'sacrificed', and does he at the end round upon his fellow-victim and denounce her to his wife as 'horrid' as a last act of self-protection?[2] Finally there is the ambiguity of Grace Brissenden's own dramatic face-about. She appears to have seen the change in Gilbert Long as clearly as the narrator, and the change in May Server very much more clearly (and much sooner) than he; yet in the last scene she repudiates both changes as wholly

[1] *The Sacred Fount*, 2, pp. 20–3.
[2] *Ibid.* 8, pp. 121–2; 10, pp. 155–6.

delusory. Is her explanation the true one, namely, that she was infected by his 'fine fancy' and simply talked into seeing what was never there to be seen; or is the narrator's the true explanation—that, with Gilbert Long's help, she has been made conscious, or partly conscious, of her 'vampire' relation to her husband and, terrified of losing her hold on him, first brings him to heel, and then demolishes the narrator and his 'crazy' theories?

In connexion with the ambiguity of *The Sacred Fount* it is interesting to note that the number of apparent confirmations of what the narrator 'sees' is almost exactly balanced by the number of real confirmations. In about half the crucial instances the witnesses do indeed confirm the narrator's impressions only after receiving the cue from him;[1] but in the rest they receive their impressions independently;[2] and in at least one important instance, the recognition of the change in May Server, the narrator himself, as we saw, notices nothing until *he* has received a cue, first from Ford Obert and then from Mrs Brissenden. This careful balancing of the 'evidences' for both sides is perhaps part of what James meant by his rather cryptic statement about *The Sacred Fount* in a letter quoted by Mr Edel: 'As I give but the phantasmagoric I have, for clearness, to make it *evidential*'.[3] In any case, the narrator's last encounter with Mrs Brissenden would entirely lose its point and the conclusion the force of its inconclusiveness if all the confirmations the narrator received were merely apparent, and his 'craziness' therefore established beyond the possibility of a doubt. James's epistemological theme requires an ambiguity perfect and complete; and this is ensured, as in *The Turn of the Screw*,

[1] For instance, Gilbert Long's confirmation of the change in Grace Brissenden (*The Sacred Fount*, 1, p. 6), and Ford Obert's of the change in Guy Brissenden (*ibid.* 2, pp. 23–4).

[2] Grace Brissenden notices the change in Long without any prompting from the narrator (*ibid.* 1, pp. 8, 9), and Obert, though he denies this afterwards, notices a change in May Server *before* the narrator has told him his theory about the Brissendens (*Ibid.* 2, pp. 16–17).

[3] Leon Edel, Introduction to *The Sacred Fount*, Grove Press ed., p. xxxi.

by so balancing the 'evidential' with the 'phantasmagoric' as to let each cancel out the other, so that no solution can be reached by an appeal to external evidences but only, if at all, by the interpretation of the motives of the participants—the strictly 'psychologic signs', as Obert calls them.[1]

The ambiguity of *The Sacred Fount* reaches, however, far beyond this comparatively formal aspect of the epistemological theme. As in *The Turn of the Screw* (and presently, as we will see, in *The Golden Bowl*) its operation is seen at its most powerful and subtle in the colloquies between the narrator and his several interlocutors. Here as there what the interlocutors in each instance say admits of two distinct readings equally self-consistent and self-complete. What they say can signify all that the narrator believes it to signify;

[1] Mr Edel himself interprets the 'phantasmagoric-evidential' antithesis rather differently. He believes it is intended to draw attention to the fundamental clash between appearance (the phantasmagoric) and reality (the evidential). My own view is that the clash is rather between two distinct and contradictory kinds of truth of which either may be reality or appearance. On this view, accordingly, what is contrasted in *The Sacred Fount* is the reality *or* appearance apprehended by the inferential ('phantasmagoric') powers of the artistic imagination and the reality *or* appearance apprehended by sense perception or common sense (the 'evidential').

This view of the Jamesian metaphysic in *The Sacred Fount* also suggests an explanation different from Mr Edel's of the rather obscure symbolism of the Man-and-Mask portrait (*The Sacred Fount*, 4, pp. 44–7; Leon Edel, Introduction, pp. xvi–xx). Mrs Server expresses the normal, common-sense view when she 'sees' the Man to be life—that is, reality—and the Mask death—that is, appearance (the negation of reality); the narrator, taking the unnatural, 'perverse' artist's view, characteristically sees the opposite—that the Mask, the work of art, is life or reality, and the Man death or appearance. One is surely reminded of James's *obiter dictum* in the letter to Wells, that 'Art *makes* life, makes interest, makes importance', in the narrator's plea for his interpretation: 'Isn't it much rather the Mask of Life? It's the man's own face that's Death. The other one, blooming and beautiful . . . is Life, and he's going to put it on; unless indeed he has just taken it off.' (*The Sacred Fount*, 4, p. 45). But, finally: both the Man and the Mask form a *picture*—that is, both owe their existence or 'life' to the phantasmagoric powers of some artist's imagination; and this gives a last Jamesian turn to the portrait colloquy as a symbolic statement of James's metaphysical position in *The Sacred Fount*. For it ensures, as competently as the ambiguity, that the metaphysical problem itself—which *is* reality, which appearance?—shall remain unresolved, while at the same time allowing a bias in favour of the narrator's (artist's) view of the superior reality of the phantasmagoric over the evidential.

but it can also signify nothing at all—nothing, that is, that in any way confirms, or indeed has any relevance to, his theory of the relations between the four principals. And if the first is the true reading, the narrator is seeing what is really there to be seen and is as 'wonderful' as he believes himself to be; and if the second is the true reading he is as monstrously deluded—as 'crazy'—as Grace Brissenden at the end declares him.

The narrator's earlier exchanges with Grace Brissenden are charged with ambiguities of this kind. Here (granted the narrator's hypothesis) the dramatic irony turns chiefly on Mrs Briss's unconsciousness of the way in which she is 'eating up' her husband; and since at this stage the more sinister implications of the narrator's own probings have not yet become apparent, the irony is comparatively light-hearted, and free as yet of the serious, bitter note that is presently to creep into it. In his first long colloquy with her he is developing his theory about Gilbert Long's still unidentified mistress, and finds he cannot resist the temptation to press the analogy with Mrs Brissenden's own case. 'It's my belief', he says, 'that he [Gilbert Long] no more goes away without her than you go away without poor Briss'. But her rejoinder shows her to be innocent of any inkling of a connexion: 'She surveyed me with splendid serenity. "But what have we in common?"'[1] He returns to his analogy a moment later:

> 'It's a relation, and they work the relation: the relation, exquisite surely, of knowing they help each other to shine. Why are they not, therefore, like you and Brissenden? What I make out is that when they do shine one will find—though only after a hunt, I admit, as you see—they must both have been involved.'

She protests that the point is, surely, that the lady they are looking for *doesn't* shine, having been robbed of all her lustre by the man. The narrator answers:

> 'Not at all. It's a case of shining as Brissenden shines,' I wondered if I might go further—then risked it. 'By sacrifice.'

[1] *The Sacred Fount*, 3, p. 33.

I perceived at once that I needn't fear: her conscience was too good—she was only amused. 'Sacrifice, for mercy's sake, of what?'

'Well—for mercy's sake—of his time'.

'His time?' She stared. 'Hasn't he all the time he wants.'

'My dear lady' I smiled, 'he hasn't all the time *you* want!'

But she evidently had not a glimmering of what I meant. 'Don't I make things of an ease, don't I make life of a charm, for him?'[1]

Presently a fresh dimension of irony is introduced when Mrs Briss, having triumphantly identified the missing woman as May Server, shows the narrator, to his growing dismay, how she has bettered her instruction in 'working things out'. As she dilates enthusiastically on Long's relationship with Mrs Server he is struck afresh, only more bitterly now, by her 'sustained unconsciousness':

'Oh, the man's not aware of his own change', [says Mrs Briss] 'He doesn't see it as we do. It's all to his advantage.'

'But *we* see it to his advantage. How should that prevent?'

'We see it to the advantage of his mind and his talk, but not to that of—'

'Well, what?' I pressed as she pulled up.

She was thinking how to name such mysteries.

'His delicacy. His consideration. His thought *for* her. He would think for her if he weren't selfish. But he *is* selfish—too much so to spare her, to be generous, to realise. It's only, after all', she sagely went on, feeding me again, as I winced to feel, with profundity of my own sort, 'it's only an excessive case, a case that in him happens to show as what the doctors call "fine", of what goes on whenever two persons are so much mixed up. One of them always gets more out of it than the other. One of them—you know the saying—gives the lips, the other gives the cheek. . . . The cheek accordingly is Mr Long's. The lips are what we began by looking for. We've found them. They're drained—they're dry, the lips. Mr Long finds his improvement natural and beautiful. He revels in it. He takes it for granted. He's sublime.'

It kept me for a minute staring at her. 'So—do you know?—are *you*!'

She received this wholly as a tribute to her acuteness, and was therefore proportionately gracious. 'That's only because it's

[1] *The Sacred Fount*, 3, pp. 34–5.

catching. You've *made* me sublime. You found me dense. You've affected me quite as Mrs Server has affected Mr Long. I don't pretend I show it', she added, 'quite as much as he does.'[1]

The ambiguity is most brilliantly sustained, and yields most for the epistemological theme of *The Sacred Fount*, in the narrator's long colloquy with Guy Brissenden (ch. VII) and his final contest with Mrs Briss (chs. XII–XIV). On the narrator's hypothesis, we remember, 'poor Briss' (like May Server) is at least partly conscious of his role as the 'sacrificed'; and it is an effect (we are perhaps meant to see) of the special sensibility induced by this role that the narrator's evident interest in him should have made him feel vaguely uneasy. Nevertheless he is pleased to see him. He says:

> 'I'm glad you turned up. I wasn't especially amusing myself.'
> 'Oh, I think I know how little!' [replies the narrator] . . . There was no curtness, but on the contrary the dawn of a dim sense that I might possibly aid him, in the tone with which he came half-way. 'You "know"?'
> 'Ah', I laughed, 'I know everything!'
> 'You know I decidedly have too much of that dreadful old woman?'[2]

The thrill of suspense created by the ambiguity of the last question is not wholly dissipated when we learn, a moment later, that Brissenden is referring to Lady John, not to his wife; it is in any case to be revived again and again in the conversation that follows concerning Mrs Server. Brissenden, it transpires, is deeply and uncomfortably puzzled by May Server, and in particular by the way in which she persistently seeks his company. He 'divines' that she is unhappy, that she is desperately trying to hide it, and that she is, unaccountably, turning to him for comfort and support in her secret affliction. He also divines that she is in danger of breaking down under it, and finds himself (again unaccountably) wanting to be 'kind' to her—wanting indeed to save her from this disaster; he even (most unaccountably)

[1] *The Sacred Fount*, 5, pp. 63–4. [2] *Ibid.* 7, pp. 86–7.

finds himself 'liking' to be kind to her, though he finds her too 'queer' to be charming, and because of the queerness even rather terrifying. But (he assures the narrator) he has no idea what is the matter with her, nor why she should seek his—of all people's—help, nor why he should want to give it and like wanting to give it. He pleads with his interlocutor to tell him what he 'knows', and when the latter laughingly refuses, saying, 'You know for yourself far more than I do', he answers sharply, 'No, I don't . . . For you know *how* you know it—which I've not a notion of.'[1]

As usual, the sustained ambiguity of this dialogue springs from the two possible meanings of everything that Brissenden says. If the narrator's hypothesis concerning the bond between him and Mrs Server is correct, Brissenden does indeed know more than he knows he knows: he knows (as he himself puts it) but does not know how he knows. Everything he says may then be consistently interpreted as the narrator interprets it—as proof of his 'intuitive' understanding of the bond between himself and Mrs Server as the sacrificed; and if at the end he does in fact tell his wife (for which, of course, we have only her word) that May Server has been making love to him and is 'horrid', the narrator's implied explanation of this may well be accepted.[2] On the other hand, if the narrator's whole hypothesis is the fantastic nonsense that Grace Brissenden at the end pronounces it to be, then of course poor Briss's words mean nothing but what they say. He is then merely expressing his genuine bewilderment at Mrs Server's strange behaviour; and what he subsequently tells his wife—about May Server's being 'horrid'—must then be taken to be nothing but the truth: that *was* what was the matter with her, and that was why she had been pursuing him.

Apart from its moral implications, the colloquy brilliantly illuminates James's epistemological theme by focusing

[1] *The Sacred Fount*, 7, pp. 97–8.
[2] *Ibid.* 8, pp. 121–2, 10, pp. 155–6.

attention on the kinds and degrees of knowledge or consciousness exhibited in *The Sacred Fount*. A kind of hierarchy emerges. The fullest knowledge and the fullest consciousness —in Plato's sense, 'knowledge' or 'wisdom' as distinct from mere 'opinion'—belongs (a claim Plato, of course, would never have allowed) to the artist—here the novelist-narrator supported by the painter Obert. They are the philosophic spirits who are forever indulging their 'wasteful habit or trick of a greater feeling for people's potential propriety or felicity or full expression than they seem able to have themselves', and persistently read into things in front of them 'more than the conscience of the particular affair itself is developed enough to ask of it'.[1] They both know and know how they know; and, like Plato's philosopher-kings, they owe their fullness of knowledge to their disinterested passion for the truth. Immediately below them in the hierarchy are the Guy Brissendens and May Servers, who know but don't know how they know. They have what Plato would have called 'true opinion'; they know 'intuitively', but not analytically; and they owe their knowledge not at all to a philosophic spirit of enquiry but, simply, to their power of love and their capacity for self-sacrifice for the sake of love. Lowest in the scale come the Gilbert Longs and Grace Brissendens who don't 'know' at all but can under stress, by the instinct of self-preservation, act as if they did. They are fundamentally stupid or selfish or both; like Plato's 'appetitive' men, they are dominated by their desire for pleasure—for the sheer enjoyment of life; and it is when they sense that they are about to be thwarted in their unreflective enjoyment of life that, like animals at bay, they are capable of the minimal knowledge necessary for self-preservation. This in essence is the picture of Grace Brissenden that emerges from her magnificent *tour de force* at the end; and it is characteristic of Henry James that, though he stands as firmly as Plato on the side of the contemplative spirit, he should yet

[1] Cp. p. 132 above.

be capable of a vivid, inward appreciation of the magnificence of the appetitive fighting for its right to pursue the life of appetite.

James, however, does not only respond keenly to the animal vitality of the totally unconscious like Mrs Briss, or to the deeper beauty and pathos of the half-conscious, like Guy Brissenden and Mrs Server. His view of the elect themselves—those, like the novelist-narrator, who are committed to the quest for the fullest knowledge and consciousness—is hedged about with reservations. Mr Wilson Follett, in a challenging note on *The Sacred Fount*, calls it a 'parody' of the artist and the artist's imagination ('Henry James deliberately turning a searchlight on Henry James').[1] My own view, like Mr Edel's,[2] is that it is James's most serious and most exhaustive study of the creative imagination, and of the moral and philosophical difficulties inherent in its characteristic operations. It is not a parody but an analysis, an elucidation, an anatomy; and what is most likely to have misled Mr Follett into seeing it as he does is the deceptive lightness of touch with which the anatomy is conducted. The Jamesian irony, unfalteringly urbane, ensures the consistent absence of solemnity; and it is rendered the more deceptive by the Jamesian energy in the pursuit of the analytic task itself, and the sustained fascination ('amusement') at all that the process of analysis yields to the enquiring mind.

The novelist-narrator in *The Sacred Fount* is accordingly a much more elaborate affair than the corresponding figure of the governess in *The Turn of the Screw*. Moreover, in so far as he is used also to exhibit as fully as possible the moral hazards of the pursuit of knowledge, he looks back most directly to the narrator in *The Aspern Papers*. The emphasis, to

[1] Wilson Follett, 'Henry James's "Portrait of Henry James"' in the *New York Times Book Review*, 23 August, 1936.

[2] Leon Edel, Introduction to the Grove Press ed. of *The Sacred Fount*, p. vi.

begin with, on its purely intellectual incentives and rewards is strongly reminiscent of *The Aspern Papers.* The moment his hypothesis forms itself in his mind, the narrator is 'conscious . . . of being on the track of a law, a law that would fit, that would strike me as governing the delicate phenomena . . . that my imagination found itself playing with'.[1] We learn that the probing and ferreting into people's private lives demanded by the search for such laws is 'a high application of intelligence' so long as it restricts itself to the 'psychologic signs' and eschews 'the detective and the keyhole'; [2] and presently we hear that for those for whom the vision of life is an obsession 'reflexion was the real intensity',[3] that 'for real excitement there are no such adventures as intellectual ones',[4] that 'it could *not* but be exciting to talk, as we talked [the narrator and Mrs Briss] on the basis of those suppressed processes and unavowed references which made the meaning of our meeting so different from its form'.[5]

The narrator's hubristic pride and exultation in his knowledge exceeds that of the governess in *The Turn of the Screw* by the same measure as his intellectual passion exceeds hers. He can rejoice to feel at the end of his talk with Guy Brissenden that 'poor Briss' was now 'intellectually speaking, plastic wax in my hand'.[6] With Lady John he experiences 'a rare intellectual joy, the oddest secret exultation, in feeling her begin instantly to play the part I had attributed to her in the irreducible drama'; [7] presently, in the course of his talk with her, he feels 'an undiluted bliss in the intensity of consciousness' he has reached;[8] and with Mrs Brissenden in the last scene his imminent defeat does not prevent him from confessing his pride in 'the kingdom of thought' he has won.[9] The idea that 'art makes life' expressed in the famous

[1] *The Sacred Fount*, 2, p. 19.
[2] *Ibid.* 4, p. 52.
[3] *Ibid.* 6, p. 71.
[4] *Ibid.* 11, pp. 168–9.
[5] *Ibid.* 13, p. 212.
[6] *Ibid.* 7, p. 99.
[7] *Ibid.* 6, p. 81.
[8] *Ibid.* 9, p. 139.
[9] *Ibid.* 12, p. 198.

letter to H. G. Wells is repeatedly touched on here. Comparing notes with Obert in the smoking room, he feels 'the joy of the intellectual mastery of things unamenable, *that joy of determining, almost of creating results'*.[1] As he reflects on poor May Server's 'case', 'the fruit of his own wizardry', he feels an extraordinary elation: 'I was positively—so had the wheel revolved—proud of my work. I had thought it all out, *and to have thought it was, wonderfully, to have brought it'*;[2] and (recalling another vivid phrase in the letter to Wells): 'It appeared then that the more things I fitted together the larger sense, every way, they made.... It justified my indiscreet curiosity; it crowned my underhand process with beauty'.[3]

The beauty of the process, however, and his intense intellectual enjoyment of it are not enough completely to still the doubts and misgivings that from time to time force their way into his consciousness. 'If he *were* innocent, what then on earth was I?' the governess in *The Turn of the Screw* had asked herself in her single terrible moment of self-doubt. 'What if she *should* be right?' the narrator in *The Sacred Fount* cries at an almost exactly corresponding moment in his last long exchange with Grace Brissenden.[4] But he has other similar moments. Earlier in the story, as he recognises with growing alarm and distress the exposure which is threatening Mrs Server as a result of his 'process', he finds himself questioning its precious beauty. 'What was the matter with *me*?' he asks himself,[5] and (like the narrator in *The Aspern Papers*) resolves to rid himself of his 'ridiculous obsession',[6] his 'private madness',[7] and to yield no further to his 'idle habit of reading into mere human things an interest so much deeper than mere human things were in general prepared to supply'.[8] These resolutions are of course of no avail; he

[1] *The Sacred Fount*, 11, p. 168. My emphasis.
[2] *Ibid.* 8, p. 101. My emphasis.
[3] *Ibid.* 8, p. 100.
[4] *Ibid.* 14, p. 238.
[5] *Ibid.* 6, p. 75.
[6] *Ibid.* 6, p. 71.
[7] *Ibid.* 9, p. 128.
[8] *Ibid.* 9, p. 123.

persists in making things fit and fit and fit; and when all he has so beautifully fitted together comes, or seems to come, apart in the last scene, and Mrs Briss says to him 'I think you're crazy', he finds himself laughing a long laugh which (he recognises) 'might well have seemed that of madness': 'Whether or not it was the special sound, in my ear, of my hilarity, I remember just wondering if perhaps I mightn't be'.[1]

These spasms of self-doubt bear directly on the 'epistemological' theme in that they confirm and reinforce the alternate possibilities of truth and delusion persistently suggested by the ambiguity. But there is another kind of doubt expressed in *The Sacred Fount* about the validity and value of the 'phantasmagoric' life of the artist which is more strictly moral in character and relates it most closely to *The Aspern Papers.* Is it not, Grace Brissenden hints in the last scene, the least bit *unhealthy*?

> 'You mean I see so much?' [asks the narrator].
> It was a delicate matter, but she risked it. 'Don't you sometimes see horrors? . . . They [people] certainly think you critical.'
> 'And is criticism the vision of horrors?'
> She couldn't quite be sure where I was taking her. 'It isn't, perhaps, so much that you see them—'
> I started. 'As that I perpetrate them?'
> . . . . 'Dear no—you don't perpetrate anything. Perhaps it would be better if you did!' she tossed off with an odd laugh. 'But—always by people's idea—you like them.'
> I followed. 'Horrors?'
> 'Well, you don't—'
> 'Yes—?'
> But she wouldn't be hurried now. 'You take them too much for what they are. You don't seem to want—'
> 'To come down on them strong? Oh, but I often do!'
> 'So much the better then.'
> 'Though I do like—whether for that or not', I hastened to confess, 'to look them first well in the face.'[2]

To look them well in the face, however, entails a ruthless-

[1] *The Sacred Fount*, 13, p. 217. [2] *Ibid.* 14, pp. 233–4.

ness, a 'sacrifice of feeling', which is the heaviest price that has to be paid for the artist's fullness of knowledge. This is what Mrs Briss and her kind are really referring to when they speak of his 'liking horrors'; and in *The Sacred Fount* James's artist-narrator is fully conscious of it, and testifies to it with the utmost explicitness. Reflecting in the course of his last colloquy with Mrs Briss on the terror of exposure which (he believes) has led her and Gilbert Long into their self-protective collusion, he finds himself not only unmoved by their predicament but also in the end curiously equable about his 'sacrifice of feeling':

> I could only say to myself that this was the price—the price of the secret success, the lonely liberty and the intellectual joy. There were things that for so private and splendid a revel. . . . I could only let go, and the special torment of my case was that the condition of light, of the satisfaction of curiosity and the attestation of triumph, was in this direct way the sacrifice of feeling. There was no point at which my assurance could, by the scientific method, judge itself complete enough not to regard feeling as an interference and, in consequence, as a possible check. If it had to go I knew well who went with it, but I wasn't there to save *them. I was there to save my priceless pearl of an enquiry and to harden, to that end, my heart.*[1]

He can at one moment, it is true, feel a decent regret at the loss of beauty involved in the acquisition of consciousness by two creatures who have been so 'splendid' in their unconsciousness.[2] But the regret is soon extinguished by elation—at the sheer 'marvel' of the phenomenon itself, and at his own dazzling feat in having thus 'communicated to them a consciousness':

> I could have made them uneasy, of course, only by making them fear my intervention; and yet the idea of their being uneasy was less wonderful than the idea of my having, with all my precautions, communicated to them a consciousness. This was so the last thing I had wanted to do that I felt . . . how much time I should need in the future for recovery of the process—all of the finest wind-blown intimations, woven of silence and secrecy and air—by which their

[1] *The Sacred Fount*, 14, pp. 230–1. My emphasis.

[2] *Ibid.* 8, pp. 106–7. The passage is discussed on pp. 191–2 below.

suspicion would have throbbed into life. . . . What came back to me . . . in waves and wider glimpses, was the marvel of their exchange of signals, the phenomenon, scarce to be represented, of their breaking ground with each other.[1]

Finally, reflecting again in the last scene on Mrs Briss's ferocious battle for self-preservation and on his own helplessness, in view of the certainty of her final victory, to do anything for the two victims, Guy Brissenden and Mrs Server, he reaches a conclusion remarkably similar to that of Lambert Strether at the end of *The Ambassadors*:

The only personal privilege I could, after all, save from the whole business was that of understanding. I couldn't save Mrs Server, and I couldn't save poor Briss; I *could*, however, guard, to the last grain of gold, my precious sense of their loss, their disintegration and their doom; and it was for this I was now bargaining.[2]

Like Strether, when he in his turn is vanquished by Sarah Pocock and as a result loses 'everything'—Mrs Newsome, Madame de Vionnet, Chad, Woollett—the narrator in *The Sacred Fount*, anticipating his own similar doom, already finds his most precious solace in his 'understanding'—his deeper knowledge, his fuller consciousness, and above all, his unconquerable power to 'consecrate by his appreciation'. What distinguishes the treatment of this familiar Jamesian theme in *The Sacred Fount* is, as we have seen, that the validity of the understanding itself is called in doubt. Is it real or is it delusory? is the question raised, and never answered, by the *dénouement*; and what this shows again is the overriding importance of the 'epistemological' theme.

In point of its moral preoccupations *The Sacred Fount* (along with *The Turn of the Screw*) is a model 'transition' work between the major works of the middle and late periods. The metaphor of the sacred fount gathers together and fuses, with the intensity and economy of all James's successful images in the late works, some of his most persistent moral themes. The insistence equally on the destructive

[1] *The Sacred Fount*, 13, pp. 213–14. [2] *Ibid.* 13, p. 213.

power of passion, symbolised in the 'eating up' of the adoring by the adored, and on its creative power, expressed in the miraculous transformation of the adored by the selfless passion of the adoring; the view that a love which is grounded in passion is essentially sacrificial, and as such rich in the most 'sublime' beauty and pathos; the suggestion that the spring of all human energy is ultimately in the passions, and that passion therefore (and in particular sexual passion) is the sacred fount of all significant moral life: these are some of the themes subsumed, directly or indirectly, by the image of the sacred fount; and they are to be taken up again and rehandled in *The Ambassadors, The Wings of the Dove* and *The Golden Bowl* on a scale far exceeding their comparatively modest scope in *The Sacred Fount.*

There are, however, more detailed connexions between *The Sacred Fount* and the latest of the late works. James's stories are full of handsome country-houses distinguished by their 'noble freedom' and 'overarching ease', which are 'great asylums of the finer wit'. But the moral air of Newmarch is perhaps closest to that of Matcham in *The Golden Bowl*:

> We existed, all of us together, to be handsome and happy, to be really what we looked—since we looked tremendously well . . . We were concerned only with what was bright and open, and the expression that became us all was, at worst, that of the shaded but gratified eye, the air of being forgivingly dazzled by too much lustre.[1]

This is the participant's easy, affable view of Newmarch society. The ironic overtone, however, is not difficult to detect; and it comes as no surprise that it should presently harden into the more deadly irony directed against the wordly world in *The Ambassadors, The Wings of the Dove* and *The Golden Bowl.* As the narrator watches Mrs Server listening to the music in the drawing-room after dinner and

[1] *The Sacred Fount*, 9, p. 124. Cp. ch. VIII, p. 242 below.

giving no sign of her secret fear and misery, he is 'moved to render fresh justice to the marvel of our civilised state':

> What, for my part, while I listened, I most made out was the beauty and the terror of conditions so highly organised that under their rule her small lonely fight with disintegration could go on without the betrayal of a gasp or a shriek, and with no worse tell-tale contortion of lip or brow than the vibration, on its golden stem, of that constantly renewed flower of amenity which my observation had so often and so mercilessly detached only to find again in its place.[1]

The conditions at Newmarch are, it seems, as 'highly organised', and as beautiful and terrible in what they exact from the individual, as those prevailing in Gloriani's garden in *The Ambassadors*, at Lancaster Gate in *The Wings of the Dove*, at Matcham in *The Golden Bowl*. That is why no doubt the image here is as violent as any to be found on this theme in the three later works. It's a jungle (James is saying here as there), but so beautiful, so irresistibly, heart-breakingly beautiful; and there is no way of separating its terror from its beauty. The group has to be cruel in order to secure and perpetuate its exquisite organisation, and the individual has to suffer in order to maintain himself in that exquisite organisation—with no compensation or reward for his ceaseless effort of self-discipline and self-denial other than the beauty of his own heroism in 'giving no sign' under this perpetual ordeal of adaptation.

A similar connexion may be discerned between the attitude to the destructive power of passion in *The Sacred Fount* and the later works. The passage, for instance, describing May Server's abasement by her passion is as heart-searing as any of the passages describing Maggie Verver's similar condition in *The Golden Bowl*; and the emphasis on her consciousness of her condition as at once her most intolerable burden and her most sublime moral beauty links her still more closely with Milly Theale and Maggie Verver—as well as Nanda

[1] *The Sacred Fount*, 9, pp. 131–2. Cp. ch. VIII, pp. 276–9 below.

Brookenham and all her predecessors as far back as the earliest stories:

> Beautiful, abysmal, involuntary, her exquisite weakness simply opened up the depths it would have closed. . . . I saw as I had never seen before what consuming passion can make of the marked mortal on whom, with fixed beak and claws, it has settled as on a prey. She reminded me of a sponge wrung dry and with fine pores agape. Voided and scraped of everything, her shell was merely crushable. So it was brought home to me that the victim could be abased, and so it disengaged itself from these things that the abasement could be conscious. That was Mrs Server's tragedy, that her consciousness survived—survived with a force that made it struggle and dissemble. This consciousness was all her secret—it was at any rate all mine. I promised myself roundly that I would henceforth keep clear of any other.[1]

Concerning consciousness itself, however, it is possible, I think, to see a development in James's view between *The Sacred Fount* and the later works, in particular *The Golden Bowl*. In *The Sacred Fount* the emphasis appears to be on the disastrous, or at any rate disfiguring, effects of 'communicating a consciousness' to the morally undeveloped, here represented by Gilbert Long and Grace Brissenden. This is the important passage in which the narrator reflects on what he has done, or believes himself to have done, in this connexion:

> What did [my] alarm imply but the complete reversal of my estimate of the value of perception? Mrs Brissenden and Long had been hitherto magnificently without it, and I was responsible perhaps for having, in a mood practically much stupider than the stupidest of theirs, put them gratuitously and helplessly *on* it. To be without it was the most consistent, the most successful, because the most amiable form of selfishness; and why should people admirably equipped for remaining so, people bright and insolent in their prior state, people in whom this state was to have been respected as a surface without a scratch is respected, be made to begin to vibrate, to crack and split, from within?[2]

From this it is clear that Gilbert Long and Grace Brissenden

[1] *The Sacred Fount*, 8, pp. 106–7. [2] *Ibid.* 9, p. 144.

are a pre-figuring of the Prince and Charlotte Stant in *The Golden Bowl.* The Prince and Charlotte, too, are so constituted as to practise 'the most consistent, the most successful because the most amiable form of selfishness'; they, too, are 'bright and insolent in their prior state', and 'admirably equipped for remaining so'; and the image of 'a surface without a scratch' which presently 'cracks' and 'splits' under the impact of self-knowledge or consciousness points directly to the symbol of the golden bowl itself, in its bearing, in particular, on the Prince's moral condition. But though the desire to 'respect' the beautiful surface of the morally nescient is no less strong in *The Golden Bowl* than it is here, Maggie Verver's act of redemption consists precisely in making the crack without ruining the surface. She succeeds in inducing in the Prince (though not in Charlotte) the knowledge of good and evil he previously lacked, yet without impairing in the minutest degree his adorable 'charm'; and this by itself indicates a significant development between *The Sacred Fount* and *The Golden Bowl* in Henry James's view of the power of consciousness to reconcile the moral and the aesthetic.

The connexion goes further, however. The success of Maggie Verver's redemptive undertaking, we learn, is ultimately assured by the presence of two vital elements, namely, her love and her husband's good faith. Her passionate, 'abject' love of the Prince comes first, of course; but without his good faith her love would have been helpless to effect in him the transformation of moral ignorance into moral knowledge which is the necessary condition of their common salvation.[1] There is accordingly a typically Jamesian relation to be discerned between the treatment of this fundamental theme in *The Turn of the Screw, The Sacred Fount* and *The Golden Bowl.* What James appears to be doing is what he did in respect to the children's condition of exposure in *The Turn of the Screw* and *What Maisie Knew*: [2] he produces

[1] Cp. ch. VIII, p. 245 below. [2] See ch. IV, p. 111 above.

in each instance a new equation by manipulating—dropping or modifying or re-combining—the common 'elements' of love and good faith. In *The Turn of the Screw*, they are both present; but because the governess's love is impure, tainted with possessiveness and spiritual greed, she fails to accomplish her work of salvation. In *The Golden Bowl* good faith and love are again both present; and because the Prince's good faith is here as genuine as Maggie's love is pure, passionate and intelligent, the work of salvation succeeds. In *The Sacred Fount*, it seems, there is neither good faith nor love. Gilbert Long and Grace Brissenden are conspicuously lacking in the first—as we learn from the imaginary dialogue in which they express their determination to resist any attempt on the narrator's part to make them see what they do not wish to see:

> Consciously, they could only want, they could only intend, to live. Wouldn't that question have been . . . the very basis on which they had inscrutably come together? 'It's life, you know', each had said to the other, 'and I, accordingly, can only cling to mine. But you, poor dear—shall *you* give up?' 'Give up?' the other had replied; 'for what do you take me? I shall fight by your side, please, and we can exchange weapons and manoeuvres, and you may in every way count upon me'.[1]

But if they are lacking in good faith, the narrator is equally lacking in love. We remember his own recognition of the 'sacrifice of feeling' necessarily involved in his pursuit of the fullest knowledge and consciousness; and this, we come to see, is the ultimate reason that he both fails to save the sacrificed from their sacrificial suffering and to redeem the sacrificers from their amoral enjoyment of the others' sacrifice. In respect to the latter, indeed, his success in communicating to them a consciousness actually has the effect of making them worse than they were in their 'prior state'. He 'spoiled their consciousness' and thereby made

[1] *The Sacred Fount*, 13, p. 230.

them 'cruel', he observes.[1] In *The Golden Bowl* this precisely is the initial effect upon the Prince of having his unconsciousness spoiled by his wife Maggie Verver. But it is not the ultimate effect; and what we must infer from this is that the presence or absence of love makes all the difference. Where there is no love for the morally bad or ignorant—no genuine involvement in them, no intimate feeling of responsibility for them—but only an intellectual passion to 'understand' them, the effect of communicating a consciousness may well be disastrous. For (as St Paul might have said) they have been given only a consciousness of their sinful state but no help or 'grace' to deliver themselves from it. But where the consciousness of sin is, as in *The Golden Bowl*, communicated 'for love, for love, for love', the effect is widely different, The narrator in *The Sacred Fount*, in short, is morally unqualified for the task of communicating a consciousness of good and evil without the loss of beauty, and therefore fails; Maggie Verver in *The Golden Bowl* is morally qualified, and therefore succeeds; and Henry Jame'ss own faith in the power of the moral to supersede the merely aesthetic without destroying it—when (but only when) the moral is grounded in love—is thus illustrated equally by the moral fables of *The Sacred Fount* and *The Golden Bowl.*

[1] *The Sacred Fount*, 13, p. 230.

CHAPTER VII

'THE WINGS OF THE DOVE'

My heart is sore pained within me: and the terrors of death are fallen upon me. Fearfulness and trembling are come upon me, and horror hath over-whelmed me. And I said, Oh that I had wings like a dove! then would I fly away, and be at rest.

Psalm 55

The dove descending breaks the air
With flame of incandescent terror
Of which the tongues declare
The one discharge from sin and error.

T. S. ELIOT, *Little Gidding*

IN an essay entitled *Henry James, Melodramatist* Mr Jacques Barzun drew attention to an important element of James's art which, he claimed, is as prominent in the works of the late period as in those of the early and middle periods.[1] Mr Barzun calls it 'melodramatic', a term exactly applicable to the early and middle works—*The American*, for instance, the *dénouement* of *The Bostonians, The Princess Casamassima*—but only (I believe) with certain reservations to the late. In the latter, this element is perhaps more properly described as 'legendary' or even 'heroic': the simplifications of the melodramatic mode, which by their nature exclude complexity, here give way to the simplicities of the heroic, which incorporate all complexity; and this development is significantly linked with other aspects of James's art in the late works. Nevertheless, Mr Barzun's term applies admirably to the bare plot of *The Wings of the Dove*, and it is worth exposing to view the remarkably simple melodramatic framework of this most heroic of James's late works.

There are four principal *dramatis personae*: the English lovers, Kate Croy and Merton Densher; Mrs Lowder

[1] Jacques Barzun, 'Henry James, Melodramatist', in *The Question of Henry James*, ed. F. W. Dupee, 1947.

(Aunt Maud), Kate's wealthy aunt and patroness; and Milly Theale, the Dove, an American millionairess. The principal minor characters are Lionel Croy, Kate's father, an elegant wastrel, who appears only in the first scene of the novel, but whose absent presence hangs over large stretches of the action; Kate's sister Marian, widow of the Rev. Mr Condrip, who lives with her four young children in a mean little house in Chelsea; Lord Mark, an English nobleman of high rank; and Mrs Susan Stringham, formerly a Boston journalist, who is Milly's friend and confidante.

Aunt Maud, who is as magnificently vulgar, witty and heartless as she is magnificently rich, offers to adopt her beautiful and brilliant niece Kate Croy and give her all the riches of the world—a charming set of rooms in her big house at Lancaster Gate, the finest robes and jewels, the most splendid society and the most distinguished husband (Lord Mark)—on condition that she severs all connexion with her odious father and sister, and gives up her lover Merton Densher, a clever but poor journalist, who (Aunt Maud knows) will never do anything remarkable in the world. The first condition is explicit and unqualified; the second, though equally binding, is tacit: Aunt Maud believes she can safely leave its fulfilment to Kate's honour and good sense. Kate submits to the first condition, under the merciless pressure of the father and sister themselves, who hope to gain everything from her connexion with Aunt Maud; she goes to live at Lancaster Gate; and soon finds that the great world is exceedingly delightful. But she does not give up Merton Densher; and from this crucial decision springs the main action of the story. The great game now begins—the game, as they call it, of 'squaring' Aunt Maud, that is, of somehow rendering Merton Densher acceptable to her so that they may have each other and Aunt Maud's money too. This proves to be no easy task; and a stalemate appears to have been reached when the fourth principal, Milly Theale, enters the story.

Milly Theale, American millionairess, the Heir of all the Ages, the Fairy Princess, the Poor Little Rich Girl, and ultimately also the Dove, appears at Lancaster Gate accompanied by her hand-maiden, Mrs Susan Stringham. She becomes Kate Croy's dearest friend, Aunt Maud's moneyed darling, Lord Mark's adorable Bronzino, and the toast of the London *beau monde.* But she is stricken with a mortal disease, knows that she must die young, and communicates this information to Kate Croy. By doing this, she provides the missing piece for the success of Kate's great design to have her cake and eat it. Since Milly very much 'likes' Densher (which in the Jamesian idiom means she is fifty fathoms deep in love with him), and since she knows nothing (and need know nothing) about his being secretly engaged to Kate, Densher is to make love to Milly, who will respond with the desperate passion of the sick girl 'conscious of a great capacity for life, but . . . condemned to die under short respite, while enamoured of the world'. They will marry; Milly will die; Densher will inherit her money and marry Kate; and in this way Aunt Maud will be at once 'squared' and 'dished'. This is Kate's remarkable plan. It is carried forward to its penultimate stage, but is at the last moment frustrated by Lord Mark, who gives the game away to Milly. Milly, in her hired palace in Venice, turns her face to the wall and dies. But before dying, she calls Densher to a last interview, at which something extraordinary happens which Densher afterwards finds it very difficult to describe; and she leaves him a great deal of money. But the interview with Milly has made it impossible for Densher to take the money; and when he goes back to Kate, it is to offer her himself without the money, or the money without himself. Kate, it seems, in the end chooses the second alternative; but the suspense is maintained to the very last line of the book:

> He only said: 'I'll marry you, mind you, in an hour.'
> 'As we were?'

'As we were.'

But she turned to the door, and her headshake was now the end. 'We shall never be again as we were!'

This is the skeleton, melodramatic indeed, that lies beneath the skin of the work that many will account James's masterpiece. The ultimate grounds of its greatness are to be discussed in their place; what more immediately claims our attention is that aspect of its greatness which turns upon the curious generality (or 'abstractness', as it is more commonly called) of its total effect. This appears to be the result chiefly of what may be described as a fusion, at maximum pressure, of all the principal Jamesian themes that had previously been treated separately and at a lower intensity. Of these, the international theme (incorporating among its component parts the American national character, the English national character and London society) is the most conspicuous. We have already learnt that this is one of James's principal 'objective correlatives' for his experience of the condition of modern man; and in *The Wings of the Dove* it is treated on a scale surpassing every previous attempt in magnitude and grandeur. All the familiar elements, we find, are there; but they are so magnified, heightened and intensified—so intensely 'idealised'—that they assume virtually heroic proportions. Everything is larger than life, and in that sense of heroic stature; and everything has about it that air of the legendary which is inseparable from the heroic.

This is true, to begin with, of the famous Jamesian 'types' that here as elsewhere sustain the international theme. They all stand to James's earlier renderings of the same types as the ideal to the actual. Milly Theale, the American Girl in Europe; Kate Croy, the English Girl of the pure Gainsborough breed; Merton Densher, the Young Man of developed sensibility and reflective mind who 'consecrates by his appreciation'; Mrs Lowder, the *grande dame* who (like Mrs Newsome in *The Ambassadors*) makes her impact by her lack of imagination; Lord Mark, the barely articulate English nobleman, who seems merely stupid but is in fact sinister; Susan Stringham, the lady journalist from Boston: it is impossible not to see them palimpsestically, written over their predecessors, and irresistibly fascinating beyond their intrinsic interest for their 'hereditary' characteristics.

The development of the new out of the old is, however, characteristically Jamesian in being not the addition of new elements to the old but, rather, a feat of generalisation. The old elements are all there by implication, 'assumed as known'; what is new is the scale and scope of their ordering—the comprehensiveness of the framework in which they are contained, the breadth and height, the sheer 'elevation', of the standpoint from which they are viewed. Nor does the quasi-logical character of the achievement injure in the minutest degree its life as a novel. The implied elements are all there, poetically realised, concretely 'pictured'; for the act of generalisation here is not the logician's kind (which ought properly to be called 'abstraction'), but the artist's which involves no loss of concreteness. It remains vivid, because it does not empty the final vision of the particular perceptions from which it draws its life but contains them in their full primitive intensity.

There is no certainty, of course, that James himself saw his later novels in this light—as generalisations, in the sense indicated, of the principal themes and characters of his earlier works; though it is conceivable (in view of his own sensitiveness to logical relations expressed in the recurrent logical or quasi-logical terms, expressions and images in his later works[1]) that he would at least not have been surprised to find them viewed in this way. But whether James was or was not conscious of it, and, if conscious, to what degree, this quasi-logical view does suggest an explanation of what would otherwise remain a baffling peculiarity of *The Wings of the Dove* along with the other late novels—the intense

[1] See Appendix C (ii) below.

generality of the picture (misdescribed as 'abstract') with the intense concreteness; and it does in any case help us to a better understanding of some of its more remarkable achievements.

Among the chief of them is the portrayal of Milly Theale. Milly is at once the most heroic, most legendary, element in this heroic and legendary tale and also the most real and exemplary for exhibiting one of the deepest aspects of James's mature vision of the human condition. We have already encountered this aspect in *The Awkward Age*. The principal tragic theme of *The Wings of the Dove*, like that of *The Awkward Age*, is the impact of the worldly world upon the unworldly—its power to undermine, reduce, and (in this instance) finally to destroy those who cannot accommodate themselves to its values. The chief weapon that the world here, as in *The Awkward Age*, employs for this work of destruction is the characteristic virtues of the victims themselves—their innocence, ignorance and good faith, their generosity and tenderness; and, again as in *The Awkward Age*, what is chiefly held up for exposure is the worldly world's rapacity and ruthlessness springing from its terrible single-mindedness in the pursuit of pleasure or power or both. These are the defining features of the world represented by the Lancaster Gate circle in *The Wings of the Dove* just as they were of Mrs Brookenham's circle in *The Awkward Age*; and, as in that supremely civilised society so in this, the rapacity and the ruthlessness are not something distinct from the charm, intelligence and civility in which Lancaster Gate, like Buckingham Crescent, abounds. On the contrary, they are so inseparably bound up with each other that it is difficult, indeed impossible, for the victims to recognise the rapacity and ruthlessness in the charm, the intelligence and the brilliance; and being unable so much as to recognise them, they are of course left helpless against their destructive power.

This was the case of Nanda Brookenham in *The Awkward Age*, and it is again the case of Milly Theale, the principal vessel of consciousness in *The Wings of the Dove*. Milly Theale, we soon discover, incorporates all the long line of Jamesian American Girls from Daisy Miller and Bessie Alden in *An International Episode* to Isabel Archer in *The Portrait of a Lady*. She is as lovely as the lovely lady in the Bronzino portrait that she is taken to see by her friend Lord Mark. She is tender, generous, gay, and full of the zest for 'life'—for knowledge, that is, and friendship and love, which she passionately desires to have in abundance and in the greatest possible intensity. She is solitary, having lost in rapid succession her parents and all other near relations; she is stricken (we have already learnt) by a mysterious but mortal disease, which must cause her to die young; and above everything, she is rich—colossally, unbelievably rich.

There are two short passages that admirably evoke this high-legendary quality of Milly Theale against the background of her personal history. The first is Susan Stringham's recollected first impression of Milly: [1]

Mrs Stringham was never to forget—for the moment had not faded, nor the infinitely fine vibration it set up in any degree ceased —her own first sight of the striking apparition, then unheralded and unexplained: the slim, constantly pale, delicately haggard, anomalously, agreeably angular young person, of not more than two-and-twenty summers in spite of her marks, whose hair was somehow exceptionally red even for the real thing, which it innocently confessed to being, and whose clothes were remarkably black even for robes of mourning, which was the meaning they expressed. It was New York mourning, it was New York hair, it was a New York history, confused as yet, but multitudinous, of the loss of parents, brothers, sisters, almost every human appendage, all on a scale and with a sweep that had required the greater stage; it was a New York legend of affecting, of romantic isolation, and,

[1] Mrs Stringham, the former Boston journalist who is now Milly's confidante and handmaiden, may be seen, partly at least, as a fresh and more complex version of Henrietta Stackpole in *The Portrait of a Lady*.

beyond everything, it was by most accounts, in respect to the mass of money so piled on the girl's back, a set of New York possibilities.[1]

A similar impression of Milly and her wildly romantic personal background is received by Kate Croy, her English friend, who is to play such a devastating part in Milly's life:

They had talked, in long drives, and quantities of history had not been wanting—in the light of which Mrs Lowder's niece might superficially seem to have had the best of the argument. Her visitor's American references, with their bewildering immensities, their confounding moneyed New York, their excitements of high pressure, their opportunities of wild freedom, their record of used-up relatives, parents, clever eager fair slim brothers—these the most loved—all engaged, as well as successive superseded guardians, in a high extravagance of speculation and dissipation that had left this exquisite being her black dress, her white face and her vivid hair as the mere last broken link: such a picture quite threw into the shade the brief biography, however sketchily amplified, of a mere middle-class nobody in Bayswater.[2]

The story of Milly Theale, we have already learnt, properly begins when, accompanied by Mrs Stringham, she descends upon London in the manner common, it seems, to rich young Americans in James's day, and is there instantly drawn into the heart of 'the world', represented by the big house in Lancaster Gate. The presiding daemon, the supreme symbol of its worldliness, is the terrible Mrs Lowder, Kate Croy's Aunt Maud, who is Mrs Touchett in *The Portrait of a Lady*, Mrs Brookenham (and the Duchess) in *The Awkward Age*, Mrs Newsome in *The Ambassadors* and a host of other earlier Jamesian *grandes dames* rolled into one; and being the quintessential *grande dame*, she is of course incomparably more deadly and dangerous than any of her predecessors. Mrs Lowder is ably supported in her role of presiding daemon by a large anonymous cast of minor daemons, who circle in and out of the big house at Lancaster Gate as friends, relations or guests at the innumerable luncheon-parties and dinner-parties that form the back-

[1] *The Wings of the Dove*, I, iii, 1, p. 95. [2] *Ibid.* I, iv, 2, p. 154.

ground to the intense personal drama in which the main actors are Milly Theale, Kate Croy and Merton Densher.

What this central drama is we already know, at least in bare outline, and further discussion of the *dénouement*—Densher's last interview with Milly Theale before she turns her face to the wall, and its remarkable consequences for the world of Lancaster Gate—must for the present be reserved. The more immediate critical task in respect to James's rendering of Milly Theale is to determine what exactly it is that exposes her to the destructive power of Lancaster Gate even to the point of death; and this brings us directly back to the international theme, the encompassing framework of the central tragic experience of *The Wings of the Dove*.

What we perceive at once and with the least difficulty is that it is her American 'innocence' which in the first place lays Milly open to the rapacity and ruthlessness of her English friends. As in her predecessors among James's American Girls, this innocence in her springs from a fatal ignorance of the complex pressures operative in the complex world of Lancaster Gate—an ignorance due in the first instance, of course, to her American background. James speaks here of 'the immense profusion, but the few varieties and thin development' of the America of Milly Theale's day, and does not fail to draw again the familiar moral of the international theme, namely, the disabling effects upon the American mind of the simplicities and freedoms of American life, and their effect in particular of placing Americans at a severe disadvantage in their intercourse with the English and the Europeans.

This precisely is what happens to Milly Theale when she is thrown among the English. Her disability is plainly that she has no experience of the pressures, in particular the economic, to which the individual in such a society is perpetually exposed. As in *The Awkward Age*, these economic pressures never show on the surface of the gracious living in the big house at Lancaster Gate; but they are the most powerful subterranean force in the life of a society struggling to maintain a traditionally high standard of life on perpetually dwindling resources. The uneasy relation between an America growing steadily richer and a Britain growing steadily poorer which has become one of the commonplaces of Anglo-American relations since James's day was, it seems, already sufficiently apparent then, at any rate to his discerning eye; and it is this economic fact (with all its moral implications) that lies behind the long sigh of ecstasy and envy that is to be heard in Lancaster Gate every time Milly Theale's English friends touch upon the subject of what they call her good luck. Her 'good luck' is, simply, her money: which they desire, of course, not for its own vulgar sake but for its precious power to secure the freedom they long for—the freedom to enjoy without impediment all that Lancaster Gate would so much like to enjoy, and would know so well how to enjoy.

But Milly knows nothing of these material pressures that lie beneath the gracious surface, and therefore knows nothing of their demoralising effects upon the human spirit, even the most intelligent, most cultivated, most imaginative of human spirits. Indeed particularly (this is James's grand point) upon the intelligent and imaginative—like Milly's dear friend Kate Croy, whose range of enjoyments so greatly exceeds that of the less intelligent and less imaginative, and whose appetite therefore for the power to procure these enjoyments exceeds correspondingly. Lacking such knowledge, Milly Theale is accordingly very slow to see herself, the fabulously rich American, as a proper object of exploitation.

Besides this, however, what makes it so difficult for her to see herself as Lancaster Gate sees her is that the exploitation is not in the least vulgar; nor is it purely mercenary. What is so difficult and puzzling (and profoundly deceptive) is that the exploitation is perfectly compatible, it seems, with the most genuine devotion to Milly herself. Aunt Maud worships the very air she breathes, and is genuinely stricken when she hears of the death of the poor 'moneyed darling'. Kate Croy is genuinely enchanted with Milly: when she says that Milly is as charming as she is queer and as queer as she is charming,[1] she speaks with complete sincerity; and she enjoys their friendship with the most genuine ardour. And Merton Densher, whom Milly so much 'likes', treats her with the most tender deference; and Lord Mark, who makes a point of showing her the Bronzino that everyone says she resembles, intimates in his inexpressive English way that she really ought to 'let a fellow who isn't a fool take care of [her] a little';[2] and all the anonymous guests at the luncheon-parties and dinner-parties can't make enough fuss of her. Everybody in Lancaster Gate, in short, is as charming as possible to her; and here (James wishes us to understand) is another of the characteristic features of the English of that class, another aspect of 'the fathomless depths of English equivocation': that they can feel the most genuine, most sincere, most whole-hearted devotion for those who can serve their interests, and can as genuinely, as sincerely and whole-heartedly cast them off the moment they have ceased to serve their interests—or, alternatively, have begun to make demands that are inconvenient or irksome or just boring.

Of all this Milly Theale has no inkling when she first arrives at Lancaster Gate. She learns most of it, very painfully and slowly, as the story advances, and the most devastating thing of all only at the point of death. She acquires her knowledge in the most incidental, or seemingly incidental, flashes; James's dramatic genius ensures that they shall appear as incidental as in life itself. One of the early flashes occurs when she is talking to Lord Mark at her first dinner-party at Lancaster Gate, and presently discerns that, in spite of his deference and his seeming interest in her, he finds her only diverting, only 'funny'—'a mere little American,

[1] *The Wings of the Dove*, I, iv, 2, p. 156. [2] *Ibid.* I, v, 2, p. 194.

a cheap exotic, imported almost wholesale', who has no power to challenge his real interest, and certainly none to engage his stronger feelings.[1] Another, very important, flash occurs when she discovers that Kate Croy cannot endure her friend Susan Stringham. The reason (she discovers on analysis) is, astonishingly, that Kate has in her a streak of brutality—the kind of brutality which enables her to dismiss another human being with the easiest contempt when that human being happens merely to violate her standard of good breeding. Yet this brutality (Milly also discovers) is characteristically English, in that it has nothing to do with primitive cruelty and everything to do with what in the modern jargon is called a 'defence-mechanism'. It is an instrument of self-preservation, Milly discerns; and pursues her analysis in a passage that is as good an instance as any of the sheer quantity of analytical insight, perfectly dramatised, that can be packed into a few characteristic sentences of James's late style:

Mrs Lowder didn't feel it, and Kate Croy felt it with ease; yet in the end . . . she grasped the reason, and the reason enriched her mind. Wasn't it sufficiently the reason that the handsome girl was, with twenty other splendid qualities, the least bit brutal too, and didn't she suggest, as no one yet had ever done to her new friend, that there might be a wild beauty in that, and even a strange grace? Kate wasn't brutally brutal—which Milly had hitherto benightedly supposed the only way; she wasn't even aggressively so, but rather indifferently, defensively and, as might be said, by the habit of anticipation. She simplified in advance, was beforehand with her doubts, and knew with singular quickness what she wasn't, as they said in New York, going to like. In that way at least people were clearly quicker in England than at home; and Milly could quite see, after a little, how such instincts might become usual in a world in which dangers abounded. There were clearly more dangers round about Lancaster Gate than one suspected in New York or could dream of in Boston. At all events, with more sense of them, there were more precautions, and it was a remarkable world altogether in which there could be precautions, on whatever ground, against Susie.[2]

[1] *The Wings of the Dove*, I, iv, 1, p. 147. [2] *Ibid.* I, iv, 2, pp. 160–1.

This is the kind of insight into the complex world of Lancaster Gate that Milly is liable to receive from her most casual encounters with her English friends. Her mind, however, is to be still further enriched by her intimacy with Kate Croy. In a great scene at a critical point in the story, Kate 'lets herself go' (as Milly puts it to herself) 'in irony, in confidence, in extravagance' on those qualities of the American Mind, as represented in her friend Milly Theale, that she has come to find peculiarly exasperating—chiefly, its crude naive empiricism, its seemingly inexhaustible capacity for 'exaggerated ecstasy' and 'disproportionate shock', and its consequent propensity to produce upon more developed minds the effects of boredom and irritation. It is an exposure as brilliant as it is bold; and Milly 'follows' it, participates in it, with an intelligence, an appreciation of all Kate's finest shades of veracity, and an irony to match Kate's own, which sets her apart from all her predecessors in the line of James's American Girls and gives her a unique place in the ranks of the late-Jamesian vessels of consciousness:

The beauty and the marvel of it was that she [Kate] had never been so frank: being a person of such a calibre, as Milly would have said, that, even while 'dealing' with you and thereby, as it were, picking her steps, she could let herself go, could, in irony, in confidence, in extravagance, tell you things she had never told before. That was the impression—that she was telling things, and quite conceivably for her own relief as well; almost as if the errors of vision, the mistakes of proportion, the residuary innocence of spirit still to be remedied on the part of her auditor had their moments of proving too much for her nerves. She went at them just now, these sources of irritation, with an amused energy that it would have been open to Milly to regard as cynical and that was nevertheless called for—as to this the other was distinct—by the way that in certain connexions the American mind broke down. It seemed at least—the American mind as sitting there thrilled and dazzled in Milly—not to understand English society without a separate confrontation with *all* the cases. It couldn't proceed by—there was some technical term she lacked until Milly suggested both analogy and induction, and then, differently, instinct, none of which were right: it had to be led up to and introduced to each aspect of the monster, enabled to walk all round it, whether for the consequent exaggerated ecstasy or for the still more (as appeared to this critic) disproportionate shock. It might, the monster, Kate conceded, loom large for those born amid forms less developed and therefore no doubt less amusing; it might on some sides be a strange and dreadful monster, calculated to devour the unwary, to abase the proud, to scandalise the good; but if one had to live with it one must, not to be for ever sitting up, learn how: which was virtually in short to-night what the handsome girl showed herself as teaching.[1]

This is Kate Croy's anatomy of the famous American innocence and ignorance; and as such it is uniquely instructive to Milly. But it is intended also to illuminate the complexities of Kate's own nature, in particular her boldness, her audacity, her strange, 'perverse' courage. For Kate by this time is already in the process of conceiving her diabolical design against Milly, and the rest of her 'speech', from the most interesting mixture of motives, is intended also as a warning to Milly—to get out of Lancaster Gate before she is destroyed.[2] Milly, of course, misses the warning, and is consequently doomed; and this submerged tragic irony does much to intensify the powerful dramatic impact of the whole scene.

So Kate Croy, at any rate, is in no doubt that it is Milly Theale's American ignorance and innocence that in the first instance expose her to the destructive power of Lancaster Gate. There are, however, other more subtle reasons that contribute to this condition of exposure. The ignorance and innocence indeed might by themselves have proved a kind of protection, at any rate against the *conscious* knowledge of her final deception and betrayal. But their potential power to protect is perpetually cancelled out by her very powers of appreciation: by her intelligence, her sensibility,

[1] *The Wings of the Dove*, I, v, 6, pp. 243–4.
[2] *Ibid.* I, v, 6, pp. 244–5, 247–8.

her imagination; and above everything by her passion for 'knowledge'—her fatal curiosity. These together make Lancaster Gate irresistibly fascinating and delightful to her; and by the same token weaken her resistance to its destructive power.

What chiefly weakens her resistance in fact is her supreme Jamesian quality, her self-consciousness. For Milly Theale's passion for knowledge is principally a passion for self-knowledge; and it is for this, more than anything, that she is prepared to suffer pain, confusion and humiliation, and finally total deprivation and loss. That is why (for instance) she participates, in the way we saw, in Kate's analysis of the American mind, entering into Kate's view of herself with an avidity of interest that would be almost masochistic if it were not what it in fact is—the disinterested passion for self-knowledge, characteristic of all the great Jamesian heroes and heroines. The same is true also of her deeply intelligent understanding of the English point of view in other connexions: of the reasons for Kate Croy's streak of brutality; and for Lord Mark's indifference to her; and, most painfully (before she is made to believe he is in love with her), for Merton Densher's indifference. Having received from Kate Croy an unforgettable light on her disabilities as an American Girl, and presently also on her still graver disability, that of being a Dove ('*That* was what was the matter with her. She was a dove'), she has already by the time Densher returns from America begun to see herself through the eyes of Lancaster Gate; and in the quarter of an hour's talk she has with him alone after their first meeting in the National Gallery, she recognises simultaneously both how much she 'likes' him and how much therefore she regrets that he should share 'the view' of her:

She could have dreamed of his not having *the view*, of his having something or other, if need be quite viewless, of his own. The defect of it [the 'view'] in general—if she might so ungraciously criticise—was that, by its sweet universality, it made relations rather prosaically a matter of course. It anticipated and superseded the—likewise sweet—operation of real affinities. It was this that was doubtless marked in her power to keep him now—this and her glassy lustre of attention to his pleasantness about the scenery in the Rockies.[1]

Again and again in *The Wings of the Dove* we receive such testimonies to the range and depth of Milly Theale's self-knowledge.[2] Its tragic implications, however, are not fully disclosed until she has learnt from the great doctor that she is very sick and, on seeking to communicate her secret to Kate Croy, meets with a rebuff that is the more desolating for being so bright and brisk.[3] Then Milly also becomes fully conscious of her own ultimate solitude amidst the buzz of admiration and adulation of the Lancaster Gate circle; and it is this knowledge that adds the last intolerable weight to the burden of her self-consciousness. Her self-consciousness is her glory (James wishes us to understand): Milly is not merely the American Girl 'acting out' her nature unconsciously, like Daisy Miller and the other American girls in James's earlier stories. She is the American Girl grown conscious of herself as acting out the character of the American Girl; and it is this capacity at once for 'being' and 'seeing', for at once suffering intensely and being intensely conscious of the suffering, that defines the kind and quality of her tragedy.

Milly's desperate isolation is created in the first instance, of course, by the combination of her 'good luck', as the English call it, with her 'queerness'—that she should be so rich and yet such a saint, a dove, an exquisite thing. More plainly, what Lancaster Gate finds astonishing beyond comprehension is that Milly Theale should be so little the

[1] *The Wings of the Dove*, I, v, 7, p. 265.

[2] In view of the displayed intelligence of Milly Theale, it is astonishing indeed to learn that such a critic as Marius Bewley finds her 'stupid', and another, F. R. Leavis, both stupid and 'embarrassingly sentimental'. One can only guess at the kind of reading of *The Wings of the Dove* that could issue in such judgements; but surely it must have been literal-minded to a degree no serious reading of the later James can afford to be.

[3] See below, pp. 211–12.

'great personage' she ought by virtue of her fabulous good luck to be: that she should, besides being munificently generous, be so mild, so humble, so eager, so 'funny'—in fact, so *good*—when she could so easily afford not to be. They cannot stop marvelling at this; and they do in fact treat her as a great personage, thus consigning her to the lonely eminence symbolised in an early scene in the Swiss Alps.[1] To this even her dear devoted Susan Stringham contributes:

> The girl was conscious of how she [Susan] dropped at times into inscrutable impenetrable deferences—attitudes that, though without at all intending it, made a difference for familiarity, for the ease of intimacy. It was as if she recalled herself to manners, to the law of court-etiquette.[2]

In this aspect, Milly's story may be seen as James's rehandling of another grand melodramatic theme, that of the Poor Little Rich Girl.[3] She is 'rich' in virtue of her money, her exalted position, and the expectations of bliss that these spread all around her. She is poor and deprived because through this thick cloud of expectations, this mass of blinding preconceptions about her 'happiness', no human love can penetrate.

What, however, intensifies her solitude to the tragic pitch is her mysterious mortal disease. It is this that finally isolates her from the world she so passionately desires to know and to enjoy. When Lord Mark takes her up to the Bronzino she is supposed to resemble she looks at it with tears in her eyes ('the lady in question . . . was a very great personage—only unaccompanied by a joy. And she was dead, dead, dead'); and Lord Mark, 'though he didn't understand her was as nice as if he had'.[4] Presently in the same scene Kate comes up, and Milly asks her to accompany her on her first visit to Sir Luke Strett, the doctor:

[1] *The Wings of the Dove*, I, iii, 1. [2] *Ibid.* I, v, 4, p. 225.

[3] The phrase is virtually used at one point in Milly's meditation in Regent's Park after her second visit to the doctor (*The Wings of the Dove*, I, v, 4, pp. 227–8).

[4] *Ibid.* I, v, 2, pp. 195–6.

Kate fixed her with deep eyes. 'What in the world is the matter with you?' It had inevitably a sound of impatience, as if it had been a challenge really to produce something; so that Milly felt her for the moment only as a much older person, standing above her a little, doubting the imagined ailments, suspecting the easy complains, of ignorant youth. It somewhat checked her.[1]

She is to receive a further and final check after her second visit to the doctor, this time alone. She has spent an afternoon of anguish in Regent's Park pondering with 'her little lonely acuteness' the great man's advice, trying to make out how sick she really is, and deciding that she must, in view of all he had said, be very sick indeed. Back at her hotel Milly awaits Kate's visit. Kate arrives; and her first words of enquiry are, 'Well, what?'

The inquiry bore of course . . . on the issue of the morning's scene, the great man's latest wisdom, and it doubtless affected Milly a little as the cheerful demand for news is apt to affect troubled spirits when news is not, in one of the neater forms, prepared for delivery. She couldn't have said what it was exactly that, on the instant, determined her; the nearest description of it would perhaps have been as the more vivid impression of all her friend took for granted. The contrast between this free quantity and the maze of possibilities through which, for hours, she had been picking her way, put on, in short, for the moment, a grossness that even friendly forms scarce lightened: it helped forward in fact the revelation to herself that she absolutely had nothing to tell. . . . Almost before she knew it she was answering, and answering beautifully, with no consciousness of fraud, only as with a sudden flare of the famous 'will-power' she had heard about, read about, and which was what her medical adviser had mainly thrown her back on. 'Oh it's all right. He's lovely.'[2]

After this, there are no further direct references to Milly's sickness; but there is one final comment upon the inaccessibility to death of the living. 'I'm a brute about illness. I hate it', says Kate Croy to Densher, telling him about Milly's case; and adds, 'It's well for you, my dear, that you're as sound as a bell'.

[1] *The Wings of the Dove*, I, v, 2, pp. 200–1. [2] *Ibid.* I, v, 4, pp. 227–8.

'Thank you!' Densher laughed. 'It's rather good then for yourself too that you're as strong as the sea'.

She looked at him now a moment as for the selfish gladness of their young immunities. It was all they had together, but they had it at least without a flaw—each had the beauty, the physical felicity, the personal virtue, love and desire of the other. Yet it was as if this very consciousness threw them back the next moment into pity for the poor girl who had everything else in the world, the great genial good they, alas, didn't have, but failed on the other hand of this. 'How we're talking about her!' Kate compunctiously sighed. But there were the facts. 'From illness I keep away.'[1]

This inaccessibility of the living to the experience of death and dying is the immediate cause of Milly's tragic deprivation.[2] The living of Lancaster Gate admire and adore Milly Theale; but they all withhold from her the one thing that would relieve the terrors of her state—their participation, at once intelligent and generous, in 'the ordeal of consciousness' from hour to hour of a young creature with a great capacity for life condemned to die while hating and fearing death. From this terror of Milly Theale's condition they all, like Kate Croy, withdraw. They are all prodigiously intelligent, but not intelligent enough to know what such a condition means; and they are all brave, but not so brave as to risk participation in the twilight life of a soul awaiting death. This, we are meant to see, is the last dreadful infirmity of the brave and beautiful souls that inhabit Lancaster Gate. A final incapacity for love is intimately linked with a final incapacity to confront the fact of death; and, conversely, the incapacity to confront death is the final measure of the coldness, ruthlessness and egotism of the worldly world figured here.

Milly Theale on her side responds to the indifference

[1] *The Wings of the Dove*, II, vi, 4, pp. 48–9.

[2] Readers of Mr Lionel Trilling's novel *The Middle of the Journey* will remember that the immunity of the strong and healthy to the experience of death and dying is one of its principal themes, and is handled by Mr Trilling with a penetration and a delicacy that one likes to think James would have admired.

with her own last infirmity, which is the sin of pride. She refuses to speak of her illness; she is determined to die (as Kate puts it) 'without smelling of drugs or tasting of medicines'. It is of course a sublime virtue, this perfect exercise of fortitude in the face of death: but it is also the last temptation of the devil. For it isolates her more completely than ever from her fellow creatures, cutting her off from her last chance to draw some remnant of loving-kindness out of the cold heart of the world. If Milly Theale (like Maggie Verver in *The Golden Bowl*) had been humble enough, or fearless enough, to renounce her pride, a saving connexion might have been established between herself and the enemy—enough at any rate to render impossible the diabolical design that finally kills her. But she does not renounce it, and thus deprives herself of the last possibility of being saved.

These accordingly are the qualities that together incapacitate Milly Theale against the powers of Lancaster Gate—her American innocence and ignorance, her appreciation, her consciousness, her solitude, her pride. And her mysterious disease is perhaps best seen as at once 'real' and 'symbolic', physical and spiritual. On the one hand, it is a real sickness of the body, which saps her physical resistance; on the other, it is a sickness of the spirit, induced in the first instance by her early intimations, vividly communicated to us by the scene in the Swiss Alps,[1] of the lonely, loveless condition to which she is condemned in spite of (or because of) her fabulous 'luck'. Her spiritual sickness is presently intensified by her experience of the world, and finally confirmed by the ultimate betrayal which causes her to turn her face to the wall and die. She would live if she could be happy, Sir Luke Strett had said;[2] but Milly Theale is so constituted that she cannot wrest happiness out of a world by its nature implacably hostile to her very being. Though she longs to the very last moment to be happy and to live, no mutual accommodation is possible

[1] *The Wings of the Dove*, I, iii, 1, pp. 110–13. [2] *Ibid.* II, vii, 1, p. 99.

between her and the world she inhabits; and with no physical, 'animal' strength to fall back upon when, for the last time, she struggles to live after the knowledge of her betrayal by her dearest friends Kate Croy and Merton Densher, there is no escape for her from death.

The question that has still to be answered is why the story is called *The Wings of the Dove*. This turns our attention more directly to the world of Lancaster Gate and, in particular, to Kate Croy and her diabolical design. That the design shall finally be judged to be diabolical James sufficiently (but not more than sufficiently) ensures by his use of one of the time-honoured devices of the tragic dramatist—he shows us the slaughter of the innocent by the wicked followed by the just punishment of the wicked in the last scene of the drama. It does not help Densher that he should have been moved to repentance and expiation by his victim's forgiveness; he still has to lose the prize for which the sin was committed. Nor does it help Kate that her design should have been a miracle of intelligence, courage, good sense, good will—everything in fact that the world ever asks of any worldly design, provided that it succeeds; she still has to lose Densher, for whose sake the courage, lucidity and self-command were so superbly exercised. In the Preface to *The Portrait of a Lady* James tells us that he deliberately forswore the use of those aids to 'interest' of which the older dramatists have always availed themselves—the 'comic relief and under-plots', the 'murders and battles and the great mutations of the world'. There is no lack of great mutations in James's dramas, but they are solely those of the moral world; and the murders and battles all take place upon the ground of the moral consciousness of his protagonists. The defeat of Kate's design is the Actium of these most magnificent of James's lovers, and their parting in the last scene a re-enactment of the parting in the Monument.

Kate's design is central to James's fable, for by means of

it he accomplishes one of his principal purposes: to exhibit the wordly world in the perfection of its horror and its glory, and thus as a world prepared for the descent of the Dove. The horror is in the fact that a design so dreadful should find such a natural place in this world—that the beautiful, gracious circle of Lancaster Gate should find it so damnably, so infernally, easy to accommodate this piece of evil; the glory is in the treasures of intelligence, courage, good will and good humour with which it renders its homage to the devil. If on the one side any part of the bright beauty of Kate Croy and Merton Densher is missed or minimised, or on the other any shade of the horror in the diabolism of Kate Croy's design, so much in either case is lost of James's achievement. Here supremely James has made the 'difficulty' as great as possible for himself; for the design is at once as monstrous as any that passion conjoined with the love of pleasure and power could devise, and is presented with a surface as brilliant and a style as great, and protected by justifications as deep and sound and satisfying, as only a great novelist could imagine and execute.

The justifications (or 'motivation') in this part of the story testify again to James's profound sense of the conditional character of our knowledge of the world and the life of man.[1] The wonderful early scenes of the novel unforgettably fix in our minds the outrage that Kate's domestic pieties —her 'narrow little family feeling', as she calls them— received from a cold mercenary father and a selfish mean-spirited sister; and are afterwards meant to remind us constantly that it was their combined pressure that in the first place precipitated her into Aunt Maud's world. We are also expected never to forget that the whole design began as a fine, 'amusing' game, that of 'squaring' Aunt Maud, and by nothing more reprehensible than the exercise of natural wit and the neatest, cleverest diplomacy. Who being Kate Croy, who 'always gave Densher finer things

[1] See Appendix B (ii), pp. 399 ff. below.

than anyone to think about and banished the talk of other women . . . to the dull desert of the conventional', would *not* be tempted to outwit Aunt Maud in this way? Who would not agree that Aunt Maud thoroughly deserved to be so outwitted—for a dozen reasons, but chiefly for the prodigious cynicism with which she can admit to liking Densher, oh liking him immensely, only for herself, not Kate?[1] And who being Densher would not respond to the daring and the fun of the thing—Densher with his developed aesthetic sense, to whom 'it had really, her sketch of the affair, a high colour and a great style, at all of which he gazed . . . as at a picture by a master'.[2] The challenge to two such people as Kate Croy and Densher really is irresistible, and to fail to take it up would be—well, rather stupid, rather spiritless; showing a narrow, unimaginative kind of rectitude, a mean sort of pusillanimity. James, in short, by the high colour and great style of his opening sketch of the lovers wins us over entirely to their side.

But Aunt Maud resists squaring; Milly Theale with her money and her mortal disease appears on the scene; and what began as a daring piece of fun is slowly transformed into the diabolical design. And here, where the going becomes more and more difficult, the justifications press most irresistibly. Is not Milly passionately, desperately, in love with Densher? Is she not to die very soon? Would not the illusion of

[1] *The Wings of the Dove*, II, vii, 1, pp. 107–8. One of the richest, subtlest strokes of the Jamesian irony occurs in the scene between Mrs Lowder and Mrs Stringham in which the two ladies settle the futures of their respective 'girls'. Having exhibited to Mrs Stringham (and to us) the breathtaking scope of her machiavellian diplomacy, and having concluded her 'beautiful' pact with Mrs Stringham—that she, Mrs Lowder, will help her, Mrs Stringham's, girl Milly to get what she wants, *viz.* Densher, if she, Mrs Stringham, in turn will help her, Mrs Lowder's, girl Kate *not* to get what she wants, *viz.* again Densher—Mrs Lowder pronounces their pawn Densher to be 'charming' nevertheless; and then, reflectively, and with perfect seriousness and sincerity, throws out the aside which explains the pious principle on which she has acted and the renunciations she has made for its sake. 'One lives for others', she says to Mrs Stringham. '*You* do that. If I were living for myself I shouldn't at all mind him . . . Of course he's all right in himself.' (*Ibid.* II, vii, 1, p. 107.)

[2] *Ibid.* I, ii, 1, p. 66.

Densher's love do as much for her last happiness as the reality? Would it not therefore be an act of loving-kindness to 'give' her Densher for that time, in order that she might die in the blissful belief of having 'lived'? Where is the harm? asks Kate Croy, with all the sincerity and good faith with which the worldly always ask the question whenever there are, or seem to be, vast splendours of power and pleasure to be gained by means only minutely tainted. All one needs is singleness of purpose, a cool head, strong nerves, and (where possible) a decent sincere regret that there should be even so minute a taint as there is in the whole magnificent business. 'I don't like it', says Kate Croy to Densher on the night of Milly's great reception in the Palazzo Leporelli, while their hostess stands on the other side of the *sala* smiling towards them: 'I don't like it, but I'm a person, thank goodness, who can do what I don't like'.[1]

When we reach this point in the story, we may well feel that here is the extreme verge of the world. It is 'extreme' in a quasi-logical sense: for here the logical implications of the values of the world are drawn out, ineluctably, to their last particle of meaning. It is 'extreme' poetically: for here is the world of appearances presented with colours so intense, lines so sharp, qualities, tones and cadences so finely discriminated and rendered with such a felicity as to give an intelligible meaning to the notion of an absolute in poetic achievement. And it is also 'extreme' in the deepest moral sense—a world *in extremis* from its own perfection of beauty and freedom. It has reached its *non ultra*, with no taint of the decay that we are soon to meet in *The Golden Bowl*; and beyond lies that of which neither Kate Croy nor Merton Densher nor Aunt Maud have any knowledge or imagination. Into this world, stretched to its limit and taut for the impact, the Dove descends. The meaning, indeed, is obscure:

He saw a young man far off and in a relation inconceivable, saw him hushed, passive, staying his breath, but half understanding,

[1] *The Wings of the Dove*, II, viii, 3, p. 203.

yet dimly conscious of something immense and holding himself painfully together not to lose it . . . The essence was that something had happened to him too beautiful and too sacred to describe. He had been, to his recovered sense, forgiven, dedicated, blessed; but this he couldn't coherently express.[1]

That is all we are told—that Densher, in his last interview with Milly Theale, when she knew that he and Kate had hideously deceived and betrayed her, had been 'forgiven, dedicated, blessed'. It becomes plain, however, from the subsequent course of the fable, that this interview marks the descent of the Dove into the world of Lancaster Gate. Not indeed with flame of incandescent terror; but quietly and unobtrusively the Dove descends, covering them all (as Kate herself puts it) with its wings.

After that, it seems, Lancaster Gate is no longer the same. Nothing spectacular happens, of course: there are no confessions, no conversions, no breast-beatings, no guilt or shame: Lancaster Gate continues to behave as beautifully as ever, with perfect lucidity and composure; and Densher still wants more than ever to marry Kate Croy, and Kate still wants to marry Densher. But the action of the Dove is known by its effects; and the ending of James's fable leaves us in no doubt that these have been shattering. Kate Croy and Merton Densher find in the end that they cannot after all marry. Densher still desires it to the last moment; but Kate, superior to the last in her clear-headedness, knows that it is no longer possible. The last dialogue between them, with which the book ends, makes it plain that Kate at least has discerned the full effect of the Dove's descent—though, characteristically, she cannot assign the proper cause to the effect. Densher is still begging her to marry him, and Kate is apparently still wavering:

'Your word of honour (she says to Densher) that you're not in love with her memory?'

'Oh—her memory!'

[1] *The Wings of the Dove*, II, x, 2, pp. 304–5.

'Ah'—she made a high gesture—'don't speak of it as if you couldn't be. *I* could, in your place; and you're one for whom it will do. Her memory's your love. You *want* no other'.

He heard her out in stillness, watching her face, but not moving. Then he only said: 'I'll marry you, mind you, in an hour'.

'As we were?'

'As we were.'

But she turned to the door, and her headshake was now the end. 'We shall never be again as we were!' [1]

In that last sentence Kate Croy, speaking for Lancaster Gate and so for all the unredeemed world, proclaims that the Dove has triumphed. It has triumphed, not indeed by redeeming the world—for James's fable of redemption we have to wait until *The Golden Bowl*; but by injecting into it its first knowledge of an order of goodness and power greater than any this world by itself can show.[2] As the religious might put it: by the holy life and holy death of one Milly Theale, God has too evidently made foolish the wisdom of the world; and Lancaster Gate, being as intelligent as it is, does not fail to grasp the point.

This is the deepest theme of *The Wings of the Dove*; and if (as I suggest elsewhere[3]) the story of Milly Theale is intended not only as a final commemoration of the beloved cousin Minny Temple but also as an expiation of the young Henry James's refusal to 'reconcile her to a world to which she was essentially hostile', it has to be allowed that the expiation is handsome indeed. The Jamesian moral passion seems here to reach a pitch, the Jamesian vision of human possibility to acquire a depth and a breadth, which brings it to the edge of the religious. If in the end it remains on this side of the dividing line, the parallels with the religious are nevertheless striking: in the use, to begin with, of the Dove as a central image; but even more in the conception of the tragic conflict

[1] *The Wings of the Dove*, II, x, 6, pp. 358–9.

[2] This is the phrase used by James to describe the religious spirit of his father, the elder Henry James (*Notes of a Son and Brother*, ch. 6, p. 335).

[3] Appendix A, p. 368 n below.

as a clash between the powers of light and darkness—between the power of the world, figured in Lancaster Gate, to undermine and destroy the noble and the good, and the power of the good, figured in the person of Milly Theale, to abase the proud by answering it with forgiveness, loving-kindness and sacrificial death.

What is perhaps more masterly than anything else in this master-novel is James's handling of the whole difficult *dénouement* in the last book, which begins with Densher's return to London after the momentous events in Venice and ends with his final parting from Kate Croy. Here Densher is the central figure: it is as if James, having cast him for the part of the male lead to the second leading lady of the drama and kept him strictly subordinate to her up to this point, at last gives him the centre of the stage; and it is wonderful to see how he is 'brought out' in the process—how all that before was implicit or only intimated is now made fully explicit, and how this justifies the special kind and quality of interest that Merton Densher had invited from the start.

Viewed palimpsestically,[1] Densher shows most clearly the lineaments of that long and distinguished line of Jamesian heroes 'who consecrate by their appreciation', which starts with Roland Mallett in *Roderick Hudson*, includes Ralph Touchett, 'little' Hyacinth Robinson (and in some aspects also Nick Dormer), and reaches its apotheosis in Gray Fielder in *The Ivory Tower* and Lambert Strether in *The Ambassadors*. This is James's opening sketch of Densher:

He was a longish, leanish, fairish young Englishman, not unamenable, on certain sides, to classification—as for instance by being a gentleman, by being rather specifically one of the educated, one of the generally sound and generally civil; yet, though to that degree neither extraordinary nor abnormal, he would have failed to play straight into an observer's hands. He was young for the House of Commons, he was loose for the Army. He was refined, as might have been said, for the City, and, quite apart from the cut of his

[1] Cp. p. 199 above.

cloth, he was sceptical, it might have been felt, for the Church. On the other hand he was credulous for diplomacy, or perhaps even for science, while he was perhaps at the same too much in his mere senses for poetry and yet too little in them for art. You would have got fairly near him by making out in his eyes the potential recognition of ideas. . .[1]

What establishes Densher's place in the brotherhood, we soon learn, is 'his weakness for life, his strength merely for thought'. Thus, in respect to Kate Croy,

Merton Densher had repeatedly said to himself—and from far back—that he should be a fool not to marry a woman whose value would be in her differences. . . . Having so often concluded on the fact of his weakness, as he called it, for life—his strength merely for thought—life, he logically opined, was what he must somehow arrange to annex and possess. This was so much a necessity that thought by itself only went on in the void; it was from the immediate air of life that it must draw its breath. So the young man, ingenious but large, critical but ardent too, made out both his case and Kate Croy's.[2]

But what links him with Lambert Strether in particular is the quality of 'intellect', as distinct from mere intelligence. Like Strether he is a 'writer', a journalist of the superior breed not uncommon, it seems, in James's day; the difference is that in Densher this quality is more integral to the man and more actively important than it ever really is in Strether. It enters intimately, for instance, into his relationship with Kate; she too, on her side, we learn, 'had quickly recognised in the young man a precious unlikeness':

He represented what her life had never given her and certainly, without some such aid as his, never would give her; all the high dim things she lumped together as of the mind. It was on the side of the mind that Densher was rich for her and mysterious and strong; and he had rendered her in especial the sovereign service of making that element real. She had had all her days to take it terribly on trust, no creature she had ever encountered having been able in any degree to testify for it directly. Vague rumours of its existence had made their precarious way to her; but nothing

[1] *The Wings of the Dove*, I, ii, 1, p. 44. [2] *Ibid.* I, ii, 1, pp. 46–7.

had, on the whole, struck her as more likely than that she should live and die without the chance to verify them. The chance had come—it was an extraordinary one—on the day she first met Densher; and it was to the girl's lasting honour that she knew on the spot what she was in the presence of.[1]

Densher, however, is also over-written with another 'line' of Jamesian heroes, which includes some members of the previous line but is distinct from it. This, in the works already discussed, is represented principally by Vanderbank in *The Awkward Age*; and it is to culminate in the Prince in *The Golden Bowl.* As we have already learnt from the case of Van, the common characteristic of this fraternity is its combination of the most engaging personal charm and the most sincere goodwill and good faith with a constitutional disposition to evade moral issues—or, rather, moral decisions. The weakness is an inseparable part of the charm, goodwill and good faith; and being for this reason so difficult to isolate as a weakness, it is exceedingly dangerous to its victims. In *The Wings of the Dove* Densher has this sacred terror chiefly, of course, for Milly; for Kate it is reinforced by the 'intellect' (which is absent in Van) and even more by the passion, the distinctively male quality which is absent in all the Jamesian heroes of this line before Densher.[2]

In any case, it is this moral personality of Merton Densher in which intellect, sensibility and passion co-exist with a

[1] *The Wings of the Dove*, I, ii, 1, p. 46.

[2] It is present only in the rough-diamond heroes, like Basil Ransom in *The Bostonians* and Caspar Goodwood in *The Portrait of a Lady*. That Densher has the 'sacred terror' for Milly is clearly intimated in the scene of the luncheon party at Milly's hotel after her meeting with Densher and Kate in the National Gallery when she grieves secretly over his, too, having 'the view' of her (see pp. 209–10 above), and recognises that 'whatever he did or he didn't, [she] knew she should still like him—there was no alternative to that.' (I, v, 7, pp. 264–5.) It is powerfully confirmed by Kate at the end when she says to Densher, 'She never wanted the truth. She wanted *you*. She would have taken from you what you could give her, and been glad of it, even if she had known it false. You might have lied to her from pity, and she have seen you and felt you lie, and yet—since it was all for tenderness—she would have thanked you and blessed you and clung to you but the more. For that was your strength . . .—that she loves you with passion.' (II, x, 1, p. 291.)

fatal moral indecisiveness that is chiefly brought out in Book X. We have, of course, seen it repeatedly before this. We remember Densher at his most Van-like when, at a crucial point in his relationship with Milly when he knows that to call on her alone would commit him irrevocably to Kate's plan, he contrives nevertheless to talk himself into the necessity, the desirability, the simple decency of doing so:

> It wasn't so much that he failed of being the kind of man who 'chucked', for he knew himself as the kind of man wise enough to mark the case in which chucking might be the minor evil and the least cruelty. It was that he liked too much everyone concerned willingly to show himself merely impracticable. He liked Kate, goodness knew, and he also clearly enough liked Mrs Lowder. He liked in particular Milly herself; and hadn't it come up for him the evening before that he quite liked even Susan Shepherd? He had never known himself so generally merciful. It was a footing, at all events, whatever accounted for it, on which he would surely be rather a muff not to manage by one turn or another to escape disobliging.[1]

The moral indecisiveness appears conspicuously at another crucial point in the story when, reflecting on the fearful implications of Kate's design in one of his interior monologues, Densher explicitly recognises that so far as he was concerned, 'Kate's design was something so extraordinarily special to Kate that he felt himself shrink from the complications involved in judging it'.[2] In Book X, however, these characteristics expose themselves most fully because tested in the most challenging situation of Densher's life. There accordingly we have Vanderbank writ large; there James 'goes behind' his hero as he did not in *The Awkward Age*, and as a consequence brings to light new facets of the type, of its graces and virtues equally with its weaknesses, which in the end make Densher one of the principal triumphs of the book. The chief of the new facets disclosed is, we shall see, the sustained self-deception that a man like Densher is capable of when life thrusts upon him an experience that

[1] *The Wings of the Dove*, II, vi, 5, p. 63. [2] *Ibid.* II, vi, 5, p. 68.

demands a total reorientation of his previous attitudes and beliefs; and this extraordinary power of self-deception, though a function of the moral weakness, is shown to be at the same time a function of his developed moral sensibility (his 'conscience'), his intelligence, his charm and his passion.

The anatomy of Merton Densher actually begins before the opening of Book X when he is left alone in Venice to bring Kate's scheme to its consummation and finds himself, suddenly, portentously, and at first unaccountably, denied access to Milly. As he wanders about in the cold lashing rain, he sees Lord Mark sitting in Florian's, guesses what has happened, and is at first stricken. But presently:

> His business, he had settled . . . was to keep thoroughly still; and he asked himself why it should prevent this that he could feel, in connexion with the crisis, so remarkably blameless. He gave the appearances before him all the benefit of being critical, so that if blame were to accrue he shouldn't feel he had dodged it. But it wasn't a bit he who, that day, had touched her [Milly], and if she was upset it wasn't a bit his act. The ability so to think about it amounted for Densher during several hours to a kind of exhilaration. The exhilaration was heightened fairly, besides, by the visible conditions—sharp, striking, ugly to him—of Lord Mark's return. . . . He didn't need, for seeing it as evil, seeing it as, to a certainty, in a high degree 'nasty', to know more about it than he had so easily and so wonderfully picked up. You couldn't drop on the poor girl that way without, by the fact, being brutal. Such a visit was a descent, an invasion, an aggression, constituting precisely one or other of the stupid shocks that he himself had so decently sought to spare her. Densher had indeed drifted by the next morning to the reflection . . . that the only delicate and honourable way of treating a person in such a state was to treat her as *he*, Merton Densher, did. With time, actually—for the impression but deepened—this sense of the contrast, to the advantage of Merton Densher, became a sense of relief, and that in turn a sense of escape.[1]

He cannot, of course, sustain this mood of 'exhilaration,' and accordingly, a few chapters on, when he meets Sir Luke Strett who has just come away from Milly, finds the sweetest

[1] *The Wings of the Dove*, II, ix, 2, pp. 236–7.

consolation in Sir Luke's complete and (as Densher interprets it) gentlemanly abstention from any reference to Milly or Milly's condition or Densher's relation to her:

He had hoped for it, had sat in his room there waiting for it, because he had thus divined in it, should it come, some power to let him off. He was *being* let off; dealt with in the only way that didn't aggravate his responsibility. The beauty was also that this wasn't on system or any basis of intimate knowledge; it was just by being a man of the world and by knowing life, by feeling the real, that Sir Luke did him good. There had been in all the case too many women. A man's sense of it, another man's, changed the air; and he wondered what man, had he chosen, would have been more to his purpose than this one. He was large and easy—that was the benediction; he knew what mattered and what didn't; he distinguished between the essence and the shell, the just grounds and the unjust for fussing.[1]

Sir Luke, however, just before he boards his train, tells him that Milly has asked to see him, and Book IX ends with Densher arriving at the palace for the last fateful interview.

The first lines of Book X inform us that Densher has been back in London for a fortnight and has only just called to see Kate at Lancaster Gate. The colloquy that follows confirms this first hint of the abyss that has opened between Kate and Densher as a result of his last interview with Milly. Yet throughout the scene (we are told) Kate's beauty, high sobriety and exquisite self-command have lost none of their power for him; on the contrary, with the memory of the consummation of their passion in Venice still unforgettably present to his mind, they inspire in him a joy, pride, tenderness and gratitude greater than ever before; and it is this, we soon perceive, as in all the succeeding scenes between them, that pulls against his growing knowledge of the change in their relationship, perpetually threatening it with extinction.

But the knowledge does come, against all resistance. In the course of their first meeting, Densher tells Kate that it

[1] *The Wings of the Dove*, II, ix, 4, p. 271.

was Lord Mark's visit that had made Milly turn her face to the wall. Kate instantly asks him why he did not deny what Lord Mark had told Milly:

> 'To tell her he lied?' [asks Densher].
> 'To tell her he's mistaken' [answers Kate].
> Densher stared—he was stupefied: the 'possible' thus glanced at by Kate being exactly the alternative he had had to face in Venice and to put utterly away from him. Nothing was stranger than such a difference in their view of it. . . . Of course, it was to be remembered, she had always simplified, and it brought back his sense of the degree in which, to her energy as compared with his own, many things were easy; the very sense that so often before had moved him to admiration. 'Well, if you must know—and I want you to be clear about it—I didn't even seriously think of a denial to her face. The question of it—*as* possibly saving her—was put to me definitely enough; but to turn it over was only to dismiss it. Besides', he added, 'it wouldn't have done any good'.[1]

What this discloses, among other things, is Densher's special kind of 'stupidity'—the intellectual counterpart, so to speak, of his moral weakness of which we are to have repeated evidence in Book X. Why, if he knows Kate (as by this time he has every reason to know her), should he 'stare' and be 'stupefied' by her suggesting something that is perfectly consistent with the grand scheme in which, up to that point, he had actively participated, and is also, granted the validity of the scheme (which he *had* implicitly granted), perfectly reasonable and 'moral'—at any rate as reasonable and moral as any of the other consequences of Kate's scheme that he had previously assented to? The answer, or one part of it, is that his mind, here as elsewhere, is as confused and self-contradictory as Kate's is clear and rigorously self-consistent; that his right hand appears not to know what his left is doing; and that he is as 'stupid' in this as Kate is in her tendency to 'simplify'.

But what we are also expected to see is that this stupidity, though present in Densher from the beginning, is now, since

[1] *The Wings of the Dove*, II, x, 1, pp. 287–8.

the shattering experience of his last meeting with Milly, acutely intensified by the bitter remorse, grief and horror with which the experience has impressed him. He is here so confused and contradictory because, still wanting Kate and still needing therefore to persuade himself that he remains loyal to her and her design, he will not recognise that he has, since he was 'forgiven, dedicated, blessed' by Milly Theale, totally repudiated the dreadful design and with it Kate herself. And that is why in this scene he 'stares' and is 'stupefied' at Kate's suggestion. It is his way of trying, characteristically, to have his cake and eat it: at once to remain loyal to Kate and to repudiate her design—an endeavour in which he is defeated, as we learn in the last line of the book, by Kate's implacable clear-headedness and consistency. This in fact is the *leitmotif* of the whole of Book X: to show Densher, on his side, as incorrigibly confused and inconsistent, and persistently—literally to the last line of of the book—refusing to acknowledge with his mind what he has recognised with his moral sensibility, that his last meeting with Milly has made a radical alteration in his relationship with Kate; while Kate, on her side, is shown to be totally deficient in moral sensibility in having to the end no knowledge of what Densher's transforming experience might have been (and probably no great curiosity to know), yet being perfectly clear and self-consistent throughout, and capable both of inferring accurately from the minimal signs she receives what the experience has done to him and of drawing the inescapable conclusions—in particular the most inescapable, that 'we shall never be again as we were'.

If the principal interest of Book X is this gradual, painful disclosure of the differences between Kate Croy and Merton Densher who had seemed such a mutual pair, what makes it especially instructive and poignant is the further disclosure that the differences had been there from the beginning, had previously been obscured by their common participation in the life of the world, but had now been brought to light by the spiritual crisis created for Densher by Milly Theale' extraordinary act of loving kindness. And this (the religious would say) is the characteristic effect of the irruption of the divine order into the natural. It pierces through the appearances, exposing to view the reality that lies beneath—the real identities and differences constituting the natural order; and by the sheer truth of its revelation in the end commands the obedience of those who have received it.

On the view of *The Wings of the Dove* proposed in this chapter, this, or something like it, would seem to be the ultimate meaning of the theme of Book X. If this is the meaning, the power and authority with which it is enunciated is due entirely to James's art—which here, as elsewhere, succeeds in projecting the theme as fully articulated drama. As in *The Awkward Age* and all the works of the late period, the style re-creates or re-enacts the succession of minute steps, each by itself barely cognisable, by which the momenttous alteration is effected: Densher's flashes of recognition alternating with his withdrawals and evasions; [1] the stresses and tensions that hover all the time below the surface of their mutual consideration, admiration, enjoyment; and towards the end, when their suppressed knowledge can barely any longer be held down, the delicate, desperate subterfuges to which they resort in the effort to hide from themselves what is happening. And, with all this and in spite of it, we also have conveyed to us a powerful sense of the bond of passion that still holds them together right to the end. It is expressed in their essential candour with each other through all the subterfuges and evasions, in their loyalty to each other, and in a kind of toughness or resiliency, which is the ultimate expression of their marvellous vitality,

[1] For instance, when Densher feels at one point 'a horror, almost of her [Kate's] lucidity', but by the end of the scene finds that she still 'prevented irresistibly . . . the waste of his passion' (II, x, 1 ,p. 311); or when he finds himself tacitly acquiescing in Mrs Lowder's view of him as 'the stricken suitor of another person', and spending more and more time with her because she does not know the truth and less and less with Kate because she does know it (II, x, 2, pp. 298 ff.).

and succeeds—as in *Antony and Cleopatra*—in turning, or almost turning, their final defeat into a triumph. The effect, if one follows the process closely enough, is as overwhelming as it is in *Antony and Cleopatra*, and leaves one with the same sense of an affirmation of life so powerful as to transcend the proper limits of tragedy.

But the tragic is there, whether or not *The Wings of the Dove* as a whole is to be accounted a tragedy. It makes its unmistakable impact in those moments when the suppressed disharmonies, misunderstandings, hostilities gathering between them momentarily break the surface: when at their first meeting, for instance, Densher tells Kate that he could not have denied to Milly what Lord Mark had told her 'only to take it back afterwards', and Kate, 'her colour flaming' as she grasps his meaning, replies 'You would have broken with me to make your denial a truth? You would have "chucked" me to save your conscience?'[1] Or when, in a later scene, having listened to Kate's explanation of Lord Mark's presence in London, Densher remarks 'You see in everything, and you always did, something that, while I'm with you at least, I always take from you as the truth itself', and Kate, 'consciously and even carefully extracting the sting of his reservation', presently answers ('with a quiet gravity') 'Thank you.'[2] Again the sense of a marriage of true minds irreparably shattered is never stronger than in the passage in which we learn of Densher's secret, silent grieving over the unread letter that Milly wrote him before she died;[3] and it is perhaps most poignant in the moment in which Densher perceives how 'damned civil' he and Kate are being to each other, and how their passion is now a way not of showing but of concealing their knowedge of each other, expressing 'the need to bury in the dark blindness of each other's arms the knowledge of each other that they couldn't undo'.[4] When one remembers the beauty and the

[1] *The Wings of the Dove*, II, x, 1, p. 290.

[2] *Ibid.* II, x, 5, p. 336.

[3] *Ibid.* II, x, 6, pp. 350–1.

[4] *Ibid.* II, x, 6, p. 347.

freshness of that early scene in Kensington Gardens when Kate pledged him every spark of her faith, every drop of her life, and he responded with breathed words and murmured sounds and lighted eyes,[1] it is hardly possible to question the tragic intention of the *dénouement*; it remains only to admire again the way in which James succeeds in suggesting a redemption of the suffering and loss by the saving power of a human passion reinforced by courage, dignity, intelligence, and good faith.

[1] *The Wings of the Dove* I, ii, 2, pp. 85–6.

CHAPTER VIII

'THE GOLDEN BOWL' (I)

Or ever the silver cord be loosed, or the golden bowl be broken, or the pitcher be broken at the fountain, or the wheel be broken at the cistern: then shall the dust return to the earth as it was: and the spirit shall return to God who gave it.

Ecclesiastes, xii, 6–7

THE story of *The Golden Bowl* is even more simple, bare and melodramatic than that of *The Wings of the Dove*. There are again just four principal personages: Adam Verver, American millionaire and art-collector; his daughter Maggie; Prince Amerigo, scion of an ancient Roman house, who marries Maggie Verver at the opening of the story; and Charlotte Stant, American *cosmopolite*, former mistress of the Prince and Maggie's dearest friend, who is presently to marry Adam Verver and become Maggie's stepmother. Of the two subsidiary characters only one is fully articulate. Colonel Assingham is an Englishman, his wife Fanny an expatriate New Yorker who is a devoted friend to all the principals and passionately concerned in their affairs; he is as unimpressionable and seemingly unresponsive as his wife is vivacious and expressive; and between them they perform admirably the function of a sustained choric commentary on the main action.

This rigid economy in the matter of *dramatis personae* is one aspect in which *The Golden Bowl* resembles the classical Greek drama. Another is the intense singleness and simplicity ('unity') of the action, in Aristotle's sense of the word; and in both aspects its quasi-classical character is reinforced by an almost text-book observance—for a modern novelist, at any rate—of the unity of place: the scene of the action moves strictly between Fawns, the Ververs' country-house, and their town-houses in Eaton Square and Portland Place, the only exceptions being an excursion to Brighton (where Mr Verver makes his proposal of marriage to Charlotte) and a memorable week-end party at a country-house called Matcham. These, however, are only the external or technical signs of the grand classic style and scope of *The Golden Bowl.* The more significant, and distinctively Jamesian, signs are to be referred to that generality and comprehensiveness of the creative impulse and passion which James speaks of in a passage in the Preface;[1] and if the degree of achieved generality and comprehensiveness is indeed the measure of poetic excellence, *The Golden Bowl* may stand as James's most ambitiously conceived and most brilliantly executed long poem.

The terms 'general' and 'comprehensive' are to be interpreted in a quasi-logical sense not commonly intended when they are used by literary critics.[2] There is a sense in which the experience of *The Golden Bowl,* like that of *The Wings of the Dove,* presupposes all that has gone before in James's poetic experience, and all that went before implies what is unfolded here. This aspect is conveniently illustrated by a short passage in the First Book in which the Prince, standing on the terrace at Matcham, reflects upon the English national character. Like other Jamesian foreigners before him, he is especially struck, it seems, by 'the fathomless depths of English equivocation':

> He knew them all, as was said, 'well'; he had lived with them, stayed with them, dined, hunted, shot and done various other things with them; but the number of questions about them he couldn't have answered had much rather grown than shrunken, so that experience struck him for the most part as having left in him but one residual impression. They didn't like *les situations nettes*—that was all he was sure of. They wouldn't have them at any price; it had been their national genius and their national success to avoid them at every point. They called it themselves, with complacency, their wonderful spirit of compromise—the very influence of which actually so hung about him here from moment to moment that the earth and the air, the light and the colour, the fields and the hills and

[1] *The Golden Bowl,* p. xx.

[2] This point is more fully discussed in Appendix C, pp. 393 ff. below.

the sky, the blue-green counties and the cold cathedrals, owed to it every accent of their tone. Verily, as one had to feel in presence of such a picture, it had succeeded; it had made, up to now, for that seated solidity, in the rich sea-mist on which the garish, the supposedly envious, peoples have ever cooled their eyes. But it was at the same time precisely why even much initiation left one at given moments so puzzled as to the elements of staleness in all the freshness and of freshness in all the staleness, of innocence in the guilt and of guilt in the innocence. There were other marble terraces, sweeping more purple prospects, on which he would have known what to think, and would have enjoyed thereby at least the small intellectual fillip of a discerned relation between a given appearance and a taken meaning. The inquiring mind, in these present conditions, might it was true, be more sharply challenged; but the result of its attention and its ingenuity, it had unluckily learned to know, was too often to be confronted with a mere dead wall, a lapse of logic , a confirmed bewilderment.[1]

The passage may be seen as a recapitulation or synopsis, at a pitch of generality not previously attempted, of all that has been exhibited *in extenso* of the English national character in such earlier stories as *The Tragic Muse*, *The Awkward Age*, *What Maisie Knew*, *The Spoils of Poynton*, and the Lancaster Gate portions of *The Wings of the Dove*. What is remarkable about it is that it really does seem to recover the multiplicity of particular perceptions, judgments and generalisations contained in those earlier works in their full vivid particularity. 'They didn't like *les situations nettes;* they wouldn't have them at any price': that, one feels, explains as comprehensively as may be desired the British hatred of art that was exposed in *The Tragic Muse*, where Nick Dormer (we remember) incurred ridicule and hostility precisely because he would insist on pursuing his portrait-painting as *une situation nette*; and it explains also, with the same satisfying completeness, a good many other British antipathies. The puzzle about 'the elements of staleness in all the freshness and of freshness in all the staleness, of innocence in the guilt and of guilt in the innocence', is the very puzzle that is so

[1] *The Golden Bowl*, I, iii, 9, pp. 317–18.

intensively explored and so instructively exhibited in *The Awkward Age* and *The Wings of the Dove.* What is it, after all, but the freshness in her staleness that makes the terrible Mrs Lowder so irresistible; and before Mrs Lowder, Mrs Brookenham in *The Awkward Age,* Mrs Gereth in *The Spoils of Poynton,* Sir Claude in *What Maisie Knew* and even Ida Beale and Mrs. Beale? Then—catching one's breath a little at the sheer quantity of illumination contained in the simple phrases—one recognises how often indeed in English society the enquiring mind is confronted in the end 'with a mere dead wall, a lapse of logic, a confirmed bewilderment'; and one recalls a dozen other delightful instances in James's works of this bewilderment of the British mind in the presence of 'ideas'—Lord Lambeth's in *An International Episode,* Mrs Ambient's in *The Author of Beltraffio,* Lady Agnes's and Julia Dallow's in *The Tragic Muse,* Lord Mark's in *The Wings of the Dove.* Finally, one understands also why the enquiring mind of a clever foreigner like the Prince should crave in that intellectual desert for even so humble a pleasure as 'the small intellectual fillip of a discerned relation between a given appearance and a taken meaning'. He wouldn't mind not understanding the English (as he did understand his Europeans), he wouldn't care that in this instance his 'taken meaning' should be a total misreading of the 'given appearance', so long as the gap itself might be admitted as matter for enquiry, the 'relation' between the given situation and his own misreading of it open to the free play of mind. For then it would be at least a relation 'discerned', and as such something to sustain a mind to which criticism and analysis came as naturally as leaves on a tree.

The high generality or 'universality' of *The Golden Bowl* is also intimately connected with the principles and method of James's later works,[1] which are here supremely exemplified. The principle of internal relations, for instance, is observed

[1] See Appendix C (ii) below.

with an ideal completeness unparalleled in any previous work of James's maturity. Everything in the world of this novel is involved in everything else, everything is modified by everything else, and this 'rich interpenetration' defines its very essence. Similarly, the principle which James called his 'law of successive aspects' is here observed with a rigour of economy not previously attempted. There are but two centres of consciousness, the Prince in the First Book, Maggie Verver in the Second, and they are used strictly in succession, without recourse to the relief of alternation. The other two principals, Charlotte Stant and Adam Verver, are never at any crucial point in the story directly exhibited —or (as James prefers to put it) are never exposed to 'that officious explanation which we know as "going behind" ';[1] and the Assinghams are there merely to assist in 'going behind' the Prince and Maggie Verver. Finally, the indirect method of presentation predominates here to the almost complete exclusion of direct statement; and as one grunts and sweats one's way through this most late of Jamesian works, perpetually losing one's way amidst the qualifications and parentheses, struggling to keep a hold on the proliferating subleties of analysis, the relentlessly sustained metaphors, the tormenting crypto-statements of the elliptical, allusive, digressive dialogues, one has reason to believe that James meant what he said when, in a letter to Hugh Walpole at about this time in reply to some unforgivable question Walpole had asked about *The Ambassadors*, he commented, 'How can you say I do anything so foul and abject as to "state"?'[2]

The generality of vision projected by these means does indeed produce an air as rarefied as any we have yet been asked to breathe in James's works. To adopt his own metaphor about *The Awkward Age*,[3] his 'process' here, as there, has been 'to pump the case gaspingly dry, dry not

[1] *The Awkward Age*, p. xxvi.
[2] *Letters*, ed. Lubbock, II, p. 254.
[3] *The Awkward Age*, p. xxiii.

only of superfluous moisture, but absolutely . . . of breathable air'; and the 'exemplary closeness', the compression 'ferocious, really quite heroic' which James proudly remarks in *The Awkward Age*, are many times more exemplary, ferocious and heroic in *The Golden Bowl*. Indeed it is for the later masterpiece rather than the earlier that one would wish to reserve the superlative praise that James bestows upon *The Awkward Age*, that it is 'triumphantly scientific'.[1]

In what sense *The Golden Bowl* is supremely 'scientific', in what sense it exemplifies and vindicates James's conception of the logic of the perfect novel, is best shown by tracing in outline the development of the central story.

Charlotte Stant, brilliant, accomplished, and beautiful in the Florentine style of 'the great time', and Prince Amerigo, Roman *galantuomo*, with a taste particularly inclined to the art of the great time, have been before the opening of the story passionately and splendidly in love with each other. But because (like Kate Croy and Merton Densher) they are both poor and both too 'great' to live without money, they do not marry; and it is evident to all, but especially to their intimate friend Mrs Assingham, that each must make a suitably splendid marriage. This is the first premise or *donnée* of the story. The first necessary consequence is that the Prince marries Maggie Verver, who is the daughter of Adam Verver, American millionaire and famous collector, whose collection of European art-treasures is finally to be taken back to American City, there to be enshrined in the greatest art-museum the continent has yet seen. Maggie adores her husband, and is blissfully happy. But she also adores her father, with whom since her mother's death sne has enjoyed a tender and deeply harmonious intimacy of companionship; and she is now full of anxious fear that her marriage will leave her father solitary and sad. Goaded by this anxiety—'her stupid little idol', as she is afterwards to

[1] *The Awkward Age*, pp. xxv–xxvi.

call it—she urges her father to marry her dear friend Charlotte. This marriage, which is the second necessary consequence of the first premise, also in due course takes place; and it is now generally felt that the best possible solution has been reached to the problems of everyone concerned. Charlotte Stant has made her splendid marriage; Adam Verver has been supplied with the best of companions to compensate him for the loss of Maggie; Maggie's own stupid little anxiety has been relieved; and the Prince is in the agreeable position of having the best of wives, the best of fathers-in-law, and now also the best of former mistresses more or less on the premises. Maggie and her father know nothing, of course, of the Prince's former relations with Charlotte.

These consequences, however, themselves produce a set of fresh relations, from which the rest of the 'argument' follows by a necessity equally ineluctable. The admirable situation created by the two marriages begins gradually to alter its character; and the alteration is all in the direction of an ironical reversal of everyone's expectations. Maggie and her father, so far from being separated by their respective marriages, are drawn together more closely than before, in particular after the birth of Maggie's son, who sets the bloom of perfection, so to speak, on their domestic happiness; and as a consequence of this increased intimacy between the father and daughter, the former lovers, the Prince and Charlotte, are in their turn thrown more and more together. The grand irony of the situation is that it is all a perfectly open secret. It had been one of Maggie's main arguments at the time she was urging her father to marry Charlotte that Charlotte would supply them with what she called 'greatness'—meaning by this a certain high distinction, in the sphere of social relations in particular, that Charlotte possessed in a pre-eminent degree and the Ververs not at all. She and her father accordingly now take the comfortable, cosy view of themselves as the dear old stay-at-homes whose special office it is to form the domestic background to the brilliant public appearances of the Prince and Charlotte; and they in turn, with the comfortable complacent approval of the Ververs, take every opportunity to exercise their developed social gifts in the interests of the two families. They appear at all the season's most important receptions, banquets and balls, while Maggie and her father remain at home, sitting together by the cradle of the Principino, rejoicing in the child, each other, their absent *sposi*, and the whole happy arrangement. Maggie and her father on their side honestly believe that the arrangement can continue indefinitely; and the Prince and Charlotte on theirs honestly desire that it may so continue.

But, of course, it can't, and doesn't. The Prince and Charlotte cannot indefinitely continue to 'go about' (as the Prince puts it to himself in a crucial interior monologue) in 'the state of our primitive parents before the Fall'. It becomes too absurd in the end that such a mutual pair as they more and more find themselves to be should continue to go about in this way. And so, partly because the situation itself is so absurd, partly because they are still bound by their old passion, and in spite of their resolution to be sane and sensible and to remember the advantages they both enjoy from not being married to each other, Charlotte and the Prince become lovers again; and this in the story of *The Golden Bowl* constitutes the act of betrayal which is presently to precipitate the suffering of Maggie Verver, the principal vessel of the central tragic experience. The fact is disclosed to us at a grand reception, at which the Prince and Charlotte encounter the Assinghams and the Prince gives Mrs. Assingham 'a quintessential wink', which makes it plain to that well-intentioned lady what has happened and sends her back in terror to her husband to communicate it all to him in a monologue longer and more intensely analytical than any she has yet embarked upon. Presently, when the Prince and Charlotte, having gone to a grand house-party at a grand country-house, stay away longer than is natural or proper, Maggie's own eyes are at last opened to the true state of affairs; and this discovery ends the first part of the story, entitled *The Prince.* The second part, entitled *The Princess,* is concerned to show, through Maggie's consciousness alone, how what has been lost is restored: how the Prince is restored to Maggie, Charlotte to Adam Verver; and how this is accomplished entirely, or almost entirely, by Maggie's solitary effort.

This, in bare outline, is the story of *The Golden Bowl,* the telling of which occupies more than eight hundred pages of the closest late-Jamesian writing. What emerges from it is a great fable—one of the greatest in modern European literature—of the redemption of man by the transforming power of human love. The instrument of the redemptive act is Maggie Verver; its ultimate source, her father; the principal recipient of the grace, her husband the Prince. But the fourth principal, Charlotte Stant, also enjoys its beneficent influence in ways accommodated to her needs and capacities; and the way in which this is accomplished by Maggie Verver, drawing her power from her father, is the heart of James's tale.

In the story the redemptive theme is contracted into a simple act of *restoration*: Maggie Verver has to restore what has been lost, or fatally impaired, by the adultery of her husband the Prince with her friend Charlotte Stant. In the concrete human situation, this means that she must draw her husband back to herself, separate him from Charlotte, and restore Charlotte to her father; and on this plane Maggie's act of restoration is characteristically simple, personal and domestic. It consistently maintains this character, with never the breath of a suggestion, never an intrusive hint, that it is anything but what it appears to be. Yet it is more; and *The Golden Bowl* is a triumph of the poet's art because it succeeds in projecting the universal in and through the intensely concrete and particular. By the profundity and intensity of his insight into the private domestic suffering of Maggie Verver, and by his power to render the felt quality of that suffering with a poet's fullness, minuteness and exactness, James exhibits to us the representative or 'exemplary' nature of that suffering; and since to be representative or exemplary in this sense is to be universal, Maggie Verver's act of restoration becomes a 'figure' (as the older critics would have called it) of a larger act—a restoration of the universal moral order which has been disordered by the immorality of an ugly betrayal.

On this view, what has disordered the moral universe in *The Golden Bowl* is the destructive passion of lust figured in the adultery of the Prince and Charlotte. The nature of this 'lust', however, is not simple but exceedingly complex, and the act of betrayal that springs from it is correspondingly complicated. Its several immediate causes are to be traced back to a single source—the fundamental clash between the moral code of the Ververs and that of the Prince and Charlotte. This indeed is the mainspring of the whole drama, and accordingly requires to be closely examined.

Prince Amerigo, we soon discern, is James's quintessential Aesthetic Man. Compared with the Prince's aestheticism, that (for instance) of Gilbert Osmond, which had seemed to go so far in sophistication and so deep in its power to dominate his life, appears crude and superficial; and also artificial, 'acquired', in a way in which the Prince's, the product of centuries of breeding, is not. The Prince's aestheticism also has nothing to do with 'fine things' as such; nor is it tainted, as it was in Osmond, by a mean, shabby conventionality, a concern about mere social appearances. The Prince's aestheticism is pre-eminently a view of life, dangerously complete and coherent, whose basic, unexamined assumption is that the aesthetic criterion, 'the touchstone of taste' (as the Prince himself is to call it at a crucial point in the story), is the ultimate criterion in the conduct of life. The aesthetic, on this view, is the measure of the good; the good is a function of the beautiful; and the beautiful, in this context, means something uncommonly large and comprehensive. It is the product of intelligence, sensibility and imagination, all developed to the highest degree; and in personal relationships it expresses itself in the pursuit not merely of the graceful and charming but also, and indeed chiefly, of the bold, the imaginative, the brilliant. That is how people are measured by the touchstone of taste—by their free play of mind, by their sense of the irony of things, by the high style in which they conduct their lives.

We receive the full flavour of this style at Matcham, the stately home from which the Prince and Charlotte make their fateful expedition to Gloucester:

> Every voice in the great bright house was a call to the ingenuities and impunities of pleasure; every echo was a defiance of difficulty, doubt or danger; every aspect of the picture, a glowing plea for the immediate. . . . For a world so constituted was governed by a spell, that of the smile of the gods and the favour of the powers; the only handsome, the only gallant, in fact the only intelligent acceptance of which was a faith in its guarantees and a high spirit for its chances.[1]

The Prince, we learn, possesses in full measure this faith in its guarantees and high spirit for its chances. As he stands on the terrace waiting for Charlotte to come down, he defines to himself the nature of his extraordinary good luck:

> The upshot of everything for him, alike of the less and of the more, was that the exquisite day bloomed there like a large fragrant flower that he had only to gather. . . . He knew [now] why he had tried from the first of his marriage with such patience for such conformity; he knew why he had given up so much and bored himself so much. . . . It had been just in order that his—well, what on earth should he call it but his freedom?—should at present be as perfect and rounded and lustrous as some huge precious pearl. He hadn't struggled nor snatched; he was taking but what had been given him; the pearl dropped itself, with its exquisite quality and rarity, straight into his hand.[2]

When the sense of the beautiful goes as far and as deep as

[1] *The Golden Bowl*, I, iii, 7, p. 297.

[2] *Ibid.* I, iii, 9, pp. 318, 321.

this, one might suppose it really was enough for all the ends of life, even the most exalted. One might suppose that the perfection of taste, when it comprehended so much, was indeed co-extensive with all human virtue and *a fortiori* with moral virtue. Yet (we learn as the story advances) it is not: these two, the aesthetic and the moral, though intimately bound up with each other, are yet not the same; indeed they can even, in certain circumstances, be mutually exclusive. We receive our first hint of this at the very beginning of the story, in a significant exchange between the Prince and Mrs Assingham in which the Prince in his charming, easy way confesses that he believes himself to be lacking in a moral sense:

'I should be interested', she presently remarked, 'to see some sense *you* don't possess'.

Well, he produced one on the spot. 'The moral, dear Mrs Assingham. I mean always as you others consider it. I've of course something that in our poor dear backward old Rome sufficiently passes for it. But it's no more like yours than the tortuous stone staircase—half-ruined into the bargain!—in some castle of our *quattrocento* is like the "lightning elevator" in one of Mr Verver's fifteen-storey buildings. Your moral sense works by steam—it sends you up like a rocket. Ours is slow and steep and unlighted, with so many of the steps missing that—well, that it's as short, in almost any case, to turn round and come down again.'

'Trusting', Mrs Assingham smiled, 'to get up some other way?'

'Yes—or not to have to get up at all. However,' he added, 'I told you that at the beginning.'[1]

We receive a further and fuller hint of the possible incompatibility of the aesthetic and the moral in another early colloquy, that between the Prince and Charlotte on their memorable shopping expedition the day before the Prince's wedding. They are talking about Maggie and the wedding gift Charlotte wants to buy her. Charlotte says, 'Anything, of course, dear as she is, *will* do for her. I mean if I were to give her a pin-cushion from the Baker Street Bazaar'; the Prince, laughing, agrees; and Charlotte goes on:

'But it isn't a reason. In that case one would never do anything

[1] *The Golden Bowl*, I, i, 2, pp. 28–9.

for her. I mean', Charlotte explained, 'if one took advantage of her character'.

'Of her character?'

'We mustn't take advantage of her character,' the girl, again unheeding, pursued. 'One mustn't if not for *her*, at least for one's self. She saves one such trouble.'

She had spoken thoughtfully, her eyes on her friend's; she might have been talking, preoccupied and practical, of some one with whom he was comparatively unconnected. 'She certainly *gives* one no trouble,' said the Prince. And then as if this were perhaps ambiguous or inadequate: 'She's not selfish—God forgive her!—enough'.

'That's what I mean', Charlotte instantly said, 'She's not selfish enough. There's nothing, absolutely, that one *need* do for her. She's so modest', she developed—'she doesn't miss things. I mean if you love her—or, rather I should say, if she loves you. She lets it go.'

The Prince frowned a little—as a tribute, after all, to seriousness. 'She lets what—?'

'Anything—anything that you might do and that you don't. She lets everything go but her own disposition to be kind to you. It's of herself that she asks efforts—so far as she ever *has* to ask them. She hasn't much. She does everything herself. And that's terrible.'

The Prince had listened; but, always with propriety, didn't commit himself. 'Terrible?'

'Well, unless one's almost as good as she. It makes too easy terms for one. It takes stuff within one so far as one's decency is concerned, to stand it. And nobody', Charlotte continued in the same manner, 'is decent enough, good enough, to stand it—not without help from religion or something of that kind. Not without prayer and fasting—that is without taking great care. Certainly', she said, 'such people as you and I are not'.

The Prince, obligingly, thought an instant. 'Not good enough to stand it?'

'Well, not good enough not rather to feel the strain. We happen each, I think, to be of the kind that are easily spoiled.'

Her friend again, for propriety, followed the argument.

'Oh I don't know. May not one's affection for her do something more for one's decency, as you call it, than her own generosity—her own affection, *her* "decency"—has the unfortunate virtue to undo?'

'Ah, of course it must be all in that.'

But she had made her question, all the same, interesting to him. 'What it comes to—one can see what you mean—is the way she believes in one. That is if she believes at all.'

'Yes, that's what it comes to,' said Charlotte Stant.

'And why', he asked, almost soothingly, 'should it be terrible?' He couldn't, at the worst, see that.

'Because it's always so—the idea of having to pity people.'

'Not when there's also with it the idea of helping them.'

'Yes, but if we can't help them?'

'We *can*—we always can. That is', he competently added, 'if we care for them. And that's what we're talking about.'

'Yes'—she on the whole assented. 'It comes back then to our absolutely refusing to be spoiled.'

'Certainly. But everything,' the Prince laughed as they went on—'all your "decency", I mean—comes back to that.'

She walked beside him a moment. 'It's just what *I* meant,' she then reasonably said.[1]

The passage discloses many significant things about Charlotte as well as the Prince; but we are concerned just now only with the Prince. What it shows is that he is a man of perfect breeding; that (like Vanderbank in *The Awkward Age*) he is thoroughly good-natured and charming; warmly affectionate; capable of the most sincere gratitude for all he has received, and is going to receive, from the Ververs; and, above everything, full of humility, goodwill and good faith. He sincerely desires to do what is right, and genuinely believes himself capable of doing what is right without undue exertion on his part, or undue modification of his view of things.[2] Yet (as he himself has recognised)

[1] *The Golden Bowl*, I, i, 5, pp. 90–92.

[2] The Prince's humility has been explicitly mentioned in the opening section of the whole book when, walking alone in Bond Street, he meditates on his qualifications and disqualifications for the 'scientific' future that is in store for him with the Ververs: 'He was intelligent enough to feel quite humble, to wish not to be in the least hard or voracious, not to insist on his own side of the bargain, to warn himself in short against arrogance and greed.' (*The Golden Bowl*, I, i, 1, p. 14). Again: 'Humble as he was, at the same time he was not so humble as if he had known himself frivolous or stupid. He had an idea . . . that when you were stupid enough to be mistaken about such a matter

he has no moral sense. His persistent evasiveness in this scene, which is not the less ominous for being so charming, good-natured and good-humoured, is ample proof of this; and Charlotte further confirms it by her own doubts and misgivings. Charlotte, it is clear, does have an inkling of one of the important truths that the fable of *The Golden Bowl* is to disclose—that there is a difference between the moral and the aesthetic, and that by the aesthetic alone no man is saved. But though Charlotte dimly understands it while the Prince understands it not at all, Charlotte does not understand it enough to avert the catastrophe that is awaiting them; and this vital defect in the Prince and Charlotte is one efficient cause of the story of suffering, expiation and final redemption that follows.

What Charlotte Stant, however, principally has in common with Maggie's husband is that she, too, conducts her life in the light of the touchstone of taste. In her, it is true, the aestheticism is acquired rather than inherited; but it is so highly developed, and so intimate an expression of her personal genius, as to appear as natural as the Prince's. The presence of the aesthetic principle in Charlotte may be discerned, first, in the kind and quality of her beauty, to the interest of which the Prince handsomely testifies;[1] and,

you did know it.' (*Ibid.* I, i, 1, p. 15.) The good faith, upon which the success of Maggie Verver's act of restoration absolutely depends, is first mentioned by the Prince himself in his talk with Fanny Assingham the day before his wedding: 'You apparently can't understand either my good faith or my humility', he finds himself constrained to say to her in the course of this talk (I, i, 2, p. 27). But Fanny, it seems, does understand: 'Amerigo's good faith was perfect', she tells Maggie at their meeting after the antiquary's visit (II, iv, 9, p. 153); and to her husband after the Matcham week-end she says, speaking of Charlotte and the Prince: 'There's nothing they're not now capable of—in their so intense good faith . . .. It's their mutual consideration, all round, that has made the bottomless gulf; and they're really so embroiled but because, in their way, they've been so improbably *good*.' (I, iii, 10–11, pp. 337, 352). It is not mentioned again until the last chapter but one when the Prince offers it as his sole word of self-justification in the moment of his reunion with Maggie: 'If ever a man since the beginning of time acted in good faith—!' he says (II, vi, 2, p. 308); and needs to say no more since Maggie, it seems, perfectly grasps the point with all its implications.

[1] *The Golden Bowl*, I, i, 3, pp. 42–3. See pp. 256–7 below.

second, in the perfection of her social accomplishments. Her tact, her presence of mind, her 'usefulness' in all social situations are never less than perfect; and her managerial capacities, though prodigious, never appear as managing but only as graceful. It may be discerned also in *minutiae* such as her dress, which is elegant in a way poor Maggie's never quite is. But, most of all, it is to be discerned in her taste for bold, free enjoyments of the kind in which, besides the boldness and freedom, the sensual element is also distinctly present; and it is this, more than anything perhaps, that defines the 'greatness' repeatedly ascribed to her by the Ververs.

As the story develops and the Prince and Charlotte are thrown more and more together, it becomes evident that the principal (and most dangerous) bond between them is their free play of mind—their capacity to see the rich irony of things, and in particular the irony of their own situation *vis à vis* the Ververs. This situation, it has already been indicated, becomes to them in the end desperately exasperating; and though it is passion that in the first instance draws them together, it is sheer exasperation with the absurdity of their situation that, equally with the passion, finally leads them to become lovers again. Yet even as their exasperation grows, they still retain intact not only their composure and good humour but (remarkably) their good faith towards the Ververs; and it is precisely this razor's-edge balance—of their good nature, goodwill and genuine gratitude for benefits received with their super-sophisticated sense of the irony of their situation—that they cannot in the end maintain. As the months pass the tension mounts and mounts, until the touchstone of taste finally triumphs and Charlotte and the Prince leap out of Mr Verver's boat and become lovers.

The interior monologue in which the Prince expresses, in the beautifully modulated accents of a *galantuomo*, his particular sense of outrage at the absurdity of his situation and the bottomless ignorance and innocence of the Ververs is among the really superb things in the book. At Matcham, where (we have already learnt) 'every voice in the great bright house was a call to the ingenuities and impunities of pleasure; every echo was a defiance of difficulty, doubt or danger; every aspect of the picture, a glowing plea for the immediate',

There were only odd moments when the breath of the day, as it has been called, struck him so full in the face that he broke out with all the hilarity of 'What indeed would *they* have made of it?' 'They' were of course Maggie and her father, moping—so far as they ever consented to mope—in monotonous Eaton Square, but placid too in the belief that they knew beautifully what their expert companions were in for. They knew, it might have appeared in these lights, absolutely nothing on earth worth speaking of—whether beautifully or cynically; and they would perhaps sometimes be a little less trying if they would once for all peacefully admit that knowledge wasn't one of their needs and that they were in fact constitutionally inaccessible to it . . .. Deep at the heart of that resurgent unrest in our young man which we have had to content ourselves with calling his irritation—deep in the bosom of this falsity of position glowed the red spark of his inextinguishable sense of a higher and braver propriety. There were situations that were ridiculous, but that one couldn't yet help, as for instance when one's wife chose, in the most usual way, to make one so. Precisely here however was the difference; it had taken poor Maggie to invent a way so extremely unusual—yet to which none the less it would be too absurd that he should merely lend himself. Being thrust, systematically, with another woman, and a woman one happened, by the same token, exceedingly to like, and being so thrust that the theory of it seemed to publish one as idiotic or incapable—this was a predicament of which the dignity depended all on one's own handling. What was supremely grotesque, in fact, was the essential opposition of theories—as if a galantuomo, as *he* at least constitutionally conceived galantuomini, could do anything *but* blush to 'go about' at such a rate with such a person as Mrs Verver in a state of childlike innocence, the state of our primitive parents before the Fall. The grotesque theory, as he would have called it, was perhaps an odd one to resent with violence, and he did it—also as a man of the world—all merciful justice; but none the less assuredly there was but one way *really* to mark, and for his companion as much as for himself, the commiseration in which they held it.[1]

From this passage there emerges what must be one of the most curious—and most subtle and persuasive—justifications of adultery to be found anywhere in imaginative literature. It is precisely because the Prince is a *galantuomo*—a Gallant Man, a man of spirit, a man who guides his life by 'the touchstone of taste,' by the standard of 'a higher and braver propriety' than any that the dear, innocent, ignorant, incorrigibly incorruptible and totally unimaginative Ververs could so much as dream of; and because, being such a man, he cannot bear the sheer ignominy of going about indefinitely 'with such a person as Mrs Verver in a state of child-like innocence, the state of our primitive parents before the Fall', that he becomes Charlotte's lover. And this is how the touchstone of taste is seen not merely to sanction adultery but positively to insist on it—as the only intelligent, the only brave, the only decent thing to do in the circumstances.

In view of the *dénouement* of *The Golden Bowl* and the overriding importance of the redemptive theme, it is tempting to minimise the significance of the exposure of the Ververs contained in the Prince's *galantuomo* speech. The cruel light in which they stand exposed (it might be argued) is merely the specious light of Matcham; the price that allegedly has to be paid for their simplicity and goodness is entirely determined by the moral arithmetic of that world. The Ververs show up as badly as this only when (like the sycamore tree) they are observed by Charlotte and the Prince—when they are measured against *their* developed sensibilities governed by the touchstone of taste, their standard of a higher and braver propriety.

James, however, leaves us in no doubt that there really is a price to be paid, and that it is as heavy as it is genuine. The law of successive aspects may rule that no single aspect

[1] *The Golden Bowl*, I, iii, 7, pp. 298–300.

yields the whole truth. But it also rules that every aspect is an aspect of the truth; and what the Prince sees in the light of the touchstone of taste, though it is not the whole of what there is to see, is in fact there to be seen.

Adam Verver's unique Homeric quality, we already know, is his 'simplicity'. Though he is a multi-millionaire, and as such a Great Personage in the worldly world, he is shy, modest and simple—in particular simple; and one important aspect of his simplicity (we soon learn) is manifested in his attitude to the aesthetic, which is now theoretically the ruling passion of his life since he ceased money-making and became a collector. Adam Verver's passion for the beautiful, it transpires, is not a particularly exacting passion. It does not, it seems, involve any radical upheaval in his spiritual economy; on the contrary, it is all too easily accommodated to the habits and tastes formed in the first instance by the money-making activity:

> It was all at bottom in him, the esthetic principle, planted where it could burn with a still cold flame; where it fed almost wholly on the material directly involved, in the idea (followed by appropriation) of plastic beauty, of the thing visibly perfect in its kind; where, in short, in spite of the general tendency of the 'devouring element' to spread, the rest of his spiritual furniture, modest, scattered and tended with unconscious care, escaped the consumption that in so many cases proceeds from the undue keeping-up of profane altar-fires. Adam Verver had, in other words, learnt the lesson of the senses, to the end of his own little book, without having for a day raised the smallest scandal in his economy at large; being in this particular not unlike those fortunate bachelors or other gentlemen of pleasure who so manage their entertainment of compromising company that even the austerest housekeeper, occupied and competent below stairs, never feels obliged to give warning.[1]

Or again, with the emphasis more explicitly on the acquisitive aspect of Adam Verver's love of the beautiful:

> Nothing perhaps might affect us as queerer . . . than this application of the same measure of value to such different pieces of property as

[1] *The Golden Bowl*, I, ii, 5, pp. 175–6.

old Persian carpets, say, and new human acquisitions; all the more indeed that the amiable man was not without an inkling on his own side that he was, as a taster of life, economically constructed. He put into his one little glass everything he raised to his lips, and it was as if he had always carried in his pocket, like a tool of his trade, this receptacle, a little glass cut with a fineness of which the art had long since been lost. . . . As it had served him to satisfy himself, so to speak, both about Amerigo and about the Bernadino Luini he had happened to come to knowledge of at the time he was consenting to the announcement of his daughter's betrothal, so it served him at present [when he is about to propose to Charlotte] about Charlotte Stant and an extraordinary set of oriental tiles of which he had lately got wind.'[1]

In respect to the Prince himself, what Mr Verver appears to find most irresistible is his exquisite breeding, which for him, the quintessential American collector, has all the beauty of its rarity value and all the rarity value of its perfect beauty. 'You're round, my boy', he says to the Prince, 'You're *all*, you're variously and inexhaustibly round, when you might, by all the chances, have been abominably square. . . . It's the sort of thing in you that one feels—or at least I do—with one's hand. . . . For living with, you're a pure and perfect crystal.'[2] Yet the Prince's being like a pure and perfect crystal is for Adam Verver, it seems, perfectly compatible with his being also like a banker's draft. The Prince perceives this when at a dinner-party at the house in Eaton Square he catches his father-in-law's eye fixed upon him:

[Mr Verver's] directed regard rested at its ease, but it neither lingered nor penetrated, and was, to the Prince's fancy, much of the same order as any glance directed, for due attention, from the same quarter, to the figure of a cheque received in the course of business and about to be enclosed to a banker. It made sure of the amount—and just so, from time to time, the amount of the Prince was certified. He was being thus, in renewed instalments, perpetually paid in; he already reposed in the bank as a value, but subject, in this comfortable way, to infinite endorsement.[3]

[1] *The Golden Bowl*, I, ii, 5, p. 175. [2] *Ibid.* I, ii, 1, pp. 122–3.
[3] *Ibid.* I, iii, 6, p. 290.

The exposure of Adam Verver's curious philistinism is not the less deadly for being so amiable; and James is equally unsparing about the Ververs' provinciality, which (according to the Arnoldian doctrine) is inseparable from any philistinism however curious. This shows itself in their general attitude to the Prince:

> There were plenty of singular things they [Maggie and her father] were *not* enamoured of—flights of brilliancy, of audacity, of originality, that, speaking at least for the dear man and herself, were not at all in their line; but they liked to think they had given their life this unusual extension and this liberal form, which many families, many couples, and still more many pairs of couples, wouldn't have found workable.[1]

The edge of the criticism here is sharp indeed, especially when one takes in the note of self-congratulatory complacency along with the provinciality; and one can easily see how these features in particular of the good, kind Ververs might come to work on the Prince's patrician nerves.

Maggie herself, as we may expect, is treated more tenderly than her father in the matter of their common weaknesses. But—leaving aside for the moment the complex questions arising from certain Jamesian ambiguities in her attitude to the Prince and to Charlotte, which are to be taken up in a later section[2]—we are left in no doubt about the effect upon her husband and her friend of her American simplicities. She may be, like all James's American heroines, generous, tender and passionate; she may be lovely and thoroughly charming (the Prince compares her to 'a little dancing-girl at rest, ever so light of movement but most often panting gently, even a shade compunctiously, on a bench'[3]). Yet, unavoidably, she is also 'funny', in the special sense in which all James's American heroines are. In this comprehensive Jamesian sense, the word denotes an irreducible compound whose elements (we have seen) the sophisticated

[1] *The Golden Bowl*, II, iv, 1, p. 5.

[2] Ch. IX, pp. 281–2, 314–19 below.

[3] *The Golden Bowl*, I, iii, 6, p. 288.

English and Europeans are particularly quick to discern, and always find fascinating and amusing when they do not find them excruciatingly boring. They are, first, the provinciality already noted; a moral rectitude remarkable—by metropolitan standards—for its simplicity, directness and candour; a passion for analysis and generalisation which is so 'funny' because it is either terribly banal or surprisingly acute, and when acute nevertheless not in the least sophisticated; and a conspicuous absence of the higher social accomplishments. The last, though the least *sub specie aeternitatis*, is the most obtrusive in day-to-day intercourse. It shows itself in a certain absence of composure or 'poise', both of the inward and the outward kind: in the light of the touchstone of taste, Maggie's numerous 'little' anxieties—about her father's happiness, her husband's, her friend Charlotte's—would be a sign of the first kind, the inward lack of composure here being the product of an over-scrupulous conscience and an over-eager desire to do only what is right; while her anxiety about appearances—her dress, for instance (she is constantly tormented by the fear that her *toilet* on any given occasion will not measure up to Charlotte's exacting standards), is meant to show her lack of that outward poise which comes so naturally, it seems, to the Kate Croys and Charlotte Stants of her world. Mrs Assingham, immediately before the scene in which the golden bowl is broken, has occasion to note Maggie's 'perfect little personal processes':

Nothing more pathetic could be imagined than the refuge and disguise her [Maggie's] agitation had instinctively asked of the arts of dress, multiplied to extravagance, almost to incoherence. She had had visibly her idea—that of not betraying herself by inattentions into which she had never yet fallen, and she stood there circled about and furnished forth, as always, in a manner that testified to her perfect little personal processes. It had ever been her sign that she was for all occasions *found* ready, without loose ends or exposed accessories or unremoved superfluities; a suggestion of the swept and garnished, in her whole splendid yet thereby more or less encumbered and embroidered setting, that reflected her small still passion for order and symmetry, for objects with their backs to the walls, and spoke even of some probable reference in her American blood to dusting and polishing New England grandmothers.[1]

In the end, indeed, the 'funniness' is seen to be merely another aspect of the familiar American innocence—the simple-heartedness which is so closely linked with the simple-mindedness as to be often (but not always) co-extensive with it. The story of *The Golden Bowl* is designed to show, among other things, how Maggie Verver starts by being as 'funny' as may be desired—as simple-minded as she is simple-hearted; and ends still simple-hearted but no longer simple-minded.

The causes of the 'act of shame' committed by the Prince and Charlotte are accordingly complex indeed. This complexity, of course, makes it very difficult to see their adultery as vicious at all, let alone as an act of shame. Yet the course of James's fable, and in particular the *dénouement*, can leave us in no doubt about the way in which we are meant to view it; and what the fable implicitly affirms is explicitly confirmed by a multitude of details designed to exhibit a fatal flaw in the relationship between the Prince and Charlotte which reduces it, in the final analysis, to a relationship of lust rather than love.[2] If this taint is in fact present, and if its proper name is lust, it is this that has violated the moral order in *The Golden Bowl*; and if lust is one of the deadliest of the deadly sins because it is so deceptively like the love that redeems while being in fact its diabolical counterpart, it is the lust figured in the adultery of the Prince and Charlotte that has to be exorcised in order that the moral order may be restored and reaffirmed.

[1] *The Golden Bowl*, II, iv, 8, p. 134.

[2] These details are examined in a later section (ch. IX, pp. 291–9 below), where it is also suggested that they justify the use of the old-fashioned word 'lust' in spite of (or indeed because of) their Jamesian complexities and refinements.

This, taken at its highest pitch, is the ultimate scope of the fable. The restoration and reaffirmation of the moral order, we already know, is in fact accomplished. It is effected by Maggie Verver's love; and what we are shown in the second part of the story is the three-fold source of the redemptive power of her love. First, it is essentially selfless;[1] second, it is grounded in anguish and humiliation; third, it is informed by intelligence: it fights to win, and uses all the resources of the mind to accomplish its end.

Socrates' definition of love in the *Symposium* appears to be peculiarly applicable to the case of Maggie Verver. Diotima, says Socrates, had told him that love is the child of Penury and Resource. What she meant was that love is, in the first instance, 'poor': poor in spirit, humble, submissive; even weak and wretched—prostrating itself before the beloved, 'seeking that which it lacks', longing only to be filled by that which is the object of its desire. But love is also 'resourceful': it knows what it wants; it seeks by all means to secure the object of its desire; and pursues its object with all the energy and purposefulness of a hunter in pursuit of his quarry. And this, which Diotima called Resource, is only another name for the intelligence by which love, the ragged pauper, is able to see its object steady and whole, and devise the means by which it may come into the blessed possession of the beloved.

Maggie Verver, when she embarks on her task of redemption and restoration, is likewise 'poor'. She is pitifully weak and wretched: pitifully diffident, of course, about her power to accomplish her task; and pitifully afraid of the three people—her husband, her father and her friend—she most cares for in the world. She is terrified, to begin with, of the Prince's 'sovereign personal power', as she calls his sexual power. For the Prince (we have already discovered) is not

[1] Or, rather, it is at once selfless and selfish; and the sense in which it is 'selfish' yet is not therefore the less selfless is to be considered later (ch. IX, pp. 282–4 below).

only charming, good-natured and affectionate, gracefully compliant, and full of humility, gratitude and goodwill towards his benefactors. He is also, unexpectedly, powerful; and the source of his power is twofold. For his father-in-law Adam Verver, as we have seen, it is his breeding; for his wife Maggie it is his sexual virility. Though Prince Amerigo's breeding is so exquisite, he does not for that reason (like the men, for instance, in D. H. Lawrence's stories: Lou's husband in *St Mawr*, or Clifford Chatterley and his circle in *Lady Chatterley's Lover*) suffer any loss or diminution of sexual energy; and though his sensuality is overlaid with his aestheticism, the aestheticism is plainly not debilitating. The passage in which Amerigo reflects on Charlotte's physical beauty at their first meeting in Mrs Assingham's house is an early indication of the kind and quality of his sexuality:

It was, strangely, as a cluster of possessions of his own that these things in Charlotte Stant now affected him; items in a full list, items recognised, each of them, as if, for the long interval, they had been 'stored'—wrapped up, numbered, put away in a cabinet. . . . He saw again that her thick hair was, vulgarly speaking, brown, but that there was a shade of tawny autumn leaf in it for 'appreciation'—a colour indescribable and of which he had known no other case, something that gave her at moments the sylvan head of a huntress. He saw the sleeves of her jacket drawn to her wrists, but he again made out the free arms within them to be of the completely rounded, the polished slimness that Florentine sculptors in the great age had loved and of which the apparent firmness is expressed in their old silver and old bronze. He knew her narrow hands, he knew her long fingers and the shape and colour of her finger-nails, he knew her special beauty of movement and line when she turned her back, and the perfect working of all her main attachments, that of some wonderful finished instrument, something intently made for exhibition, for a prize. He knew above all the extraordinary fineness of her flexible waist, the stem of an expanded flower, which gave her a likeness also to some long loose silk purse, well filled with gold pieces, but having been passed empty through a finger-ring that held it together. It was as if, before she turned to him, he had weighed the whole thing in his open palm and even heard a little the chink of the metal.[1]

The aesthetic emphasis is of course unmistakable, and it blends smoothly, we observe, with the commercial and the erotic. It is a dangerous mixture; and in the Prince's attitude to Maggie this rare blend of sophisticated refinement with sexual power is made the more dangerous by the presence of a real tenderness, or at least affection, for her. These elements are beautifully distinguished in two important passages in the Second Book, in which the operation of the Prince's 'sovereign personal power' is directly exhibited and its power to sap Maggie's resolution and strength for her redemptive task particularly emphasised. In their contexts the passages are as heart-rending for what they show of Maggie's heroic struggle against her own susceptibilities as they are terrifying for what they suggest of the power of the sexual element, in a man like Maggie's husband, to dominate and subdue:

He had possession of her hands and was bending toward her, ever so kindly, as if to see, to understand more, or possibly give more —she didn't know which; and that had the effect of simply putting her, as she would have said, in his power. She gave up, let her idea go, let everything go; her one consciousness was that he was taking her again into his arms. It was not till afterwards that she discriminated as to this; felt how the act operated with him *instead* of the words he hadn't uttered—operated in his view as probably better than any words, as always better in fact at any time than anything. Her acceptance of it, her response to it, inevitable, foredoomed, came back to her, later on, as a virtual assent to the assumption he had thus made that there was really nothing such a demonstration didn't anticipate and didn't dispose of. . . . He had been right, overwhelmingly right, as to the felicity of his tenderness and the degree of her sensibility, but even while she felt these things sweep all others away she tasted of a sort of terror of the weakness they produced in her. It was still for her that she had positively something to do, and that she mustn't be weak for this, must much rather be strong.[2]

[1] *The Golden Bowl*, I, i, 3, pp. 42–3. [2] *Ibid.* II, iv, 2, pp. 25–6.

Presently again, in the carriage:

What her husband's grasp really meant, as her very bones registered, was that she *should* give it up [her 'idea']: it was exactly for this that he had resorted to unfailing magic. He *knew how* to resort to it—he could be on occasion, as she had lately more than ever learned, so munificent a lover: all of which was precisely a part of the character she had never ceased to regard in him as princely, a part of his large and beautiful ease, his genius for charm, for intercourse, for expression, for life. She should have but to lay her head back on his shoulder with a certain movement to make it definite for him that she didn't resist. To this as they went every throb of her consciousness prompted her—every throb, that is, but one, the throb of her deeper need to know where she 'really' was. By the time she had uttered the rest of her idea therefore she was still keeping her head and intending to keep it; though she was also staring out of the carriage-window with eyes into which the tears of suffered pain had risen. . . She was making an effort that horribly hurt her, and as she couldn't cry out her eyes swam in her silence.[1]

So Maggie is abjectly afraid of her husband's sexual power. But she is almost equally afraid of Charlotte's formidable managerial powers; and she lives in hourly terror, of course, of her father's coming to know what he must on no account know if they are not all to be ruined. Nor are her weakness and wretchedness diminished but rather increased by her passion. Her love of her father, always tender and passionate, is now reinforced by a fierce protectiveness of the 'perfect little man' whose goodness, as she sees it, has been hideously betrayed by his wife and son-in-law. At the same time she adores the Prince her husband with an adoration that is incapacitating; she admires Charlotte's 'greatness' with a generosity that her fear of Charlotte has no power to destroy; and while she is swamped and submerged in this way by her terror and her passion, she knows all the while that to the Prince and Charlotte she has no hope of appearing as anything but a fool—'saintly', of course, 'rotten with goodness' (like Mitchy in *The Awkward Age*), but still a poor, simple-

[1] *The Golden Bowl*, II, iv, 3, pp. 50–51.

minded fool. This, it is indicated,[1] is what in fact happens after the Matcham episode: the Prince and Charlotte, now bound together by the most intimate of bonds, tacitly agree to treat Maggie with a compassionate consideration more cruel than contempt; and Maggie, being fully conscious of this, is spared none of its pain or humiliation.

All this, one might suppose, would already sufficiently disable Maggie Verver for the task of restoration she has assumed. But these disabilities are as nothing compared with her ultimate disability—the ultimate condition, supremely exacting and absolutely binding, under which she has to accomplish her task. She must effect it in such a way that the precious uniqueness of each of the three beloved persons concerned shall be unimpaired. The Prince must retain his adorable Roman 'charm'; Charlotte must retain her 'greatness'—her social gifts and high administrative abilities; and her father must retain his mysterious 'simplicity', his beautiful 'innocence': he must never know what has happened—never know the shameful act of betrayal that has been perpetrated under his eyes.

There can accordingly be no question of *exposing* the Prince and Charlotte. There is to be nothing so crude and mortal as an exposure; nor is there to be anything that would be tantamount to it. For to expose them (she comes to see in a crucial scene later in the story [2]) would be to reject them: to sever the connexion which (she discerns) is as precious to them as it is to her, and is the foundation of their common life together. To destroy this, the connexion and the common life, is what she cannot bring herself to do; and that is why the Prince and Charlotte are to be 'spared', whatever the cost to herself.

The lengths to which Maggie is prepared to go to spare first her husband and presently also her friend are to be touched on in a later section.[3] In the meantime, the interest

[1] *The Golden Bowl*, II, iv, 2, pp. 31, 38–9. [2] See pp. 264–6 below.
[3] See pp. 273–5 below.

of this particular condition of Maggie's task is that it is the immediate (though not the only) cause of the extraordinary central situation that dominates the Second Book of *The Golden Bowl*. As this situation is James's main dramatic device for projecting simultaneously almost all the important aspects of his redemptive theme, it invites the closest attention.

Its simplicity is the first extraordinary thing about it. What 'happens' is merely that Maggie, her father, the Prince and Charlotte maintain a total, unbroken silence about the drama in which they are all involved. After the Matcham episode, each 'knows' that the other 'knows'; or, rather, each knows that the other knows something but none knows exactly what the other knows. Maggie herself does not know for certain until the incident with the golden bowl; up to then she is only in an anguish of doubt and uncertainty. Charlotte and the Prince do not know how much Maggie knows; and neither Charlotte nor the Prince even knows what the other knows of what Maggie knows, since (we are made to understand) they hold no private communication after their return from the Gloucester expedition. When the golden bowl is broken, the Prince in the subsequent scene [1] does indeed learn that his wife Maggie knows 'everything'. But immediately after that the silence is resumed; and in the critical period that follows at Fawns, Mr Verver's country-house, Maggie speaks never another word about it to the Prince, the Prince speaks never a word to Charlotte, Charlotte never a word either to the Prince or Maggie, and none of them, of course, utters a syllable to Adam Verver who knows (or appears to know) nothing whatever about the whole matter from the beginning to the end of the story.

So there they hang, the four of them, 'in the upper air, united in the firmest abstention from pressure'—Maggie abstaining from pressure upon the Prince and Charlotte,

[1] *The Golden Bowl*, II, iv, 10.

they abstaining from pressure upon her and one another, and all of them abstaining from pressure upon Adam Verver; and it is in this condition of total silence about what concerns them all so intimately that Maggie accomplishes her task of restoration.

On the face of it, it is a situation so extraordinary as to seem almost grotesque. At first glance it looks like some huge super-subtle jest; and if this is what it is, the jest, being at the expense of a situation we are otherwise invited to treat with the utmost seriousness, would be in rather bad taste. Or (as some of James's more unsympathetic critics would urge), it might be merely another instance of that 'hypertrophy of sensibility' which led James in his later works to lose all, or almost all, sense of reality and all sense of proportion in his treatment of human relationships, and to indulge his passion for elaboration and refinement as a mere exercise of technical virtuosity.

In fact, however, it is neither. As a dramatic device it is super-subtle indeed, but for reasons wholly creditable to James's genius; and it is of the first importance to understand the several complex ends it achieves in the total plan of *The Golden Bowl.*

The first of these is most conveniently approached by recalling one important theme in the account of *The Turn of the Screw* set out in an earlier chapter. The governess, it was suggested,[1] failed in the end to accomplish her work of salvation because at a crucial point in the story she had insisted on extracting from little Miles a confession which in that situation it was sheer cruelty to insist upon. Goaded on (as she afterwards realised) by her mad 'pride', her desire to bring her work to a decisive victory, she had pressed and harassed the child in her determination to 'have all'. She had been unable to let the knowledge of good and evil grow in him of itself, naturally and sweetly, until it should finally separate him from the powers of evil and

[1] Ch. IV, pp. 125–7 above.

restore him to the powers of good; and this in the governess was as much a failure of intelligence as of character. She did not in the first instance see that if love is to save it must be perfectly selfless; nor was she capable, it seems, of the effort of self-discipline that such love demands and (paradoxically) makes possible—in this instance, the power to abstain from pressure.

This is the failure which is gloriously redeemed by Maggie Verver in *The Golden Bowl.* Maggie's task, we gradually come to see, is accomplished precisely by not insisting: by not pressing or harassing her husband the Prince but, instead, simply letting him alone—to see for himself the shamefulness of his act of betrayal, to come by his own effort to the knowledge of good and evil, and so to supply himself in the end with that moral sense which (he had confessed to Mrs Assingham) he so lamentably lacked. By letting him alone,[1] moreover, the main condition of his transformation is also perfectly fulfilled—that it shall be accomplished without the smallest injury to his personal gifts and graces. His adorable Roman charm is to remain intact, the beautiful 'pride of his manhood' (as Maggie later sees it) is to be left unimpaired. He must, in the common phrase, 'remain himself' even while he is radically transformed by his new knowledge of good and evil; he must be humbled by the consciousness of his guilt but not diminished by it. The knowledge of good and evil must effect, in short, a transfiguration in a quasi-religious sense: the old elements are all to remain, but so glorified as to make a 'new man' who, brought to birth in this way, will stand as a living testimony to the redeeming power of human love.

It is easy to see how the seemingly fantastic situation in the Second Part of *The Golden Bowl* perfectly dramatises this aspect of the theme. Maggie's total silence, her absolute

[1] This phrase, it will be remembered, is actually used by Miles in *The Turn of the Screw* when the governess, kneeling by his bed after his midnight encounter with Peter Quint, is pressing him to confess what he had 'done' at school (see ch. IV, pp. 117 above).

abstention from pressure throughout the period in which the Prince is plunged in his dark night of the soul, is now seen to be the final measure of her love. It is because she loves him with a passion untainted by the spiritual greed of the governess in *The Turn of the Screw* that she can abstain from pressing him or harassing him or preaching to him; and it is by the strength of the same love that she can silently forgive him his trespass against her, silently suffer with him and watch over him in his anguish as he struggles to come to his knowledge of good and evil.

So this is the strength of Maggie Verver's love. Maggie herself, however, we already know, is a weak, timid, quavering girl. (Her voice always quavers in the most absurd way, especially when she is speaking to Charlotte.) In the pursuit of her redemptive task she accordingly passes through purgatorial fires of anguish, humiliation and terror, in a solitude more dark and dense even than any that Milly Theale had known; and the heroic effort it costs her to persist in her total abstention from pressure is repeatedly emphasised. As in the following passage, appropriately cast in a Waste Land image, in which the effort and the pain, the unnatural self-discipline, and the aching desire to relieve the solitude and re-establish the connexion she yearns for, are powerfully evoked:

Maggie had become more conscious from week to week of his [the Prince's] ingenuities of intention to make up to her for their forfeiture, in so dire a degree, of any reality of frankness—a privation that had left on his lips perhaps a little of the same thirst with which she fairly felt her own distorted, the torment of the lost pilgrim who listens in the desert sands for the possible, the impossible plash of water. It was just this hampered state in him none the less that she kept before her when she wished most to find grounds of dignity for the hard little passion which nothing he had done could smother. There were hours enough, lonely hours, in which she let dignity go; then there were others when, clinging with her winged concentration to some deep cell of her heart, she stored away her hived tenderness as if she had gathered it all from flowers. He was walking ostensibly beside her, but in fact given over without a break to the grey medium in which he helplessly groped; a perception on her part which was a perpetual pang and might last what it would—for ever if need be—but which if relieved at all must be relieved by his act alone.[1]

This 'perception', however, among others of the same order, follows as a consequence of the single, all-illuminating, perception that visits Maggie in an earlier scene. As in *The Portrait of a Lady* Isabel Archer's midnight vigil before the dying fire of her sitting-room marks the highest point of her growth in self-knowledge, so in *The Golden Bowl* Maggie Verver reaches her peak of self-knowledge as she walks on the terrace at Fawns passing and re-passing the smoking-room where her father, her stepmother and her husband sit playing their game of bridge.[2] Before coming out on to the terrace, as she sat on a sofa watching the players, she had been seized for a moment by a dreadful temptation to speak the word that would tear through the appearances they were all so wonderfully and prodigiously keeping up and expose once and for all the reality that lay behind:

> The amount of enjoyed or at least achieved security represented by so complete a conquest of appearances was what acted on her nerves precisely with a kind of provocative force. She found herself for five minutes thrilling to the idea of the prodigious effect that, just as she sat there near them, she had at her command; with the sense that if she were but different—oh, ever so different! —all this high decorum would hang by a hair. There reigned for her absolutely during these vertiginous moments that fascination of the monstrous, that temptation of the horribly possible, which we so often trace by its breaking out suddenly, lest it should go further, in unexplained retreats and reactions. . . . After it had been thus vividly before her for a little that, springing up under her wrong and making them all start, stare and turn pale, she might sound out their doom in a single sentence, a sentence easy to choose among several of the lurid—after she had faced that blinding light and felt it turn to blackness she rose from her place . . . and moved slowly round the room, passing the card-players and pausing an instant behind the chairs in turn.[3]

[1] *The Golden Bowl,* II, v, 4, pp. 247–8.

[2] *Ibid.* II, v. 2.

[3] *Ibid.* II, v, 2, p. 206.

She meets the eyes of each of the four players (Mrs Assingham is the fourth) as she passes out of the room on to the terrace, conscious of 'the secret behind every face', and receives her first intimation of her role as sufferer and redeemer. She reads in each pair of eyes

> an appeal, a positive confidence . . . that was deeper than any negation and that seemed to speak on the part of each of some relation to be contrived by her, a relation with herself, which would spare the individual the danger, the actual present strain, of the relation with the others. They thus tacitly put it upon her to be disposed of, the whole complexity of their peril, and she promptly saw why: because she was there, and there just *as* she was, to lift it off them and take it; to charge herself with it as the scapegoat of old, of whom she had once seen a terrible picture, had been charged with the sins of the people and had gone forth into the desert to sink under his burden and die.

They did not, however, want her to *die*:

> That indeed wasn't *their* design and their interest, that she should sink under hers; it wouldn't be their feeling that she should do anything but live, live on somehow for their benefit, and even as much as possible in their company, to keep proving to them that they had truly escaped and that she was still there to simplify.[1]

Then, as she walks on the terrace, pondering the implications of this, she receives another great shock of recognition. She sees, at last, why she had all this time persisted in her chosen course, and what it was that had supported her through all the anguish, terror and humiliation. She sees why, from the beginning, there had been no question for her of succumbing to the more commonplace passions that her situation might, all too excusably, have provoked in another: why 'she had been able to give herself from the first so little to the vulgar heat of her wrong'; why (though she had 'yearned' for it) she had had to renounce 'the straight vindictive view, the rights of resentment, the rages of jealousy, the protests of passion'; why, even, she had had to forgo the sense of horror itself—'the horror of

[1] *The Golden Bowl*, II, V, 2, p. 207.

finding evil seated all at its ease where she had only dreamed of good; the horror of the thing hideously *behind*, behind so much trusted, so much pretended, nobleness, cleverness, tenderness'; why, in short, she had been unable 'to feel about them in any of the immediate, inevitable, assuaging ways, the ways usually open to innocence outraged and generosity betrayed'. The reason, she discerns, was that to feel in any of these ways 'would have been *to give them up*'—to reject them, to break the connexion; and this, 'marvellously', never had been and was not now to be thought of. Her task all along, she now sees, had not been in the first instance to preserve her own dignity, her own self-respect, even her own integrity; nor had it been to preserve theirs. It had been, rather, to preserve the connexion itself, by guarding, jealously and tenderly, the very appearances she had a little while back wanted to tear apart—those 'serenities, dignities and decencies' (as she now calls them) which were the common ground of their life together; and within this connexion and this common life to achieve a common salvation for them all.[1]

This, she now knows, is what had caused her on her sofa in the smoking-room to draw back 'from that provocation of opportunity which had assaulted her . . . as a beast might have leaped at her throat'[2]; and as she reaches this point in her meditation, she sees Charlotte standing in the empty drawing-room—'a splendid shining supple creature . . . out of the cage'—and knows that she is to be exposed in her rôle as scapegoat and redeemer to another terrifying, humiliating ordeal.

I return to the central situation in the Second Book of *The Golden Bowl* to suggest another aspect of its complex meaning. I mentioned in an earlier section that Henry James's particular contribution to the anatomy of love is the idea that love in the modern world must be informed by

[1] *The Golden Bowl*, II, v. 2, pp. 209–10. [2] *Ibid.* II, v, 2, p. 208.

intelligence.[1] If the love of a Maggie Verver is to triumph in this world; if its redemptive work is to be accomplished, wholly and perfectly, within the human order and without reference to an order transcending the human; if, therefore, love is to triumph by the visible annihilation of death, and Maggie, the vessel of the redemptive love, is not (like the scapegoat of old) to die but to live, love must fight to win, and must win a visible victory. And to win such a victory requires not only humility and selflessness, and the power to forgive and to suffer—not only, that is, the saving virtues recommended by historic Christianity; it requires also a virtue not generally much emphasised in the Christian scheme and even held to be a little suspect.

The reason why Maggie Verver's love absolutely must be informed by intelligence is to be discovered by considering again the nature of the enemy she has to engage. Maggie is not, like Shakespeare's Desdemona or Cordelia, fighting the devil in the comparatively simple, tangible shape of an Iago or a Goneril and Regan. She is fighting him in a shape more subtle and insidious than any that even Shakespeare appears to have had any knowledge of—for the reason, perhaps, that it had not yet fully emerged in the consciousness of man at the time Shakespeare wrote. The destructive element that the Prince and Charlotte embody in the aesthetic principle, their 'touchstone of taste', is a distinctly modern phenomenon, peculiar to the modern consciousness; and in the story of *The Golden Bowl*, its diabolical character is most fully exposed in that interior monologue of the Prince on the terrace at Matcham[2] in which the touchstone of taste says in effect 'Evil be thou my good', and argues, with the utmost cogency and persuasiveness, that the Prince's adultery with Charlotte is not merely justified but is positively the only natural, the only decent, the only properly moral thing to do.

It is the touchstone of taste accordingly that Maggie must

[1] P. 255 above.

[2] Pp. 248–9 above.

annihilate in order to accomplish her task. But since this is in its essence a function of the finest of human qualities—of sensibility and imagination, and of goodwill and good faith; since it looks so much like the work of God and not at all like the work of the devil, the difficulty of recognising it for what it is would seem almost beyond the power of human discernment. And perhaps it is beyond the power of human discernment, and perhaps (as the religious would say) Maggie Verver is acting by a power other than and greater than herself. But the fact is that she does discern, by whatever power, that the touchstone of taste must be annihilated.

Or, rather, it must be transformed. The aesthetic must be superseded by the moral; yet the moral must, somehow, incorporate the aesthetic. For if the good is not also beautiful, and if it is not *seen* as beautiful, it will have no power to draw to itself those who are in the grip of the infernal principle. But the beautiful for the Prince and Charlotte, we already know, is inseparable from the intelligent (we remember the Prince on the terrace at Matcham reflecting bitterly on the dear good Ververs' constitutional inaccessibility to knowledge, and correspondingly rejoicing in Charlotte's free play of mind and rich sense of the irony of things); therefore the good must have the specific beauty of intelligence; and that is the first important reason why Maggie Verver's love has to be informed by this specific quality.

But, further (she also discerns), her intelligence must be the kind that the Prince will be able to recognise. It must be, in other words, the intelligence of 'the world'—the Prince's world, the worldly world. Though directed to ends transcending in dignity and power anything that this world can conceive, it must yet be as acute, as shrewd, as calculating, as cool and self-possessed, and as perfectly disciplined as the intelligence that the world honours and understands; and since this, it seems, is the character that an intelligence animated by love has to assume in the modern world, it does in fact assume it when (like the divine love in the Pauline scheme) it is prepared to be all things to all men in order that it may by any means save some.

In the personal domestic story of Maggie Verver's struggle to regain the husband she has lost, what this means is that Maggie has to prove to the Prince that she is not the charming simpleton he and Charlotte have taken her to be but a person (in the phraseology of the world) to be reckoned with. In this, we know, Maggie succeeds; she succeeds by the exercise precisely of the worldly qualities required; and in succeeding she satisfies the world's ultimate criterion of virtue. She achieves her triumph, however—and this is the point to be stressed—entirely within the framework of the strange situation she has created, by which she, her husband, her father and her friend are held together in the upper air, united by the firmest abstention from pressure; and to understand how she does it, and why, is to understand another aspect of the dramatic significance of this remarkable situation.

Having discovered that she has been betrayed by her husband and her friend, Maggie Verver abstains from pressure (we are now expected to see) because this is not only the most loving thing to do in the circumstances but also the most intelligent. To begin with, it is intelligent to exploit —yes, exploit—her husband's and her friend's terror of exposure. It is intelligent to exploit their compunction at what they have done. It is intelligent to hold them in an unbroken suspense, first, about how much Maggie knows and, presently, about what if anything she is going to do. It is supremely intelligent to keep them always in the wrong, herself always in the right—perpetually 'one up' on them— by never breaking the silence she had resolved to maintain from the moment the golden bowl was broken and she said to the Prince 'Find out the rest. Find out for yourself'.[1] For by remaining absolutely and perfectly silent she can never provoke the kind of show-down in which they would

[1] *The Golden Bowl*, II, iv, 10, p. 179.

certainly gain the mastery over her; she can never ask them for an explanation or excuse, and so never give them a chance to lie to her or snub her or in any other way put her in the wrong, themselves in the right. This, in the current phrase, is lifemanship; and this, it seems, is what a love informed by intelligence must know how to exercise in the modern world for the ends of salvation. In any case, it is by exercising her intelligence in this thoroughly worldly way that Maggie achieves her first decisive victory. She gains it by winning, in the phrase of the world, the Prince's 'respect'—for her purposefulness, her shrewdness, her coolness, her self-possession; and in so doing, she completes the first necessary stage of her task of restoration and redemption.

There is, however, a further reason why Maggie's total silence, which is the pivot of the strange situation we are trying to understand, should gain for her the respect of her husband. For, simultaneously with its being an exercise of the worldly intelligence, it happens also to satisfy completely the touchstone of taste itself—that standard of a higher and braver propriety which, it appears, is so much too high and too brave for any simple-minded openness and candour. Is there not (one may imagine the Prince asking himself in the course of his silent brooding at Fawns) something extraordinarily delicate and charming about this silence of Maggie's—something so entirely expressive of the right sort of restraint, the right sort of forbearance, the right sort of abstention from every kind of tediousness? There had been no reproaches or recriminations (he would have noted to himself); no martyred airs, no moralising, no discussion or analysis even; nothing at all of what in the Prince's world variously adds up to being tedious. Apart from her matter-of-fact statement of what she 'knew' when the golden bowl was broken, there had been only this perfect silence, expressive of perfect civility, perfect composure, perfect good manners; and it is this that in the first instance must win the Prince's admiration and respect—that his wife should be capable of such scrupulously good manners in the face of (as he would put it) such a very trying situation. She is standing up to the touchstone of taste in a way completely unexpected, and to him thoroughly instructive.

Then, as his admiration and respect for her grow, he suddenly also finds her interesting, in the way Charlotte was interesting; and presently, indeed, more—positively more—interesting than Charlotte. For he begins to perceive, dimly and confusedly at first, but as the months pass more and more clearly, that her intelligence and her manners in this most trying of situations are not ends in themselves but are subordinated to another end. That end remains unnamed, and is perhaps unnameable; but though he never names it, he recognises it as something other than and superior to the touchstone of taste by which he has always conducted his life. The moment in which the Prince recognises this is climactic, and marks the resolution of one of James's principal themes in *The Golden Bowl.* Characteristically, it is given to us as casually and unemphatically as are all the great moments in James's greatest stories.[1] Maggie has announced to her husband that Mr Verver and Charlotte are coming to spend a last evening with them before they sail for America, and has suggested that he might like to spend it alone with Charlotte. The Prince's first reaction is to let Maggie see 'that he took [this] for no cheap extravagance either of irony or of oblivion'.[2] Then, as he reflects intently on this offer of 'an opportunity to separate from Mrs Verver with the due

[1] Mr Percy Lubbock has made the point very beautifully in his discussion of a similar climactic moment in *The Wings of the Dove:* 'Turning back, looking over the pages again, I can mark the very point, perhaps, at which the thing [i.e. the vital piece of knowledge] was liberated and I became possessed of it; I can see the word that finally gave it to me. But at the time it may easily have passed unnoticed; the enlightening word did not seem peculiarly emphatic as it was uttered, it was not announced with any particular circumstance; and yet, presently—there was the piece of knowledge that I had not possessed before.' (*The Craft of Fiction*, p. 176.)

[2] *The Golden Bowl*, II, vi, 2, p. 303.

amount of form', he seeks grounds for condemning Maggie's suggestion by an appeal to his touchstone of taste. But, for the first time in his life, it fails him. He finds himself 'in so pathetic way, unable to treat himself to a quarrel with it on the score of taste'; and the reason, we are explicitly told, is that:

> Taste in him as a touchstone was now all at sea; for who could say but that one of her [Maggie's] fifty ideas, or perhaps forty-nine of them, wouldn't be exactly that taste by itself, the taste he had always conformed to, had no importance whatever? [1]

This is what the Prince has at last learnt, solely as a result of the conduct of his wife. For her conduct, he now sees, has been motivated by love and by love alone; and by the side of such love, he also sees, the touchstone of taste has indeed 'no importance whatever'.

There is soon after this, and following directly from it, another climactic moment which is given to us even more economically. The Prince, having seen what Maggie really is, is suddenly struck with the fact that Charlotte does not see it. He registers this insight to Maggie in a single simple sentence: 'She's stupid', he says, in a context that makes the pregnant reference of the statement plain enough to Maggie.[2] Again it comes out as casually and unemphatically as any remark at the tea-table. But when one remembers the weekend party at Matcham and the glory that had hung about the Prince and Charlotte then; when one remembers in particular their shared ironies at the expense of the poor simple-minded Ververs, and their shared sense of that 'higher and braver propriety' which had seemed to make their passion self-justifying, this simple remark of the Prince has all the significance and force of an illumination. As such, it marks his final repudiation of the aesthetic standard and his final recognition of the moral—of the surpassing dignity, power and beauty of the moral by which it transcends the inferior dignity, power and beauty of the merely aesthetic.

[1] *The Golden Bowl*, II, vi, 2, p. 304. [2] *Ibid.* II, vi, 2, p. 307.

Maggie disputes her husband's judgement on Charlotte, and presently succeeds in showing him that his rejection of Charlotte is as unjust as it is unnecessary for the end of their common salvation. This, however, is not the main point in the present context.[1] The point is that Maggie Verver has won back her husband and restored the right relations of their moral universe which had been disordered by his act of betrayal by bringing him to see the insufficiency of the touchstone of taste for the conduct of life—and thus effecting in him the final supersession of the aesthetic by the moral.

This process, however, it has already been indicated,[2] is in the nature of a transformation rather than an annihilation. In *The Golden Bowl* the aesthetic is indeed annihilated in the form in which it governs the life of the wordly world; but in the form in which the beautiful is always an intimate, inseparable part of the good, the touchstone of taste is not annihilated but incorporated into the greater and more glorious beauty of the good.

In an essay on Flaubert published in 1893, James speaks of the ultimate source of Flaubert's limitations as a lack of 'faith in the power of the moral to offer a surface'.[3] This memorable phrase exactly defines the faith he himself did possess—an absolute, inextinguishable faith in the supreme beauty of goodness, and in the consequent 'power' of goodness to offer to the artist the richest opportunities for exhibiting this beauty; and in *The Golden Bowl* the power is conclusively shown and the faith triumphantly vindicated in the story of the moral transformation of the Prince by his wife's love.

That Maggie herself recognises the inseparable unity of the beautiful and the good is sufficiently proved by her passionate concern, already touched on,[4] to leave intact and inviolate her husband's princely 'charm'. He must acquire

[1] The point is to be taken up again in its relation to Charlotte in a later section (pp. 295, 298, 303 ff. below).

[2] P. 268 above.

[3] Quoted by Quentin Anderson in *The American Henry James*, p. 5.

[4] P. 259 above.

the moral sense he lacks, but he must not acquire it at the expense of his 'personal serenity', his 'incomparable superiority'. She feels this very powerfully on the momentous occasion when the golden bowl is broken and the Prince's duplicity is about to be exposed. As she bends to gather up the pieces under his eyes, knowing that he now knows that she knows 'everything',

> There was even a minute . . . when her back was turned to him, during which she knew once more the strangeness of her desire to spare him, a strangeness that had already fifty times brushed her, in the depth of her trouble, as with the wild wing of some bird of the air who might blindly have swooped for an instant into the shaft of a well, darkening there by his momentary flutter the far-off round of sky.[1]

She accordingly finds herself silently entreating him to take all the *time* he needs to compose himself:

> 'Take it, take it, take all you need of it; arrange yourself so as to suffer least, or to be at any rate least distorted and disfigured. Only *see*, see that *I* see, and make up your mind on this new basis at your convenience. . . . Above all don't show me, till you've got it well under, the dreadful blur, the ravage of suspense and embarrassment produced, and produced by my doing, in your personal serenity, your incomparable superiority.'[2]

Presently, when the beginning of the end is in sight, we are given a vivid sense of the plenitude of peace, power and joy that flows for Maggie from her vision not, in the first instance, of the Prince's new moral goodness but of his moral *loveliness* —of 'the beauty shining out of the humility, and the humility lurking in all the pride of his presence':

> It was as if she had passed in a time incredibly short from being nothing for him to being all; it was as if, rightly noted, every turn of his head, every tone of his voice, in these days, *might* mean that there was but one way in which a proud man reduced to abjection could hold himself. During those of Maggie's vigils in which that view loomed largest the image of her husband thus presented to her gave out a beauty for the revelation of which

[1] *The Golden Bowl*, II, iv, 10, p. 164. [2] *Ibid.* II, iv, 10, p. 163.

she struck herself as paying, if anything, too little. To make sure of it—to make sure of the beauty shining out of the humility and of the humility lurking in all the pride of his presence—she would have gone the length of paying more yet, of paying with difficulties and anxieties compared to which those actually before her might have been as superficial as headaches or rainy days.[1]

Finally, in the very last scene, when Adam Verver and Charlotte have gone and the love that has flowered between Maggie and her husband out of the depths and intensities of their new understanding of each other is about to be consummated in the body, she has a last spasm of anxiety for him. Amerigo enters the room, and

His presence alone, as he paused to look at her, somehow made it [her reward] the highest, and even before he had spoken she had begun to be paid in full. With that consciousness in fact an extraordinary thing occurred; the assurance of her safety so making her terror drop that already within the minute it had been changed to concern for his own anxiety, for everything that was deep in his being and everything that was fair in his face. . . . What instantly rose for her between the act and her acceptance was the sense that she must strike him as waiting for a confession. This, in turn, charged her with a new horror: if *that* was her proper payment she would go without money. . . . All she now knew accordingly was that she should be ashamed to listen to the uttered word; all, that is, but that she might dispose of it on the spot for ever.[2]

Here again, and for the last time, she cannot bear the thought of his being disfigured by anything so ugly as a 'confession'.

The Prince's recognition of the power of the moral to offer a surface is, of course, a vital part of his transformation. When he repudiates the touchstone of taste, he does so because he has perceived at last not only the goodness of Maggie's love but also the beauty of that goodness. This is what he means—or part of what he means—when he says of Charlotte 'She's stupid' (not to see what Maggie is); and this is what is intimated again in his prolonged moment with Maggie in the scene just before the arrival of the

[1] *The Golden Bowl*, II, v, 1, pp. 201–2.   [2] *Ibid.* II, vi, 3, p. 324.

Ververs on their last visit, when his passion almost overmasters his prudence about 'waiting' until the Ververs have gone:

On him too however something had descended. . . . 'Ah, but I shall see you—! No?' he said, coming nearer.

She had, with her hand still on the knob, her back against the door, so that her retreat under his approach must be less than a step, and yet she couldn't for her life with the other hand have pushed him away. He was so near now that she could touch him, taste him, smell him, kiss him, hold him; he almost pressed upon her, and the warmth of his face—frowning, smiling, she mightn't know which; only beautiful and strange—was bent upon her with the largeness with which objects loom in dreams. She closed her eyes to it, and so the next instant, against her purpose, she had put out her hand, which had met his own and which he held.[1]

So the touchstone of taste is finally transcended by incorporation into the moral, where beauty and goodness are, at last and indissolubly, one; and this is accomplished by Maggie Verver's love operating through her deeply intelligent scheme of maintaining a total unbroken silence about 'everything'. This, I believe, is the principal meaning of the situation in *The Golden Bowl* which had seemed at first sight so fantastic. There is, however, still another and final aspect to be discerned, which is in a sense comprehended by the other yet is also distinct from it.

One may call this the 'social' aspect; and it is recognisably present already in the social themes of *The Awkward Age* and, further back, of *The Tragic Muse* and *The Portrait of a Lady*. This aspect is used by James to express a final criticism of modern society, meaning by 'society' here as everywhere in James the ideally civilised, ideally sophisticated society of Buckingham Crescent, Lancaster Gate, and now also Matcham and Portland Place and Eaton Square.

In this aspect, the central situation in the Second Book of *The Golden Bowl* is, I believe, a colossal symbol, as audacious

[1] *The Golden Bowl*, II, vi, 2, pp. 310–11.

as it is brilliant, for expressing (in the Prince's phrase) the fathomless depths of equivocation that a sophisticated society is by its nature committed to. Reviewing the situation from such a point of view, what is the familiar picture that emerges? A calamitous thing, we know, has happened: Maggie Verver's adored husband has entered into an adulterous relationship with Maggie's beloved friend Charlotte Stant, who is also her father's wife. The calamity is, in the first instance, in the anguish of loss which Maggie herself suffers to satiety; but it is equally in the fact that the 'serenities and dignities and decencies' of their common life appear, by the act of betrayal, to be shattered beyond repair. Yet everyone concerned remains, or appears to remain, perfectly unmoved. No one registers shock or horror, no one explains or apologises, no one so much as comments on what has happened or asks a single question about it. A perfect unbroken silence about it is maintained by everyone concerned. They remain perfectly easy and natural, perfectly civil to each other, chatting in the ordinary way, sharing their normal interest in each other and the world around them, carrying on the domestic and social round as if nothing whatever had happened.

Yet the calamity *has* occurred; and it is vitally necessary for the moral health and happiness of all concerned in it, and in order that the crooked may be made straight and the right relations of things restored, that it should be explicitly acknowledged and openly discussed. Nevertheless though there is nothing to prevent them from 'speaking out'—telling what they know, asking what they want to know, challenging those who will neither tell nor ask—this is in fact the last thing any of them would dream of doing. In particular they would not dream of doing anything so simple, straightforward and candid as to ask. For though to ask and to receive an answer would instantly clear the air, yet it would also (we are made to understand) tear the little society to pieces by exposing it to itself in a way that would somehow bring it to ruin.[1] So the vital, saving question is never asked; there is never a show-down, never a face-to-face encounter; but everyone tries to read the answer in everyone else's eyes, to 'find out' what he desperately wants and needs to know, while remaining totally silent.

We have already in James's later works met this particular object of his irony: most prominently in *The Awkward Age*, *The Sacred Fount* and *The Wings of the Dove*; but also in *The Turn of the Screw*, where the governess, we remember, cannot until the end bring herself to name Peter Quint and Miss Jessel to the children—cannot, that is, bring herself to challenge them directly about their relations with the dead servants. We have already, in other words, been invited to share the threefold aspect of James's vision of modern sophisticated societies: his profound sense of the prevailing absence of candour, the prevailing presence of obliqueness, evasiveness, 'ambiguity'; his sense, equally profound, of its necessity—as, somehow, a means of corporate self-preservation; and his sense, finally, of its beauty. For there *is* a beauty (James here as elsewhere insists [2]) in reticence, composure and civility inflexibly maintained, with every appearance of naturalness and ease, when the heart is being torn to pieces by anguish, terror and humiliation; and though the over-civilised—the Edwardian English, for instance—had perhaps too much of it, the under-civilised—James's simpler Americans—had too little; and James himself, we may suppose, would not have chosen to live among the more civilised rather than the less if he had not seen its beauty as well as its ugliness. Nothing in Henry James is ever made simpler than it is; but nowhere perhaps is his refusal to

[1] The point is made explicitly in the last chapter of *The Golden Bowl* when Maggie, watching her father walk out on to the balcony of the house in Portland Place, 'asked herself but for a few seconds whether reality, should she follow him, would overtake or meet her there', and then recognises as she joins him 'how impossible such a passage would have been to them, how it would have torn them to pieces, if they had so much as suffered its suppressed relations to peep out of their eyes'. (II, vi, 3, p. 319.)

[2] Cp. ch. VI, pp. 189–91 above.

simplify and his fidelity to the experienced complexity of the actual more complete and more admirable than in his handling of this theme in *The Golden Bowl.*

If, as James intimates, the necessity and the beauty, as well as the horror, of this prevailing lack of candour is to be observed at its richest and ripest in modern English society, it has to be added that it is more likely to be recognised by the perceptive foreigner than by the Englishmen concerned, whose degree of immersion in it (as James would have said) is generally as complete as it is unconscious. Nor, of course, will one ever see it in operation in real life as absolutely as in *The Golden Bowl.* But allowing for the difference between art and life, between the ideal perfection of the artistic situation and the imperfect approximations of life, the central situation in the Second Book may stand as James's most devastating comment on an aspect of civilised society that he had, from far back, found to be appalling, fascinating and illuminating all at once. As such, it is in one sense the super-subtle jest that some critics have taken it to be. But the jest in that case is a very serious one, and the irony (as in *The Awkward Age*) is predominantly tragic, not comic. For the main intention of the ironic exposure is to show the price in human suffering that may have to be paid for this lack of candour—which, we learn from the exemplary story of the four persons in *The Golden Bowl* who remained to the end united by the firmest abstention from pressure, can be colossal indeed.

CHAPTER IX

'THE GOLDEN BOWL' (II)

In an illuminating chapter on *The Golden Bowl* in his little book on the later novels of Henry James,[1] Mr F. C. Crews remarks on the presence, in the later chapters in particular, of a 'wealth of Christian overtones' which, he says, must be accounted for if we are to understand the 'ultimate meaning' of the fable. The evidences he cites, though not exhaustive, are striking indeed. He notes that Maggie is 'surrounded with images linking her to Christ', and that her function as 'an agent of mercy' becomes increasingly prominent as the story draws to a close. He shows how Adam Verver's role as the God to Maggie's Christ, which has already been hinted at by the emphasis throughout the story on his power, and the 'formlessness, colourlessness and inaccessibility' which are its essence, appears now to be reinforced by the suggestion that the power is unlimited; and he quotes passages in the later chapters that would seem to argue in James a deliberate intention to present Adam as a God figure whose relation to Maggie resembles in many important respects that of the Father to the Son in the Christian scheme.[2]

Mr Crews rightly declines to conclude from these admittedly challenging details that James is here writing as a Christian, or even in any strict sense projecting the Christian scheme of salvation; he contents himself with the observation that 'by enlarging his characters through religious analogies he introduced the whole Christian system as an available means of moral judgment'.[3] The sense in which Henry James might be regarded as a 'religious humanist', and his later writings, in particular *The Golden Bowl*, as religious in that sense, is to be the subject of a

[1] Frederick C. Crews, *The Tragedy of Manners: Moral Drama in the Later Novels of Henry James* (1957).

[2] *Ibid*. pp. 105–8.

[3] *Ibid*. p. 106.

separate enquiry.[1] In the meantime Mr Crews' formula, modest though it is, is of great value: first, in drawing attention to a dimension of meaning in *The Golden Bowl* that invites further examination; second, in suggesting the direction in which the answer to an important problem in the Second Book is to be sought. This turns upon the case of Charlotte Stant. Granted the interpretation of *The Golden Bowl* set out in the previous chapter, that it is predominantly a fable about the redemptive power of human love, the story of Charlotte in the Second Book clearly raises doubts and difficulties. What on this account are we to make of her fate? How in particular are we to explain what has been frequently noted as strange, unpleasant, and even repulsive in the last part of *The Golden Bowl*—the seeming injustice of Charlotte's 'punishment', which is conspicuously more severe than that of her fellow-sinner the Prince, and so harsh as to seem cruel to the point of savagery?

The question of Charlotte's punishment, moreover, appears to be connected with other 'unpleasant' elements in this part of the book. There are the numerous extended images of terror and shame surrounding not only Charlotte but Maggie as well.[2] There are the strange ambiguous conversations, between Maggie and Fanny Assingham and Maggie and Adam, in which Maggie's attitude to the 'sinners', Charlotte and the Prince, seems often to carry a taint of self-righteousness, and her father's an even stronger taint of self-assertion, issuing in what appears to be a cruel, arbitrary exercise of power; and there are passages bearing specifically on Maggie's scheme for separating the Prince and Charlotte which suggest, or seem to suggest, a disturbing element of selfishness and possessiveness in her attitude of

[1] See above, p. ix.

[2] Mr Stephen Spender was one of the first to draw attention to these in his in many ways admirable essay on *The Golden Bowl* reprinted in *The Question of Henry James*, ed. W. F. Dupee (1947). The conclusion he drew from them, however—that they express 'abysses of despair and disbelief: *Ulysses* and *The Waste Land*'—is, I will try to show, seriously incomplete.

which neither she nor anyone else in the story appears to be conscious. The total impression left upon the reader is that in the later parts of *The Golden Bowl* there is a strain of grimness, pessimism, even bitterness in James's view of the human condition; and though this is hinted at by the title (and should therefore perhaps cause no surprise), it is at any rate not easy to reconcile with the positive redemptive theme of the story.

Before considering the scheme within which the seemingly contradictory aspects of *The Golden Bowl* might possibly be reconciled, I want to take up briefly the question of Maggie's 'selfishness', in relation to the Prince in particular.

In an earlier section [1] I suggested that the most interesting thing about Maggie Verver's love was that it was at once completely selfless and thoroughly selfish, and that the sense in which it was selfish yet not therefore the less selfless needed to be understood if we were not to miss what was perhaps Henry James's most original contribution to the anatomy of love. The selfishness, in one word, is all in Maggie's wanting of her husband the Prince. She wants him passionately, possessively, jealously. Through all her anguished doubts and misgivings, it never for a moment occurs to her to concede Charlotte a prior or superior 'right' to him. She too in fact, like Charlotte, regards her passion as self-justifying; she needs no further reason for wanting to get the Prince back from Charlotte than that she desperately, abjectly, abysmally wants him back. This is how she puts it to her father in the garden at Fawns:

> When you only love a little you're naturally not jealous—or are only jealous also a little, so that it doesn't matter. But when you love in a deeper and intenser way, then you're in the very same proportion jealous; your jealousy has intensity and, no doubt, ferocity. When however you love in the most abysmal and unutterable way of all—why then you're beyond everything, and nothing can pull you down.[2]

[1] Ch. VIII, p. 255 n, above. [2] *The Golden Bowl*, II, v. 3, p. 231.

This is the selfishness of Maggie's love of the Prince; in this respect it is no different from Charlotte's; and the moral James perhaps means us to draw is that love by definition is grounded in and sustained by desire, and that, whatever else it may also have to be, it is not love at all if it does not spring from and is not perpetually nourished by want and wanting.

What then is the difference between Maggie's love and Charlotte's? Charlotte's is to be more fully discussed in a later section; for the present it is perhaps enough to say that her passion for the Prince (like his for her) is grounded in the aesthetic rather than the moral, that their marriage of true minds is sustained by their common allegiance to the touchstone of taste and the standard of a higher and braver propriety than (in their view) the merely moral can yield. In Maggie's love the aesthetic is, of course, not absent; on the contrary—as we saw in the scene in the carriage[1] where in the midst of her wretchedness she can still adore him for his 'large and beautiful ease, his genius for charm, for intercourse, for expression, for life'—the aesthetic is an intimate part of it, and induces its own variety of passion. But it is not confined to the aesthetic. What she ultimately adores him for, what she finds peculiarly beautiful in him, is the moral loveliness she discerns in his charm, his tenderness, his good humour, good will, good faith—in everything that is most noble, most generous, most *good* in him. This, we will find, is what Charlotte happens to be most 'stupid' about;[2] and it is also precisely what Maggie above everything wants to preserve (or restore) in the Prince. It is for this that she suffers terror, anguish and humiliation; renounces the pride of her knowledge, letting Charlotte think her a 'fool' to the end; and is even ready, by one of the paradoxes of the true love, to lose the very object of her adoration rather than lose that which to her is most adorable in him: 'He was walking ostensibly beside her, but in fact

[1] P. 258 above. [2] Pp. 295–9 below.

given over without a break to the grey medium in which he helplessly groped; a perception on her part which was a perpetual pang and which might last what it would—for ever if need be—but which if relieved at all must be relieved by his act alone.'[1]

So Maggie's love is firmly grounded in the carnal, in want and wanting; yet it issues in something that transcends the carnal by incorporating it; and this is how the *eros* and the *agape* of the Christian account of love are reconciled in Henry James's account. But—and this is the last vital point—though (as we saw) Maggie's courage, intelligence and resolution have everything to do with the redemptive power of her love, it is her faith that ultimately guides and directs it. Maggie does not try to 'teach' the Prince; she has no theories about making him better than he is; she is conscious of no desire to alter him. She clings to and acts by her faith alone—that is, by the simple belief that so long as she loves him for what is most beautiful and splendid in him, and so long as she wants him with passion, what she does will be, *must* be, right. Here again is the reconciliation of *eros* and *agape*: the wanting, 'selfish' love—Socrates' ragged pauper in the *Symposium* pursuing the object of his desire and not resting until he possesses it; and the *agape*, the adoration of that which is most good and most beautiful in the beloved, issuing in a redemption of the beloved that is the more triumphantly found because it was never sought.

The grimmer, more pessimistic view of Maggie's 'selfishness' is to be discussed in a later section.[2] In the meantime, I return to our main problem in the latter part of *The Golden Bowl*, that turning upon the fate of Charlotte Stant. To account for this, the framework of the redemptive theme set out in the previous chapter must, I believe, be enlarged to incorporate an aspect of the inherited Judaeo-Christian scheme of salvation (with all the necessary 'humanist' modi-

[1] *The Golden Bowl*, II, v, 4, p. 248. Cp. pp. 263–4 above. [2] Pp. 317 ff, below.

fications) which is perhaps more distinctively Judaeic than Christian and has a prominent place also in the view of the human condition of that other great source of spiritual wisdom in our civilisation, the Greek. The enlarged scheme turns upon the relation of love and justice, and the supremacy of justice in a world only imperfectly and incompletely redeemed by love. On this view, the defining task of justice is to ensure the right relations of things—their right relation to reality, whatever that reality may be; and in the moral sphere specifically, its task is to ensure the stability and perpetuity of the moral order, guarding it from violation or, when it has been violated, restoring it by the best means available to it in the circumstances. The defining task of love, on the other hand, is to alter reality—to transform it, transfigure it, perfect it; and because love possesses this power to alter or transform which justice does not possess, it is greater than justice, and the God of the Judaeo-Christian tradition is first and last a Loving God perpetually offering his prevenient grace to his creatures for their salvation by love.

But, though love by its nature has this power to transform and perfect reality and therefore the power to supersede justice by incorporating it into itself, and though in a world completely and perfectly redeemed by love justice would, finding its occupation gone, cease to exist as a separate and distinguishable entity, love never in fact, particularly when exercised by imperfect or limited human agents upon imperfect or sinful fellow humans, succeeds in accomplishing its redemptive task completely and perfectly. It never therefore succeeds in rendering justice supererogatory; and in a world incompletely and imperfectly redeemed by love—in the actual moral world, that is, as we know it—justice is for this reason supreme. For where love has failed, by reason of the imperfections of the agent or of the recipient or of both, there justice has to take over; and since in our world love never succeeds completely, justice always does have the last word, and is in that sense supreme. And that is why the God of Judaism and Christianity, besides being a God of Love, is also always a God of Justice who, knowing the disposition of his creatures perpetually to resist the grace of love, is perpetually compelled to exercise his power—the 'wrath', the 'judgement', of the Old Testament—as distinct from his love to restore and maintain the moral order against its perpetual violation by the creatures.

So although love has indeed the power to supersede and annihilate justice when it is exercised perfectly, where love fails, or is exercised only imperfectly, justice prevails; and a world, or that part of the world, in which justice prevails is likely to be sterner, harsher, grimmer than one which has been brought under the sweet dominion of love. As such, it may induce a profound 'pessimism'; and we will presently examine more closely the evidences of this in *The Golden Bowl*. Meanwhile the general relevance of this view of the relation of love and justice to *The Golden Bowl* and the case of Charlotte Stant may be briefly indicated. What it suggests is that that part of the moral world in which Charlotte Stant is most prominent remains, for reasons to be examined, outside the dominion of love; that she accordingly comes under the dominion of justice; that Adam Verver is the executor of the justice, being, so to speak, a figure of the Just God of Judaism and Christianity as Maggie is a figure of the Loving God; and that Charlotte's fate at the end of the story, along with the other 'unpleasant' elements we have noted, are to be explained as a function of the quasi-divine justice executed by Adam Verver by the exercise of his power.

An easy approach to the harsher, grimmer aspects of *The Golden Bowl* is to compare its prevailing moral atmosphere with that of *The Wings of the Dove*. Modern critics of Henry James—F. O. Matthiessen, for instance, and Quentin Anderson—have tended to treat the last three complete works as if they formed virtually a single unit;

Mr Anderson indeed speaks of them as the parts of a 'spiritual trilogy' each expressing a different aspect or phase of a single spiritual theme.[1] There is no doubt, of course, about the unifying preoccupations of these three works, nor about the peculiarities of the late style that they have in common. Yet the differences are as great, and as important, as the resemblances; and *The Golden Bowl* seems to me, in point of what I have called its moral atmosphere, to stand closer to *The Ivory Tower* and some of the very late stories—*The Bench of Desolation*, for instance—than to *The Wings of the Dove* and *The Ambassadors*.[2] At any rate, the peculiar moral atmosphere of *The Golden Bowl* may be discovered in a multitude of details which cumulatively give us the measure of its difference from *The Wings of the Dove*.

These, significantly, seem almost always to be connected with the Prince and Charlotte—with their own relationship or their relationship, singly or together, to the Ververs. What we sense very soon is that 'the world' here—the worldly world—has passed beyond its climacteric. The odour of decay can already be scented; and though it does not yet hang as heavy as in *The Ivory Tower*, there is no mistaking the staleness here for the freshness of *The Wings of the Dove*. We notice before long, for instance, the absence of that primary passion which united Kate Croy and Densher in their infernal design; compared with them, Charlotte and the Prince, though they are of course 'young' and though the talk at Matcham is all of 'the bravery of youth and beauty', seem curiously middle-aged, somehow past their prime. Again, we notice the absence here of the prevailing note of discovery in *The Wings*—the perpetual freshness of surprise, wonder and excitement, shared in such abundance by Kate and Densher, by Kate and Milly, and even by Milly and Densher, which gives the relationships in that book the

[1] Quentin Anderson, *The American Henry James* (Rutgers University Press, 1957).

[2] The relation between the novels and the stories of the later period is more fully discussed in chapter x below.

irrecoverable vibration of youth. Charlotte and the Prince give the impression of discovering only what they already knew from the beginning, and of being engaged for the most part in merely manipulating with superb competence their pre-existent knowledge. The Prince's reflections on the terrace at Matcham upon 'the freshness in all the staleness and the staleness in all the freshness' have, we gradually come to see, an ironic double-reference: they refer in the first instance, of course, to the English *beau monde*, but implicitly also to his own relation with Charlotte as infected by the prevailing moral tone of that world.

There are more details of this sort to suggest the odour of decay in the moral atmosphere of *The Golden Bowl*. We receive early in the story a first hint of the Prince's 'knowledge' of women: 'He liked in these days to mark them off, the women to whom he hadn't made love: it represented . . . a different stage of existence from the time at which he liked to mark off the women to whom he had';[1] and we are jerked back to Merton Densher's lack of such knowledge, recalling how he had laughed with the excitement, intense though muted, of perpetually finding in Kate Croy's tone 'something that banished the talk of other women, so far as he knew other women, to the dull desert of the conventional'.[2] Again, when we hear Charlotte's banal, self-exhibitory chatter at tea with the Prince,[3] we discern at once that it is the 'greatness' of the Princess Casamassima rather than that of Kate Croy that we are here invited to recognise. Or there is the shopping expedition of the two women, Maggie and Charlotte,[4] to yield some nice points of comparison with a similar expedition of the other two women, Milly Theale and Kate Croy.[5] Milly and Kate are so clearly *enjoying* themselves, even though on Kate's side the air of their friendship is already filled with the perturbations that are

[1] *The Golden Bowl*, I, i, 1, pp. 19–20.
[2] *The Wings of the Dove*, I, ii, 1, p. 63.
[3] *The Golden Bowl*, I, iii, 5. [4] *Ibid.* II, iv, 2, pp. 33–4.
[5] *The Wings of the Dove*, I, iv, 2, pp. 154–9.

soon to grow into her infernal design. Their enjoyment nevertheless is real, and springs from the spontaneity of their liking for each other, the freshness of their mutual interest and curiosity—from the sheer contagion of friendship which the ardent young seem able to enjoy even in the felt presence of the destructive element. For Charlotte and Maggie there is no such saving exhilaration to come to the rescue. The Matcham episode has already taken place, and Charlotte, not knowing what Maggie 'knows' or indeed whether she knows anything at all, seeks relief from the oppression of her anxiety and compunction by the warmest, sincerest civilities and affabilities to her victim. But nothing can turn appearance into reality. The air between them is rancid with Charlotte's guilt on the one side and Maggie's confusion and terror on the other; and all they can do is bravely to observe the forms of friendship, hoping and praying all the while that (as Maggie is to phrase it at the end [1]) reality may not break in to tear them both to pieces.

There are similar differences to be discerned between the passionate moments of Charlotte and the Prince and those of Kate Croy and Densher. The heavily patterned prose and the violence of the sexual imagery of the one stand in sufficient contrast with the directness and simplicity of the other to suggest the different qualities we are expected to take cognisance of:

> They were silent at first, only facing and faced, only grasping and grasped, only meeting and met. 'It's sacred,' he said at last. 'It's sacred', she breathed back to him. They vowed it, gave it out and took it in, drawn, by their intensity, more closely together. Then of a sudden, through this tightened circle, as at the issue of a narrow strait into the sea beyond, everything broke up, broke down, gave way, melted and mingled. Their lips sought their lips, their pressure their response and their response their pressure; with a violence that had sighed itself the next moment to the longest and deepest of stillnesses they passionately sealed their pledge.[2]

[1] *The Golden Bowl*, II, vi, 3, p. 319. [2] *Ibid.* I, iii, 5, p. 279.

> He went on with that fantasy, but at this point Kate ceased to attend. He saw after a little that she had been following some thought of her own, and he had been feeling the growth of something determinant even through the extravagance of much of the pleasantry, the warm transparent irony, into which their livelier intimacy kept plunging like a confident swimmer. Suddenly she said to him with extraordinary beauty: 'I engage myself to you for ever'. The beauty was in everything, and he could have separated nothing—couldn't have thought of her face as distinct from the whole joy. Yet her face had a new light. 'And I pledge you—I call God to witness!—every spark of my faith; I give you every drop of my life'. That was all, for the moment, but it was enough, and it was almost as quiet as if it were nothing. They were in the open air, in an alley of the Gardens; the great space, which seemed to arch just then higher and spread wider for them, threw them back into deep concentration. They moved by a common instinct to a spot, within sight, that struck them as fairly sequestered, and there before their time together was spent, they had extorted from concentration every advance it could make them.[1]

Finally, Densher's encounter with Aunt Maud[2] may be compared with similar profit with the Prince's encounters with Mr Verver.[3] They both 'like' their benefactors, they both find them tremendously 'interesting'; and they both acquiesce, in ways we are invited to judge as equally culpable, in the conditions tacitly laid down for them. Yet the difference of man and man, the qualitative difference between the two complicities, is conveyed with the most convincing exactness. Everywhere we detect the staleness in the one, the freshness

[1] *The Wings of the Dove*, I, ii, 2, pp. 85–6. The passionate episode in Venice (*ibid.* II, ix, 1, pp. 211 ff.) is, characteristically, not described directly but entirely by its effects—by evoking the enchantment that for Densher hangs upon the air of his small room for many days after Kate had come to him. We are expected in this connexion to remember James's comment on the representation of physical love in the novel in a letter to H. G. Wells: 'I think the exhibition of "Love"—functional Love—always suffers from a certain inevitable and insurmountable flat-footedness (for the readers' nerves etc.); which is only to be counterplotted by roundabout arts—as by tracing it through indirectness and tortuosities of application and effect—to keep it somehow interesting and productive . . .' (*Letters*, ed. Lubbock, II, p. 189).

[2] *The Wings of the Dove*, I, ii, 2, pp. 73 ff.

[3] *The Golden Bowl*, I, ii, 1, pp. 122–3.

in the other, and in consequence the relative proportions of the guilt and the innocence in both.

With these preliminary suggestions about the moral atmosphere of *The Golden Bowl* present to our minds, we may look more closely at the Prince's relationship with Charlotte in an effort to determine in what sense, if any, the old-fashioned word 'lust' may be applied to it.[1] The course of the fable, I have suggested, can leave us in no doubt about James's intention to present the relationship as, in some sense, evil. In spite of the powerful justification provided by the Ververs' culpable ignorance and innocence, it does remain, in some vital sense, an act of shame which has to be expiated by the suffering of the three persons most intimately concerned—first Maggie, then the Prince, finally Charlotte; and the problem is therefore to discover what, if anything, there is in the relationship itself—in the nature of the love or passion or whatever between the Prince and Charlotte—that renders it intrinsically self-destructive and therefore an act of betrayal *vis-à-vis* Maggie and Adam, an assault on the dignities, decencies and serenities of their common life, and ultimately also a violation of the universal moral order.

The answer, at this stage of our argument, is not difficult to find. To begin with, we have it on the authority of that invaluable choric commentator, Mrs Assingham, that the Prince does not really 'care for' Charlotte. Her husband stares when she throws out this statement in the course of their long analytical session after the Matcham episode; so she explains: 'Men don't when it has all been so easy. That's how, in nine cases out of ten, a woman *is* treated who has risked her life.'[2] That Fanny Assingham is right about the Prince's never 'really' having cared for Charlotte is most explicitly confirmed in the scene in which the golden bowl is broken and Maggie tells her husband what she

[1] Cp. ch. VIII, p. 254 above. [2] *The Golden Bowl*, I, iii, 11, p. 357.

'knows'. As she reaches the point of explaining that she is now aware of the real reason for his shopping expedition with Charlotte the day before their wedding, Amerigo is listening intently. Maggie says: 'The reason of that was that there had been so much between you before—before *I* came between you at all'; and Amerigo, who had been moving about the room, at this stands still 'as to check any show of impatience', and answers: 'You've never been more sacred to me than you were at that hour—unless perhaps you've become so at this one.' From the 'assurance of his speech' and the way in which he meets her eyes as he says it, and from the effect of the words upon Maggie ('it was as if something cold and momentarily unimaginable breathed upon her, from afar off, out of his strange consistency'), we are meant to infer that the declaration is as true as it is sincere.[1]

An apparently trivial episode earlier in the same scene further confirms the truth of Fanny Assingham's insight. Maggie is telling the Prince about the purchase of the bowl when, suddenly and seemingly irrelevantly, he asks her how much she paid for it. Maggie does not tell him because, she says, she is 'rather ashamed to say'—it was so high; and does not, of course, attach any importance to the question except to find it 'quaint'.[2] But we are expected to know why Amerigo asks the question: we are expected to remember that on the day of the shopping expedition for the golden bowl, when Amerigo, on seeing the crack in the bowl, had stepped outside leaving Charlotte in the shop with the dealer, she had afterwards told him that the price of the bowl was remarkably low. 'Five pounds', she had said, 'Really so little'—though the man had in fact asked fifteen pounds and she had refused to take the bowl chiefly for this reason. 'Five pounds?' Amerigo had asked. 'Five pounds', Charlotte had firmly answered.[3] Amerigo, it seems, had

[1] *The Golden Bowl*, II, iv, 10, p. 176. Cp. ch. IX, p. 312 n. below for further discussion of this passage.

[2] *Ibid.* II, iv, 10, p. 175.

[3] *Ibid.* I, i, 6, p. 106.

suspected that she was lying, and had bethought himself at this moment with Maggie to confirm his suspicion; and though we may suppose that as a European he did not—or did not at the time—particularly mind the lie itself, we are surely meant to see a significance in the fact that it should have lingered still in his memory, and (more significantly) that it should have been recalled just at the moment when Maggie's own candour and directness were already making an impact on him very different from any that Charlotte had ever made.[1]

The most telling evidence of the Prince's not 'really' having cared for Charlotte comes later: first, when after the episode of the broken bowl he deliberately withholds from Charlotte what Maggie now knows about their relationship, thus contributing more than anyone to her state of tormented fear and suspense; and finally, in the last scene but one, when he gives Maggie the brief assurance of his good faith from the beginning ('If ever a man, since the beginning of time, acted in good faith—!'). The first point is to be taken up again in another context; but it is already evident that there has been from the beginning some fatal flaw in the golden bowl of the Prince's and Charlotte's happiness, and that Fanny Assingham's diagnosis was cruelly accurate.

The reason Fanny had put forward was, however, equally

[1] In this connexion it is interesting to remember that James had at least in one other important work made a dramatic issue of the difference between the European and the American (or Anglo-Saxon) attitude to the glib, wanton untruth. In *The Europeans* what finally decides Robert Acton that he cannot propose to the Baroness is the fact, simply, that she lies to him about having signed the document dissolving her marriage (or supposed marriage) to her German Prince (*The Europeans*, 11, p. 178; 12, p. 204). He finds the Baroness in a hundred ways fascinating and adorable; as a result of his European travels, he has himself adopted a score of her European attitudes, and has reconciled himself to a dozen others which he cannot adopt. But the ingrained Anglo-Saxon or 'Puritan' revulsion from lying of the easy, habitual kind practised by the Baroness cannot, it seems, be exorcised by any amount of acquired European culture; nor can it be compensated for by any European virtues, however brilliant; and Robert Acton's decision is finally determined by this seemingly most trivial of considerations—that he cannot marry a woman who lies.

accurate and even more cruel. 'Men don't [care] when it has all been so easy', she had told her husband; and the truth of this too we are able to verify almost from the beginning of the story. Charlotte does indeed, all the time, make it too easy for the Prince—from the day of their shopping expedition for the golden bowl to the Matcham week-end which virtually ends their relationship. When on that shopping expedition they stop to rest in Hyde Park, and she openly declares her passion in a heart-searing speech in which she explicitly tells him that she doesn't ask anything of him except that he should know that she adores him, that she is 'giving herself away' and 'perfectly willing to do it for nothing', we (like the Prince) are left in no doubt about the fact that she is 'letting him off'. Amerigo observes that 'she let him off, it seemed, even from so much as answering'; and he accordingly allows his 'handsome, slightly anxious yet still more definitely "amused" face' to register all the attention her speech deserves, but otherwise remains totally silent and unresponsive.[1] Again, at the crucial meeting in Portland Place, when the Prince is awaiting Maggie for tea and Charlotte arrives instead,[2] the impression throughout the scene is that Charlotte is leading, all the time; and the Prince is again justified in the view he had expressed to himself in an earlier scene—that he could always get what he wanted from women 'without lifting a finger', that 'he only had to wait with a decent patience, to be placed, in spite of himself, it might really be said, in the right'.[3]

But it is at Matcham most conspicuously that Charlotte's high competence makes everything easy. She so 'arranges' everything, down to the train-times for their several departures and arrivals, that it is little wonder that Amerigo should reflect again, with a still greater intensity of satisfaction, that 'he had, after all, gained more from women than he had ever lost by them'. They seemed all, the

[1] *The Golden Bowl*, I, i, 5, pp. 86–8. [2] *Ibid.* I, iii, 4–5.
[3] *Ibid.* I, i, 3, p. 45.

'wonderful creatures'—Charlotte, his wife Maggie, Mrs Assingham, even his hostess Lady Castledean—to do nothing but 'combine and conspire for his advantage'; and all there was left for him to do was to justify their unspoken faith in him—'that he wasn't, as a nature, as a character, as a gentleman, in fine, below his remarkable fortune'.[1]

The fatal taint in the relationship is already apparent, and becomes unmistakable before the end of the Matcham episode. 'You're terrible', Amerigo says to Charlotte when she tells him about the train-times; and this is like an answer —in anticipation, as it were—to Maggie's secret prayer at a later stage in the story, that her husband may before long tire of 'Mrs Verver's too perfect competence'.[2] Already at Matcham her competence is proving too perfect for his nerves, his 'finer irritability'; there is a shade of revulsion, along with the admiration and delight, in the cry 'You're terrible'; and the short colloquy with which the Matcham section ends is, as we have cause to remember afterwards, the first ominous sign of the crack in their golden bowl. He says to her laughingly, 'How shall I ever keep anything [from you] —some day when I shall wish to?' And she replies, 'Ah for things I mayn't want to know I promise you shall find me stupid.'[3]

The source of the taint, the reason for the crack in the golden bowl, is threefold: first, the aestheticism we have already examined;[4] second, the purely erotic element in their passion, which is closely connected with the aesthetic; third, the 'utilitarian' aspect of their relationship—which is a consequence of the other two. The three are so intimately linked that they are inseparable in experience and can barely be distinguished in analysis. The primary bond between Charlotte and the Prince, we remember, was their touchstone of taste; and we received an early insight into the sense of beauty which nourished and sustained this common

[1] *The Golden Bowl,* I, iii, 9, p. 315. [2] *Ibid.* II, iv, 8, p. 126.
[3] *Ibid.* I, iii, 9, p. 325. [4] Pp. 241–9 *passim*, 256–7, 267–8, 271–2, 273–6, above.

view. In the passage describing the Prince's first impression of Charlotte at Mrs Assingham's,[1] his appreciation of her beauty, we recall, is conveyed by images at once erotic and commercial. These images signify an attitude simultaneously *detached* and *possessive*; and since both the detachment and possessiveness are of the kind with which we normally view things rather than persons, they are as such inimical to a real involvement in the person who is being thus viewed as a thing. This absence of the kind of involvement which is the basis of love is still more powerfully suggested by another passage in the same scene in which the Prince's recognition of Charlotte's state of 'abjection' is recorded. It is as searing a comment as any to be found in James's works on male sexuality in its cruellest, most destructive aspect; and the cruelty and destructiveness are not mitigated but intensified by the characteristic grace and good humour with which the Prince conducts his reflections:

Once more, as a man conscious of having known many women, he could assist, as he would have called it, at the recurrent, the predestined phenomenon, the thing always as certain as sunrise or the coming round of saints' days, the doing by the woman of the thing that gave her away. She did it, ever, inevitably, infallibly—she couldn't possibly not do it. It was her nature, it was her life, and the man could always expect it without lifting a finger. . . . It produced for [him] that extraordinary mixture of pity and profit in which his relation with her, when he was not a mere brute, mainly consisted; and gave him in fact his most pertinent ground of being always nice to her, nice about her, nice *for* her. She always dressed her act up, of course, she muffled and disguised and arranged it, showing in fact in these dissimulations a cleverness equal to but one thing in the world, equal to her abjection. . . . She was the twentieth woman, she was possessed by her doom, but her doom was also to arrange appearances, and what now concerned him was to learn how she proposed. He would help her, would arrange *with* her—to any point in reason; the only thing was to know what appearance could best be produced and best be preserved. Produced and preserved on her part of course; since on his own

[1] Pp. 256–7 above.

there had been luckily no folly to cover up, nothing but a perfect accord between conduct and obligation.[1]

The seed of self-destruction in the relationship that is about to develop lies in the phrase about the 'pity and profit', and in the repeated emphasis on the Prince's marvellous 'luck' in having to do nothing about it except (like Densher in *The Wings of the Dove*) refrain from being a 'brute' and co-operate in whatever Charlotte proposes. We see the destruction taken a stage further in the episode at Matcham, where the Prince's consciousness of his 'luck', of his 'profit', and of the beauty and virtue of co-operating with Charlotte, is never more intense; only now the 'pity' is absent, having been replaced by a pleasure in which the aesthetic, the erotic and the commercial blend in images as richly evocative as any to be found in *The Golden Bowl.* There he hears 'the chink of gold in his ear' when Charlotte tells the Assinghams that they are staying on to luncheon at Matcham,[2] there everything melts together 'to feed his sense of beauty',[3] the exquisite day blooms 'like a large fragrant flower that he had only to gather',[4] his freedom is 'as perfect and rounded and lustrous as some huge precious pearl';[5] and when Charlotte appears at an upper window of the house,

> Something in her long look at him now out of the old grey window, something in the very poise of her hat, the colour of her necktie, the prolonged stillness of her smile, touched with sudden light for him all the wealth of the fact that he could count on her. He had his hand there, to pluck it, on the open bloom of the day.[6]

He does pluck it; and he and Charlotte are on that unforgettable occasion as mutual a pair as any two people have ever perhaps succeeded in being by the strength of the touchstone of taste, reinforced by passion and courage. But (as we have remarked) in the very moment, so to speak, of plucking the wonderful bloom, the signs of the imminent decay are

[1] *The Golden Bowl*, I, i, 3, pp. 45–6.
[2] *Ibid.* I, iii, 8, p. 309.
[3] *Ibid.* I, iii, 9, p. 315.
[4] *Ibid.* I, iii, 9, p. 318.
[5] *Ibid.* I, iii, 9, p. 321.
[6] *Ibid.* I, iii, 9, pp. 319–20.

already to be noticed. The dangerous detachment is one of them. The Prince can even at this moment jest (or half-jest) about some day wishing to 'keep things' from her; she can strike him as 'terrible' in her very splendour; and he can revert again and again to the 'profit' *motif*. The result is that already, before the end of the Matcham episode, we have an inkling of what may be the crucial defect in a passion grounded solely in the touchstone of taste. We perceive that such a passion is ultimately external—directed in the end only to the beautiful surface of the other, making this the entire object of its delight and desire, but evading the deeper involvements and responsibilities of love. That is why it is also possessive in the sense indicated: it can so easily treat the other as a 'thing'—a valuable, even a precious thing, but still a thing—because it has so little care for it as a human being. That is why, too, it can 'exploit' the other, with the good conscience and perfect lack of scruple with which we have seen the Prince use Charlotte—or, rather, allow Charlotte to allow herself to be used as (he knows) she wants to be used, thereby absolving himself from all moral responsibility for the using. It is because his passion is external in this sense that, after the Matcham episode, the Prince can treat Charlotte with the refined brutality which, when she recognises it, brings tears to Maggie's eyes: keeping from Charlotte everything he 'knows', leaving her to suffer the torments of fear and anxiety in solitude, sharing with her nothing of the profound inner change that he himself is undergoing all that long summer at Fawns, and finally, when he knows they are to be separated for ever, pronouncing her 'stupid'.

These, James tells us, are the wages of sin—the common degradation of the sinners, which in the Prince takes the form of inflicting pain, in Charlotte that of suffering it. That is the price to be paid when two human beings take the appearance for the reality, the simulacrum for the thing itself; and if in this instance the thing itself is love, the simulacrum that shone with such brilliance and splendour at Matcham may well receive the old-fashioned name of lust.[1]

Turning now from the Prince's side of the relationship to Charlotte's, we at once encounter certain familiar difficulties. As in *The Wings of the Dove* James had made it as difficult as possible to pronounce judgement on Kate Croy and her infernal design by supplying her with justifications irresistibly cogent and persuasive, so in *The Golden Bowl* he makes similar provision for Charlotte Stant. In the opening chapters of the story we learn, first from Mrs Assingham[2] and then from Maggie,[3] that she has always been alone and unprotected; and we have this indirectly but poignantly confirmed by her own declaration of her passion to the Prince. We learn, again separately from Mrs Assingham[4] and Maggie,[5] that she has 'loved and lost', and from Mrs Assingham, who knows so much more about the matter than Maggie, that there has been a peculiarly 'magnificent' heroism in her giving up the Prince in order that he might be free to court Maggie.[6] Presently, in the proposal scene with Adam Verver, we receive direct proof of Charlotte's remarkable honesty, courage and pride. As Kate Croy, when she had already formed her dreadful plan and desperately needed Milly's co-operation in it, had nevertheless in her 'bright perversity' openly warned Milly to get out of Lancaster Gate before she was destroyed,[7] so Charlotte here, 'oddly conscientious', intimates to Adam, first, that he does not perhaps know her as well as he thinks, and then, in spite of her openly expressed desire to marry, that his reasons for wanting to marry her are not perhaps as good as they might be.[8] Both Kate Croy and Charlotte Stant know what

[1] The cruel 'unfairness' of it—that Charlotte should suffer so much for their common sin, the Prince by comparison so little—is to be considered in the next section.

[2] *The Golden Bowl*, I, i, 4, p. 77.

[3] *Ibid.* I, ii, 4, pp. 161–2.

[4] *Ibid.* I, i, 4, pp. 64–5, 67–8.

[5] *Ibid.* I, ii, 4, pp. 165–6.

[6] *Ibid.* I, i, 4, p. 76.

[7] *The Wings of the Dove*, I, v, 6, pp. 247–8. Cp. ch. VII, pp. 207–8 above.

[8] *The Golden Bowl*, I, ii, 6, pp. 195–202. See also ch. V, pp. 163–4 above.

they want and know how to get it; but neither will have it cheaply. They not only take all the necessary risks but some gratuitous ones as well—partly no doubt for conscience' sake, but chiefly out of that 'perversity' which is the form taken by their courage and pride; and Charlotte's offer to show Adam the Prince's telegram [1] is meant as a final, spectacular proof of this.

After the marriage our sympathies are still more strongly engaged for her in the ironic situation that develops. Charlotte shows herself to be (in the phrase Adam Verver had used at Brighton) 'very very honourable' in the fulfilment of her part of the contract. She 'does the worldly' for the two families not only with energy and zeal but also with grace and good will; the Ververs' complacent acceptance of her services shows at its least agreeable at this point in the story; and Charlotte's final resentment at being so conspicuously neglected by Adam and so much taken for granted by both Ververs strikes us as more than justified.[2] And after the disastrous Matcham week-end which leads to Maggie's finding out everything, when Charlotte is left alone with her fear and doubt and suffers unspeakable torments in her isolation, we hardly need Maggie's outbursts of compassion to Fanny Assingham to convince us that (as Maggie says to the Prince at the end) 'it's *always* terrible for women'.

The seemingly monstrous severity of Charlotte's 'punishment' is accordingly very difficult to explain, let alone to justify. The completeness of her subjugation is conveyed in images which, for their sustained violence and ferocity, have no parallel in James's works. Repeatedly, Charlotte is described as a creature 'in a cage': in the scene with Maggie which ends in the Judas kiss, she is a 'splendid shining supple creature out of the cage'; [3] at another moment, she stands in 'the hard glare of nature . . . , virtually at bay and yet denied the last grace of any protecting truth'.[4] Again,

[1] *The Golden Bowl*, I, ii, 7, p. 215.
[2] *Ibid.* I, iii, 1, 4, 5.
[3] *Ibid.* II, v, 2, p. 211.
[4] *Ibid.* II, v, 5, p. 267.

as *cicerone* to the visitors at Fawns, Maggie imagines her going about with 'a long silk halter looped round her beautiful neck', the end of which is firmly held by her father in one of his pocketed hands. ('He didn't twitch it, yet it was there; he didn't drag her, but she came');[1] and she seems to hear Charlotte's 'high coerced quaver before the cabinets in the hushed gallery'.[2] The cumulative effect is horrible and terrifying; and it is reinforced by the images of desperate, back-to-wall conflict between the two women, Maggie and Charlotte, in their two crucial encounters in the last part of the book,[3] and (most of all perhaps) by the strange and fearful imaginary dialogue between Maggie and her father as they watch Charlotte conduct the visitors round the galleries. This is what Maggie imagines her father to be saying:

> Yes, you see—I lead her now by the neck, I lead her to her doom, and she doesn't so much as know what it is, though she has a fear in her heart which, if you had the chances to apply your ear there that I, as a husband, have, you would hear thump and thump and thump. She thinks it *may* be, her doom, the awful place over there—awful for *her*; but she's afraid to ask, don't you see? Just as she's afraid of not asking; just as she's afraid of so many other things that she sees multiplied all about her now as perils and portents. She'll know, however—when she does know.[4]

James has made the case of Charlotte as 'difficult' as possible; and to determine the nature and extent of her 'guilt' is accordingly not easy.

The first indication of a moral taint in Charlotte is given in her exchange with Fanny Assingham at the Foreign Office reception, at which she virtually tells Mrs Assingham that she and Amerigo are, or are about to become, lovers. We learn that she has 'an easy command' and 'a high enjoyment' of her 'crisis':[5] unlike Maggie, she does not 'quake' but

[1] *The Golden Bowl*, II, v, 4, p. 253. [2] *Ibid.* II, v, 4, p. 259.

[3] In the first encounter on the terrace, for instance, Maggie's terror of Charlotte is expressed in the picture of herself as 'having been thrown over on her back with her neck from the first half broken and her helpless face staring up' (*Ibid.* II, v, 2, p. 214).

[4] *Ibid.* II, v, 4, p. 253. [5] *Ibid.* I, iii, 1, p. 220.

positively enjoys the dangers of her situation. Presently again we hear that she actually wants Fanny to 'know' and, again, positively enjoys her knowing.[1] In the exchange itself Charlotte is as usual 'magnificent', and her charges against the Ververs are unanswerable. But there is a note of defiance in it, a hardness (her face shows a 'fine and slightly hard radiance'),[2] an absence of tenderness, and—most significant—an absence of the least sign of grief or even regret that the situation should be as it is; which, taken together, are revealing indeed. Charlotte *is* hard, is fundamentally un-tender. Nor does she really mind the badness of the situation because it is bad: she minds it only in so far as it affects her unpleasantly; she does not mind it at all in so far as she can triumph over it. That is why she can have such an 'easy command' and 'high enjoyment' of her crisis: because she is never for a moment undermined, much less disabled, by any distress or shock or grief; because she is in fact fundamentally detached from it, uninvolved in it, indeed only interested in it as a challenge—a challenge to herself to master it. In the present scene, she triumphantly succeeds; and it is the knowledge of her mastery that blends with her consciousness of her own splendid appearance and the brilliance of the whole occasion to produce in her a sense of power and pride that (we are meant to see) is charged with danger. As she stands alone on the grand staircase feeling as never before that she has been 'justified of her faith',[3] she suggests vividly a modern allegorical figure of the deadly sin of Pride placed against a symbolic background of the modern world at its worldliest:

> The air had suggestions enough . . . to constitute those conditions with which, for our young woman, the hour was brilliantly crowned. She was herself in truth crowned, and it all hung together, melted together, in light and colour and sound: the unsurpassed diamonds that her head so happily carried, the other jewels, the other perfections of aspect and arrangement that made her personal scheme

[1] *The Golden Bowl,* I, iii, 1, p. 226.

[2] *Ibid.* I, iii, 1, p. 230.

[3] *Ibid.* I, iii, 1, p. 219.

a success, the *proved* private theory that materials to work with had been all she required and that there were none too precious for her to understand and use . . .

Then, as the Prince joins her,

She had an impression of all the place as higher and wider and more appointed for great moments; with its dome of lustres lifted, its ascents and descents more majestic, its marble tiers more vividly overhung, its numerosity of royalties, foreign and domestic, more unprecedented, its symbolism of 'State' hospitality both emphasised and refined. This was doubtless a large consequence of a fairly familiar cause, a considerable inward stir to spring from the mere vision, striking as that might be, of Amerigo in a crowd; but she had her reasons, she held them there, she carried them in fact, responsibly and overtly, as she carried her head, her high tiara, her folded fan, her indifferent unattended eminence; and it was when he reached her and she could, taking his arm, show herself as placed in her relation, that she felt supremely justified.[1]

This is the pitch that Charlotte maintains in all the scenes that follow, culminating in the week-end at Matcham. At Matcham, we have seen, she is as 'young' and brilliant as she has ever been: she enchants the Prince as never before by her beauty, her intelligence, her good humour, and (as at the Foreign Office reception) by her easy command and high enjoyment of their crisis. And there also, in the scrap of dialogue already quoted,[2] we receive our clearest hint of the fundamental moral flaw in Charlotte:

'How shall I ever keep anything [from you]—some day when I shall wish to?' [the Prince says].

'Ah for things I mayn't want to know I promise you shall find me stupid.'

Here, I believe, is the key to our understanding of the complex nature of Charlotte's guilt; it is confirmed in the subsequent scenes in which the kind and quality of her 'stupidity' are directly and indirectly exhibited. This stupidity, we gradually come to see, consists in her refusal to

[1] *The Golden Bowl*, I, iii, 1, pp. 220, 221.

[2] P. 295 above.

recognise her guilt. Though she has repeated opportunities to 'confess', she refuses each time: persistently, on each successive occasion, she refuses to humble herself by admitting—even to herself, we may presume—that she has done anything wrong; and her 'stupidity' accordingly reveals itself to be a fundamental moral insensibility, a fundamental lack of grasp of the moral realities of her situation, which is at the same time 'willed'—that is, deliberate and conscious. Such a failing, in a person of Charlotte's specific gifts and endowments, is deeply culpable. (For who could plead for Charlotte Stant that she was too simple to understand and must therefore be exonerated on the grounds of invincible ignorance; or, remembering her 'too perfect competence', that she was too weak to act on her understanding?) With such gifts and endowments, she could have understood, and could therefore have recognised and acknowledged her guilt. But she refuses, deliberately and consciously, to do so: refuses to eat the bread of humiliation, to abase her pride before a creature like Maggie Verver whom she despises, to admit for a moment that she has 'failed'; and it is for this reason that she is damned, and has to suffer the purgatorial fire of that long agonising summer.

Our first direct view of Charlotte after the move to Fawns is in her encounter with Maggie on the terrace when she challenges Maggie to say whether she knows of any wrong she, Charlotte, has done her. What we recognise as damnable here is the perfect coolness and self-possession with which Charlotte can speak the necessary lie, and the absence of any hint of a recognition of the wrong she has been guilty of, much less of any shame or penitence. She is brazening it out, and not defensively but aggressively, using all the formidable resources of her 'greatness' to frighten and subdue Maggie and ensure her absolute victory in the contest:

'I'm aware of no point whatever at which I may have failed you', said Charlotte, 'nor of any at which I may have failed any one in whom I can suppose you sufficiently interested to care. If I've been guilty of some fault I've committed it all unconsciously. . . .'[1] The episode ends appropriately with the 'high publicity' of the Judas kiss, which Charlotte forces upon Maggie as the final mark of her victory.

In the scenes that follow, Charlotte's suffering in her growing isolation is poignantly exhibited; and it is in these scenes also that we receive our most explicit intimations of the reason for her suffering. It is her 'stupidity', we see again and again, her infernal pride, her dogged refusal to recognise the moral reality of her condition, that condemns her to her suffering. We have already had Maggie's vision of Charlotte at one point as standing 'in the hard glare of nature . . . virtually at bay and yet denied the last grace of any protecting truth'.[2] In a later scene, Maggie compares the Prince's 'caged' condition with Charlotte's and sees what the difference is—that he is 'lurking there by his own act and his own choice' while Charlotte has had to be forced into it, against her own act and choice, resisting all the time.[3] Then there is Charlotte's imagined address to Maggie, in which her own anguish at the loss of her lover is as moving as her contempt of Maggie (and her total insensibility to Maggie's suffering) is reprehensible and—in the sense explained—'stupid'. 'You don't know what it is to be loved and broken with', Maggie imagines her saying,

> You haven't been broken with, because in *your* relation what can there have been worth speaking of to break? Ours was everything a relation could be, filled to the brim with the wine of consciousness; and if it was to have no meaning, no better meaning than that such a creature as you could breathe upon it, at your hour, for blight, why was I myself dealt with all for deception? why condemned after a couple of short years to find the golden flame—oh the golden flame!—a mere handful of black ashes? [4]

Finally, there is Charlotte's last despairing stand in her second and final encounter with Maggie in the garden at Fawns, in which the pride that at once ruins and sustains

[1] *The Golden Bowl*, II, v, 2, p. 219.
[2] *Ibid.* II, v, 5, p. 267.
[3] *Ibid.* II, vi, 2, p. 298.
[4] *Ibid.* II, vi, 1, pp. 290–1.

her is most fully exhibited. Charlotte is in anguish, knowing herself to be 'doomed to a separation that was like a knife in her heart', and she has wandered out of the house on this hot afternoon in her 'uncontrollable, her blinded physical quest for a peace not to be grasped'.[1] Maggie, who knows all about her impending separation from the Prince, and is now filled with a boundless compassion for Charlotte, has followed her into the garden with a single object in view—'to make somehow, for her support, the last demonstration',[2] to 'allow her, . . . fairly to produce in her, the sense of highly choosing'[3]—the sense, that is, of choosing to go to America with Adam Verver, when in fact she is being forced to it and is full of bitter loathing of the plan. As Charlotte sees the other approach, she is momentarily seized with fear: has Maggie come to retract the 'lie' she had told on the terrace, that she knew of no wrong Charlotte had done her; and is there to be an exposure after all? But as she perceives her rival is looking as 'little dangerous', as 'abjectly mild' as usual, she decides that Maggie has after all only 'presented herself once more to . . . grovel'; and this gives her her cue and her inspiration to do exactly what Maggie wishes her to do—to give the appearance of 'highly choosing'.[4] Maggie perceives how this produces in her an 'instant stiffening of the spring of pride':

Pride indeed had the next moment become the mantle caught up for protection and perversity; she flung it round her as a denial of any loss of her freedom. To be doomed was in her situation to have extravagantly incurred a doom, so that to confess to wretchedness was by the same stroke to confess to falsity. She wouldn't confess, she didn't—a thousand times no; she only cast about her, and quite frankly and fiercely, for something else that would give colour to her having burst her bonds. Her eyes expanded, her bosom heaved as she invoked it, and the effect upon Maggie was verily to wish she could only help her to it.[5]

[1] *The Golden Bowl,* II, v, 5, pp. 274–5.
[2] *Ibid.* II, v, 5, p. 271.
[3] *Ibid.* II, v, 5, p. 273.
[4] *Ibid.* II, v, 5, pp. 273–6.
[5] *Ibid.* II, v, 5, p. 275.

There follows a dialogue, the most openly hostile yet on Charlotte's side, in the course of which Charlotte once more asserts her 'greatness', in the grand style with which she plays out the illusion of free choice; and it ends with Maggie's last act of self-abasement directed to the single end of ensuring that Charlotte's sense of highly choosing shall be as complete and perfect as possible:

'How I see that you loathed our marriage! . . . How I see that you've worked against me!' [says Charlotte].

'Oh, oh, oh!' the Princess exclaimed.

Her companion, leaving her, had reached one of the archways, but on this turned round with a flare. 'You haven't worked against me?'

Maggie took it and for a moment kept it; held it, with closed eyes, as if it had been some captured fluttering bird pressed by both hands to her breast. Then she opened her eyes to speak. 'What does it matter—if I've failed?'

'You recognise then that you've failed?' asked Charlotte from the threshold.

Maggie waited; she looked, as her companion had done a moment before, at the two books on the seat; she put them together and laid them down; then she made up her mind.

'I've failed!' she sounded out before Charlotte, having given her time, walked away. She watched her, splendid and erect, float down the long vista; then she sank upon a seat, Yes she had done all.[1]

So Charlotte's pride with all its implications is the cause of her damnation and the reason for her terrible 'purgatorial' suffering at Fawns; but it is also the groundwork of her salvation. There is a first hint of this in one of Maggie's colloquies with Fanny Assingham at Fawns. Mrs Assingham is speaking of America, the penal colony to which Charlotte is before long to be exiled:

'I see the long miles of ocean and the dreadful great country, State after State. . . . I see the extraordinary "interesting" place

[1] *The Golden Bowl*, II, V, 5, pp. 279–80.

[American City]—which I've never been to, you know, and you have—and the exact degree in which she [Charlotte] will be expected to be interested'.

'She *will* be', Maggie presently replied.

'Expected?'

'Interested'.[1]

Of Charlotte's defiant intention to be 'interested' we have already been given sufficient notice in her address to Maggie in their encounter in the garden. Then, when the Prince and Maggie are back in their house in London, we hear of Charlotte's energetic supervision of the removal of the art-treasures from Fawns, which (it seems) absorbs her so completely as to leave her no time for social calls, even on her step-daughter and former lover; and this is the immediate occasion for a pregnant remark which the Prince addresses to Maggie. They have been speaking of Charlotte and the life that lies before her in America: 'As you say, she's splendid', he says, 'but there is—there always will be—much of her left. Only, as you also say, for others'.[2]

It seems perfunctory, but it is in fact an important clue for our understanding of the redemptive power of Charlotte's 'greatness'. What it chiefly intimates is that her pride, which is the foundation of her 'greatness', has given her in the most testing situation of her life a remarkable resilience, resourcefulness, courage and resolution with which to meet it; and that this is its positive, affirmative side, as the other was negative and destructive. The Prince's remark thus also suggests the double-view we are ultimately expected to take of the case of Charlotte Stant. Because her pride is deadly and damnable, she has to suffer the torments of rejection and isolation, and the final punishment of separation and exile; and because at the same time it is a source of energy and beauty, life-giving and life-affirming, it redeems her suffering and turns her final 'punishment' into a fresh opportunity for the exercise of her gifts. Both aspects, James wishes us to see, are equally real;

[1] *The Golden Bowl*, II, v, 5, p. 268. [2] *Ibid.* II, vi, 2, p. 305.

neither cancels out the other. They simply co-exist, seemingly contradictory and incompatible, yet reconciled in living experience, and as such forming one of the paradoxes of the moral life.

The redeeming power of the sin of pride is memorably figured in Charlotte when she comes with her husband on her last visit to Portland Place and speaks of her 'mission' to the citizens of American City:

> The question of the amount of correction to which Charlotte had laid herself open rose and hovered for the instant only to sink conspicuously by its own weight; so high a pitch she seemed to give to the unconsciousness of questions, so resplendent a show of serenity she succeeded in making. The shade of the official, in her beauty and security, never for a moment dropped; it was a cool high refuge, like the deep arched recess of some coloured and gilded image, in which she sat and smiled and waited, drank her tea, referred to her husband and remembered her mission. Her mission had quite taken form—it was but another name for the interest of her great opportunity: that of representing the arts and the graces to a people languishing, afar off, in ignorance. . . . The difficulty now indeed was to choose, for explicit tribute of admiration, between the varieties of her nobler aspects. She carried it off, to put the matter coarsely, with a taste and a discretion that held our young woman's attention. . . . to the very point of diverting it from the attitude of her over-shadowed, her almost superseded companion'.[1]

The ironic overtones here do, of course, sufficiently indicate the limitations of Charlotte's redemption by pride; yet they do not diminish its reality. Charlotte's 'greatness' has remained unimpaired; and this, we learn in the last exchange between Maggie and her father, is to be her salvation. 'She wasn't to be wasted', Maggie perceives: 'her gifts, her variety, her power' were to be used to capacity; she was to be 'great for the world that was before her'; there was to be no loss for her but only gain. She was, in short, to realise herself more fully and splendidly in the service of Adam's 'idea' than she had ever before been able;

[1] *The Golden Bowl*, II, vi, 3, pp. 314–15.

and though her greatness at Matcham may have been more brilliant, her greatness in American City will be more worthwhile and enduring. And because the triumph of good over evil, especially when achieved at the cost of much suffering, is the ultimate form of success, and because the pure in heart rejoice particularly in such successes, Maggie Verver's last words to her father are 'It's success, father' and his to her, 'It's success'.[1]

Among the many problems presented to the critic of *The Golden Bowl*, one important one (at least) remains to be considered: that of James's particular use of ambiguity in this work. Technically speaking, the ambiguity of *The Golden Bowl*, like that of *The Turn of the Screw* and *The Sacred Fount*, is a direct consequence of James's 'law of successive aspects'[2] which leads him here as in all the works of the late period (and, though less rigorously, also in the main works of the early and middle periods) to present his story at every point through the consciousness of a single interpreter, so that everything that happens is seen from that interpreter's point of view and no other. In *The Golden Bowl* the two principal centres of consciousness are the Prince in the First Book, Maggie in the Second; the only deviations that James allows himself are Fanny Assingham's analytical sessions with her husband, and Adam Verver's brief reflections on Maggie's happiness early in the First Book and Charlotte's on her own happiness at the grand reception later in the First Book.

As a technical device, its primary intention is to ensure the maximum economy and intensity of effect, and this it achieves wherever it is employed—in *Washington Square* and *The Portrait of a Lady* no less than in *The Awkward Age* and *The Ambassadors*. What produces the peculiar ambiguity which *The Golden Bowl* has in common with *The Turn of the Screw* and *The Sacred Fount* is the deliberate exploitation

[1] *The Golden Bowl*, II, vi, 3, p. 322.

[2] See Appendix C, pp. 401–6 below

of the device to cast the shadow of a huge doubt over the validity of any given interpretation. This, as we saw, was accomplished in *The Turn of the Screw* and *The Sacred Fount* by so arranging the dialogues and interior monologues that they could with perfect self-consistency yield two distinct and, in the context, contradictory meanings, one confirming the validity of the interpreter's point of view, the other putting it in doubt. In *The Golden Bowl* the effect is accomplished in exactly the same way; and James's conscious deliberation in the matter is attested by explicit hints of, or even direct references to, the prevailing ambiguity.

As Maggie, on the night of her encounter with Charlotte on the terrace at Fawns, is made by Charlotte to pause before the window of the smoking-room where the others are playing their game of bridge, she reflects that 'this picture of quiet harmonies, the positive charm of it and, as might have been said, the full significance . . . could be no more after all than a matter of interpretation, differing always for a different interpreter'.[1] Fanny Assingham, in one of her conversations with Maggie, is allowed an explicit doubt about the validity of what she is 'seeing': 'She saw her [Maggie] —or believed she saw her—look at her chance for straight denunciation, look at it and then pass it by'.[2] Even more significantly, Maggie herself is allowed a spasm of self-doubt—or rather two spasms—as radical and portentous as that of the governess in *The Turn of the Screw* asking herself at a crucial point in the story, 'If he *were* innocent, what then on earth was I?'[3] Maggie's moment comes in the same scene on the terrace with Charlotte. As Charlotte is approaching her, she 'literally' catches herself 'in the act of dodging and ducking', and recognises 'vividly, in a single word, what she had all along been afraid of'—that Charlotte might go to Adam, tell him openly about Maggie's suspicions of her, and convince Adam that they were wickedly false:

[1] *The Golden Bowl*, II, v. 2, p. 215. [2] *Ibid.* II, iv, 9, p. 143.

[3] See ch. IV, p. 134 and ch. VI, p. 185 above.

Such a glimpse of her [Charlotte's] conceivable idea . . . opened out wide as soon as it had come into view; for if so much as this was still firm ground between the elder pair [Charlotte and Adam], if the beauty of appearances had been so consistently preserved, it was only the golden bowl as Maggie herself knew it that had been broken. The breakage stood not for any wrought discomposure among the triumphant three—it stood merely for the dire deformity of her attitude toward them.[1]

It is this fear that decides Maggie that she must 'of her own prudence' persuade Charlotte to believe that she has no quarrel with her; and so, 'with a rare contraction of the heart', she proceeds to do.

It is true that we have in *The Golden Bowl* the kind of 'check' that was completely absent in *The Turn of the Screw*: we have actually seen the Prince and Charlotte together at Matcham (and at Portland Place when they passionately seal their pledge[2]), and there can accordingly be no doubt about the adultery—as there could be a doubt in *The Turn of the Screw* about whether the children in fact saw the apparitions of the dead servants and had any relations with them. But there can still be a doubt about Maggie's moral attitude to what has happened, and about her view of its moral consequences. Is it really as wicked and destructive (a 'wrought discomposure') as it appears to her to be; or is this merely an illusion induced principally by her desire to get her husband back from Charlotte and ensure her own happiness ('the golden bowl as she herself knew it')? The emphasis in what follows on the 'prudence' of her lying to Charlotte in order to prevent her from going to Adam makes it clear that the ambiguity is intended to put Maggie's motive in doubt; and since the most ambiguous passages in the book do impugn precisely Maggie's motive (and Adam's), it is consistent that her moment of self-doubt should turn upon this.[3]

[1] *The Golden Bowl*, II, v, 2, p. 212.

[2] P. 289 above.

[3] There is a seemingly similar moment earlier in the Second Book which, however, is not quite the same, and is in any case much less explicit. It occurs in the scene between Maggie and the Prince which follows the breaking of the

The Golden Bowl abounds in dialogues as impenetrably ambiguous as those of *The Turn of the Screw* and *The Sacred Fount*. There is, for instance, Maggie's conversation with her father on their walk in Regent's Park soon after the Matcham episode when she is at the peak of her terror about his coming to 'know' what he must on no account know. Again and again Adam makes a remark or rejoinder that could mean that he does know 'everything', yet could also be perfectly innocent; Maggie as the scene advances chooses more and more, by reasonings often remarkably circuitous, to interpret everything he says as a sign that he does know; and we are left with no key to the true state of affairs.[1] The same is true of that other crucial talk between Maggie and her father in the garden at Fawns. Again everything Adam says may mean nothing more than it appears to, or it may mean all that Maggie reads into it; and again the reader is left with nothing conclusive to tip the scales either way—except the fact that Adam, in this instance as in the other, in fact does what Maggie wants him to. But though these acts—the cancellation of the holiday in Spain and the return to America with Charlotte—visibly happen, they are no conclusive proof of Adam's having known what Maggie supposes him to know; and the more so since it is an important part of their ambiguity that we are in both instances

golden bowl, when the Prince says to her 'You've never been more sacred to me than you were at that hour—unless perhaps you've become so at this one' (II, iv, 10, p. 176. Cp. p. 292 above). Upon this follows the passage: 'The assurance of his speech, she could note, quite held up its head in him; his eyes met her own so for the declaration that it was *as if something cold and momentarily unimaginable breathed upon her, from afar off, out of his strange consistency*. She kept her direction still however under that.' The italicised words seem to suggest that she has a momentary doubt, very chilling to her, about the validity of the conclusions she has drawn from what the antiquary told her, which she is at that moment imparting to the Prince. If this is what the words mean (and if they do not, it is difficult to know what they do mean), the 'doubt' would clearly not be of the same radical kind as the one cited above. For we know that the Prince's 'strange consistency' is due to his never 'really' having cared for Charlotte (see pp. 291–3 above); and since Maggie does not at this stage know it, there is no ambiguity here of the kind we are examining, but only straightforward dramatic irony.

[1] *The Golden Bowl*, II, iv, 5, pp. 77 ff.

uncertain whether Adam made his decision independently (as Maggie believes) or whether Maggie, however 'unconsciously', put the idea into his head, and he, being the devoted father he was, responded to her suggestion. (In the talk in the garden, for instance, is it really Adam who first thinks of returning to America—or is it Maggie who insinuates the idea into his mind by first mentioning American City?) [1]

The most interesting and most baffling ambiguities, however, are those which bear on the question of the Ververs' motives. Again and again in the Second Book, as we listen to Maggie and her father talking about Charlotte or the Prince, or themselves in relation to either or both, the question arises, often very insistently: Are they really as 'good' as everyone—the Prince, Charlotte, Fanny Assingham—says they are? Are their motives as disinterested as the others seem to assume, and they themselves certainly believe? What, for instance, are we to make of their attitude to Charlotte, with its constant and seemingly shameless emphasis on her 'usefulness' to them? In the talk in Regent's Park, they touch on the question of their returning to Fawns. Maggie asks, 'Is Charlotte really ready?' and Adam answers,

> 'Oh if you and I and Amerigo are. Whenever one corners Charlotte . . . one finds that she only wants to know what *we* want. Which is what we got her for!'
>
> 'What we got her for—exactly!' [Maggie answers] [2].

Later, in a conversation with Fanny Assingham, Maggie has a momentary inkling of the kind of cruelty it might have been to Charlotte to know that Adam had 'got her in' chiefly for the sake of her, Maggie's, happiness; but she repudiates it as a serious criticism of Adam almost as soon as it occurs to her.[3] In the garden at Fawns, again, when her father announces his decision to return to America, Maggie for a moment has a vision of Charlotte 'removed, trans-

[1] *The Golden Bowl*, II, v, 3, p. 238.

[2] *Ibid.* II, iv, 5, p. 83.

[3] *Ibid.* II, iv, 9, pp. 150, 152–4.

ported, doomed'; [1] and soon after this, when her compassion for Charlotte leads her in imagination to beg her father to desist from his 'punishment', we have this extraordinary imagined conversation between the daughter and the father:

> The high voice [Charlotte's] went on; its quaver was doubtless for conscious ears only, but there were verily thirty seconds during which it sounded, for our young woman, like the shriek of a soul in pain. Kept up a minute longer it would break and collapse—so that Maggie felt herself, the next thing, turn with a start to her father. 'Can't she be stopped? Hasn't she done it *enough*?' Some such question she let herself ask him to suppose in her. Then it was that, across half the gallery—for he had not moved from where she had first seen him—he struck her as confessing, with strange tears in his own eyes, to sharp identity of emotion. 'Poor thing, poor thing'—it reached straight—'*Isn't* she, for one's credit, on the swagger?' After which, as, held thus together they had still another strained minute, the shame, the pity, the better knowledge, the smothered protest, the divined anguish even, so overcame him that, blushing to his eyes, he turned short away.[2]

On the view of Adam as the figure of the Just God administering a just punishment,[3] the passage makes reasonably coherent sense. The 'strange tears' in Adam's eyes and the 'sharp identity of emotion' would refer to the peculiar intimacy of his relation with Maggie; the 'shame' would presumably be Charlotte's shame, the 'pity' would be for Charlotte (or perhaps the pity of her condition—oh, the pity of it), the 'protest' that is smothered and the 'anguish' he divines would again be Charlotte's, and the 'better knowledge' (of the reality of her condition perhaps) would be his. But the alternative interpretation presses hard here: that the 'shame' is Adam's; that, having divined Charlotte's 'anguish', he recognises (and Maggie recognises with him) that his punishment of Charlotte is shamefully cruel; and that this is the 'better knowledge' which causes him to 'blush to the eyes'.

The question is raised again, for the last time and most

[1] *The Golden Bowl*, II, v, 3, p. 239. [2] *Ibid.* II, v, 4, p. 257.
[3] P. 286 above.

acutely, by the exchange between Maggie and her father when he and Charlotte come on their final visit to Portland Place before their departure. I have already indicated[1] the interpretation that seems to me consistent with the redemptive theme of *The Golden Bowl*; and I will have something more to say about it presently. Granted that this is one valid account, the ambiguity nevertheless leaves the way open for the alternative interpretation which unsympathetic readers of *The Golden Bowl* have not hesitated to give. As Maggie and her father stand on the balcony looking into the room where Charlotte and the Prince are talking together for the last time, the Ververs' 'collectors'' view of them is heavily emphasised:

> The two noble persons seated in conversation and at tea fell thus into the splendid effect and the general harmony: Mrs Verver and the Prince fairly 'placed' themselves, however unwittingly, as high expressions of the kind of human furniture required esthetically by such a scene. The fusion of their presence with the decorative elements, their contribution to the triumph of selection, was complete and admirable; though to a lingering view, a view more penetrating than the occasion really demanded, they also might have figured as concrete attestations of a rare power of purchase. There was much indeed in the tone in which Adam Verver spoke again, and who shall say where his thought stopped? '*Le compte y est.* You've got some good things.' Maggie met it afresh—'Ah, don't they look well?'[2]

Presently when Adam says of Charlotte, 'She's beautiful, beautiful', Maggie detects in this 'the note of possession and control'; and when at the end she says 'It's success, father' and he answers 'It's success',[3] the reader is meant to see that it might be one of two kinds of success—either the good and noble kind consistent with the redemptive theme, or a success fundamentally power-seeking and acquisitive, and not the more attractive for its admixture of self-righteousness.

[1] Pp. 309–10 above. [2] *The Golden Bowl*, II, vi, 3, pp. 317–18.
[3] *Ibid.* II, vi, 3, p. 322.

The ambiguities bearing on Maggie's relation to the Prince are equally striking; and the question they repeatedly raise is whether Maggie's motives are as selfless as she herself and everyone else (including the Prince) believes them to be, or whether there is not a strong taint of selfishness, indeed of greed and possessiveness, in her determination to separate him from Charlotte and draw him back to herself. In an earlier section [1] I suggested an account of Maggie's selfishness compatible with her role as scapegoat and redeemer in James's fable of salvation; but again, as in all the other instances I have cited, the ambiguities are so striking and so consistent that it is impossible to suppose that James did not intend the alternative meanings to be taken seriously. Soon after the Matcham episode, for instance, when Maggie is being the princess for the first time in her life, Fanny Assingham notes her 'blameless egoism' in 'using' them, the Assinghams, to capacity, and finds her 'as hard . . . in spite of her fever as a little pointed diamond' showing 'something of the glitter of consciously possessing the constructive, the creative hand'. [2] That the egoism is 'blameless' is Fanny's view, and since her view, like everyone else's in the book, is necessarily partial, the reader is invited to wonder whether it is in fact correct. The same is true of Maggie's declaration to Fanny at Fawns that the Prince now understands what she wants. 'I want happiness without a hole in it big enough for you to poke in your finger . . . The golden bowl—as it *was* to have been. The bowl with all our happiness in it. The bowl without the crack', she says; [3] and here it is the assurance of the tone and the inflexibility of purpose it expresses that creates the ambiguity. It is the same again in all the scenes between Maggie and the Prince himself, where there is always a phrase or tone or emphasis to raise a similar doubt, right up to the last scene and the last lines of the book.

[1] Pp. 282–4 above. [2] *The Golden Bowl*, II, iv, 8, p. 128. Cp. the narrator in *The Sacred Fount*, ch. VI, pp. 184–5 above. [3] *Ibid.* II, v, 1, p. 191.

'I see nothing but *you*', says the Prince on the closing page; and upon this follow the lines:

And the truth of it had with this force, after a moment, so strangely lighted his eyes that as for pity and dread of them she buried her own in his breast.[1]

Mr R. P. Blackmur sees in these lines 'a shade embracing a shade . . . in the shades of poetry', and is convinced that Maggie 'under the presidency of [her] goodness, the sovereignty of her love, and the tyranny of her conscience' has in fact effected the 'break-down' of the other three, the Prince, Charlotte and Adam—though (Mr Blackmur adds) this destructive outcome of Maggie Verver's efforts 'is all the nearer to reality because it is protected and sustained by the cover of manners, by the insistence on equilibrium, the preservation of decorum'.[2] If the account of the redemptive theme of *The Golden Bowl* set out in the previous chapter is correct, Mr Blackmur's 'break-down' theory, if not false, is not the only possible interpretation; and the same is true of his interpretation specifically of the 'pity' and 'dread' in the last lines. For he appears not to have taken into account what there is in this last passage to link it intimately with the redemptive theme. Since immediately before this we have been told that Maggie, as the Prince re-enters the room and advances towards her, is 'charged with a new horror' at the thought that he might want, or feel obliged, to 'confess' to her, the pity and the dread in the last lines may surely be taken to refer to this—to the confession and repentance implied in his 'I see nothing but *you*' (no longer Charlotte but only 'you', Maggie), and in the light that 'the truth of it'—that is, the 'confessional' implication of now seeing only her—kindles in his eyes. If we recall the other crucial places in the story where Maggie has been shown to have the same impulse to 'spare' the Prince,[3] it need cause no surprise that James

[1] *The Golden Bowl*, II, vi, 3, p. 325.

[2] R. P. Blackmur, Introduction to *The Golden Bowl* pp. xx–xxi (Grove Press, New York 1952).

[3] Pp. 273–5 above.

should have chosen to emphasise this again in the closing scene as the supreme expression of the moral beauty of his heroine.

Nevertheless, as in all the other instances I have cited, the 'pity and dread' does admit of an alternative interpretation; the ambiguity here does therefore at least give colour to Mr Blackmur's interpretation, just as the ambiguities in *The Turn of the Screw* and *The Sacred Fount* gave colour to Mr Wilson's; and if it is correct to suppose that all this is perfectly deliberate—that James, so far from being 'unconscious' of the ambiguity (as Mr Wilson supposed), has deliberately put it there to ensure just such a double reading of some of the most crucial passages—it becomes necessary to find an explanation of the ambiguity compatible with the various themes of *The Golden Bowl* discussed in these chapters, and in particular the redemptive theme.

The explanation has in fact already been touched on. The ambiguity is perhaps best defined as a huge, elaborate metaphor for James's experience of the unavoidable, unalterable mixed motive of all human action, and the consequent dual ('ambiguous') character of all human endeavour. The selfless motive is inseparable in experience from the selfish, the beneficent action from the acquisitive, the courage and intelligence of love from the cravenness of fear, the beauty of good faith and good will from the meanness of moral evasion and the cruelty of sexual power. Nor are they merely conjoined but rather causally connected: the good is somehow the result of evil, the base is somehow a necessary condition of the noble—is, indeed, the very soil from which it springs and in which it is nurtured. If Maggie Verver had not wanted the Prince, passionately and possessively, she would have had no motive for undertaking her redemptive task with all its terrifying difficulties. If the Prince had not wanted the ease and freedom supplied by Adam Verver's money, he would have had no motive for acquiring the moral sense he lacked;

if Charlotte likewise had not wanted the security from loneliness and want, the status and opportunities provided by her position as Adam Verver's wife, she would never have consented to go to American City and so would have missed her finest opportunity for the exercise of her 'greatness'. As for Adam Verver: if Adam had not been passionately acquisitive, he would not have made his millions; if he had not made his millions, he would not have had his limitless power at once to bestow benefits upon the three souls in his care and to exact submission or 'obedience' from them to the conditions of the gift; while they—Maggie equally with the Prince and Charlotte—would have had no motive for wanting to stay in his 'boat', nor therefore for making themselves, in their various ways, good enough to stay in it; and Henry James in that case would have had no story to tell.

To recognise this interdependence in human life of the good and the evil, the noble and the base, the beautiful and the sordid, is by itself perhaps no special distinction; there is no great novelist or dramatist who has not recognised it and attempted to render it in his art. James's distinction is that he invented a literary technique, the late style, which enabled him to render his sense of the fusion, or rather fusedness, of these co-existent and interdependent elements with a peculiar immediacy. In James's works the double aspect of everything in human life is never described or analysed or commented upon or in any manner directly treated. It is projected by the late style itself in a strictly poetic and dramatic mode—'enacted' in such a way as to make the experience of the fusedness directly accessible to us; and here James's achievement has no parallel in that of any other novelist, nor indeed anywhere in European literature except perhaps in the early Socratic dialogues of Plato and in Shakespeare's mature drama.

Recalling the pervasive Jamesian irony in *The Golden Bowl* and how it is directed equally against the 'good' Ververs and the 'bad' Prince and Charlotte; and having in mind the significant change in the tone and mood of the irony between the First and Second Books—how it is comparatively light, even light-hearted, in the First, but in the Second grows steadily grimmer and harsher until it reaches a peak of savage 'unpleasantness' in the scenes relating to Charlotte—we ought to have no difficulty in discerning the profoundly pessimistic side of James's vision. 'Everything is terrible, *cara*—in the heart of man', says the Prince to Maggie near the end of the story; and this sentence might be the epigraph for that side of *The Golden Bowl* which relates it to the prophetical book of the Old Testament from which the title is taken. The blandness of the Jamesian manner does not (and is not meant to) obscure the bitterness; on the contrary, it intensifies it. When Adam Verver in his loving daughter's imagination is allowed to make his savage comments on Charlotte's tormented state in the coolest, most matter-of-fact tones, what this signifies is not the brutality or diabolism of Adam Verver but the grief of Henry James, speaking through his vessel of consciousness Maggie Verver, at all that is terrible in the heart of man. Oh, the pity of it, and the horror: that the wages of sin should by their nature be so desolating; that the execution of justice should by its nature be so merciless; that pride and fear, the first so wicked and the second so mean, should be the only ground of salvation for those who cannot be saved by love; that the cost of salvation in this world, the cost in pain, terror and humiliation, should be so bitterly heavy.

This is how the dominant mood and tone of the Second Book of *The Golden Bowl* are linked with those of Ecclesiastes. The possible reasons, in James's personal life and his life as an artist, for their presence in the latest of his late works are to be briefly considered in the next chapter [1]. Meanwhile, it remains to add that the Jamesian pessimism is, of course, only one side of the picture. The other is the faith, hope and charity embodied in the story of Maggie Verver's triumphant

[1] Ch. x, pp. 349 ff. below.

work of redemption; and viewed from this aspect, the scene in the last chapter, in which Maggie and her father stand together on the balcony looking at 'the two noble persons' inside, brings together in a grand recapitulation all the components of James's complex vision. If Charlotte and the Prince 'might have figured as concrete attestations of a rare power of purchase', if Adam Verver can say to Maggie '*Le compte y est.* You've got some good things', and Maggie can answer 'Ah, don't they look well', it is because the acquisitive passion in Adam was from the beginning, and remains to the end, the source of the limitless wealth which is the foundation of his limitless power, which in turn was the ground of their salvation. If when Adam says of Charlotte 'She's beautiful, beautiful', and Maggie detects in this 'the note of possession and control', the point again is that power by definition implies these qualities, and without Adam's possession and control of his vast resources they would all have been lost. Finally when Maggie, rejoicing at the knowledge that Charlotte 'wasn't to be wasted', says 'It's success, father' and he answers 'It's success', they are summing up in that phrase the whole story of the redemption that has been accomplished, by love where that was possible, by justice where love was rendered inoperative by pride and fear. The 'pessimism' is there, in the unforgettable knowledge of the price that has had to be paid—Maggie's suffering, Charlotte's, the Prince's; the 'optimism' is there, in the faith that the good can nevertheless be affirmed so long as there are people willing to pay in suffering. And that is why they all emerge more wonderful and prodigious at the end than they were at the beginning. For each (to adapt a famous formula) has contributed according to his means and has received back according to his need. Adam has given his power and wisdom; Maggie has given her love, informed by intelligence and sustained by courage; the Prince has given his good faith; Charlotte has given her pride (her 'greatness'). Between them they *have* in the end succeeded: in restoring the dignities, decencies and serenities of their common life, which figure the harmony and stability of the universal moral order; and in finding their individual salvation within that larger restoration.

To say this, however, is not to say that the pessimism is cancelled out by the faith and hope, or by the 'success' that in the end crowns them. Tempting as this conclusion may be, especially to those who find in James's handling of the redemptive theme in *The Golden Bowl* the supreme achievement of his mature genius, what forbids it is precisely the ambiguity. Even as we listen again to Maggie's last dialogue with her father, and presently to Maggie's with the Prince in the moment of their ultimate reunion, the Jamesian ambiguity is persistently, relentlessly, impenetrably there. Certainly each exchange could have the meaning consistent with the redemptive theme; and this would seem to argue the annihilation of all the pessimistic bitterness and horror. But it could also, and as consistently, have the other meaning. The 'high power of purchase' could as well signify nothing but the vulgar acquisitiveness of a vulgar American millionaire turned art-collector; the 'possession and control' could signify nothing but the passion of such a man for power, in this instance reinforced by complacency and a strong streak of (perhaps 'unconscious') sadism; and the talk about 'success' could be nothing but the gratification, vulgar or naive or both, of the simple but cunning American pair who have outwitted the two clever Europeans, and have succeeded in getting what they want while forcing the others to take what they are given. Again, in the last scene, the 'pity' and 'dread' with which Maggie buries her eyes in her husband's breast can mean what I suggested; but it can also mean what Mr Blackmur thought it to mean—that Maggie 'pities' the Prince because she knows that this moment marks his final subjugation to her moral 'tyranny', and 'dreads' her own remorse about what she had done, or the

Prince's recognition of his state of subjection, or perhaps both.

But it is not really a question of alternative meanings. The question is not whether the ambiguous passages *could* have the meaning consistent with the redemptive theme: they do have that meaning. Nor need it be asked whether they could have the meaning consistent with the bitter, pessimistic, all-is-vanity view: for they do have that meaning too. If the general hypothesis about the Jamesian ambiguity in *The Golden Bowl* advanced in this chapter is valid, its presence at these crucial points in the resolution of the drama can itself then have only one meaning: that, in Henry James's total vision, the sense of the grimness and bitterness of human life is inseparably fused with the sense of its beauty and blessedness; that neither cancels out the other; and that the ambiguity is intended to express this experience of their permanent, inseparable fusion.

CHAPTER X

THE BEEF AND THE LITTLE TARTS

In a letter to Mrs G. W. Prothero, written in September 1913, James charmingly indicates his own view of the relation between his novels and his tales. An earnest young man from Texas had, it seems, expressed to Mrs Prothero his desire to study James's works, and had appealed to her for help in compiling a reading-list. She had written to James about it, and he—'amused by the request', says Percy Lubbock—immediately sent off two alternative lists of the novels, the first more 'elementary', the second more 'advanced', adding the following comment on the tales:

> When it comes to the shorter Tales the question is more difficult (for characteristic selection) and demands separate treatment. Come to me about that, dear young man from Texas, later on—you shall have your little tarts when you have eaten your beef and potatoes.[1]

Since James distinguished fairly consistently between his shorter tales and his *nouvelles*, it may be presumed that the 'little tarts' do not include such works as *The Aspern Papers*, *The Turn of the Screw*, *The Beast in the Jungle* or *The Bench of Desolation*. It is interesting nevertheless that he should be so unequivocal about the relative importance and value of his novels and tales; and the critic ought no doubt to take this as a hint for the treatment of the tales. In proposing to discuss in this chapter some of the later tales and *nouvelles*, in particular the two collections originally published under

[1] *Letters*, ed. Lubbock, II, p. 345. The alternative lists of the novels are themselves interesting. The first consists of the following five works: (1) *Roderick Hudson*, (2) *The Portrait of a Lady*, (3) *The Princess Casamassima*, (4) *The Wings of the Dove*, (5) *The Golden Bowl;* the second—the more 'advanced'—of: (1) *The American*, (2) *The Tragic Muse*, (3) *The Wings of the Dove*, (4) *The Ambassadors*, (5) *The Golden Bowl.*

the titles *The Better Sort* (1903) and *The Finer Grain* (1910), I have accordingly a limited object in view. This is to indicate what has seemed to me to be their illuminating relation to the novels of the late period, and—with the later collection particularly in mind—to draw attention also to certain features of these stories which seem to link them with the harsher, grimmer, more pessimistic side of *The Golden Bowl* and thus to point the way to *The Ivory Tower*.

Generally speaking, the relation between these stories and the novels appears to be that of the sketch or study to the finished portrait. Again and again we come upon themes, characters, situations, 'ideas' recognisably similar to those we have encountered in the novels. But besides the difference in scale—which is, of course, microcosmic compared with that of the novels—the treatment in the stories is curiously different. In the first place, it is tentative, exploratory, 'experimental', and in that respect suggests the preliminary (or contemporaneous) sketch or study; in the second, it is remarkable for a directness and a degree of explicitness not to be found in the novels. It is as if James in his stories (though never in his novels) had consented, from time to time at least, to be so abject as to *state*; [1] and this, besides being a pleasure and relief in itself, provides valuable corroborative evidence of James's main preoccupations in the novels.

The stories in *The Better Sort* contain telling instances both of the overlapping of themes, situations and ideas and of the invaluable explicitness. This is evident, for instance, in the tone of the comments on London life and London society. In *The Awkward Age* and *The Wings of the Dove* the exposure of Buckingham Crescent and Lancaster Gate, we remember, owed its deadliness to the inexplicitness of the irony—its characteristic obliqueness and indirectness, its never being stated but always only implied. Here, on the contrary, we have the most explicit ironic references to essentially the same phenomena. In *The Beldonald Holbein*,

[1] Cp. p. 236 above.

for instance, we hear about the peculiar charm of scoring a personal triumph in 'our superior sophisticated world', ' "our set" with its positive child-terror of the *banal*' [1]; and in *The Tone of Time* the artist-narrator can marvel, after his second interview with Mrs Bridgenorth, at the typically 'London' manner in which 'everything was vivid between us and nothing expressed'.[2] The type of the handsome, serene, 'sublimely' egotistical London *mondaine*, drawn at full-length in Grace Brissenden in *The Sacred Fount* and Charlotte Stant in *The Golden Bowl*, frequently recurs in these stories. Mrs Cavenham in *The Special Type* and Lady Beldonald in *The Beldonald Holbein* are conspicuous instances: Mrs Cavenham, who can take Alice Dundene's extraordinary sacrifice as her due, accepting it with the best conscience in the world ('it put roses in her cheeks and rings on her fingers and the sense of success in her heart' [3]) and without so much as a flicker of recognition of the magnitude of the sacrifice, let alone any sign of gratitude; and Lady Beldonald, with her 'high serenity' and 'supreme stupidity', who cannot conceive of any interest that might be found in the wizened 'Holbein' face of her aged companion Mrs Brash, but the moment she recognises it and sees in the old lady a threat to her own social pre-eminence has no hesitation in getting rid of her. Again, in Lady Wantridge in *Mrs Medwin*, 'the hard depository of the social law', we recognise Aunt Maud Lowder in *The Wings of the Dove*—much simplified, of course, and drawn with crisp, cruel strokes more reminiscent of the brilliant thumb-nail sketches in *The Bostonians* than of the *pointilliste* portraiture of the later novels: 'She was no younger, no fresher, no stronger, really, than any of them; she was only, with a kind of haggard fineness, a sharpened taste for life, and, with all sorts of things behind and beneath her, more abysmal and more immoral, more secure and more impertinent'; [4] and Miss

[1] *The Beldonald Holbein*, pp. 355, 356.
[2] *The Tone of Time*, p. 456.
[3] *The Special Type*, p. 62.
[4] *Mrs Medwin*, p. 440.

Mamie Cutter in the same story, the expatriate American who fills the office of a kind of universal aunt to the tight little society dominated by Lady Wantridge, is a miniature Fanny Assingham in *The Golden Bowl* who, however, requires to be *paid* for her services.

Another, more striking, parallel in this collection of stories is that between the young couple in *The Papers* and Kate Croy and Merton Densher in *The Wings of the Dove*. Maud Blandy and Howard Bight distinctly do not belong to the Lancaster Gate *milieu*. They are poor obscure young journalists, who have to earn their living, are passionately ambitious for success and fame in the already ferociously competitive world of Fleet Street, and know London high-life only as potential material for their 'columns'. Yet poverty and obscurity, it seems, are relative, while the zest for life, especially in two gifted, ardent, adventurous young people, is absolute; and it is therefore not surprising that there should be a kinship between this Jamesian couple and the other. The opening sketch of the young lovers meeting for a meal at a 'small and not quite savoury pothouse a stone's throw from the Strand', takes us straight back to the atmosphere of the Kate–Densher relationship—its freshness, its ardour, its intelligence and good humour:

Their general irony, which they tried at the same time to keep gay and to make amusing at least to each other, was their refuge from the want of savour, the want of napkins, the want, too often, of shillings, and of many things besides that they would have liked to have. Almost all they had with any security was their youth, complete, admirable, very nearly invulnerable, or as yet inattackable; for they didn't count their talent, which they had originally taken for granted and had since then lacked the freedom of mind, as well indeed as any offensive reason, to reappraise. They were taken up with other questions and other estimates—the remarkable limits, for instance, of their luck, the remarkable smallness of the talent of their friends. They were above all in that phase of youth and in that state of aspiration in which 'luck' is the subject of most frequent reference, as definite as the colour red, and in which it is the elegant name for money when people are as refined as they are poor.[1]

This fine buoyancy sustains the story to the end, rising in pitch and volume as the satiric exposure of 'the papers' gains momentum, until in Howard Bight's merciless baiting of poor Mr Mortimer Marshal, who hungers and thirsts after publicity, it reaches a peak of the comic-diabolical which bears comparison in James's works with the wonderful comic-melodramic finale of *The Bostonians*.[2]

The deeper themes of the late novels are also clearly discernible, on a suitably reduced scale, in these stories. The problem of the artist's 'vision', for instance, and the price that has to be paid for it in 'feeling', which was the principal moral theme of *The Sacred Fount*, is repeatedly glanced at here. The narrator in *The Beldonald Holbein* seeks to excuse his passionate interest in the 'little wonderful career' of Mrs Brash on grounds recognisably similar to those of the narrator in *The Sacred Fount:* 'It's not my fault', he pleads, 'if I am so put together as often to find more life in situations obscure and subject to interpretation than in the gross rattle of the foreground'[3]; and another Jamesian narrator (in *The Special Type*) confesses himself to be 'a man habitually ridden by the twin demons of imagination and observation', and consequently always involved—always 'in' things, 'never—enough for his peace—out of anything'.[4] The authentic *timbre* of the voice of the narrator in *The Sacred Fount* is, however, best heard in two of the later stories, *Mora Montravers* and *The Velvet Glove*. Sidney Traffle, the Strether-like vessel of consciousness in *Mora Montravers*, reflects at the end of his great adventure on the gains and losses involved in the exercise of an 'imagination' like his:

He was asking himself . . . what would have been the use, after all, of so much imagination as constantly worked in him. Didn't it

[1] *The Papers*, pp. 77–8.
[2] *Ibid.* pp. 152–63.
[3] *The Beldonald Holbein*, p. 348.
[4] *The Special Type*, p. 57.

let him into more deep holes than it pulled him out of? Didn't it make for him more tight places than it saw him through? Or didn't it at the same time, not less, give him all to himself a life exquisite, occult, dangerous and sacred, to which everything ministered and which nothing could take away? [1]

The same conviction, only at a higher pitch, is expressed by the super-Jamesian author in *The Velvet Glove*. Having built as grandiose a 'palace of thought' about the handsome, distinguished young couple on the train from Cremona to Mantua as the narrator in *The Sacred Fount* had built about his two victims on the train to Newmarch, he recognises in this 'an inveterate habit of abysmal imputation, the snatching of the ell wherever the inch peeped out'—'without which' (he adds unrepentantly) 'where would have been the tolerability of life?' [2] And in an earlier passage the same Jamesian author proclaims, still more emphatically and sonorously, the supreme value of this habit of abysmal imputation—the marvellous flexibility, receptivity, negative capability it argues in its possessor, and the sacrifices, even to one's personal 'dignity', that it justly exacts from its votaries:

That was the disservice, in a manner, of one's having so much imagination: the mysterious values of other types kept looming larger before you than the doubtless often higher but comparatively familiar ones of your own, and if you had anything of the artist's real feeling for life the attraction and amusement of possibilities so projected were worth more to you, in nineteen moods out of twenty, than the sufficiency, the serenity, the felicity, whatever it might be, of your stale personal certitudes. You were intellectually, you were 'artistically' rather abject, in fine, if your curiosity (in the grand sense of the term) wasn't worth more to you than your dignity. What *was* your dignity, 'anyway', but just the consistency of your curiosity, and what moments were ever so ignoble for you as, under the blighting breath of the false gods, stupid conventions, traditions, examples, your lapses from that consistency? [3]

[1] *Mora Montravers*, p. 318.

[2] *The Velvet Glove*, p. 211.

[3] *Ibid*. pp. 206–7.

Advancing from *The Sacred Fount* to *The Ambassadors* and *The Wings of the Dove*, we find these stories full of echoes of familiar themes, characters and episodes. *The Special Type*, which turns upon a heartless scheme involving the sacrifice of one woman to ensure the happiness of another woman and her lover, can hardly fail to bring back to mind Kate Croy's diabolical scheme at the expense of Milly Theale—even though the diabolism here is mild indeed compared with that in *The Wings of the Dove*, and the rich refinements of motive completely absent. Again, in *The Story In It* a familiar note is heard in the concluding dialogue between the clever, worldly Mrs Dyott and her lover Colonel Voyt about poor lovely Maud Blessingbourne. Do they not find her 'charming' in almost exactly the way that Kate Croy found Milly Theale as charming as she was queer and as queer as she was charming? And—allowing for the difference in the degree of seriousness—is there not the same worldly cynicism mixed with admiration and 'compunction' in the Colonel's final comment on poor Maud's hidden passion for his own splendid person as there was in Kate's reaction to Milly's passion for Densher? 'Her consciousness', he tells Mrs Dyott, '*was*, in the last analysis, a kind of shy romance. Not', he adds 'a romance like our own, a thing to make the fortune of an author up to the mark . . . ; but a small, scared, starved, subjective satisfaction that would do her no harm and nobody else any good.'[1]

These, however, are fugitive echoes compared with the powerful reverberation of the *dénouement* of *The Wings of the Dove* which we find in the semi-apparitional story *The Friends of the Friends*. Here, as other critics have noted,[2] we have the curious situation of James's treating an almost identical idea, that of a man falling in love with the memory of a dead woman, as a quasi-supernatural phenomenon in the

[1] *The Story In It*, p. 387. Cp. ch. VII, p. 223 n above.

[2] F. O. Matthiessen, for instance, in his comment on the story in his edition of the *Notebooks* (p. 245).

story, as perfectly naturalistic (if not wholly natural) in the novel. Though the novel was published some six years later than the story, the *Notebooks* show that they were worked out more or less contemporaneously;[1] and this is only one instance of the evidence supplied by the *Notebooks* to support the view suggested earlier, that James's stories of this period (as of his earlier periods) often treat, on a reduced scale and with a tone and emphasis often interestingly different, a theme or situation or relationship developed on a more ambitious scale in one or more of his novels.[2]

The theme of '*Too late*', as James himself calls it—'of some friendship or passion or bond, some affection long desired and waited for, that is formed too late'[3]—is another important case in point. It is treated most fully in *The Ambassadors*, where the 'passion' and the 'bond' are extended beyond the purely personal relationship envisaged in the *Notebooks* to embrace a whole view of life, indeed a whole dimension of human experience; and here the pain of the loss and waste implied by the 'too late' experience—which the famous anecdote from which the novel sprang poignantly expresses[4] —is virtually annihilated by the redeeming power of consciousness. The two stories on the same theme, *The Beast in the Jungle* and *The Jolly Corner*, treat it in significantly different, though related, ways.[5] Allowing again—as one must all

[1] See *Notebooks*, pp. 169–74, 187–8, 231, 241–4.

[2] In James's earlier works, the relation of the 'international' stories—*A Bundle of Letters, An International Episode, Daisy Miller, Lady Barbarina et al.*—to the 'international' novels from *Roderick Hudson* to *The Portrait of a Lady* is the most obvious instance. In *A London Life* (a story of the 'middle' period) the relationship between Laura and her wicked sister Selina bears a recognisable resemblance to that between Nanda and her mother in *The Awkward Age*—with the characteristic difference that the story 'states' it with a directness and explicitness, indeed with a bluntness and violence, wholly absent from the novel.

[3] *Notebooks*, pp. 182–3.

[4] *Ibid.* p. 226.

[5] *The Friends of the Friends* is also, of course, in a sense on the 'too late' theme. To the extent that it does treat this theme, however, it treats it superficially and a trifle mechanically compared with *The Beast in the Jungle* and *The Jolly Corner*; what is really interesting in this story is, as I suggested, the connexion of the 'supernatural' part with the *dénouement* of *The Wings of the Dove*.

the time in these comparisons—for the difference in scope between even the most ambitious Jamesian *nouvelle* and a full-scale Jamesian novel, it is possible, I think, to see *The Beast in the Jungle* as a deliberately tragic version of *The Ambassadors*. Here the perfusive irony of *The Ambassadors* is completely absent; here the pain of the 'too late' experience is not annihilated, and John Marcher's final recognition of the loss and waste of a life not lived fails to be redeemed by the act of recognition; and the anguish and remorse he suffers in the moment of revelation at May Bartram's grave are, in a way virtually unique in James's writing up to this point, as painfully raw as they are in life itself.

Leaving aside the possible personal reasons for this departure from the normal mode of the late works, that the central experience of *The Beast in the Jungle* was perhaps nearer to a direct autobiographical experience than that of *The Ambassadors*, what is interesting again from the point of view of our enquiry is the relation of *The Beast in the Jungle* to *The Ambassadors* as the sketch to the final portrait.[1] What it suggests is that James, here as elsewhere, found it helpful to 'try out' an important theme first in a story or *nouvelle*, confining himself to a single personal relationship and a single central situation, and not hesitating to give the experience in a comparatively raw, crude state, before embarking on its definitive rendering in the novel. And if it may also be assumed that the experience was in a special sense personal or autobiographical, this procedure might well have served a double purpose: in the first instance that of mastering the experience in the purely artistic sense—exploring its possibilities, discovering its potentialities,

[1] *The Beast in the Jungle* and *The Ambassadors* were published in the same year (1903), and they appear to have been written practically simultaneously. The entry in which James first discusses the 'too late' idea is dated 5th February 1895 (*Notebooks*, pp. 182–3), the first entry about *The Ambassadors* starting with the Howells anecdote is dated 31st October 1895 (*ibid.* pp. 225–8); the scenario of *The Ambassadors* sent to his American publishers is dated 1st September, 1900 (*ibid.* pp. 370 ff.), the single full entry about *The Beast in the Jungle* 27th August 1901 (*ibid.* p. 311).

learning (in James's favourite phrase) to 'see all round it'; but also that of mastering it as personal, private experience—'writing it out of his system', as we say, purging himself of the personal private pain so that he might the better command the experience for the end of artistic creation.

The Jolly Corner, published in 1909, a full six years later than *The Ambassadors*, cannot of course be called a sketch 'for' *The Ambassadors*. But the internal evidences (and the fact that James put it in the same volume as *The Beast in the Jungle* and *The Friends of the Friends* in the New York Edition) sufficiently indicate that it is another rendering of the 'too late' theme.[1] Or rather, in this instance, of the almost-too-late theme: for here the hero's encounter with his apparitional *alter ego* has the effect of vanquishing it; and the work of redemption begun by his own courage in pursuing it and in the end meeting it face to face (this last act, one may suppose, a figuring of the cataclysmic moment of illumination in the quest for self-knowledge) is completed by the love proffered to him at the end by the woman whose faith in him through the years has been as steadfast as it was intelligent. *The Jolly Corner* accordingly is *The Beast in the Jungle* with a happy ending, so to speak: John Marcher is

[1] There are other external evidences, admittedly circumstantial, to suggest that *The Jolly Corner* may have been conceived, though not executed, very much earlier than its date of publication would lead one to suppose. Since this is one of the few stories James does not discuss at all in the *Notebooks* and since, Matthiessen tells us, James ceased to keep his *Notebooks* regularly only after about 1904, it is of course reasonable to conclude that *The Jolly Corner* was not conceived until well after the appearance of *The Ambassadors* in 1903. Yet the important entry about the too-late theme dated 5th February 1895 mentions as a possible story something very similar to that of *The Jolly Corner* (*Notebooks*, pp. 183, 184); and (more important) there are two references to it in the Notes to *The Sense of the Past* (*Notebooks*, pp. 364, 367) which draw attention to the resemblance between its ghostly apparatus and that of *The Jolly Corner*. These Notes were in fact not written until 1914; but we know that James had started *The Sense of the Past* as far back as 1900 (there is a long entry about it dated 9th August 1900) and dropped it as 'too difficult'; and it is this that has led me to think that the theme of *The Jolly Corner* may (like that of *The Golden Bowl* in the previous decade) have been present to James's mind as many as ten or more years before it was published—that is, at approximately the same time as *The Ambassadors*.

doomed because he learns too late that to 'live all you can' is in the end nothing but to give and to receive love; Spencer Brydon is saved because he learns the same lesson just in time. The emphasis in both stories is, I believe, on the power to receive love even more than the power to give it. For in James's gentle, gentlemanly egotists (Strether, Marcher, Brydon) the capacity merely to receive love would already by itself be a sufficient sign of renunciation of the false gods—the missions, ambitions, scruples and decorums—they have been pursuing to their ruin, and therefore the first sign also of their recognition of and submission to the law of love.[1] If this interpretation is correct, the morality finally affirmed in *The Jolly Corner* departs significantly from that affirmed in *The Ambassadors.* It repudiates the claim for the redeeming power of consciousness alone and proclaims instead the power of love as the ultimate redemptive force in human life; and in this it points directly towards James's last (and perhaps most poignant) story, *The Bench of Desolation*, in which the redeeming power of the mere capacity to receive love shows as the last flickering pin-point of light in the dark night of a world sunk in helpless, hopeless suffering.

The Bench of Desolation is the last of the stories in *The Finer Grain* (1910), the collection which, I suggested, is peculiarly related to *The Golden Bowl* and *The Ivory Tower.* What chiefly establishes the connexion is the prevailing mood and atmosphere of these stories, which strikingly resemble that of *The Golden Bowl*, in particular in the Second Book. The elements of harshness, grimness, pessimism—the Ecclesiastes note—that we discerned there are all here, only greatly intensified. Henry James's love and faith seem here, for the first time, to be seriously threatened by a

[1] Witness also the characters of the two women—both distinctly of the type whose genius is wholly for giving; the *dénouement* of *The Jolly Corner* (ch. 3); and the climactic scene in *The Beast in the Jungle* (ch. 4) when May Bartram rises from her invalid's chair, stands close to Marcher, and asks 'Don't you know—now?'

profound disenchantment with humanity and human life, verging sometimes on a positive repulsion for all that is vile in man; by an ever more aching sense of the waste and loss seemingly inseparable from human life, and of the price in human suffering that has to be paid for every creative achievement; and by an increasingly bitter consciousness of the quantity of moral *ugliness*—petty self-interest, heartlessness, meanness—in man's nature. In the end (as we see in *The Bench of Desolation*) the love and the faith prevail, but at an expense of spirit even greater than in *The Golden Bowl;* and the result is a collection of stories strangely unlike anything else James ever wrote.

The literary features of *The Finer Grain* are the index to the temper of these stories. The style is as 'late' as in all the works of the late period: if anything, it is 'later'—more elaborately circuitous, more tortuously qualified, more super-subtle in its distinctions, magniloquent in its eloquence, violent and melodramatic in its imagery than even in *The Ambassadors, The Wings of the Dove* and *The Golden Bowl.* But it is here no longer used, or used noticeably less than in the novels, for the end (to adopt James's own phrase) of 'some kinder, some merciful indirection'.[1] On the contrary, the uncharacteristic directness and explicitness we noted in *The Better Sort* is more marked than before; and so also is the rawness and bareness of the experience itself, which seems hardly to have been submitted to the operation of the Jamesian transmuting power but appears to be given to us straight from 'life'. Again, the ironic mode frequently here gives way to the frankly satiric, and the urbanity of tone to a sharpness, a harshness, a bitterness which suggests that the author is out to draw blood. Indeed, the total impression is that Henry James, for whatever reasons, is seeking a temporary relief or respite from the sustained effort of a creative lifetime to maintain that 'distance' from his life's experience which he knew to be the necessary condition of a perfected art.

[1] *The Wings of the Dove*, p. xxv.

He is, it seems, determined for once to let himself go—to speak his mind without any 'mere twaddle of graciousness' about those phenomena in the human scene that have thrust the iron into his soul; and he seems not to mind for once being a little crude to do it.

In two of the five stories, *A Round of Visits* and *Crapy Cornelia*, the phenomena in question are those features of the new America which he had found particularly repellent on revisiting his native land, for the first time in some twenty-five years, in 1904–5. The 'round of visits' is undertaken in New York by Mark Monteith, an American expatriate who has come back to America from Europe to find he has been defrauded of his 'poor dividends' by the dear friend, Phil Bloodgood, to whose care he had entrusted his property in his absence. In his anguish of spirit at 'the ugliness, the bitterness, . . . the sinister strangeness' of this betrayal, he longs for the comfort and relief of sharing his grief with another human being. But in the great heartless pre-occupied city (as James calls it in the *Notebooks* [1]) there is, it seems, no such human being to be found. He calls first on an old friend, Mrs Folliott, and is immediately precipitated into the 'vast rankness' of the New York hotel world:

> He threaded the labyrinth, passing from one extraordinary masquerade of expensive objects, one portentous 'period' of decoration, one violent phase of publicity, to another: the heavy heat, the luxuriance, the extravagance, the quantity, the colour, gave the impression of some wondrous tropical forest, where vociferous, bright-eyed and feathered creatures, of every variety of size and hue, were half smothered between undergrowths of velvet and tapestry and ramifications of marble and bronze. The fauna and the flora startled him alike, and among them his bruised spirit drew in and folded its wings.[2]

Mrs Folliott has also employed Phil Bloodgood as her agent but, having grown suspicious of him long before her friend Monteith, has managed to save most of her property. She

[1] *Notebooks*, p. 281. [2] *A Round of Visits*, p. 370.

too, however, has been defrauded of some ten thousand dollars, and in the half-hour that Monteith spends with her she talks of nothing but 'her peculiar, her cruel sacrifice', abuses Bloodgood with uninhibited zest, and shows too plainly that she has no inkling of Monteith's own view of the catastrophe. This, we learn, is as typically late-Jamesian a view of the horror attaching to an act of betrayal by a friend or kinsman as Maggie Verver's in *The Golden Bowl* or Gray Fielder's in *The Ivory Tower*:

It wasn't that he wished to be pitied—he fairly didn't pity himself; he winced, rather, and even to vicarious anguish . . . for poor shamed Bloodgood's doom-ridden figure. But he wanted, as with a desperate charity, to give some easier turn to the mere ugliness of the main facts; to work off his obsession from them by mixing with it some other blame, some other pity, it scarce mattered what —if it might be some other experience; as an effect of which larger ventilation it would have, after a fashion and for a man of free sensibility, a diluted and less poisonous taste.[1]

But Mrs Folliott has no conception of the way in which a man who has suffered an injury may yet feel himself to be his injurer's keeper; and the passage in which Monteith expresses his revulsion at her moral insensibility is in the violence of its attack and the 'roughness' of its tone as atypical of the master of the exquisite-ironic mode who wrote *The Awkward Age* and *The Ambassadors* as it is typical of the mood and style of these stories:

The rapid result of her egotistical little chatter was to make him wish he might rather have conversed with the French waiter dangling in the long vista that showed the oriental *café* as a climax. . . . She bewailed her wretched money to excess—she who, he was sure, had quantities more; she pawed and tossed her bare bone, with her little extraordinarily gemmed and manicured hands, till it acted on his nerves; she rang all the changes on the story, the

[1] *A Round of Visits*, p. 372. The close resemblance between the central act of betrayal in *A Round of Visits* and (according to James's Notes for this unfinished novel) in *The Ivory Tower* illustrates again James's habit of treating an important preoccupation first in miniature, so to speak, in a story and only afterwards *in extenso* in a novel.

dire fatality of her having wavered and muddled, thought of this and but done that, of her stupid failure to have pounced, when she had first meant to in season. She abused the author of their wrongs —recognising thus too Monteith's right to loathe him—for the desperado he assuredly had proved, but with a vulgarity of analysis and an incapacity for the higher criticism, as her listener felt it to be, which made him determine resentfully, almost grimly, that she shouldn't have the benefit of a grain of *his* vision or *his* version of what had befallen them. . . . She had, in a finer sense, no manners, and to be concerned with her in any retrospect was—since their discourse was of losses—to feel the dignity of history incur the very gravest.[1]

James returns to this question of manners 'in a finer sense' in *Crapy Cornelia*. There in Mrs Worthingham—another version of the Grace Brissenden–Charlotte Stant type, only without Charlotte's 'greatness' or Mrs Brissenden's vitality —the elderly hero, White-Mason, finds an absence of manners in a sense still finer than in *A Round of Visits*: the exposure accordingly is here even more plain-speaking and hard-hitting, and its tone even rougher and angrier. The special object of the attack is the distinctively 'modern' character of Mrs Worthingham's vulgarity. This James reduces to two fundamental features: first, the disposition to flaunt her 'advantages' in a way as heartless as it is cheap, second, the insatiable appetite for 'amusement' of the most superficial kind; and as one reads the scorching passage in which they are exposed, one is persuaded to believe that things really have grown worse even since Mr Longdon in *The Awkward Age* found Mrs Brook's modernity—so mild and decorous (and so engaging) compared with Mrs Worthingham's— more than he could stomach. White-Mason has perceived that Mrs Worthingham is 'frankly diverted' by his confusion at not having recognised his old friend Cornelia Rasch, whom she herself has been treating as if she were a mere piece of furniture in the room:

[This] was precisely an example of that newest, freshest, finest

[1] *A Round of Visits*, pp. 372–3.

freedom in her, the air and the candour of assuming, not 'heartlessly', not viciously, not even very consciously, but with a bright pampered confidence which would probably end by affecting one's nerves as the most impertinent stroke in the world, that every blest thing coming up for her in any connection was somehow matter for her general recreation. There she was again with the innocent egotism, the gilded and overflowing anarchism, really, of her doubtless quite unwitting but none the less rabid modern note. Her grace of ease was perfect, but it was all grace of ease, not a single shred of it grace of uncertainty or of difficulty—which meant, when you came to see, that, for its happy working, not a grain of provision was left by it to mere manners. This was clearly going to be the music of the future—that if people were but rich enough and furnished enough and fed enough, exercised and sanitated and manicured, and generally advised and advertised and made 'knowing' enough, *avertis* enough, as the term appeared to be nowadays in Paris, all they had to do for civility was to take the amused ironic view of those who might be less initiated.

He recalls that 'in his time' manners and morals were not quite so disconnected:

In *his* time, when he was young or even when he was but only a little less middle-aged, the best manners had been the best kindness, and the best kindness had mostly been some art of not insisting on one's luxurious differences, of concealing rather, for common humanity, if not for common decency, a part at least of the intensity or the ferocity with which one might be 'in the know';

and his bitterest censure is reserved for Mrs Worthingham's abysmal ignorance of these older, traditional values, which is all of a piece with her lack of manners in the finer sense:

Oh, the 'know'—Mrs Worthingham was in it, all instinctively, inevitably and as a matter of course, up to her eyes; which didn't, however, the least bit prevent her being ignorant as a fish of everything that really and intimately and fundamentally concerned *him*, poor dear old White-Mason. . . . That indeed—he did her perfect justice—was of the very essence of the newness and freshness and beautiful brave social irresponsibility by which she had originally dazzled him: just exactly that circumstance of her having no instinct for any old quality or quantity or identity, a single historic or social value, as he might say, of the New York of his already almost legendary past.[1]

These are some of the disillusionments connected specifically with the American scene; and they are only a special case of the deeper disillusionments, with human nature and human life itself, which these stories express with so much power and poignancy. The experience of the ultimate selfishness or self-centredness of human motive, already touched on in *The Golden Bowl*, is a subsidiary theme of *A Round of Visits* and the principal theme of *The Velvet Glove*. In *A Round of Visits* Monteith finds at last in Newton Winch the one human being to whom he can confide his secret sorrow. He had known him at Harvard Law School, and had found him then 'constitutionally common', 'powerfully coarse', and 'clever only for uncouth and questionable things'. He now finds him miraculously altered—'mysteriously educated', charming, refined, and (most remarkable of all) intuitively aware, it seems, of the sickness of soul that is oppressing his visitor. Monteith accordingly tells him all, and Winch's intelligent, sympathetic participation is a sweet balm to his wounds. Nor does he hesitate, with such a listener, to speak about his passionate concern for the friend who has betrayed him. The horror of Phil Bloodgood's situation revives for him in an image powerfully reminiscent of the images of pain in *The Golden Bowl*:

It was as if a far-borne sound of the hue and cry, a vision of his old friend hunted and at bay, had suddenly broken in—this other friend's, this irresistibly intelligent other companion's, practically vivid projection of that making the worst ugliness real. . . . A great rush of mere memories, a great humming sound as of thick, thick echoes, [rose] now to an assault that he met with his face indeed contorted. If he didn't take care he should howl. . . .[2]

The melodramatic climax breaks upon them soon after. Monteith notices an object on the floor, which Winch has been trying to push out of sight, and recognises it as a revolver;

[1] *Crapy Cornelia*, pp. 338–9.   [2] *A Round of Visits*, pp. 394–5.

and when Winch sees that he has seen it, he drops 'the dazzling glitter of intelligence' he had desperately been keeping up, and cries in anguish, 'I beg of you in God's name to talk to me—to *talk* to me!' The principal moral of James's tale emerges at this point:

> 'It's you, my good friend, who are in deep trouble' [says Monteith], 'and I ask your pardon for being so taken up with my own sorry business.'
>
> 'Of course I'm in deep trouble'—with which Winch came nearer again; 'but turning you on was exactly what I wanted.'
>
> Mark Monteith, at this, couldn't, for all his rising dismay, but laugh out; his sense of the ridiculous so swallowed up, for that brief convulsion, his sense of the sinister. Of such convenience in pain, it seemed, was the fact of another's pain, and of so much worth again disinterested sympathy! 'Your interest was then—?'
>
> 'My interest was in your being interested. For you *are*! And my nerves—!' said Newton Winch with a face from which the mystifying smile had vanished, yet in which distinction . . . still sat in the midst of ravage.[1]

The *dénouement* follows: Winch tells Monteith that he has been guilty of the same crime as Phil Bloodgood, but has 'stayed back to take it'; and Monteith now understands what has produced the transformation in Winch, and feels that 'nothing in life had ever been so strange and dreadful to him' as this perception. Within a few moments the police officers arrive and, as Monteith is opening the door to them, Winch shoots himself.

The treatment of the self-interest theme here is, in its miniature way, very close to that in the second part of *The Golden Bowl*. 'Of such convenience in pain, it seemed, was the fact of another's pain, and of so much worth again disinterested sympathy.' There is, in other words, no such thing as disinterested sympathy because human nature cannot, simply, afford the luxury. The power to give in weak, erring human beings is determined by the need to receive; plenitude is wholly dependent on penury, and penury alone yields

[1] *A Round of Visits*, pp. 401–2.

plenitude. If Newton Winch had not needed to listen, he would not have been able to meet so perfectly Mark Monteith's need to talk; and if Monteith had not so desperately needed to talk, he could not have met so perfectly Winch's desperate need to listen. The noble motive and the base are here, as in *The Golden Bowl*, shown to be correlative: one is the necessary condition of the other, each entails the other, neither exists without the other. If James in his original plan for this story had reason to fear that its moral would seem 'obvious and banal',[1] his fear ought surely to have been banished by the profound interest and value of the moral that finally found its way into it.

The Velvet Glove is perhaps best described as James's most deliberately anti-romantic story. It reminds one curiously of Shakespeare's 'bitter' sonnets; for though the treatment is ironical, the irony is not light-hearted but grim and saturnine —not the mood of 'My mistress' eyes are nothing like the sun' but rather that of 'Alas, 'tis true I have gone here and there And made myself a motley to the view'. An author, John Berridge, who (like most of the Jamesian authors in the later stories) is very distinguished and virtually unread, is approached by a dazzling young English nobleman at an evening party in Paris with the humble request to read and 'criticise' the unpublished novel of a dear friend. The friend turns out to be an exquisite French princess, a quintessential Princess Casamassima who, with striking success, stoops to conquer the poor author, and within an hour or two leads him, bewitched and bemused, into her motor to have supper at her house. The pages describing Berridge's transports at the imperious beauty, noble grace, Olympian freedom of the lovely lady, and his own dazed delight at being the object of her attentions, mark a fresh peak in the late-Jamesian baroque eloquence. But in the motor, alas, the base purpose of her attentions is disclosed: she wishes him to write a 'preface' for her book 'The Velvet Glove'—'a lovely, friendly,

[1] *Notebooks*, p. 281.

irresistible log-rolling preface'—which (she explains) 'would do so much for the thing in America'. As the terrible truth dawns on him, 'Where are we', Berridge in his torment asks himself, 'Where, in the name of all that's damnably, of all that's grotesquely delusive, are we?':

He felt the dire penetration of two or three of the words she had used; so that after a painful minute the quaver with which he repeated them resembled his drawing, slowly, carefully, timidly, some barbed dart out of his flesh. . . . It was as if she had lifted him first in her beautiful arms, had raised him up high, high, high, to do it, pressing him to her immortal young breast while he let himself go, and then, by some extraordinary effort of her native force and her alien quality, setting him down exactly where she wanted him to be—which was a thousand miles away from her.[1]

Ignoring her sad, bewildered protests (for she does not of course in the least understand why he will not do what she asks), he leaves her at the door of her house with a 'Good-night, Princess. I shan't see you again'; and in case she should afterwards think, or pretend to think, that he wouldn't write her wretched preface because he couldn't, or (worse) because he didn't 'like' her enough to do what 'any proper Frenchman, master of the *metier*, would so easily and gallantly have promised', he kisses her, passionately, violently, as she leans towards him through the open window of the car:

He uttered, in a deep-drawn final groan, an irrepressible echo of his pang for what might have been, the muffled cry of his insistence. 'You *are* Romance!'—he drove it intimately, inordinately home, his lips, for a long moment, sealing it, with the fullest force of authority, on her own.[2]

The 'live-all-you-can' theme of *The Ambassadors* dominates the opening section of this story. Berridge's reflections, for instance, on the splendid young Englishman who is engaging him in conversation are only a more explicit and more analytical statement of Strether's feelings about Chad Newsome, but with the edge of the criticism sharpened, and the note of nostalgia more open and unashamed:

[1] *The Velvet Glove*, pp. 232, 233. [2] *Ibid.* p. 239.

His *Seigneurie*, at all events, delightfully, hadn't the least real idea of what any John Berridge was talking about, and the latter felt that if he had been less beautifully witless, and thereby less true to his right figure, it might scarce have been forgiven him. . . . His right figure was that of life in irreflective joy and at the highest thinkable level of prepared security and unconscious insolence. What was the pale page of fiction compared with the intimately personal adventure that, in almost any direction, he would have been all so stupidly, all so gallantly, all so instinctively and, by every presumption, so prevailingly ready for? Berridge would have given six months' 'royalties' for even an hour of his looser dormant consciousness—since one was oneself, after all, no worm, but an heir of all the ages too—and yet without being able to supply chapter and verse for the felt, the huge difference.[1]

Then, when Berridge suspects that the young man will forget all about his gifted friend's book:

Such again was a note of these high existences—that made one content to ask of them no whit of other consistency than that of carrying off the particular occasion, whatever it might be, in a dazzle of amiability and felicity and leaving *that* as a sufficient trace of their passage. Sought and achieved consistency was but an angular, a secondary notion; compared with the air of complete freedom it might have an effect of deformity.[2]

But it is under the spell of the Princess that his sense of what he has missed is at its keenest. Oh, if *he* were an Olympian, he cries to himself, coming as near as Henry James probably ever came to a *trahison de clercs*:

He would leave his own stuff snugly unread, to begin with; that would be a beautiful start for an Olympian career. He should have been as unable to write those works in short as to make anything else of them; and he should have had no more arithmetic for computing fingers than any perfect-headed Apollo mutilated at the wrists. He should have consented to know but the grand personal adventure on the grand personal basis.[3]

When accordingly the promise of the single grand personal adventure on the grand personal basis held out by the Olympian princess is blasted by the abysmal vulgarity of

[1] *The Velvet Glove*, p. 207. [2] *Ibid.* p. 208. [3] *Ibid.* pp. 216–17

Amy Evans, author of 'The Velvet Glove', he laments his loss in words essentially the same as Strether's in Gloriani's garden: 'You *are* Romance . . . You don't need to understand. Don't attempt such base things. Leave those to us. Only live. Only be. *We'll* do the rest.'[1]

The passionate moment at the end, so rare in James's works, has the special poignancy of a last assertion of the will and the capacity to 'live'. Berridge–Strether claims the right to wrest a last remnant of a grand personal adventure on a grand personal basis out of the grotesque delusion from which he has just been awakened; and by the dignity, the confidence and the authority with which he claims it persuades us that he has succeeded in doing at least so much.

The kiss at the end of *The Velvet Glove* represents virtually the last flicker of the high-romantic, heroic, essentially youthful spirit that dominates *The Ambassadors, The Wings of the Dove* and (up to a point) even *The Golden Bowl.* In the remaining four stories there are no lovely princesses, no Kate Croys and Denshers, no Paris, no Matcham: the spirit of late middle age, subdued by the knowledge of its past failures and present infirmities, replaces that of youth; and the old Jamesian glamour evaporates in the light of a day as common as any to be found in the most strenuously naturalistic of his contemporaries.

We have already glanced at the un-Jamesian commonness of the women in *A Round of Visits* and *Crapy Cornelia*; we meet this commonness again in the Traffles in *Mora Montravers.* Sidney Traffle may by virtue of his consciousness be a near relation of Lambert Strether; but by virtue of his philistinism he is equally a near relation of Sarah Pocock. And his wife Jane is more bottomlessly bourgeois (the phrase James applied to Ibsen) than any figure yet encountered in James's works. Indeed, a key passage early in the story suggests a resemblance between her and the depressed,

[1] *The Velvet Glove*, p. 237.

deprived women in Ibsen—Aline in *The Master Builder*, for instance, or Ella in *John Gabriel Borkman*. As her husband tries, unsuccessfully, to make her understand Mora's complicated point of view about her 'elopement',

> He had felt how more than ever her 'done' yellow hair—done only in the sense of an elaborately unbecoming conformity to the spasmodic prescriptions, undulations and inflations of the day, not in that of any departure from its pale straw-coloured truth—was helped by her white invalidical shawl to intensify those reminders of their thin ideals, their bloodless immunity, their generally compromised and missed and forfeited frankness, that every other feature of their domestic scene had just been projecting for him.[1]

This sardonic, bitter-indulgent tone of a husband about a wife is something new in the Jamesian register. It remains the dominant note of the Traffles' relationship; and it is not dissipated but reaffirmed by the super-sardonic *dénouement*, in which Jane Traffle, having lost a niece because she had forced her to marry against her will, possesses herself of a nephew in the person of the niece's discarded husband, and contrives to turn this feat of self-contradiction into a subtle triumph at the expense of her husband.

If *Mora Montravers* has a little touch or taint of Ibsen, *The Bench of Desolation*, James's last *nouvelle*, is Hardyesque. For the first and only time since *The Princess Casamassima* the two principals are members of the wage-earning class. Kate Cookham, who strikingly resembles Arabella in *Jude the Obscure*, is a schoolteacher—this being, one must suppose, as close as James is able to approach to the Hardyesque barmaid;[2] Herbert Dodd keeps a small, shabby, unremunerative bookshop, and in so far as he loves his books, is sufficiently cultured, and thinks and feels sufficiently like a gentleman, he resembles his predecessor Hyacinth Robinson. But no American princess appears to rescue him from obscurity; and there are no anarchists to induce moral

[1] *Mora Montravers*, p. 250.

[2] She is, however, at one point described as looking like a 'vindictive barmaid' (*The Bench of Desolation*, p. 411).

conflicts of the kind productive of high tragedy. Herbert Dodd is doomed to remain obscure; his suffering is intense and protracted enough to be heart-rending but too blind and confused, too ugly and sterile, to be tragic; and his weakness, helplessness and hopelessness in the face of the disasters that successively overtake him rob him of any last claim to tragic stature.

It is a picture of human wretchedness and degradation such as is to be found nowhere else in James's works: a figuring of the bare pitiableness of man's condition unqualified by the smallest particle of dignity or beauty. And the language, we find, exactly matches the conception. The terrible Kate Cookham stands before Herbert Dodd threatening him with ruin 'in all the grossness of her native indelicacy, in all her essential excess of will and destitution of scruple';[1] and he in his turn fears that his face could never show her 'the quantity of hate he felt'.[2] When he presently woos Nan Drury he does it as 'a refuge from poisonous reality';[3] and though he finds solace in her pretty teeth and pretty eyes, he finds also that she has 'forms of speech, familiar watch-words, that affected him as small scratchy perforations of the smooth surface from within'.[4] Years later, when Nan is dead and he has been left to 'the worship of an absolutely unpractical remorse', he is haunted by the 'faint wail' of her life-long reproach: 'he seemed to hear it sound as by the pressure of some weak broken spring';[5] and when Kate Cookham returns—'a handsome, grave, authoritative, but refined and, as it were, physically re-arranged person'—he shrinks from her with repulsion, remembering that this was the woman 'the outrageous vulgarity of whose prime assault had kept him shuddering so long as a shudder was in him.'[6] The language, in short, is as harsh and strident, as uncompromisingly bleak and ugly, as the conception; and

[1] *The Bench of Desolation*, p. 409.
[2] *Ibid.* p. 411.
[3] *Ibid.* p. 419.
[4] *Ibid.* p. 421.
[5] *Ibid.* p. 430.
[6] *Ibid.* p. 438.

again there is nothing quite like it anywhere else in James's writing.

The *dénouement* is 'happy'—as happy as the case permits. It is a happiness that reinforces the sense of the pitiableness of man by reaffirming on the one hand his essential wretchedness, weakness and helplessness, and on the other the truth of the Gospel saying 'Blessed are they that mourn, for they shall be comforted.' The late-Jamesian view of 'self-interest'—that is, *need*—as the deepest spring of human relationships (which we noted as a major theme in *The Golden Bowl* and in the story *A Round of Visits*) here receives its definitive formulation. Herbert Dodd, sitting on his bench of desolation, has been resisting Kate Cookham's offer of her money and her love; but he knows (and she knows) that he must in the end capitulate. He knows

> that he wasn't really free [to choose], that this was the thinnest of vain parades, the poorest of hollow heroics, that his need, his solitude, his suffered wrong, his exhausted rancour, his foredoomed submission to any shown interest, all hung together too heavy on him to let the weak wings of his pride do more than vaguely tremble.[1]

This is King Lear, in the guise of a shabby broken little bookseller, saying 'I am a very foolish fond old man. . . . Pray you now, forget and forgive'; and Kate Cookham, who once looked like a 'vindictive barmaid', responds with the only form of Cordelia's tenderness that the situation admits of:

> He leaned forward, dropping his elbows to his knees and pressing his head on his hands. So he stayed, saying nothing; only, with the sense of her sustained, renewed and wonderful action, knowing that an arm had passed round him and that he was held. She was beside him on the bench of desolation.[2]

The student of Henry James will know that there were compelling personal reasons for the black mood of disillusion that appears to have overtaken him. The long-postponed visit to America was as exciting and stimulating

[1] *The Bench of Desolation*, p. 465. [2] *Ibid.* p. 474.

an experience as any he had been exposed to in his mature years; yet (we have learnt) a great deal of what he saw he found both disturbing and depressing in itself and personally desolating. For it could leave him in no doubt that the Old New York of his childhood and youth had become a part of the 'almost legendary past'; and for someone whose sense of the past was as intense and intimate as Henry James's, to be robbed in this way of a vital part of it was a loss indeed. Its full effects, however, appear not to have been felt immediately. *The American Scene*, written within a year of James's return to England, is dominated by the thrill, the excitement, the absorbing interest of it all; the other side, as if subject to a delayed reaction, is more slowly assimilated. He needed time, it seems, to absorb the shock and grasp the implications of all he had found painful and unpleasant in the America of 1904; and this side accordingly seeps slowly and only bit by bit into the writings of the next three or four years.

Then, within a few years of the American experience, came the failure of the New York Edition. It should not be difficult for an admirer of Henry James to imagine his disappointment and discouragement at the languid reception of the handsome 24-volume 'collective and revised and prefaced' edition of his works. Such a response indeed was by this time not new to him. He had already, in such stories as *The Middle Years* and *The Figure in the Carpet*, and most poignantly in *Broken Wings*, found occasion to lament the unresponsiveness of the reading public to the offerings of the serious artist. 'We're simply the case of having been had enough of', says Straith to Mrs Harvey in *Broken Wings*; and adds, 'No case is perhaps more common, save that for you and for me . . . it did look in the good time—didn't it?—as if nobody *could* have enough'.[1] By the time James was preparing the New York Edition his own 'good time' was already long since past, and the Prefaces are full of

[1] *Broken Wings*, pp. 140–41.

ironic references to the 'limp state' of the criticism of his time and the 'odd numbness of the general sensibility'.[1] When the expected blow fell, it could therefore not have surprised him; it could only have confirmed his certainty of having been had enough of; and since he was now in his middle sixties, the finality of the confirmation must have been depressing indeed.

James's sense of professional failure must accordingly have been especially acute in the years immediately preceding the publication of *The Finer Grain*. To this was added in these same years a sense of personal failure to which the autobiographical flavour of certain stories of this period—*The Beast in the Jungle*, for instance, *The Jolly Corner*, *The Velvet Glove*—seems to testify. The knowledge that he had not 'lived' all he could, the fear that he had perhaps sacrificed too much for the sacred end of art, the deeper fear that there might have been a sharp taint of egotism in the sacrificial business itself, appears in these years to have grown more and more oppressive, and the pain of 'too late' almost unendurable. The fears could, of course, have been exorcised and the sacrifice of 'life' at least partly compensated for by the miracle of a public recognition such as he confessed himself—in the Preface to *The Portrait of a Lady*, for instance—occasionally to have dreamed of. But this miracle did not happen; and the sense of personal failure, reinforced by the objective proof of professional failure in the fate of the New York Edition, may be supposed to have had a great deal to do with the nervous disorder to which he succumbed at the beginning of 1910, which for two wretched years virtually incapacitated him for serious work. The death of his brother William in the autumn of 1910—'the nearest and dearest friend of his whole life', Percy Lubbock calls him—no doubt prolonged this dark night of the soul, if that is what it was; and it was not until a year later that he was able to undertake the autobiographical

[1] *The Lesson of the Master* and other Stories, pp. xvii–xviii.

works *A Small Boy and Others* and *Notes of a Son and Brother*.

It is to be hoped that the later volumes of Mr Leon Edel's biography of James will throw some light on this mysterious nervous collapse, about which the biographical material at present available is on the whole unilluminating. Meanwhile, the bare fact that it happened, and that it should have happened at the time when James appears to have had most cause to feel himself alone and deserted of men, suggests a special connexion between the personal experiences of the years following the publication of *The Golden Bowl* and the experiences embodied in the stories in *The Finer Grain*. Without falling into the error of seeing them as wholly autobiographical, it is yet safe, I think, to postulate here a more immediate and intimate connexion between the man that suffered and the mind that created than even in the semi-autobiographical stories of the previous decade (*The Middle Years*, *The Figure in the Carpet*, *The Altar of the Dead*, *The Great Good Place*); and since in this respect too it is the only instance of its kind in James's works, *The Finer Grain* has, besides its intrinsic interest, also the value of rarity.

The main works that follow *The Finer Grain* are—besides the two unfinished novels *The Ivory Tower* and *The Sense of the Past* and the unfinished volume of autobiography *The Middle Years*—the two complete autobiographical works *A Small Boy and Others* and *Notes of a Son and Brother*. These, though in the first instance commemorative, are also works of art of the maturest Jamesian vintage; as such they form an integral part of the Jamesian *œuvres*; and along with *The Ivory Tower* and *The Sense of the Past* they testify as decisively as may be desired to James's remarkable powers of recovery. As one reads these works, one recognises that nothing, after all, has been lost in the abyss: neither the unquenchable energy of interest in the human scene, nor the faculty of appreciation, nor the passion for criticism and analysis, nor the tenderness, nor the 'amusement'; and the qualities of the spirit that Mr Eliot noted [1]—the precious 'reasonableness' and 'benignity', and the absence of any trace of 'violence' or 'bitterness'—shine again with all their old lustre. Henry James, true to his lifelong practice of converting every scrap of his life's experience into the material of his art, has once more and for the last time succeeded in 'using' to capacity his recent experiences of doubt, fear, disillusion and despair; and in thus using them, he masters them, and effects his restoration and recovery.

If an external proof should be needed of the perfection of the mastery and the completeness of the recovery, it is to be found in the letter James wrote to Henry Adams at the age of seventy, two years before his death. Besides other things, it proclaims his own triumphant survival of the ordeal of consciousness which he had explored with so much passion and so much art in the greatest of his works. It is dated 21st March 1914, and is James's reply to the gloomy letter Adams had evidently written him in acknowledgement of the copy of *Notes of a Son and Brother* he had sent him. It reads:

My dear Henry,

I have your melancholy outpouring of the 7th, and I know not how better to acknowledge it than by the full recognition of its unmitigated blackness. *Of course* we are lone survivors, of course the past that was our lives is at the bottom of an abyss—if the abyss *has* any bottom; of course, too, there's no use talking unless one particularly *wants* to. But the purpose, almost, of my printed divagations was to show you that one can, strange to say, still want to—or at least can behave as if one did. Behold me therefore so behaving—and apparently capable of continuing to do so. I still find my consciousness interesting—under *cultivation* of the interest. Cultivate it *with* me, dear Henry—that's what I hoped to make you do—to cultivate yours for all it has in common with mine. *Why* mine yields an interest I don't know that I can tell you, but I don't challenge or quarrel with it—I encourage it with a ghastly grin. You see I still, in the presence of life (or what you deny to be such), have reactions—as many as possible—and the book I sent

[1] Ch. 1, p. 2 above.

you is a proof of them. It's, I suppose, because I am that queer monster, the artist, an obstinate finality, an inexhaustible sensibility. Hence the reactions—appearances, memories, many things go on playing upon it with consequences that I note and 'enjoy' (grim word!) noting. It all takes doing—and I *do*. I believe I shall do yet again—it is still an act of life. But you perform them still yourself—and I don't know what keeps me from calling your letter a charming one! There we are, and it's a blessing that you understand —I admit indeed alone—your all-faithful

HENRY JAMES.[1]

[1] *Letters*, ed. Lubbock, II, pp. 373–4.

APPENDICES

APPENDIX A

TWO PROBLEMS IN 'THE PORTRAIT OF A LADY'

AT the end of Chapter II I suggested that there were two critical problems arising from the story of Isabel Archer which were important enough to require separate treatment. The first turned upon the question, Why does Isabel go back to Osmond?, the second upon James's treatment of the sexual theme in *The Portrait of a Lady*.

(1) WHY DOES ISABEL GO BACK TO OSMOND?

This problem has, I believe, been somewhat artificially created for modern critics by a failure in critical perspective which arises from the disposition to ignore or minimise the context, historical and dramatic, in which Isabel Archer's final decision is made. I have heard it seriously argued that Isabel 'could after all have done something else'—walked out into freedom (like Nora in *A Doll's House*, presumably), or gone in for charitable works (like Dorothea Brooke in *Middlemarch*), or even perhaps taken a degree and become a pioneer in women's education, or whatever. The short answer to these bracing proposals is that Isabel Archer could have done none of these things. Her circumstances, historical, psychological and dramatic—in particular the dramatic—absolutely proscribe any 'end' to her life other than marriage, and any duties, responsibilities or even serious interests other than those belonging to or arising out of that estate. This is part of James's *donnée* in the story; and to intrude other, extrinsic possibilities—or, rather, pseudo-possibilities—is to fall into a vicious abstractionism that is fatal to literary criticism.

This is the failure in critical perspective at its most elementary level. At a less elementary level, it springs from a preconception almost as intrusive and misleading as the other—namely, a disposition to take too emancipated a view of the marriage-bond and the 'naturalness' of divorce. Why did not Isabel divorce Osmond? is now the question; and the answer is that what we are shown of Isabel Archer's nature and of her view of marriage (as distinct from her modern critics') makes it abundantly clear that divorce would be for her the least natural form of deliverance from her predicament. Leaving aside the special motive for going back to Osmond provided by Pansy and Pansy's need of her, which is explicitly emphasised, we are expected to remember that loyalty or 'devotion' was a conspicuous element of Isabel Archer's nature. Gilbert Osmond, we remember, had recognised it from the beginning: 'I like her very much', he had said to Madame Merle, 'She's all you described her, and into the bargain capable, I feel, of great devotion'.[1] In Isabel's midnight vigil we have this confirmed in a particularly decisive (and moving) way when, reflecting on Osmond's hatred of her 'ideas', she calls her soul to witness that 'she had no opinions . . . that she would not have been eager to sacrifice in the satisfaction of feeling herself loved for it';[2] and this devotion or loyalty may be seen as a function of the moral consistency that springs so naturally, it seems, from her moral seriousness.

Her view of the marriage bond as in the highest degree solemn and serious is closely linked with it. Marriage for her is a complete commitment of one person to another, and as such not to be set aside even from the gravest causes; and though there is, of course, no suggestion of a Christian-theological sanction in the strict sense, it would nevertheless be true to say that Isabel Archer takes a 'sacramental' view of marriage, as a 'sanctified' union which is to be regarded as substantially indissoluble. In the earlier parts of the story, this is implicit in the exalted view she takes of her marriage to Osmond, and her faith in all that this most intimate of

[1] Cp. p. 55 above. [2] Cp. p. 49 above.

bonds can yield for the exercise of virtue as well as for personal happiness; in the later parts, it is several times explicitly mentioned as a prime reason for her reluctance to leave, or even to defy, her husband. Long before the end of the story, when her cousin Ralph Touchett is lying sick in his hotel in Rome, we learn that she is filled with 'shame' and 'dread' at the thought of deliberately flouting Osmond's wishes by going to see him:

She had not as yet undertaken to act in direct opposition to his wishes; he was her appointed and inscribed master; she gazed at moments with a sort of incredulous blankness at this fact. It weighed upon her imagination, however; constantly present to her mind were all the traditionary decencies and sanctities of marriage. The idea of violating them filled her with shame as well as with dread, for on giving herself away she had lost sight of this contingency in the perfect belief that her husband's intentions were as generous as her own. She seemed to see, none the less, the rapid approach of the day when she should have to take back something she had solemnly bestown. Such a ceremony would be odious and monstrous; she tried to shut her eyes to it meanwhile.[1]

She cannot indeed for long shut her eyes to it; for the crisis is precipitated soon after this when Osmond virtually forbids her to go to Ralph, now dying at Gardencourt. But though she does in the end defy him and go, she still, we learn, finds the ceremony 'odious' and 'monstrous'. She has gone to her room after the scene with Osmond:

It seemed to her that only now she fully measured the great undertaking of matrimony. Marriage meant that in such a case as this, when one had to choose, one chose as a matter of course for one's husband. 'I'm afraid—yes, I'm afraid', she said to herself more than once, stopping short in her walk. But what she was afraid of was not her husband—his displeasure, his hatred, his revenge; it was not even her own later judgement of her conduct—a consideration which had often held her in check; it was simply the violence there would be in going when Osmond wished her to remain. A gulf of difference had opened between them, but nevertheless it was his desire that she should stay, it was a horror to him

[1] *The Portrait of a Lady*, II, 45, pp. 215–16.

that she should go. She knew the nervous fineness with which he could feel an objection. What he thought of her she knew, what he was capable of saying to her she had felt; yet they were married, for all that, and marriage meant that a woman should cleave to the man with whom, uttering tremendous vows, she had stood at the altar.[1]

Isabel's deepest and most decisive reason, however, for going back to Osmond is to be inferred from those passages in her midnight vigil in which she comes to her painful self-knowledge, in particular the knowledge of the degree in which she herself has been responsible for Osmond's self-deception about her, and the extent therefore to which she has contributed to the failure of their marriage. ('She had made herself small, pretending there was less of her than there really was . . .'; 'Yes, she *had* been hypocritical; she had liked him so much', and so on.[2]) What she comes to feel is that, having this degree of moral responsibility, she must accept the consequences; and this means going back to Osmond and enduring, simply *enduring*, her life with him as the only expiation open to her. She never, of course, puts it to herself so explicitly; but she comes as near as she can to seeing it (and saying it) in a brief passage in her last reflections at Gardencourt, when she recognises once again that 'certain obligations were involved in the very fact of marriage, and were quite independent of the quantity of enjoyment extracted from it'[3]—and then acts on that insight.

The most explicit statement of this final position, however, comes from Osmond himself, in the bitter exchange between them when he forbids her to go to Ralph at Gardencourt; and it is like a last turn of the screw that she should have to take her most compelling reason for continuing in her wretched condition from the man who is its principal cause. The passage, though long, is worth quoting in full because, besides giving us the poignancy of Isabel's situation, it also

[1] *The Portrait of a Lady*, II, 51, pp. 315–16.

[2] Cp. p. 57 above.

[3] *The Portrait of a Lady*, II, 55, p. 368.

throws a last vivid light on Osmond's view of it, and shows us how the strange *sincerity* that lurks in his care for appearances has, more than anything, the power to break down Isabel's resistance. Osmond is speaking:

'I've never liked him [Ralph] and he has never liked me. That's why you like him—because he hates me,' said Osmond with a quick, barely audible tremor in his voice. 'I've an ideal of what my wife should do and should not do. She should not travel across Europe alone, in defiance of my deepest desire, to sit at the bedside of other men. Your cousin's nothing to you; he's nothing to us. You smile most expressively when I talk about *us*, but I assure you that *we*, *we*, Mrs Osmond, is all I know. I take our marriage seriously; you appear to have found a way of not doing so. I'm not aware that we're divorced or separated; for me we're indissolubly united. You are nearer to me than any human creature, and I'm nearer to you. It may be a disagreeable proximity; it's one, at any rate, of our own deliberate making. You don't like to be reminded of that, I know; but I'm perfectly willing because—because—' And he paused a moment, looking as if he had something to say which would be very much to the point. 'Because I think we should accept the consequences of our actions, and what I value most in life is the honour of a thing!'

Upon this speech follows the comment:

He spoke gravely and almost gently; the accent of sarcasm had dropped out of his tone. It had a gravity which checked his wife's quick emotion; the resolution with which she had entered the room found itself caught in a mesh of fine threads. His last words were not a command, they constituted a kind of appeal; and, though she felt that any expression of respect on his part could only be a refinement of egotism, they represented something transcendent and absolute, like the sign of the cross or the flag of one's country. He spoke in the name of something sacred and precious—the observance of a magnificent form. . . . Isabel had not changed; her old passion for justice still abode within her; and now, in the very thick of her sense of her husband's blasphemous sophistry, it began to throb to a tune which for a moment promised him the victory. It came over her that in his wish to preserve appearances he was after all sincere, and that this, as far as it went, was a merit. Ten minutes before she had felt all the joy of irreflective action—a joy to which she had for so long been a stranger; but action had been suddenly changed to slow renunciation, transformed by the blight of Osmond's touch.[1]

Isabel does go to Ralph, and to that extent does temporarily resist the blight of Osmond's touch. But his words, she presently discovers, have struck a deeper response in her than she knew at the time. What she finds in the end is that though she repudiates his reasons as blasphemous sophistry, the fact he insists on commands her most inward assent; and it is the fact that finally compels her to go back to him in despite of the reasons.

(2) THE SEXUAL THEME

To speak of James's 'treatment' of the sexual theme in *The Portrait of a Lady* would be virtually meaningless, but for the striking episode between Isabel and Caspar Goodwood in the very last pages of the book. Apart from the hint about the 'male' quality in Caspar Goodwood that troubles Isabel from the beginning,[2] there is, or seems to be, until this episode no reference to it either explicit or implicit; and if the sexual theme in *The Portrait of a Lady* were indeed to rest entirely on this episode it would seem hardly worth examining. This, however, is only apparently the case. The last encounter between Isabel and Caspar Goodwood is not only peculiarly significant in itself but also illuminates previous, less conspicuous, episodes bearing on the sexual theme; and by tracing these connexions one can, I believe, arrive at a reasonably complete view of James's treatment of this theme in *The Portrait of a Lady*.

The fact that in this last vivid scene Isabel should again and finally turn down Caspar Goodwood raises by itself no problem. As he kisses her, 'it was extraordinarily as if, while she took it, she felt each thing in his hard manhood that had least pleased her, each aggressive fact of his face, his figure, his presence, justified of its intense identity

[1] *The Portrait of a Lady*, II, 51, pp. 311–12.

[2] P. 34 above.

and made one with this act of possession';[1] and what this means is that Goodwood will no more 'do' now than he would have 'done' before she married Osmond. For he is still, in a word, too crude; and the fact that Osmond's refinement has turned out to be terrible delusion does not make Goodwood's lack of it any more acceptable. In this I think, we are meant to see a last proof of Isabel's ultimate integrity. Even in her misery and despair at the prospect of resuming her life with Osmond, her judgement in this vital connexion remains unimpaired: she knows that she ought not to give herself to Caspar Goodwood now any more than she ought to have given herself to Gilbert Osmond then; and this perhaps is part of what she has learnt from her disastrous mistake with Osmond.

What does raise a problem, however, is the kind and quality of the fear that Isabel appears to experience in this climactic episode. This is powerfully evoked by the sea-image[2] (more than sufficiently 'Freudian') which expresses it here. As Goodwood ends his passionate speech, she feels herself 'floating' upon a sea in an ecstasy of incipient surrender:

> The world . . . had never seemed so large; it seemed to open out, all round her, to take the form of a mighty sea, where she floated in fathomless waters. She had wanted help, and here was help; it had come in a rushing torrent . . . She believed just then that to let him take her in his arms would be the next best thing to her dying. This belief, for a moment, was a kind of rapture, in which she felt herself sink and sink. In the movement she seemed to beat with her feet, in order to catch herself, to feel something to rest on.[3]

Then he speaks again, in a voice 'harsh and terrible', and her sensation now is that of sinking: 'The confusion, the noise of waters, all the rest of it were in her . . . swimming head';[4] and as he kisses her ('His kiss was like white lightning, a flash that spread, and spread again, and stayed') and she is

[1] *The Portrait of a Lady*, II, 55, p. 381.
[2] *Ibid.* II, 55, p. 380.
[3] *Ibid.*
[4] *Ibid.*

seized with her final revulsion, this is succeeded by a sensation of drowning: 'So she had heard of those wrecked and under water following a train of images before they sink.'[1] The next moment the 'darkness' returns (after the flash of white lightning), and through it she speeds to 'freedom'—away from Caspar Goodwood, back to the house, and ultimately to Rome and Gilbert Osmond.

In a way unusual in James's works, the image here is left to express the whole meaning; there is none of the help so often provided by somebody's analytical comment or interior monologue; and this is significant not because the help is in fact needed but because it suggests on James's part a deliberate intention to leave as open as possible the question of the 'rightness' or 'wrongness' of Isabel's action. She is afraid—that is clear enough; but is she *right* to be afraid? Is she right in particular in view of what she herself has just a moment before recognised, 'that she had never been loved before'? This sensation, too, is conveyed by an image as violent as the white-lightning image of the kiss. Goodwood has ended his first speech with the question, 'Why should you go back—why should you go through that ghastly form?'; to which she answers,

> 'To get away from *you*!'. . . But this expressed only a little of what she felt. The rest was that she had never been loved before. She had believed it, but this was different; this was the hot wind of the desert, at the approach of which the others dropped dead, like mere sweet airs of the garden. It wrapped her about; it lifted her off her feet, while the very taste of it, as of something potent, acrid and strange, forced open her set teeth.[2]

So Isabel Archer knows she is being for the first time 'loved'; yet she resists it fiercely (it 'forced open her set teeth'), and finally flees from the love, the lover, indeed from the knowledge itself. What frightens and repels her is plain enough. It is the sheer violence of it—'the hot wind of the desert'; and this fear and distaste in Isabel of the element

[1] *The Portrait of a Lady*, II, 55, p. 381. [2] *Ibid.* II, 55, p. 379.

of violence in the passion of love has (we now remember) already shown itself before this. There is, for instance, a significant passage in the early scene of Lord Warburton's proposal in the garden at Gardencourt, to which we are sent back by the reference here to the 'mere sweet airs of the garden' which drop dead before the 'hot wind of the desert.' Warburton has told her he is 'a very judicious animal' and does not 'go off easily', but when he does it's for life:

> 'It's for life, Miss Archer, it's for life', Lord Warburton repeated in the kindest, tenderest, pleasantest voice Isabel had ever heard, and looking at her with eyes *charged with the light of a passion that had sifted itself clear of the baser parts of emotion—the heat, the violence, the unreason—and that burned as steadily as a lamp in a windless place.*[1]

Again, in an earlier passage, when Isabel dismisses Lord Warburton with seeming coldness, we are told explicitly that 'her coldness was not the calculation of her effect. It came from a certain fear';[2] and when, much later, she has a strenuous encounter with Caspar Goodwood in Florence and bursts into tears 'five minutes after he had gone',[3] the main reason for the tears is again, we may suppose, 'a certain fear'.

If from these episodes we may legitimately infer that Isabel Archer has a fear of sexual passion, particularly in its more 'violent' aspect, two questions arise: first, to what extent is this fear 'culpable' in Isabel; second, how conscious was James himself of its presence in his portrait of his engaging young woman, and if he was conscious of it, what view did he mean us to take of it?

That a young woman of Isabel Archer's sensibilities should, in that time and place in particular, feel a fear of the sexual need cause no surprise. Its mystery and terror is something that not only the young and immature experience;

[1] *The Portrait of a Lady* I, 12, p. 130. My emphasis.
[2] *Ibid.* I, 9, p. 100. [3] *Ibid.* II, 32, p. 45.

and only the most doctrinaire of modern theorists would want to dispute the naturalness of the fear, and to that extent also its 'rightness', in someone like Isabel. This, however, seems not to be the whole explanation. The rest has to do with what we feel in Isabel as a tendency to *withdraw*—a tendency to withold herself, to refuse to surrender herself to the relationship as a whole and *a fortiori* to its sexual demands. She herself appears to recognise this, or something like it, when she asks herself at the end of one of her agitating encounters with Lord Warburton 'if she were not a cold, hard, priggish person' to find herself so unable to accept a man of such splendid parts; and the question for us is whether this seeming coldness and hardness are due to what would nowadays be called sexual frigidity, or, if they are not due to this, what their cause in fact is.

I believe it has nothing to do with frigidity, either in intention or effect, and has everything to do with that aspect of Isabel's nature already touched on [1] which James himself saw as the centre of interest in his engaging young woman. When a young woman is so constituted as to have, besides an enquiring mind and an independent spirit, an unquenchable passion for knowledge derived from direct, first-hand experience, the most serious threat to such aspirations, especially in an earlier age than the present, is that constituted by marriage and the completeness of the surrender it involves—for someone at any rate who, like Isabel Archer, takes this absolute view of the marriage bond. With the 'right person,' as we say, there is of course no problem; and Isabel, we saw, joyfully embraced the opportunity to surrender herself to the right person when she thought she had found him in Gilbert Osmond. But the right person, never to be had for the wanting, was particularly not to be had for the wanting in the circle to which Isabel Archer's life was confined; her story amply confirms this—indeed is intended to exhibit this among other unalterable facts of her

[1] Pp. 42–4 above.

condition; and so long as there *is* a doubt that the person in question (Lord Warburton, Caspar Goodwood) is 'right', a young woman like Isabel Archer cannot be careful enough. The seeming coldness and hardness are accordingly to be seen as self-protective indeed; but the end for which the self is being protected is (James wishes us to see) in the highest degree noble and worthwhile, and as such invites not censure but compassion for the means—the 'coldness' and the 'hardness', and the fear from which they spring—to which Isabel must have recourse in order to safeguard that precious end.

This, I believe, is James's principal intention in emphasising his heroine's 'fear' at certain crucial moments in the story; and it is again characteristic of James's mastery of the psychological and dramatic verisimilitudes of these moments that Isabel herself should in each instance appear puzzled and confused about its meaning, and disposed therefore to put the least creditable interpretation on her own reactions. The problem that remains turns upon Isabel's revulsion from the 'violence' of the sexual passion itself, which is so clearly apparent in the final episode with Caspar Goodwood but (I suggested) is hinted at before. On the explanation I have proposed of Isabel's fear in general, it would presumably be justified on the ground that it is intrinsically incompatible with all that is *civilised* in the ideal that Isabel aspires to realise in her life. In that case, it would seem that the element of violence in sexual passion is being equated with the uncivilised or anti-civilised; and in the passages cited this indeed appears to be Isabel's attitude. In so far as it is only Isabel's attitude, there can of course be no quarrel with it. But in so far as it may also be James's own attitude, it is a cause if not for quarrel at least for further enquiry. For (as James himself is to show in some of the most important of his later works) the 'violent' element—the importunate, the wanting and desiring, jealous and possessive element—in sexual passion, so far from being incompatible with the perfection of civilised virtue, is in fact (as James is to show in *The Golden Bowl* in particular), the necessary condition of this, as of all, virtue; [1] and the question is whether James when he wrote *The Portrait of a Lady* knew what he later came to know, or whether he knew at this time as little as his heroine and consequently identified himself with her on this vital matter.

The internal evidences of the text suggest that the latter was the case—that James shared his heroine's fear of, and even revulsion from, the sexual passion in its more violent, importunate forms, and for reasons *mutatis mutandis* essentially similar to hers.[2] He, too, at this stage of his life felt it as a threat to the two things, one 'public', the other 'private' or personal, that were most precious to him—his ideal of civilisation on the one side, his aspiration to dedicate his life to the practice of his art on the other. Both ends, it would have seemed to him, were better—that is, more safely—

[1] See ch. IX, pp. 255, 282–4 above.

[2] The main external evidences to support this view are to be found in the curious letters, recently made available by Mr Leon Edel (in *Selected Letters of Henry James*, London 1956), that James wrote to his family about the beloved cousin Minny Temple immediately after her death (*op. cit.*, pp. 60–64). Though they are sincere enough, and often beautiful and moving, they seem nevertheless to be tainted with a degree of detachment of the wrong kind—a holding back, an ultimate refusal to be really deeply and painfully involved in the life of the suffering girl, a refusal in fact to share her suffering—which brings back (with all the necessary qualifications) Isabel Archer's phrase about herself as 'cold, hard and priggish'. 'To have known her is certainly an immense gain', he writes to his mother on 26th March 1870, 'but who would have wished her to live longer on such a footing—*unless he had felt within him (what I felt little enough!) some irresistible mission to reconcile her to a world to which she was essentially hostile.* There is absolute balm in the thought of poor Minny and *rest*—rest and immortal absence!'. (*Op. cit.* p. 61. My emphasis.) The 'irresistible mission' James speaks of needed nothing more abstruse than love to inspire and sustain it; and what he is saying here is that he adored and admired Minny Temple but did not love her. If the suggestion, frequently made, that Isabel Archer is one of James's renderings of Minny Temple is correct, it would be confirmed by the connexion between James's own imperfect capacity for love at this period of his life and the similar defect in his heroine Isabel Archer; and if, as everyone believes, Milly Theale in *The Wings of the Dove* is James's final rendering of this cousin whose life and death appears always to have haunted him, it could be argued with this same connexion in mind that James's object there is not only commemorative but also expiatory. (Cp. ch. VII, p. 220 above.)

served by a passion that (in Isabel's phrase) 'had sifted itself clear of the baser parts of emotion—the heat, the violence, the unreason—and that burned as steadily as a lamp in a windless place'; and both (so again it would have seemed to him) were in mortal danger when exposed to 'the hot wind of the desert' which Isabel experiences in the last scene of the book.

The *prima facie* reasonableness of this view is obvious, and has in any case been argued fully and eloquently enough by James himself in the group of stories—*The Lesson of the Master* and the rest—dealing with the life of the artist and the insoluble problems created for him by the involvements of marriage. (The sexual theme as such, it is true, is not mentioned in these stories; but readers of the story *John Delavoy* will have no difficulty in discerning the reason for this.) What is interesting to the student of Henry James's development as man and artist is that he came in time to change his view. His life's experience, it seems, contrived to teach him what he appears not to have known at the time he wrote *The Portrait of a Lady*—that passion, with all its dangers, is the sacred fount of all creative endeavour, and that to deny or sacrifice it in the name of any ideal, however noble, is a delusion which succeeds only in defeating the noble end for which the denial or sacrifice was made. *The Beast in the Jungle* is, I believe, Henry James's most poignant testimony to this hardest, most painful lesson of his life; and having learnt it, he characteristically redeems his tragic error in the most important works of his late period—*The Sacred Fount* to begin with, followed by *The Ambassadors*, *The Wings of the Dove* and *The Golden Bowl*—in which the power of sexual passion to redeem (as well as destroy) is exhibited with a fullness of knowledge to be found nowhere else in the English novel.

APPENDIX B

EDMUND WILSON AND OTHERS ON 'THE TURN OF THE SCREW'

(1) EDMUND WILSON

MR WILSON's account of *The Turn of the Screw* in the essay entitled 'The Ambiguity of Henry James' [1] deserves attention for several reasons. In the first place, it has a strong period interest, being a specimen of the type of literary criticism that the Freudian psychology inaugurated and caused to flourish in the late twenties and thirties of this century; and on this ground there are many useful morals to be drawn from it for the principles and practice of literary criticism. But it happens also to be an instructive instance of the kind of incomplete interpretation that James's works (like Shakespeare's) seem particularly to invite. This is the kind that is substantially false, yet is not wholly without truth; and it is for this reason chiefly that I have chosen to take issue with Mr Wilson's essay, which has already received so much attention (too much, some will think) in recent years. My object is to show, rather more fully perhaps than other critics have done, that his account of *The Turn of the Screw*, while being as wrong-headed, perverse and irresponsible as his critics have shown it to be, nevertheless does draw attention to elements of the story that are of vital importance for its proper understanding.[2]

[1] Reprinted in *The Triple Thinkers* (London, 1952).

[2] Mr John Lydenberg in an article on 'The Turn of the Screw' in *Nineteenth-Century Fiction* (xii, 1, June 1957) pronounces Mr Wilson's interpretation to be 'a dead horse, oft beaten.' I submit that it has indeed been much beaten but never yet (to pursue the rather grim metaphor) to death. So the death-blow still remains to be administered, and a decent burial if possible provided. Besides the article by Mr Heilman already mentioned (pp. 106–7 above), and another by the same author to be discussed in the second section of this Appendix (pp. 381–4 below), I have found the following critical comments on Mr Wilson's essay relevant to my topic in this section: A. J. A. Waldcock,

Mr Wilson's thesis depends, it will be remembered, on two principal points of interpretation: first, that the story is really 'about' the governess, the first-person narrator of the story, not—as the common reader has always supposed—about the children and their relations with the dead servants; and second, that the governess is a classic case of neurotic sex-repression who, having fallen in love with the children's charming uncle at her first and only meeting with him in London, sublimates her frustrated passion for the uncle by the elaborate device of the apparitions and their supposed relations with the children. The apparitions, in other words, are purely hallucinations of the governess's disordered psyche; the children are in fact perfectly innocent of all the dreadful goings-on with the dead servants of which she imagines them to be guilty; and only the governess herself is guilty—of a monstrous invention which is merely a rationalisation of her sex-fantasy, causing her to torment the poor innocent children with portentous questionings and frenzied pursuits until she drives the little girl Flora to a nervous breakdown and the boy Miles to his death. ('She has literally frightened him to death', declares Mr Wilson.) The ambiguity of the *Turn of the Screw* consists then, on this hypothesis, in James's appearing to say one thing, about the children and their corrupt dealings with the servants, but actually saying something quite different, about the governess and the psychology of the 'thwarted Anglo-Saxon spinster'.

Mr Wilson rests much of this sexual interpretation upon the fact that the governess sees the apparitions in what would appear to be the most correct Freudian circumstances. The man-servant, Peter Quint, first appears to her hallucinated brain on a high tower of the house [1]—and this of course makes it perfectly plain what *he* is there for. Again,

'Mr Edmund Wilson and *The Turn of the Screw*' (*Modern Language Notes*, Vol. LXII, 1947, pp. 331–4); E. E. Stoll, 'Symbolism in Coleridge' (*P.M.L.A.*, Vol. LXIII, 1948, pp. 229–33); Glenn Reed, 'Another Turn on James's *Turn of the Screw*'. (*American Literature*, Vol. XX, January 1949, pp. 413–23.)

[1] Edmund Wilson, *The Triple Thinkers*, p. 91.

in the climactic scene with little Flora, Miss Jessel, the dead governess, appears to her on the other side of the lake in the park. And for the completion of the sexual case on the female side, little Flora in this same scene, when she is supposed to be communicating with the apparition of Miss Jessel across the lake (but is of course, on this interpretation, doing no such thing), is observed by the governess to be engaged in some highly symbolic play with two bits of wood; and this again is meant to show us how the governess's subconscious mind is working.[1]

The larger sexual symbolism of the story is explained just as neatly and persuasively. Being unable to satisfy her passion for the children's guardian, the governess has searched in her deep subconscious for a substitute lover, and found him, psychologically speaking, in the apparition of Peter Quint, the master's dead valet. The other apparition, that of Miss Jessel, the dead governess, has been conjured up by her neurotic fear of her predecessor as a rival for the affections of Peter Quint—or, rather, the apparition of Peter Quint symbolising the children's guardian with whom she is in love. And as a last refinement of the prevailing ambiguity, Mr Wilson further intimates that the apparitions of Peter Quint and Miss Jessel symbolise also the governess's subconscious fear of possible rivals for the affections of the children, to whom (and in particular to the boy Miles) she has by now formed a neurotically possessive attachment. The main point is that the governess does not really see the apparitions of the dead servants but only imagines that she is seeing them; and the children do not see the apparitions at all, much less have any relations with them, but are in fact throughout as perfectly innocent as they appear to be.

The most glaring flaws of Mr Wilson's interpretation have been sufficiently exposed by the critics already mentioned. They may for convenience be summarised in the following list:

[1] Edmund Wilson, *op. cit.*, pp. 90–1.

(1) Mr Wilson ignores, in a really inexcusable way, James's own explicit statement of his intention in his Preface, which leaves no room for doubt that the corruption of the children by the servants was the *donnée* of his 'bogey-tale', that the children *were* therefore guilty, and that everything else in the story, including the governess's part in it, was subordinate to this central theme and could only be properly interpreted in relation to it.[1]

(2) He does not consider the negative evidence against his 'hallucination' theory, of which the most conspicuous is the fact (pointed out by Mr Waldock, 'Mr Edmund Wilson and *The Turn of the Screw*', p. 332) that the governess, who has up to this moment never heard of Peter Quint, is able to give the housekeeper Mrs Grose a description of the male apparition that immediately enables the housekeeper to recognise it as that of the dead valet.[2]

(3) He completely disregards the testimony to the governess's perfect normality carefully set out in the prologue to the story. This is a point that Mr Glenn Reed stresses ('Another Turn on Henry James's *Turn of the Screw*',

[1] In view of the explicitness with which this is stated in the Preface (see ch. IV, pp. 107–8 above for the relevant passages), it is remarkable indeed that Mr Wilson should apparently have needed the entry about *The Turn of the Screw* in the *Notebooks* to convince him of James's intention. In a postscript dated 1948 to the 1952 edition of his essay (originally published in 1938, before the *Notebooks* had appeared), Mr Wilson writes: 'The recent publication of Henry James's note-books seems . . . to make it quite plain that James's conscious intention, in *The Turn of the Screw*, was to write a *bona fide* ghost story' (*The Triple Thinkers*, p. 121). But this surely was plain enough already in the Preface, which was as available to Mr Wilson in 1938 as it was to everyone else; and in any case, if the postscript is meant to be a recantation of his former errors, to admit so much is to admit a good deal too little. For what Mr Wilson still does not admit is that the children, not the governess, are the centre of the story, and that this makes nonsense of his 'governess' theory as such even before the validity of the repressed-sex hypothesis is considered; and so far from recanting his misguided Freudianism, he reaffirms and further elaborates it (*ibid.* pp. 122–3), drawing upon what he believes to be certain relevant facts of James's personal history and arriving at conclusions which are no longer even perverse but merely fatuous.

[2] See, however, p. 385 below for H. C. Goddard's brilliant analysis of this episode which, if correct, would overrule this objection to Mr. Wilson's theory.

p. 419) quoting the relevant passage. ('She was a most charming person', says Douglas, the cultivated man of middle age who, as an undergraduate at Cambridge, had met her when she was his sister's governess, about ten years after the events at Bly. 'She was the most agreeable woman I've ever known in her position: she'd have been worthy of any whatever. . . . We had, in her off-hours, some strolls and talks in the garden—talks in which she struck me as awfully clever and nice . . . I liked her extremely and am glad to this day to think she liked me too'.[1])

(4) Above everything, as Mr Rahv excellently puts it,[2] Mr Wilson 'lets off too many of the agents', in particular the children—and thereby stands condemned, by the pleasantest irony, of a thoroughly unscientific treatment of the story. For the least one expects of a theory that claims to be scientific, not merely (to adopt Mr Wilson's own idiom) obscurantist or mystical, is that it shall take account of all the facts. But to 'let off' the children in *The Turn of the Screw* as Mr Wilson does is surely tantamount to ignoring a huge, palpable fact. For it is plain that on Mr Wilson's theory the children are reduced to nothing more than the instruments of the governess's neurotic hallucinations: apart from this bare instrumental function, they have, on his view, no special interest or value. But this is a supposition that is decisively refuted by the literary evidences of the text. The prominent place the children occupy in the story—the sheer space that is devoted to them; the thoroughness and minuteness with which James explores their psychology; the quantity of exquisite craftsmanship he expends on the task of rendering them with the utmost vividness and intensity: these surely condemn as preposterous any suggestion that they are nothing but the instruments of the governess's sex-fantasy. Mr Wilson's view can only be maintained on the supposition that James

[1] *The Turn of the Screw*, p. 131.

[2] Philip Rahv, Introduction to *The Turn of the Screw* in *The Great Short Novels of Henry James*, ed. Rahv (Dial Press, 1944).

in his treatment of the children in *The Turn of the Screw* was guilty of a shocking wastefulness, a clumsy inept lack of economy—in short, a singular lack of artistry—which even those who read him with the least pleasure would acknowledge him to be incapable of. That Mr Wilson should nevertheless have been able to take this view argues the kind of insensibility to the literary evidences before him which may well be taken as a disqualification for the task of interpreting such a work.

So the weaknesses of Mr Wilson's theory are patent enough, the criticisms listed above are just and pertinent, and the whole theory deserves to be execrated by all right-minded readers of James. Yet what Mr Wilson's critics have tended to ignore, or at least seriously to minimise, is all that his theory does try to take account of in *The Turn of the Screw*. There are at least three vital elements in the story that previous critics had either completely missed, or at least not seen with the clarity and vividness with which Mr Wilson evidently saw them; and they had certainly not given them the importance that Mr Wilson rightly does. I refer, first, to the ambiguity; second, to our persistent impression that the governess is, in some sense, guilty, in particular of little Miles's death at the end; and, third, to the significance of the governess's being the first-person narrator of the whole story.

Taking the last first: the fact that the governess is the narrator means that the whole strange action is presented entirely and exclusively through her consciousness; and this most of Mr Wilson's critics have recognised as a fact lending colour to his hallucination theory. But what they have tended to minimise is the disturbingly consistent support it gives to Mr. Wilson's theory. For since, from beginning to end, we have in the strictest sense only the governess's word for what 'happened', it is surely significant that the story should offer no shred of independent confirmation of the truth of her account. To mention the prime instance: dismissing for the moment the most untenable part of Mr Wilson's thesis, his hallucination theory, and allowing that the governess herself really saw the apparitions of the dead servants, it still remains true that there is no shred of independent evidence of the children's having seen them. Consequently, if the governess were self-deceived, for whatever reasons, creditable or discreditable (and I have tried to show [1] that she was self-deceived, though for reasons totally different from those Mr Wilson assigns and perfectly compatible with the high distinction of mind and character attributed to her in the prologue), it is surely significant that there is nothing in the story to save it from being interpreted as the governess's purely 'subjective', even if not 'hallucinatory', view of what happened. James has not—this is the capital point—made any provision against the possibility of such an interpretation. On the contrary, he appears rather to have been at pains to leave the way wide open for just such alternative interpretations; and this is something that cannot be dismissed as irrelevant to the total intention of the story.

This sense of a deliberate (and deliberately hidden) purpose in presenting the story entirely through the governess's consciousness is reinforced by the pervasive ambiguity and the persistent impression of the governess's being in some sense guilty. Some of Mr Wilson's critics have thought he makes too much of the ambiguity: Mr Heilman, for instance, thinks that 'a great deal of unnecessary mystery has been made of the apparent ambiguity of the story',[2] and Mr Glenn Reed that 'there is little possibility of ambiguity of interpretation regarding the governess'.[3] But Mr Wilson is surely right in insisting that it cannot be made too much of. It is certainly there; it is as prominent and as profoundly puzzling as Mr Wilson finds it; and it operates in exactly the way

[1] Ch. IV above.

[2] R. B. Heilman, 'The Freudian Reading of *The Turn of the Screw*', p. 441.

[3] Glenn Reed. 'Another Turn on James's *Turn of the Screw*', p. 422.

Mr Wilson says (before he spoils everything by his theorising): 'Nowhere does James unequivocally give the thing away: almost everything from beginning to end can be read equally in either of two senses.'[1]

Anyone who is in doubt about this need only look again at such a key-scene as the exchange between the governess and little Miles on their Sunday-morning walk to church[2] to see just how consistently, and with what peculiarly terrifying effect, this ambiguity is maintained. The child is asking to be sent back to school, and the governess is resolved to prevent him: that is the bare substance of the exchange. But everything, literally everything, that is said by the boy admits of a double interpretation. *If* the boy's words in fact mean what the governess believes them to mean, then he is indeed as corrupt as she believes him to be and for the reasons she herself gives. But since everything the child says also admits of a perfectly innocent interpretation, if what he says *is* innocent, then it is of course the governess who is guilty—as monstrously guilty as Mr Wilson wishes us to believe she is, and she herself, at certain critical moments in the story, fears she may be.[3]

What is true of this important scene is true also, without any undue forcing of the meaning, of every other scene in the story, and most particularly and significantly of the climactic scenes which end in the catastrophe of the boy's death. As to the scenes between the governess and the housekeeper Mrs Grose, in which the latter appears to confirm independently the governess's interpretations of what is happening: here I would want to argue with Mr Wilson and against his critics

[1] Edmund Wilson, *The Triple Thinkers*, p. 94

[2] *The Turn of the Screw*, Ch. 14. Cp. p. 115 above.

[3] The most striking instance, we remember, is the terrible doubt that seizes her in the very last scene, when she is pressing the boy for the last time to confess what it was he had done at school to be expelled: 'Within a minute there had come to me out of my very pity the appalling alarm of his being perhaps innocent. It was for the instant confounding and bottomless, for if he *were* innocent, what then on earth was I?' (*The Turn of the Screw*, ch. 24, p. 274. See also p. 134 above).

that it seems to me perfectly legitimate to take the view that these confirmations may have been induced by 'suggestion'. The suggestibility of comparatively simple, uneducated persons like Mrs Grose, besides being a matter of common observation in James's day as in any other, happens also to be one of the obvious explanations of at least some of the psychical phenomena which were just then being vigorously investigated by the newly formed Society for Psychical Research, whose reports (we learn) James was in the habit of studying with fascinated interest.[1] Nor is it necessary to postulate in the governess any undue exercise of 'authority' over the housekeeper—the sort of desire to 'dominate' or 'bully' that Mr Wilson, quite gratuitously, postulates[2]—to make this hypothesis plausible.

What at any rate seems to me indisputable is that it really is James's intention that everything in *The Turn of the Screw* shall be capable of being read 'in either of two senses'; and that it is for this reason that he 'nowhere . . . unequivocally gives the thing away', chiefly by ensuring that the story shall afford no independent confirmation of the governess's reading of the situation. The moment one sees this, having had one's attention drawn to it by Mr Wilson, one cannot fail to see also how real is the ambiguity in *The Turn of the Screw* and how consistently it is maintained. It then does become impossible not to take it seriously—to see it as a profoundly important element in the story which, technically speaking, is the direct outcome of the seemingly innocent device of presenting the whole story entirely through the governess's consciousness, and is also intimately connected with our feeling that the governess is in some sense guilty. Mr Wilson's sexual interpretation, I have tried to show, is wide of the mark; but the elements he has discerned are very much there to be discerned, and must

[1] See Francis X. Roellinger, Jr., in the article 'Psychical Research and *The Turn of the Screw*' mentioned above, p. 130.

[2] Edmund Wilson, *op. cit.* p. 95

be fully accounted for by any interpretation that claims to be more complete than his.

This is what I have tried to do in my chapter on *The Turn of the Screw*. Concerning the governess's guilt, I have argued that Mr Wilson was right—only for quite the wrong reasons. The governess was indeed guilty, but for reasons very much more subtle, and as such more worthy of a great novelist, than any that Mr Wilson was able to discern. And concerning the ambiguity, Mr Wilson was again right, and again for the wrong reasons. *The Turn of the Screw* is indeed as profoundly ambiguous as Mr Wilson was clever enough to see. But the ambiguity has nothing to do with sex-repression, either in the governess or in Henry James, but rather (as I suggested)[1] with the problem of good and evil, and in particular the final mystery of the co-existence of good and evil in the human soul. And this again seems to me an explanation which is consonant not only with all the literary evidences of the text (as Mr Wilson's is not) but also with the level—the depth, the breadth and the intensity—of Henry James's mature vision of life.

It must now be left to the reader to judge which interpretation of *The Turn of the Screw* seems to him the more valid. Assuming that he finds cause to reject Mr Wilson's, it remains to summarise the several morals for literary criticism to be drawn from Mr Wilson's errors.

(1) A preliminary moral, admittedly Rymeresque, is that an excessive preoccupation with sexual neurosis in general and an excessive (perhaps neurotic?) antipathy to Anglo-Saxon spinsters in particular may subvert a man's powers of judgement in disastrous ways. *Could* Mr Wilson (one asks) have ignored, or mentally explained away, the testimony to the governess's sanity, intelligence and moral probity set out in the prologue if he had not come to the text with certain preconceived notions (and certain strong feelings) about the psychological make-up of the Anglo-Saxon

[1] Pp. 130–1 above.

spinster? That the governess technically belongs to this class of person may be true; but that James, either consciously or unconsciously, presented her as a member of this class, exhibiting the eternal, immutable characteristics that Mr Wilson ascribes to it, is patently false: we have only to recall Olive Chancellor in *The Bostonians* to recognise, first, that when James wanted to present a type approximating to Mr Wilson's thwarted Anglo-Saxon spinster (with all its neurotic or quasi-neurotic symptoms) he was perfectly capable of doing it, and, second, that there is no resemblance—none, at any rate, apparent to an unbiased eye—between this Anglo-Saxon spinster and that. The reader who is not interested in Mr Wilson's Platonic idea of the type but only in James's governess in *The Turn of the Screw* will accordingly reflect that Mr Wilson's bias does nothing to illuminate the story but only distorts and falsifies it.

(2) Another bias, closely connected with the other, which Mr Wilson brings to his reading of *The Turn of the Screw* appears in his use of the Freudian theory of the unconscious; and from this, too, there is a valuable moral to be extracted for the practice of literary criticism. In an astonishing passage in the 1948 postscript to his essay, Mr Wilson remarks: 'The doubts that some readers feel as to the soundness of the governess's story are, I believe, the reflection of James's doubts, communicated unconsciously by James himself.'[1] When one recalls how explicitly and unambiguously James states the 'doubt' we are meant to feel about the governess's story ('If he *were* innocent, what then on earth was I?'), one does rather gasp at the word 'unconsciously': if this was how Henry James's unconscious mind worked, one wonders what there could be left for his conscious mind to do. But it is all too evident that Mr Wilson, in his uncritical enthusiasm for the Freudian unconscious, has appropriated the concept without troubling himself about the problems it raises for literary criticism. He plainly has no usable criteria for distinguishing

[1] *The Triple Thinkers*, p. 121.

between the operations of the conscious and unconscious; his use of both terms is consequently as arbitrary as it is irresponsible; and one is forced to conclude that, like other critics who have misappropriated the Freudian method of analysis, he falls back on the unconscious whenever his sensibility lets him down and there is an awkward gap to fill—a practice which is a service neither to Freudianism nor to literary criticism.

(3) These morals, however, are only special cases of the principal moral, which is old and familiar indeed, and turns upon the disastrous effects of a misapplied theory upon the practice of literary criticism. Mr Wilson's account of *The Turn of the Screw* shows with exemplary force the wages of this particular sin: how it can nullify, or at least obscure, the critic's own best perceptions (here Mr Wilson's perception of the ambiguity, the governess's guilt, the part played by the children's absent-present guardian); how it can cause an otherwise presumably honest mind to ignore whole tracts of relevant evidence (James's treatment of the children in the story; the testimony to the governess's mind and character in the prologue; the episodes that don't quite fit, and so on); how it can paralyse the critic's sensibility, resulting in a crassly literal reading of an essentially literary, poetic text; how, finally and most disastrously, it can reduce the level of the work of art, turning it into something immeasurably less profound, less subtle, less instructive—simply, indeed, less interesting—than it in fact is. I think Henry James would have disliked Mr Wilson's theory not in the first instance because it is false but because, in view of what his little bogey-tale in fact offers to the receptive reader, it is so naive, so literal-minded, and therefore ultimately so boring.

(2) R. B. HEILMAN; H. C. GODDARD

The account of *The Turn of the Screw* set out in Chapter IV along with the first section of this Appendix was first written some six years ago, in the form of an essay called *A Modern Faustian Fable: Henry James's 'The Turn of the Screw,'* in direct response to the challenge presented by Edmund Wilson's essay. I had at the time read no other comments on *The Turn of the Screw*, and it was only when I was preparing the essay for inclusion in this book that I read Mr Heilman's earlier piece (pp. 106–7 above) and the critics mentioned in the note on pp. 370–1. When the whole book was ready to go to press, I came upon a more extended essay by Mr Heilman entitled *'The Turn of the Screw' as Poem*[1] and an essay by H. C. Goddard *A Pre-Freudian Reading of 'The Turn of the Screw'* published posthumously with a prefatory note by Leon Edel.[2] Mr Heilman's account strikingly endorses my own view of the story, the late Professor Goddard's as strikingly supports Mr Wilson's; and both are so interesting in themselves, and bear so closely not only on my interpretation of *The Turn of the Screw* but also on the larger theme of the Jamesian ambiguity discussed in that chapter and in the chapters on *The Sacred Fount* and *The Golden Bowl* that they have seemed to me to require separate treatment.

The main point in which Mr Heilman's account is in substantial agreement with mine is in his emphasis on the 'theme of salvation' as the heart of James's fable. This implies of course, a recognition of the children and their relations with the dead servants, not the governess and her psychology, as the centre of interest in the story; and indeed Mr Heilman devotes the greater part of his study to a detailed, and to my mind completely convincing, analysis of James's treatment of the children in support of his view that in *The Turn of the Screw* 'his [James's] real subject is the dual nature of man, who is a little lower than the angels and who can yet become a slave in the realm of evil'.[3] The corruption of the children

[1] In *Forms of Modern Fiction*, ed. William Van O'Connor (Univ. of Minnesota Press, 1948).

[2] In *Nineteenth-Century Fiction*, XII, 1 (June 1957), pp. 3–36.

[3] R. B. Heilman, *'The Turn of the Screw' as Poem*, p. 215.

by the evil servants and the governess's struggle to save them dramatises a well-attested truth about the nature of man, that 'what is tragic and terrifying in man is that to be capable of salvation is to be capable also of damnation;'[1] and thus 'the battle between the governess and the demons becomes the old struggle of the morality play in a new dress'.[2]

Mr Heilman goes a good deal further than I have ventured to go (in this book, at any rate) in the direction of a religious, and indeed theological, interpretation of the central fable. 'James', he declares, 'has an almost religious sense of the duality of man, and, as if to manifest an intention, he makes that sense explicit in terms broadly religious and even Christian'.[3] From there he goes on to argue—on the evidence of the persistent 'verbal patterns' associating the children with a 'more than earthly beauty', an 'extraordinary brightness', freshness and innocence which is fatally 'clouded' by their intercourse with the dead servants, and those on the other side associating the apparitions with the satanic, the damned and the damnable—that *The Turn of the Screw* is in effect a Jamesian version of the Judaeo-Christian story of the Fall of Man, with the children enacting the parts of the first Man and Woman, the servants the part of the Tempter, and Bly itself figuring as the Eden in which the momentous act of corruption is accomplished.

I am reserving a further discussion of this more theological (and controversial) side of Mr Heilman's interpretation for the supplementary study on Henry James I have mentioned elsewhere. In the meantime, its main virtues seem to me to be that it puts the children and their mysterious corruption by the servants squarely into the centre of the picture—which, it can no longer be doubted, is true to James's intention, whatever else may also be true of the story; that it assigns to the governess her principal role in

[1] R. B. Heilman, '*The Turn of the Screw*' as *Poem*, p. 220.
[2] *Ibid*. p. 215.
[3] *Ibid*. p. 220.

the story, that of 'saviour-confessor'; that it recognises the 'Faustian' aspect of the central theme of salvation ('James's story, in its central combat, is not unlike the Faustus story as it might be told by the Good Angel', says Mr Heilman explicitly; and acutely points out that on this view Miles's last terrible cry 'Peter Quint—you devil' is 'in one way almost identical with Faustus's savage attack, in Marlowe's play, upon the Old Man who has been trying to save him'); [1] and that it recognises also the hovering presence of some non-theological version of the doctrine of Original Sin in James's emphasis on the co-existence in the children of the beauty, brightness and innocence with (as Mr Heilman puts it) their 'strange maturity' and the 'cold adult calculatingness' they reveal at the moments of crisis—Flora by the lake, for instance.[2]

The main weakness of Mr Heilman's account, as I see it, is that he still appears not to recognise the ambiguity in the crucial sense defined by Mr Wilson—that 'almost everything from beginning to end can be read equally in either of two senses'; and consequently does not recognise the nature and extent, or even really the fact, of the governess's guilt. At the end of his otherwise excellent analysis of the last scene Mr Heilman remarks merely, 'It is in part through the ineptitude of the governess-confessor-saviour, we are led to understand, that Miles is lost' [3]—and leaves it at that. This does suggest that he has missed, more or less completely, the other, seamier side of James's theme of salvation—the fatal moral taint in the 'good angel' herself which directly precipitates the catastrophe—which it is one of the principal functions of the ambiguity to convey. In that case the analysis I have proposed would seem to begin where Mr Heilman's leaves off, and (if it is valid) would as such be complementary to Mr Heilman's.

The late Professor Goddard's paper is in many ways a

[1] R. B. Heilman, '*The Turn of the Screw*' *as Poem*, p. 223.
[2] *Ibid*. p. 218.
[3] *Ibid*. p. 224.

model of the kind of criticism of Henry James's works that is most valuable, and serious students of James will be heavily in Mr Edel's debt for having made it generally available. The method is simply that of the closest exegesis, of key-scenes and key-passages, conducted with an old-fashioned leisureliness which appears to be inimical to rigour in analysis but in fact covers every inch of the ground; and what Goddard's brilliant application of the method to *The Turn of the Screw* proves among other things is that no passage in this remarkable story can be too closely scrutinised, and that none of James's works yields richer rewards to those prepared to give it this kind of attention.

Mr Edel rightly singles out the analysis of the 'identification' scene—the scene in which Mrs Grose supposedly recognises the male apparition as that of Peter Quint from the governess's detailed description[1]—as the highlight of Goddard's critique. What he demonstrates with the utmost cogency (and to my mind conclusiveness) is that there is a serious doubt about whether Mrs Grose's identification is in fact based on the governess's description or merely on an antecedent disposition (induced by her own suggestibility and the governess's power of suggestion) to believe the apparition to be Peter Quint's. The whole analysis is too long to reproduce here, and only its central point can be mentioned: that Mrs Grose does not in fact identify the apparition by its most distinctive feature, namely, the red hair and whiskers, but by the two facts, significantly the first and the last mentioned by the governess, that the stranger wore no hat and that his clothes looked as if they belonged to someone else.[2] The details of the analysis, in any case, give the strongest support to Mr Wilson's insistence on Mrs Grose's suggestibility as a prime element to be taken into account in assessing her value as an independent witness;[3] and in this connexion

[1] *The Turn of the Screw*, ch. 5.

[2] Harold C. Goddard, *A Pre-Freudian Reading of 'The Turn of the Screw'*, p. 15.

[3] Cp. pp. 377–8 above.

one is struck afresh by Goddard's acuteness when knowing nothing, one may suppose, of James's ardent interest in the published Proceedings of the Society for Psychical Research since established by Mr Roellinger,[1] he remarks that 'that touch about "the missing waistcoats" [at the end of the identification scene] is precisely at Mrs Grose's intellectual level, the level, as anyone who has ever had the curiosity to attend one knows, of a fifth-rate spiritualist seance'.[2]

The essay abounds in similar examples of Goddard's insight and analytical power. Among these is his account of the governess's romantic 'myth-making' nature, which induces in her a passionate desire to participate in a 'heroic drama';[3] and his analysis of the very last scene, in which the boy's cry 'Miss Jessel, Miss Jessel', so difficult to explain on any hypothesis which accepts without reservation the governess's account of the events, is admirably explained on the hypothesis that she is 'guilty' in a sense very close to, if not identical with, Mr Wilson's. Apart from their intrinsic value for a better understanding of *The Turn of the Screw*, what Goddard's exegeses chiefly establish, and more conclusively than ever, is the completeness and perfection of the Jamesian ambiguity: how James has been at pains to make his text yield evidences for the innocence of the children and the guilt of the governess as cogent, as powerful and as persuasive as those for the corruption of the children and the innocence—subject to the 'Faustian' reservations indicated—of the governess; and how this more than ever proves the validity of Mr Wilson's perception, that 'nowhere does James unequivocally give the thing away: almost everything from beginning to end can be read equally in either of two senses'.[4]

[1] Cp. pp. 130 n above. [2] Goddard, *A Pre-Freudian Reading*, p. 15.

[3] *Ibid.* pp. 8–10.

[4] It is easy to see also how Goddard's analysis of the 'identification' scene in *The Turn of the Screw*, if it is correct, supports my account of the connexion between *The Turn of the Screw* and *The Sacred Fount*. If I had read his essay before I wrote these chapters, I should have wanted to make a stronger claim

Prof. Goddard's exegeses, however, are one thing, the conclusions he draws from them about the total meaning of *The Turn of the Screw* are—as James said about the governess's explanation of the events at Bly as distinct from her bare report of them—'another matter'. His explanation is in the end as fatally one-sided as Mr Wilson's; it is only less unjust because he is at least free of Mr Wilson's violent, almost personal, antipathy to the thwarted Anglo-Saxon spinster. Nevertheless he endorses Mr Wilson's main position, that the children are completely innocent and the apparitions purely hallucinations of the governess's brain; and he goes further than Mr Wilson in pronouncing the governess to be not merely neurotic but literally insane. '*Two children, under circumstances where there is no one to realise the situation, are put for bringing up in the care of an insane governess*':[1] this, according to Goddard, is the 'sinister romance' that James chose to develop out of the anecdote he claimed to have heard from the Archbishop of Canterbury.

The objections to this hypothesis are substantially the same as those to Mr Wilson's. James's own remarks about the story in the Preface and the *Notebooks* can leave us in no doubt that the dead servants and not the governess, no matter how self-deceived or neurotic or insane, are intended to be the agents of the evil to which the children succumb. The prologue likewise ensures that the governess was not only not mad before or during the strange events at Bly but (unlike the unfortunate woman who was put in charge of Prof. Goddard as a child)[2] also not after those events: Douglas, we remember had the story from her some ten years after she had left Bly, and was then so impressed by her charm, 'cleverness' and so on. With *The Sacred Fount*

for the importance of what I called the 'epistemological' theme in *The Turn of the Screw*. I still hold that it is subsidiary to the moral, or moral-religious, theme of salvation, only (I now think) less subsidiary than I had supposed.

[1] Goddard, *op. cit.* p. 19. The author's emphasis.

[2] The author cites a personal childhood experience of being put in the care of a woman who was afterwards found to be insane as the original clue to his understanding of the governess in *The Turn of the Screw*.

in mind, it is difficult not to see this as a deliberate precaution: James must have been all too conscious that the governess in *The Turn of the Screw*, like the narrator in *The Sacred Fount*, would be thought 'mad' (and indeed, again like the narrator in the later story, would often think herself to be mad), and accordingly took care to balance the evidences for and against this hypothesis with the nicest precision. Thus the several references to the governess's 'wild' looks to which Goddard draws attention are balanced by the emphatic testimony to her sanity in the prologue; and her subjective fears, doubts and misgivings about her sanity may be read either as proof of her actually being what in those moments she fears herself to be, or as proof of precisely the opposite—that she is too sane and balanced *not* to feel she must be mad to see what she is seeing.

Although Prof. Goddard does not explicitly speak of the ambiguity of *The Turn of the Screw*, his whole critique makes it plain that he recognises it, and is in fact attempting to explain it. In this connexion therefore he lays himself open to the same charge as that invited by Mr Wilson's treatment—and, on the side of the angels, by Mr Heilman's as well. To recapitulate: [1] what neither Goddard nor Wilson on their side nor Heilman on his appear to recognise is that the text in fact—not possibly or probably but actually—yields two meanings, both equally self-consistent and self-complete. This is what the term 'ambiguous' *means* when applied to *The Turn of the Screw* (and *The Sacred Fount* and *The Golden Bowl*): it means that on one reading the children are—not *may be* but *are*—corrupt, the governess *is* their good angel, and the apparitions are in some sense real, while on the other reading the children *are* innocent, the governess *is* a monster, and the apparitions are in some sense unreal or hallucinatory. In respect to the ambiguity, therefore, the relevant critical question is not 'Which is the "true" meaning?' but 'Why did James insist on making his text yield, with

[1] Cp. pp. 130–1, 324, 375–9 *passim* above.

this ferocious consistency, both meanings, the "innocent" and the "guilty"?' The answer to this question is not to choose one meaning to the exclusion of the other—without, that is, taking the other fully into account—and declare the preferred meaning (on whatever grounds, Freudian or Christian or commonsensical) to be the true one. The critic here is not invited to choose or prefer; he is invited only to recognise the co-existence of the two meanings as equally self-complete and self-consistent, and then to explain it—to explain this very co-existence of the two meanings which defines the ambiguity. This is what I have tried to do in my chapters on *The Turn of the Screw*, *The Sacred Fount* and *The Golden Bowl*, with what success the reader must judge. My point in the present context, however, is that even if my explanation turned out to be completely wrong, this would still remain the central problem in any discussion of the Jamesian ambiguity; and it is because both Mr Heilman and Prof. Goddard, in spite of their brilliance in the detailed exegesis of the text, appear to have missed it that it seemed to me useful to restate it once more.

APPENDIX C

THE LATE STYLE

(1) RHETORIC

JAMES's late style does not easily lend itself to discussion in the abstract, and it has therefore seemed best to indicate its most prominent characteristics as concretely as possible in the chapters on the individual late works.[1] A short view of it, however, is possible; and this is perhaps most easily reached by seeing it as a 'rhetoric' which is as intensely stylised as it is dramatic. In view of its high degree of stylisation, it is astonishingly flexible as a dramatic medium. Its main achievement, as we saw, is its power to reproduce, or rather to re-enact, every minute change in tone, pace and emphasis of the mind engaged in self-reflective discourse, every bend and turn in the stream of a consciousness essentially intelligent and coherent—not, like that of the more conventional stream-of-consciousness novel, merely associative and episodic; and as such it is an artistic achievement comparable in originality and power with the blank verse of Shakespeare's mature plays.

James's late style, however, has no equivalent of Shakespeare's prose to supplement it, and is therefore not capable of all things. It has difficulty in particular with those ordinary events which occasionally have to be reported in the late works. When, for instance, in *The Golden Bowl* the question of Charlotte's coming or not coming to lunch at Eaton Square is pondered in periods as elaborate and scrupulously qualified as those employed for the great matters in the book, one feels rather as one felt the first time one heard an opera and thought how silly the *recitativo*

[1] The further discussion of the late style as an intensely personal idiom, its finer points as the medium of the Jamesian exploration of consciousness and its connexion with the 'figure in the carpet' in James's work, are reserved for the supplementary essay on Henry James mentioned earlier (p. ix above).

sounded. But that is the price one expects to have to pay for any high degree of stylisation. And James in fact exacts it very rarely: he shows his intuitive sense of the limitations of his rhetorical medium by reducing to the smallest possible number these ordinary occasions, and thus the occasions for protest.

He is less sure, unfortunately, in his handling of his images and symbols (in particular the symbols) in the latest of his late works. Dr Leavis's dismissal of the images in *The Golden Bowl* as 'coloured diagram'[1] seems to me both sweeping and inaccurate: some of them are brilliantly successful—for instance, the images of terror and violence in the Second Book;[2] and others are unsuccessful not because they are coloured diagram but because they are too arbitrary or too clumsy or both to be dramatically effective. The image of the spaniel shaking the water from his ears is one case in point,[3] the elaborate figure of the pagoda at the opening of the Second Book is another. In each instance the oddness of the image is felt to be in excess of the originality of the experience, making it in this sense arbitrary; and its disproportionate and rather heavy-handed protraction noticeably slackens the dramatic pace at the point at which it occurs.

The main quarrel, however, is with the famous symbols, in particular the golden bowl itself and the ivory tower in *The Ivory Tower*. Mr Quentin Anderson in his book *The American Henry James* has explained in detail the complicated symbolism of the golden bowl, dividing it (as preachers in earlier ages used to divide the texts of their sermons) into its component parts—the bowl, the stem, the base etc.—and elucidating each separately. But whatever the validity of these interpretations may be, and whatever the interest of their connexion with the symbolic system of the elder Henry James's theodicy,[4] neither has the power to transform the golden bowl into a good *poetic* symbol. It remains, to my

[1] F. R. Leavis, *The Great Tradition*, p. 168.

[2] Pp. 263–4, 266, 281, 300–1, 315 above.

[3] p. 398 below.

[4] This is one of the themes of Mr Anderson's book.

mind, a clumsy, artificial graft—a scissors-and-paste image (to adopt Collingwood's term), depressingly reminiscent of Ibsen's symbols—which is not organic to the poetic structure of the novel, and merely illustrates what is already so magnificently exhibited as to stand in no need of illustration. The fact that there should be no mention of the golden bowl in the two entries about *The Golden Bowl* in the *Notebooks* [1] or of the ivory tower in the Notes to *The Ivory Tower* [2] is in this connexion significant. A symbol that *expresses* the theme as distinct from merely illustrating it would surely be an integral part of the original conception of the theme, and might surely therefore be expected to be intimately present to the author's mind at the time of its conception. The total absence of these seemingly vital symbols from James's notes seems to give circumstantial proof of their being as artificial and inorganic as I have suggested.

Besides drawing attention to the Ecclesiastes theme, the golden bowl has its use, of course, in helping to advance the plot at two important points. But this is too small a matter to justify so elaborate an affair; and James's further purpose in introducing it, to symbolise by a really prodigious collector's piece the moral taint that infects all the main characters and relationships in the story, is more effectively accomplished, I think, by those unobtrusive 'occasional' images scattered throughout the book, which expose the fatal mixture of the commercial with the aesthetic in the collecting passion.[3] Finally, there is even a certain physical incongruity, so to speak, in the presence of this large, hard, shiny, insistently material object in a world otherwise composed entirely of the non-material substance of consciousness. At any rate, for those who feel this it produces, each time it reappears in the story, an effect of disharmony distinctly jarring—like a

[1] *Notebooks*, pp. 130–1, 187–8.

[2] *The Ivory Tower*, ed. Percy Lubbock (Collins, 1917).

[3] See above, pp. 250–1, 256–7, 297, 298, 316, 322, 323.

false note in music or a bad distinction in logic or a banal remark in a sensible conversation.

What I have said about the golden bowl seems to me equally true of the ivory tower in the unfinished novel of that name: this also seems to me a foreign graft on the native Jamesian tissue. If this is a fair judgement, the presence of these 'symbols' in the last works may be seen as the weaker side of James's late-Victorian bent towards the melodramatic, and suggests that towards the end of his life, when he was beginning to weary (in his own phrase) of 'the wear and tear of discrimination', he succumbed to some of the less rewarding practices of the nineteenth-century literary tradition. One would like to fancy that if he had lived to revise these works for some new New York Edition fifteen years or more after they were written, he might have recovered sufficiently to discard completely the golden bowls and ivory towers, leaving it to the force of the late style alone to accomplish all his artistic purpose in those works.

(2) LOGIC AND METAPHYSICS

In the Preface to *The Golden Bowl,* James sets out a definition of the poet which does much to illuminate the distinctive character of his own poetic gift:

> The title we give him [the poet] is the only title of *general* application and convenience for those who passionately cultivate the image of life and the art, on the whole so beneficial, of projecting it. The seer and speaker under the descent of the god is the 'poet', whatever his form, and he ceases to be one only when his form, whatever else it may nominally or superficially or vulgarly be, is unworthy of the god: in which event, we promptly submit, he isn't worth talking of at all. He becomes so worth it, and *the god so adopts him, and so confirms his charming office and name, in the degree in which his impulse and passion are general and comprehensive*—a definitional provision for them that makes but a mouthful of so minor a distinction, in the fields of light, as that between verse and prose.[1]

[1] *The Golden Bowl,* p. xx. My emphasis.

This splendid affirmation of faith in the generalising power of the poetic mind makes a mouthful also of distinctions rather less minor than that between verse and prose. It suggests, for instance, that the received distinction between the philosophic mind and the poetic is not as absolute as is commonly supposed: if the philosopher and the poet in question are only great enough (we are tempted to argue), their power of grasping generality is likely to be equal in scope, depth and intensity; the difference will lie only in their respective modes of rendering what they have so grasped. It suggests also, on grounds more cogent than are generally advanced for this familiar criticism, that Plato was wrong to suppose that the generalising powers of the human mind could be developed only by exercise upon strictly mathematical material. In the *Republic*, we remember, the future philosopher-kings were to be put through an arduous course of mathematical studies arranged in an ascending order of abstractness or generality with the object of preparing their minds for the final apprehension of the Form of the Good, which, whatever else it might also be, was in the first instance the supreme Form—that is, the most general, most comprehensive, most inclusive 'idea' accessible to the human mind, and as such the ultimate source of the perfect knowledge which issued in perfect virtue. Granting Plato his assumption, that the power of grasping generality is the defining property of the philosophic mind, we might argue, taking courage from James's counter-definition, first, that this power is not the exclusive property of the analytical mind (the 'philosopher' in the narrower sense of the word), but can belong equally to the poetic mind; second, that these two forms of the power, the analytic and the poetic, can co-exist in the same mind; and, third, that the generalising power in the poetic or literary mind can itself assume two broadly distinct forms, the 'creative' and the 'critical'.

Returning to Henry James with the last claim in mind,

we may venture a further distinction. In the literary mind of the highest order, the generalising power can exercise itself directly on the raw material of life; and then it will produce poetry of the highest order. Or it can exercise itself in the analysis of the poet's rendering of the raw material of life; and then it will produce criticism of the highest order. At this exalted level both gifts are rare—which is only to say that great poetry and great criticism are rare; and to find the gifts at this level combined in a single mind is still rarer. Henry James was one of the rare minds in which the two gifts were combined. His Prefaces, Letters and critical essays abundantly testify to the generality and comprehensiveness of his analytical impulse and passion; and these, I will presently try to show, contain some of his most explicit statements about the principles and method of his art. But the 'poetry' itself, the novels and stories, especially those of the late period, equally bear witness to it; and since the forms in which it appears here are also intimately, though less overtly, related to the principles and method directing James's practice as an artist, and are besides intrinsically curious and interesting, they deserve special attention.

In James's later works the generalising impulse and passion is to be detected first in certain unusual features of the language, and pre-eminently in his persistent use of what may be called logical terms, expressions and images. Such images are to be found also in the earlier works; but they occur much more frequently, and in forms conspicuously more elaborate, in the later; and they do much, I believe, to account for the 'abstract' flavour of the late style as a whole, which has often been recognised but rarely explained.

In *The Ivory Tower* (to start at an advanced point), we read that 'the general hush . . . pushed upward and still further upward the fine flower of the inferential'.[1] In the same book, one character remarks to another that a particular condition 'will cut down not a little your general possibilities

[1] *The Ivory Tower*, III, 5, p. 209.

of relation' and that 'you can't not count with a relation—I mean one that you're a party to, because a relation is exactly a *fact* of reciprocity'.[1] And in another place, the young man, Gray Fielder, meditating on 'the mere beastly fact of his pecuniary luck', uses the rather odd word *constatation* in a not readily intelligible passage: 'How was he going not to get sick of finding so large a part played, over the place, by the mere *constatation*, in a single voice, a huge monotone restlessly and untiringly directed, but otherwise without application, of the state of being worth dollars to inordinate amounts?'[2]

As we move back, through *The Golden Bowl* to *The Wings of the Dove* and *The Ambassadors*, the examples become less abstruse but not less intricate. Lambert Strether, reflecting upon his changed relations with Maria Gostrey, discerns that 'it was the proportions that were changed, and the proportions were at all times, he philosophised, the very conditions of perception, the terms of thought'.[3] Madame de Vionnet receives from Strether this special tribute to her personal genius, that 'she had taken all his categories by surprise'.[4] And on that fateful expedition into the country, when Strether comes upon Chad and Madame de Vionnet in the boat, he has time, in the idyllic mood that precedes the shock of the encounter, to reflect upon the logical properties of his felicity:

> The conditions had nowhere so asserted their difference from those of Woollett as they appeared to him to assert it in the little court of the Cheval Blanc while he arranged with his hostess for a comfortable climax. They were few and simple, scant and humble, but they were *the thing*, as he would have called it. . . . 'The' thing was the thing that implied the greatest number of other things of the sort he had had to tackle; and it was queer of course, but so it was—the implication here was complete. . . .[5]

[1] *The Ivory Tower*, III, 5, p. 227. [2] *Ibid.* IV, 1, pp. 251–2.

[3] *The Ambassadors*, II, vii, 3, p. 42. [4] *Ibid.* I, vi, 3, p. 239.

[5] *Ibid.* II, xi, 3, p. 226. It is worth noting the difference between the handling of the logical image here and that of a similar image in an earlier work like *The Portrait of a Lady*. There Madame Merle also launches into a little

The Golden Bowl, as may be expected, yields a particularly rich crop of images of this kind. At one point, Maggie Verver's 'grasp of appearances was . . . out of proportion to her view of causes'; [1] at another, she is engaged in reducing her harrowing moral problem to a disjunctive syllogism: 'Unless she were in a position to plead definitely that she was jealous she should be in no position to plead decently that she was dissatisfied. This latter condition would be a necessary implication of the former; without the former behind it it would *have* to fall to the ground'.[2] The elaborate image of the pagoda, with which the second book of the novel opens, includes a characteristic example (unfortunately not very felicitous) of the kind of running together of logical and pictorial imagery which tends to become a favourite type of 'mixed metaphor' in the late novels. The passage is worth quoting in full. It begins:

Maggie's actual reluctance to ask herself with proportionate

disquisition on the subject of personal identity: 'When you've lived as long as I', says Madame Merle to Isabel, 'you'll see that every human being has his shell and that you must take the shell into account. By the shell I mean the whole envelope of circumstances. There's no such thing as an isolated man and woman; we're each of us made up of some cluster of appurtenances. What shall we call our "self"? Where does it begin? Where does it end? It overflows into everything that belongs to us—and then it flows back again. I know a large part of myself is in the clothes I choose to wear . . . One's self—for other people—is one's expression of oneself; and one's house, one's furniture, one's garments, the books one reads, the company one keeps—these things are all expressive.' (I, 19, pp. 252–3.) Upon which follows the comment: 'This was very metaphysical; not more so, however, than several observations Madame Merle had already made. Isabel was fond of metaphysics, but was unable to accompany her friend into this bold analysis of the human personality . . .' It seems that the philosophical stamina of the James characters improved as they passed out of James's middle period into his late period. But even here James in his own person allows himself some charming touches: for instance, when the inflexible Mrs Touchett's mellowing with age is expressed as a case of stooping to the contingent: 'Isabel had reason to believe . . . that as she [Mrs Touchett] advanced in life she made more of these concessions to the sense of something obscurely distinct from convenience —more of them than she independently exacted. She was learning to sacrifice consistency to considerations of that inferior order for which the excuse must be found in the particular case.' (I, 21, p. 279.)

[1] *The Golden Bowl*, II, iv, 3, p. 46.

[2] *Ibid.* II, iv, 2, p. 30.

sharpness why she had ceased to take comfort in the sight of it [the pagoda] represented accordingly a lapse from the ideal consistency on which her moral comfort almost at any time depended. To remain consistent she had always been capable of cutting down more or less her prior term.

The image is then particularised—rendered less general (though still remaining logical) by restriction to the specifically moral domain; and is finally abandoned for a concrete, pictorial image:

Moving for the first time in her life as in the darkening shadow of a false position, she reflected that she should either not have ceased to be right—that is to be confident—or have recognised that she was wrong; though she tried to deal with herself for a space only as a silken-coated spaniel who has scrambled out of a pond and who rattles the water from his ears. . . .[1]

'She should either not have ceased to be right—that is, to be confident': in which case there would be no need to 'cut down' her 'prior term'—no need, that is, to modify her initial assumptions, no need therefore to think herself wrong, and consequently to lose her confidence. Or, she should 'have recognised that she was wrong'—that is, have seen that a consequence not derivable from her 'prior term' had in fact occurred; and then it *would* be necessary to 'cut down' this prior term. The image of the silken-coated spaniel that follows is concrete and pictorial enough, but is drawn out so heavy-handedly and at such inordinate length that one can see why Max Beerbohm wrote *The Mote in the Middle Distance*.[2] The passage, however, illustrates the kind of statement that was becoming the staple of James's writing in the later novels; and this leads one to turn to his other, non-fictional writings of the period, in particular the Prefaces, in search of parallel examples that might perhaps throw further light on this curious feature of the late style.

The Prefaces for this purpose are rewarding indeed. There, where the subject-matter allows every freedom to

[1] *The Golden Bowl*, II, iv, 1, p. 6.

[2] Cp. p. 391 above.

James's generalising power, the logical and philosophical phraseology is as prominent as the sensuous and pictorial. There we hear him speak of 'the confidence of the dramatist strong in the sense of his postulate',[1] of 'the quality involved in the given case or supplied by one's data',[2] of the problem of artistic unity as a problem of 'the order, the reason, the relation, of presented aspects'; and yield to passionate utterances about 'the *arbitrary* stroke, the touch without its reason'.[3] The force of such phrases is of course best appreciated in their immediate contexts. Their most inclusive context, however, is James's theory of the art of the novel, which is also the ultimate context of the logical expressions and images we noted in the novels. This theory revolves about three seminal principles, which are not easy to define, or even to name, in a sentence. The key-words, at any rate, are 'aspects', 'conditions', and 'internal relations'; to discover the full meaning of these terms in the Jamesian critical canon is to discover at once the laws of construction, or 'logic', and the view of reality, or 'metaphysics', implicit in the world created in James's late works; and to understand this is of the utmost importance for an understanding of the late Jamesian method.

That art concerns itself to render the world of appearances; that these appearances exist only in the consciousness, indeed *are* the content of the consciousness, of human observers; that the world of art therefore is a beautiful representation of the appearances present to a particular consciousness under particular conditions, and the artist's overriding task is accordingly to exhibit in the concrete, with the greatest possible completeness and consistency, as well as vividness and intensity, the particular world of appearances accessible to a particular consciousness under the specific conditions

[1] *The Awkward Age*, p. xvii. [2] *The Princess Casamassima*, p. xiv.

[3] 'The sense of a system saves the painter from the baseness of the *arbitrary* stroke, the touch without its reason . . .' (*The Tragic Muse*, p. xvi.)

created for it by the artist: these are the elements of James's theory of art.

Nor is it difficult, once the elements have been grasped, to see how this view gives rise to those special technical problems to which so many pages of the Prefaces and the Letters are devoted. Shall the story be presented through a single consciousness, with no 'going behind' of any but this? Or shall there be more than one centre of consciousness, used 'alternatingly' or 'successively', but always with the same rigour—always, that is, keeping the presented world fixed within the compass of that reflector, never allowing a single apprehension to slip in that could not be seen to belong by intrinsic necessity to that consciousness operating under those limitations? 'To make the presented occasion', writes James in the Preface to *The Awkward Age*, 'tell all its story itself, remain shut up in its own presence and yet on that patch of staked-out ground become thoroughly interesting and remain thoroughly clear, is a process not remarkable, no doubt, so long as a very light weight is laid on it, but difficult enough to inspire great adroitness so soon as the elements to be dealt with begin at all to "size up".'[1]

The 'coercive charm' (as James explains in the same Preface) of this mode of conceiving and executing the fictive art is that it places the novelist under the most binding obligation to present exhaustively the limiting conditions of the protagonist centre of consciousness. The conditions must be exhaustive in order that it may be apodeictically certain what apprehensions—what perceptions, judgements, responses—in the particular situation in which it is placed are and are not logically possible to it; and, conversely, if the conditions are not exhaustive, the novelist will fail in one of his principal tasks, that of showing incontrovertibly—apodeictically again—that these apprehensions and only these are accessible to that consciousness in that situation. That situation, however, is itself made up of other persons,

[1] *The Awkward Age*, p. xx.

each hedged about with his own limiting conditions; and these also must be exhaustively rendered in order that their collective limiting effect upon the centre of consciousness through which the action is being unfolded may be exhibited as necessary and inevitable. And this, the complete rendering of all the conditions, is the way in which the novelist *defines* his centre of consciousness, and consequently (as we shall see) the 'aspect' or 'point of view' under which the world in that particular novel is being presented. To accomplish this is, on such a theory, the ultimate proof of the novelist's verisimilitude, the whole business of holding the mirror up to nature, the 'beautiful difficulty' of which James discusses in the Preface to *The Princess Casamassima*. 'Extreme and attaching always', he notes there, speaking of the special problems presented by his little Hyacinth Robinson, 'the difficulty of fixing at a hundred points the place where one's impelled *bonhomme* may feel enough and 'know' enough—or be in the way of learning enough—for his maximum dramatic value without feeling and knowing too much for his minimum verisimilitude, his proper fusion with the fable. This is the charming, the tormenting, the eternal little matter *to be made right*, in all the weaving of silver threads and tapping on golden nails.' [1]

If we turn our attention from the reflector to the reflected, a fresh view of James's late method presents itself. Not only is it the world of appearance, not reality, that a given centre of consciousness is conscious of; it is always the world of appearances under this or that 'aspect', under this or that set of 'conditions'. The limiting conditions, or determinants, of the reflecting consciousness find (or create) their counterpart in the object; the particular reflection, or appearance, of the real that the given consciousness projects bears the mark of its limiting conditions or determinants.

It may be supposed that this is to say no more than that

[1] *The Princess Casamassima*, p. xviii.

every protagonist can necessarily (and too obviously) give only a 'partial' view of the world—'from his point of view', 'as he sees it' are some of the common phrases. In a sense this is true; and perhaps James is doing no more than refine upon these common notions. Yet it is more, since the refinement is a matter of pursuing the notion to its furthest logical limit—a process that always yields uncommon results; and in this instance the result is a method of presentation so organically, so necessarily and inescapably, dramatic that one searches in vain for anything comparable in the history of the novel, and turns in the end to the great dramatists for the right measure.[1]

But the common notion of the partial view will not meet the Jamesian case. For it would not be true to say that the Jamesian centres of consciousness are 'partial' in the ordinary sense—in the sense of being limited, by this or that obvious blind spot, this or that obvious patch of stupidity or perversity or inconsequentiality, which shuts out from their vision some portion of the world. They see 'everything', these remarkable consciousnesses of the late novels: 'everything' is a word that frequently recurs, to denote the excess of light, of sheer intelligibility, with which their world is flooded. As we have already noted,[2] they are intensely perceptive, incessantly analytical, and marvellously articulate. They are always lucid and ironical, never muddled or tediously portentous. They are all possessed of a limitless curiosity and detachment, which renders their perceptions and analyses intensely enjoyable to themselves even while they burn in purgatorial fires; indeed, the 'enjoyment' appears to be most

[1] James's notorious failure as a playwright need not be taken as a measure of his powers as a dramatist. In his plays he was attempting to write for a theatre which happened to be dominated by a dramatic convention, the so-called 'naturalistic', that was to him uncongenial to a degree virtually incapacitating. A great dramatist will turn to whatever *genre* happens in his own time to offer him, by its superior vitality, freedom and flexibility, the best opportunities for the exercise of his gift; and *The Awkward Age* is one of the great dramatic works in the English language.

[2] Ch. I, pp. 15–19, 21–3 above.

intense when the immediate object of their detached curiosity is their own present suffering.[1] They are generous and fearless; earnest without being boring; delicate without loss of candour; civil and kind and good-humoured, and never sentimental; and intent, with the strangest passionate intentness, upon knowing themselves to the last limit of their powers, and acting upon that knowledge with an absolute consistency—as if to fail in this kind of consistency were the ultimate outrage. They are indeed, as we saw, superior people, figuring the human intelligence at its furthest reach. They can hardly therefore be 'limited' in the ordinary sense.

Yet, even at its furthest reach, the human intelligence, as it is human, can only see partially; for it *is* after all limited. But by what, in this instance? What could limit such intelligences, which seem to be as free, luminous and comprehensive as those of angels? The answer is, by that which marks the division between men (even the most prodigious men) and angels: by what old-fashioned moralists have called the passions. To match the beauty and refinement of their virtues, the destructive passions in the late novels accordingly appear in their most refined, most subtle, forms; and in these forms they are, as we have seen, so inseparably bound up with the virtues that it is not at all easy to see at what point they cease to be graces and become sins. The sins —or (better) the virtues in their sinful aspect—can, however, be named. The first is pride, with its attendant perversity and *hauteur*—the damnable damning pride of a Fleda Vetch, a Nanda Brookenham, a Milly Theale. The next is boredom, the terrible hovering *ennui* of the Prince and Charlotte in *The Golden Bowl*, of the Parisian *beau monde* in *The Ambassadors*, of Lord Mark in *The Wings of the Dove* and his well-bred

[1] In his Notes to *The Ivory Tower*, James makes the point explicitly in connexion with his hero Gray Fielder's betrayal: 'He really enjoys getting so detached from it as to be able to have it before him for observation and wonder as he does, and I must make the point very much of how this fairly soothes and relieves him . . .'. (*The Ivory Tower*, p. 309.)

friends murmuring 'I say, Mark' as they circle about the gardens at Matcham.[1] Then, as a function of the boredom, there is their revulsion from stupidity and vulgarity, which in the end they hate so much more than they love truth and goodness; and this, in turn, is intimately connected with the cankerous sexuality—most fully exposed in *The Awkward Age*, but also, though more elusively, in *The Ambassadors* and *The Golden Bowl*—which ultimately finds no delight in the aspiration of the beloved after perfect knowledge and perfect goodness, but instead takes for the object of its adoration the imperfect and the incomplete, the patches of nescience and the residual mystery. (That is why, we have learnt, Nanda Brookenham is the type of the unmarriageable girl.) And, subsuming all these, there is the last infirmity of these noble spirits, their worship of the beautiful, that infernal aestheticism by which (James lets us know in each of his late novels) such men believe themselves saved but are in fact damned. 'You've all of you here', remarks Strether in Gloriani's garden—

> 'You've all of you here so much visual sense that you've somehow all "run" to it. There are moments when it strikes one that you haven't any other.'
>
> 'Any moral', little Bilham explained, watching serenely, across the garden, the several *femmes du monde*. 'But Miss Barrace has a moral distinction', he kindly continued; speaking as if for Strether's benefit not less than for her own.
>
> '*Have* you?' Strether, scarce knowing what he was about, asked of her almost eagerly.
>
> 'Oh not a distinction'—she was mightily amused at his tone—'Mr Bilham's too good. But I think I may say a sufficiency. Yes, a sufficiency . . . I daresay, moreover,' she pursued with an interested gravity, 'that I do, that we all do here, run too much to mere eye. But how can it be helped? We're all looking at each other—and in the light of Paris one sees what things resemble. That's what the light of Paris seems always to show. It's the fault of the light of Paris—dear old light!'

[1] *The Wings of the Dove*, I, v, 2, p. 193.

'Dear old Paris!' little Bilham echoed.

'Everything, every one shows', Miss Barrace went on.

'But for what they really are?' Strether asked.

'Oh, I like your Boston "reallys"! But sometimes—yes'.

'Dear old Paris then!' Strether resignedly sighed while for a moment they looked at each other. . . .'[1]

This is how James's centres of consciousness in the late novels come to be limited after all, and therefore able to give only a partial view of the whole, only this or that aspect of the world of appearances. Nor is it anything but reassuring that the fatal limitation should be introduced by irrupting the passions into the clear stream of intelligence; for what dramatist or novelist worth remembering has not done the same? What distinguishes James from others is the amount of intelligence he affords his centres of consciousness. By allowing so much, he risks at every moment the annihilation of the very possibility of destructive passion: one more turn of the screw, one feels, and they really will be angelic intelligences; and that will be the end of all story and drama.[2] James, in other words, makes it all as difficult as possible for himself. Given such a prodigious quantity of light, what (he has to ask himself) will they not see? Where, in such a noontide of light, can the shadow fall? And since they are all bathed in this noontide radiance, how are shadows and shadows to be differentiated? What in each instance are to be the 'beautiful determinants' of the shadow that actually falls? Finally (the supreme problem): how shall each set of beautiful determinants beautifully determine every other set; and determine it 'without remainder', so completely as to leave not the minutest interval, not a single point at which there might be a 'leak of interest'?[3] These are the difficulties in which James in the late novels is constantly rejoicing; and

[1] *The Ambassadors*, I, v, 1, pp. 181–2.

[2] Cp. p. 401 above; and ch. I, pp. 16–17 above.

[3] 'There is nothing so deplorable as a work of art with a *leak* in its interest; and there is no such leak of interest as through commonness of form. Its opposite, the *found* (because the sought-for) form is the absolute citadel and tabernacle of interest.' (Letter to Hugh Walpole, *Letters*, ed. Lubbock, II, p. 246.)

rejoicing the more because they are created by and inherent in 'the blest operation . . . of my Dramatic Principle, my law of successive Aspects'.[1]

From the law of successive aspects it is an easy passage to the last intricacy of James's theory of the fictive art, his doctrine of internal relations. A work of art must have a beginning, a middle and an end; one thing must follow from another as 'inevitably' as possible; causes (in a novel, 'motivation') must be commensurate with effects, and the objective correlative adequate to the subjective content; a work of art, in short, must be an organic whole, not a mechanical contrivance. These are among the most important commonplaces of our current critical theory; and James in his Prefaces is affirming all this, but also much more. What he adds, as before, is his immeasurably deeper understanding of all that these critical commonplaces imply, and his incomparably exact analysis of their meaning for the practising novelist. Indeed, all the most memorable critical pronouncements in the Prefaces are derived, in the first and last instance, from his own practice as a novelist, and for this reason are invaluable for the understanding of the principles and method of his works.

Repeatedly, with variations only in the details, James lays down the fundamental condition of the fictive art. The 'painter' must create a world in which nothing shall happen but by an ineluctable necessity: all that follows must already have been present in the conditions laid down at the beginning, so that the story is in the nature of an unfolding, an exfoliation, of all that was from the beginning involved in the *donnée*. The process is beautifully described in the Preface to *The Portrait of a Lady*, where James reflects upon 'the whole matter of growth, in one's imagination' of such a subject as his engaging young woman, Isabel Archer. 'These are the fascinations of the fabulist's art', he writes there, 'these

[1] Notes to *The Ivory Tower*, p. 268.

lurking forces of expansion, these necessities of upspringing in the seed, these beautiful determinations, on the part of the idea entertained, to grow as tall as possible, to push into the light and the air and thickly flower there'.[1] It follows that the necessity of the action can never be merely asserted but must always be exhibited ('The novelist who doesn't represent, and represent "all the time", is lost'[2]). Every part of the action must be shown to belong intrinsically to 'the given case'; and this can only be shown by a rendering of the given conditions so precise and so exhaustive as to leave no possibility of a doubt that anything can happen as a consequence of those conditions but what does in fact happen. The deliberate extinction of all alternatives, however desolating in life, is the vital principle of every successful work of art. Wherever there is a 'leak', there is failure; and for the artist who has learnt the lesson of the master and cares for nothing but perfection, the distinction between partial failure and total failure is merely verbal.

But the doctrine of internal relations is not only a logical principle, which as such directs the method of James's later works. It is also a view of reality, a metaphysical principle; and it is in this character that it makes a memorable appearance in *The Ambassadors*. Strether is engaged in his great show-down with Sarah Pocock, and is pleading for recognition of Madame de Vionnet's services to Chad. 'Why when a woman's at once so charming and beneficent . . .', he begins. But Mrs Pocock takes him up on the ground of her Woollett metaphysic of straight and simple dichotomies: 'You can sacrifice mothers and sisters to her without a blush, and can make them cross the ocean on purpose to feel the more, and take from you the straighter, *how* you do it?' Whereupon Strether invokes in his defence another view of experience, totally distinct from Mrs Pocock's, which she will never understand: a view that sees all reality as a tissue of implications, in which everything is internally

[1] *The Portrait of a Lady*, p. vii. [2] *The Tragic Muse*, p. xxi.

related with everything else; in which causal sequences of the kind that direct Mrs Pocock's thinking are never more than arbitrary and therefore false; and a single life is never long enough to make out even a fraction of what is implied by its own most significant experience. Strether replies:

'I don't think there's anything I've done in any such calculated way as you describe. Everything has come as a sort of indistinguishable part of everything else. Your coming out belonged closely to my having come before you, and my having come was a result of our general state of mind. Our general state of mind had proceeded, on its side, from our quiet ignorance, our queer misconceptions and confusions—from which, since then, an inexorable tide of light seems to have floated us into our perhaps still queerer knowledge. Don't you *like* your brother as he is,' he went on. . . .[1]

To understand the vital place of the doctrine of internal relations in James's view of reality as a whole and the world of human relations in particular is to understand also the logical place of the famous obliqueness or indirectness of presentation in the method of the late novels. If, for the novelist, the business of intimating (and never more than intimating) the reality beneath the appearances is the business of unfolding all that is implicit in 'the given case'; if therefore personal identity (the 'individual') is nothing other than that which emerges from the process of unfolding the implications of the *donnée*; and emerges, not as something distinct from the tissue of implications, but as the tissue itself—for the individual *is* the sum total of his determinants or conditions when (but only when) the full implications of those determinants have been fully understood and exhibited: if this is the fundamental logic of James's mature thinking, the method of oblique or indirect presentation may be seen as yet another instance of that high, rare consequentiality which is the characteristic expression of his genius, and not (as some have thought) a mere perversity, or the result of a 'hypertrophy of sensibility', or (as one lady thought) a form of self-indulgence made possible by having Miss Bosanquet to

[1] *The Ambassadors*, II, X, 3, p. 179.

dictate to from ten o'clock to one o'clock each day. James's own remarks in the concluding passage of the Preface to *The Wings of the Dove* about 'his instinct everywhere for the *indirect* presentation of his main image' may, one fears, have been misleading to some of his modern critics. He notes there 'how again and again, I go but a little way with the direct—that is, with the straight exhibition of Milly: it resorts for relief, this process, wherever it can, to some kinder, some merciful indirection. . . . All of which proceeds from her painter's tenderness of imagination about her, which reduces him to watching her, as it were, through the successive windows of other people's interest in her'. This has sometimes been taken as a confession of sheer incapacity for the direct and its consequent evasion in the late novels; and since it is known that Milly Theale is a rendering of the beloved cousin Minny Temple, it has also been taken as a confession of the sentimentality that some readers have found in the portrayal. But it is neither. The passage refers to a thoroughly deliberated, wholly intrinsic, aspect of James's late method; and so far from being a confession of weakness, it may be taken to point rather to the kind of freedom of speculation upon his own practice that an artist as secure as James in the attested virtues of his method might well feel himself able to afford.

In a well-known exchange of letters with H. G. Wells,[1] James sets down an *obiter dictum* concerning the nature of art that might, at first sight, seem to imply philosophical commitments of an alarming kind. 'It is art that *makes* life', he writes to Wells, 'makes interest, makes importance, for our consideration and application of these things, and I know of no substitute whatever for the force and beauty of its process.' One is put in mind of another famous *obiter dictum*,

O Lady! we receive but what we give,
And in our life alone does nature live,

[1] *Letters*, ed. Lubbock, II, pp. 503–8.

and one wonders how near James is to dropping into the abyss of metaphysical idealism, from which (philosophers warn us) no traveller returns.

Whatever may be the philosophical difficulties, it is at any rate a position consistent with the logic of internal relations that James's thinking in his later period everywhere exhibits. To say that 'art *makes* life' is to say that the artist at once creates the conditions in which life can be 'ideally' exhibited and exhibits it thus ideally by exploring and articulating the fullest implications of the given case. Life is made to yield its fullest, richest meanings when subjected to the artistic process; indeed, to the extent that life is intelligible and significant at all, it has already been brought under the beautiful dominion of art. Art, then, *makes* life by making meaning; it makes meaning by discovering the full implications of the *donnée*; and it discovers these implications by creating the conditions in which they may most beautifully and instructively unfold themselves. That is how art exhibits life at its maximum intensity, at its highest reaches of 'interest' and 'importance'; and that is why (as James elsewhere remarks) those centres of consciousness that are endowed with 'the power to be finely aware and richly responsible' yield most to the attentive reader: 'their being finely aware—as Hamlet and Lear, say, are finely aware—*makes* absolutely the intensity of their adventure, gives the maximum of sense to what befalls them'.[1]

There remains the question of the sources of James's view of reality and its essential logic as these have been outlined here. It will be evident that it has affinities with the so-called idealist philosophies of the nineteenth century; and it is even possible that James was aware of the connexion—if his use of the logical terms and images to which I drew attention may be taken as a sign of such an awareness. I have thought it safer, however, to proceed on the hypothesis that he did not

[1] *The Princess Casamassima*, p. ix.

take it from anywhere, or anybody, in particular: neither from Hegel, nor F. H. Bradley, nor from his brother William's Pragmatism,[1] nor (least of all) from his father's Swedenborgian system. I have supposed he took it from the ambient air of nineteenth-century speculation, whose main current was the preoccupation with the phenomenon of self-consciousness. To this air he had been exposed from his earliest years; and the animating intellectual atmosphere of his remarkable home, created by his father and the circle of gifted friends and relations commemorated in the pages of *Notes of a Son and Brother*, made perhaps the heaviest contribution to Henry James's philosophical development. But he must have received much also from his studies at home and abroad (which he appears to have pursued a good deal more systematically than the circumstance of the young Jameses' desultory education would lead one to suppose) before he finally settled in England and entered upon his career as a novelist. After that, the sources of his 'thought' were identically the same as the sources of his life's experience and his literary experience. James always took his thought in solution, never neat; and therefore found what he wanted, and in the form in which he best liked to receive it, in the works of his fellow-novelists and the conversation of men and women. He read such contemporary masters of his art as Balzac, Turgenev, Tolstoy, and George Eliot, as well as humbler practitioners like W. D. Howells, Paul Bourget, Mrs Humphry Ward, and his dear friend Edith Wharton, with a passion of interest that stands in marked contrast with his always languid response to the logical edifices of systematic philosophers, his father's not excepted. And though it is true that the conversation of the society in which he moved in London was not especially rich in general ideas, owing to the dislike of the English for criticism and keen analysis,[2]

[1] He read with admiration, however, William James's *Pragmatism* and *The Meaning of Truth*, and declared himself 'lost in wonder of the extent to which all my life I have (like M. Jourdain) unconsciously pragmatised' (*Letters*, ed. Lubbock, II, p. 85).

[2] Cp. ch. I, pp. 6–7 above.

it was also true that the English were not incapable of using ideas, of incorporating them, so to speak, into their routine day-to-day intellectual acts. There was much therefore, that a mind like James's, 'as receptive . . . of any scrap of enacted story or evoked picture as it was closed to the dry or the abstract proposition',[1] could learn from intercourse with them. And, interacting with all these influences, there was James's own prodigious speculative power—the power to generalise to the furthest limit the particulars of experience, and to render these without loss of particularity in the light of the most inclusive generality.

When it happens to be the particulars of the human condition that a man is concerned to render, his aiming after the highest generality is also and at the same time a search for the deepest grounds of conduct and aspiration. He seeks to discover the standpoint from which the permanent elements of human experience may be rendered completely intelligible; and in the pursuit of this end, finds himself committed to a particular logic and a particular metaphysic. For it is a single quest that he is engaged upon, which in its logical or philosophical aspect shows as a pursuit of the highest generality, in its poetic aspect as a search for that which is at once the ground and the end of man's life.

In a mind like James's, however, which (to adopt one of Coleridge's wonderful definitions) is 'intensely watchful of its own acts and shapings', which 'thinks while it feels, in order to understand, and then to generalise that feeling', no single feature of its own activities can escape its intense watchfulness. Consequently the logic of its own ultimate view of the condition of man becomes for it a distinct object of perception; and it is this perception of the logical structure, the logical properties, of his own responses to the world that James records in those curious terms and images mentioned at the beginning of this section. But, finally: his perceptions of the world itself and his perception of the

[1] *Notes of a Son and Brother*, ch. 6, p. 350.

logic of his perceptions of the world 'happen' simultaneously, are the parts of a single inclusive experience; and what this shows is that in James the philosophic, analytic passion is all of a piece with the poetic and intuitive: they can be distinguished but never divided.

INDEX

29034499R00243

Printed in Great Britain
by Amazon